1983

William I. Kaufman's

Pocket Encyclopedia of California Wine

PUBLISHED BY
THE WINE APPRECIATION GUILD
SAN FRANCISCO

Published by The Wine Appreciation Guild
1377 Ninth Avenue
San Francisco, CA 94122
(415) 566-3532
957-1377

ISBN 0-932664-24-5

Library of Congress Catalog Card Number

Printed in The United States of America

Cover Design: Bill Lansberg
Typography: Green Valley Graphics
Managing Editor: Maurice Sullivan
Editor: Kathi Horton

Contents

Foreword

In 1858, Col. Agoston Haraszthy predicted: "It is beyond a doubt that California will produce as noble a wine as any part of Europe: when the proper varieties of grapes and the most favored localities in soil and climate are discovered."

One hundred and twenty-two years later those localities have certainly been discovered in what has become known around the world as the California Wine Country. It is also certain, as Col. Haraszthy had predicted, that California produces as noble a wine as any part of Europe.

This wine encyclopedia provides the clues to one of California's most enjoyable treasure hunts. The search through our wine Country is almost as rewarding as the tasting of our wines. This erudite but quite readable little volume will help any reader develop an appreciation for California wines and enhance an appreciation already acquired.

March Fong Eu
California Secretary of State

Introduction

The Pocket Encyclopedia of California Wines is a "first" in many ways. It is the "first" totally objective book on the subject of California wine in that I have not imposed my "favorites" on you the reader. It is a reference book with suggestions and a broad list on the subject of varietal wines that you might want to try. I do not tell you what is best. When it comes to telling you what is best, I have not backed off from making a decision, I simply made the decision that the results of the San Jose Mercury New Consumer and Professional Panels, and the Orange County Fair 1982 Commercial Wine Judging Awards were the most important recommendations that I could make to you. Judging was done on a blind basis, no labels showing, no preconceived judgements could be made. Wines were not submitted for judging. A total of 1387 wines were purchased from retail stores and divided into 17 varieties. The judges were representatives of 43 California wineries. This is what I call the best of judging and that is why I have stepped back to let the judges (many who are winemakers) make specific suggestions through the award system.

The other important factors of this book are that it will give you an easy reference guide to all of the wineries and vineyards in California and help explain some of the terminology that is associated with wine. There is always the possibility that I have omitted a winery. If I have done this and you want to bring it to my attention, please do so. Please keep in mind that this is a pocket size book and I have tried to give you a treasure of information that will help enrich your wine life and at the same time provide you with an easy reference source.

I have told you what my pocket encyclopedia is, and now I would like to tell you what it is not. It is not a vintage guide to the best wines and their years. I have purposely left out the inclusion of vintage years with each wine and have indicated whether or not wineries vintage date their wine. However, we have included a brief chart of the vintages by district, as there have been some truly outstanding years.

My reason for this is simple. All wines are not available all over the United States since the majority of wineries are small or medium size. Telling someone that the 1968 Chateau Jacqueline from Napa was one of the greatest and then that person not being able to go out and purchase it, is one of the most frustrating experiences to the wine lover.

On the other hand, I have done my best to tell you something about the winery (providing there was something to say or the winery was willing to share information with me). I tell you about the wines that are produced, vintage dated, estate bottled and the secondary label if there is one. On the matter of definition: I have included those definitions that will cover the broad range of wine drinkers from the serious winophile to the "not too serious but enjoys a good glass of wine," drinker.

Never before in the history of wine books has there been a vintage date on the cover. As life changes everyday, so does the wine business. It is the desire of the publisher and myself to add new wineries, new wines and the results of important tastings to each new year's pocket encyclopedia. This will open the door to several thousand bottles of wine depending on your pocketbook and interest. Most importantly the Pocket Encyclopedia of California Wine will help expand your knowledge of the world's most exciting wine region. I have learned from creating this book, and I am certain that the same shall be true with you.

I want to thank all of the wineries, and Kathi Horton for her assistance. I dedicate this book to Mme. Jacqueline S. Nagel.

William I. Kaufman
Master Knight of the Vine

Key to Symbols

Medal winners at competitive tastings are indicated with ★. Full results of the 1982 Orange County Fair Wine Competition are in the last pages.

Abbreviations for fairs and wines are indicated as follows:

(Sample—['80 OC] (G) '79 CA (S) '78 PN means that winery won a gold medal for a '79 Cabernet Sauvignon and a silver for '78 Pinot Noir) at the 1980 Orange County Fair. G-Gold, GG-Double Gold, S-Silver, B-Bronze, HM-Honorable Mention

OC	Orange County Fair
SJC	San Jose Mercury Consumer Panel
SJP	San Jose Mercury Professional Panel

A	Angelica
AB	Alicante Bouschet
B	Barbera
BDN	Blanc de Noir
BL	Blanc
BOT	Botrytised
BR	Burgundy
C	Chardonnay
CA	Cabernet Sauvignon
CAB	Cabernet Sauvignon Blanc
CAG	Carignane
CAR	Cabernet Sauvignon Rose
CB	Charbono
CD	Cold Duck
CF	Cabernet Franc
CH	Chenin Blanc
CHA	Champagne
CHAB	Chablis
CHD	Chenin Blanc Dry
CHS	Chenin Blanc Sweet
CHBBF	Champ. Brut Bot. Ferm.
CHEDBF	Champ. Ex. Dry Bot. Ferm.
CHCP	Camp. Charmat Proc.
CHPCP	Champ. Pink Char. Proc.

CHBPS	Champ. Spkl. Pink Rose Bulk
CHBP	Champ. Bulk Process
CL	Claret
CN	Carnelian
D	Dry
DM	Dry Malvasia
DW	Dessert Wine
DWF	Dessert Wine Flavored
EH	Early Harvest
ER	Emerald Riesling
FB	Fumé Blanc
FC	French Colombard
F	Flora
FR	Flavored Wine
G	Gewurztraminer
GA	Gamay
GAR	Gamay Rose
GB	Gamay Beaujolais
GE	Grenache
GER	Grenache Rose
GR	Green Hungarian
GRR	Grey Reisling
GS	Golden Chasselas
JR	Johannisberg (White) Reisling
LHG	Late Harvest Gewurztraminer
LHJ	Late Harvest Johannisberg Riesling
LHP	Late Harvest Pinot St. George
LHZ	Late Harvest Zinfandel
M	Merlot
MA	Marsala
MB	Merlot Blanc
MBSL	Malvasia Bianca Swt. Lt. Hvst.
MC	Muscat Canelli
MCS	Muscat Canelli Sweet
MU	Muscatel
MUA	Muscat of Alexandria
MD	Madeira
P	Port
PB	Pinot Blanc, White Pinot
PN	Pinot Noir
PNR	Pinot Noir Rose
PS	Petite Sirah
PSR	Petite Sirah Rose
PSG	Pinot St. George
R	Riesling or Rhine
RB	Ruby Cabernet
RO	Rosé
RT	Red Table Wine
RV	Rosso or Vino Rosso
S	Soft
SA	Sangria
SB	Sauvignon Blanc
SBD	Sauvignon Blanc Dry
SBO	Sauvignon Blanc Botrytis
SBS	Sauvignon Blanc Sweet
SE	Semillon

SES	Semillon Sweet
SFD	Sherry Flor Dry
SFM	Sherry Flor Medium
SFS	Sherry Flor Sweet
SG	Sweet Gewurztraminer
SH	Sherry
SHC	Cream Sherry
SHD	Sherry Dry
SHM	Sherry Medium
SHS	Sherry Sweet
SJR	Sweet Johannisberg Riesling
SLHR	Select Lt. Hvst. Jo. Ries.
SM	Sparkling Muscat
SP	Sparkling Burgundy
SR	Sweet Riesling
ST	Sauterne
SW	Sparkling Wine
SWR	Sweet White Riesling
SWZ	Sweet White Zinfandel
SY	Sylvaner (Franken) Riesling
SHG	Selec. Hvst. Gewurztraminer
T	Tokay
TB	Table Wine
TP	Tawny Port
VP	Vintage Port
VTP	Vintage Tawny Port
WF	White Flavored Wine
WR	White Riesling
WS	White Sweet
WT	White Table Wine
WZ	White Zinfandel
Z	Zinfandel
ZB	Zinfandel Blanc White
ZP	Zinfandel Port
ZR	Zinfandel Rosé

Please keep in mind that a winery may produce minimum quantities of specific types not as part of their usual production.

A

ACACIA WINERY ★ *Napa County*

2750 Las Amigas Road, Napa, CA 94559
(707) 226-9991 Founded: 1979
Storage: French oak.
Owner: Limited Partnership—General Partners: Jerry Goldstein, Michael Richmond. Winemaker: Larry Brooks.

A 50 acre Chardonnay vineyard is located in the Carneros region. Grapes are also purchased on a select vineyard basis. Label indicates vineyard and/or appellation.

100% varietal, vintage-dated, estate bottled Chardonnay is produced. Also produced are 100% varietal, vintage-dated Pinot Noir and Chardonnay.

['81 OC (B) '79 C.

Acidity

In wine, acidity is the word normally used to indicate the quality of tartness to the taste; i.e. to the presence of agreeable fruit acids, an important favorable element in wine quality. Not to be confused with "sour" or dryness or astringency.

Acids

Natural acidity in grapes (and new wines) is mostly tartaric and malic acids; after Malolactic "secondary" fermentation, the malic acid has changed into softer tasting lactic acid, but the tartaric acid remains unchanged through it all. Tartaric, in fact, remains unchanged through long-term bottle aging as well. (Tannins soften with age, but acids don't change unless the wine is chilled enough to cause cream of tarter to crystallize out of solution.) When that happens, you can see crystals on the cork or in the bottle but, even then, the taste of the wine is not usually changed significantly. Acidity gives the wine its "tart" taste, but equally important, acidity helps to protect the wine from spoilage, during fermentation and during aging later.

ADLER FELS WINERY *Sonoma County*

5325 Corrick Lane, Santa Rosa, CA 95405
(707) 539-3123
Storage: Oak casks and barrels, stainless steel.
Owners: David Coleman, Ayn Ryan & Patrick Heck. Winemaker: Patrick Heck.

Grapes are purchased on a select vineyard basis. Varietal, vintage-dated wines produced are Cabernet Sauvignon, Late Harvest Johannisberg Riesling, Gewurztraminer, Chardonnay and Champagne.

ADOBE CELLARS NEGOCIANTS

5789 Dexter Circle, Rohnert Park, CA 94928
(707) 584-5987

Negociant offers a complete line of vintage North Coast varietal wines.

Ageing

Wine develops smoothness, mellowness and character in ageing. Everything that happens to wine during ageing is not yet fully understood by scientists. However, many things are known: the grape solids are deposited, the wine clarifies itself, some oxidation occurs as the wine "breathes" through the wood casks and the many complex natural elements of the wine slowly interact or "marry" for smoothness. Other complex natural changes also occur. These changes are the most mysterious. They create in the wine elements of flavor and bouquet, substances called aromatic esters and other compounds that are not found in grapes, grape juice or new wine.

Age is not a positive guide to quality. Most of the world's wines complete their ageing quite early, even losing quality with further storage. Ageing usually begins in large tanks holding from 5,000 to 200,000 gallons each. Some wineries prefer wood, others concrete tanks lined with special coating, and others use glass-lined steel or stainless steel tanks. As wines mature, many producers complete the ageing in smaller wood containers. Oak is favored by some, but redwood is also much in use. Casks of 1,000 gallons, oval shaped to make the lees deposit in a small space at the bottom, are preferred by many. Some finish the ageing in even smaller casks or barrels. The smaller the container of wood, the greater the ratio of surface through which the wine can "breathe" and take on the flavor characteristics of the container.

AHERN WINERY ★ *Los Angeles County*

715 Arroyo Ave., San Fernando, CA 91340
(213) 365-3106 Founded: 1978
Storage: Oak tanks and barrels.
Owners: James and Joyce Ahern. Winemaker: James P. Ahern.

Grapes are purchased on a select vineyard basis. Label indicates vineyard and/or appellation.

Varietal, vintage-dated wines produced are Zinfandel, Cabernet Sauvignon, Pinot Noir and Chardonnay.

['81 OC] (B) '79 C; ['82 OC] (S) '81 C, (G) '80 Z; ['82 SJP] (B) '81 C, (B) '80 Z.

AHLGREN VINEYARD ★ *Santa Cruz County*

20320 Hwy. 9, Box 931, Boulder Creek, CA 95006
(408) 338-6071 Founded: 1976
Storage: French and American oak barrels.
Owners: Dexter and Valerie Ahlgren. Winemaker: Dexter Ahlgren.

The 12 acre vineyard is under development and located on the San Lorenzo watershed, in the Santa Cruz mountains. Grapes are also purchased on a select vineyard basis. Label indicates vineyard and/or appellation.

Varietal, vintage-dated wines produced are Chardonnay and Cabernet Sauvignon. Also Semillon and Zinfandel.

The winemaker's favorite wines are Cabernet Sauvignon & Chardonnay.

['82 OC] (B) '79 CA; ['82 SJP] (B) '79 CA.

ALAMEDA COUNTY *A North Central Coast County.*
Appellations: Livermore, Livermore Valley.

ALAMEDA, CONTRA COSTA

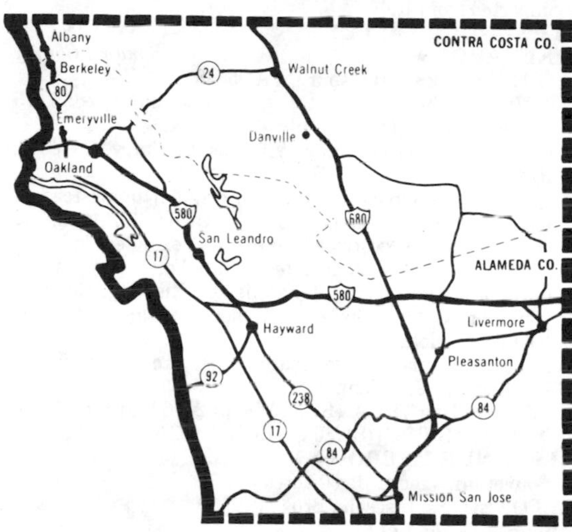

ALATERA VINEYARDS ★ *Napa County*
2170 Hoffman, Napa, CA 94558
(707) 944-2094 Founded: 1977
Storage: Oak and stainless steel.
Owners: Six individuals. Winemakers: H. T. and A. M. Mitchell. Larry Wara, consulting enologist.

Vineyards are in Napa County. Grapes are mainly supplied from Vineyard Hill Farm owned by Holbrook Mitchell in Yountville, Napa County. Label indicates vineyard and/or appellation.

Varietal, estate bottled, vintage-dated wines produced are Cabernet Sauvignon, Gewurztraminer, Late Harvest Bunch Sel. Hvst. Johannisberg Reisling, Pinot Noir and Chardonnay.

['81 OC] (S) '79 PN; ['82 OC] (B) '79 PN.

Alcohols

The major alcohol in wine is ethanol. Table wines with low ethanol content have a thin character, and those with too high a concentration often have a "hot" taste. The other alcohols, never present in large concentrations, can be considered flavor components, especially in contributing something to the "nose" of the wine.

Alcohol Content

Average % Alcohol Content of wine: Aperitif, 12% - 13%; Red, White, Rosé and Champagne, 12% - 14%; Dessert, 17% - 21%; soft wines 7% - 14%.

Aleatico

(Sweeter Fortified Wine)

A varietal grape occasionally used for sweet table or dessert wine. It is related to the muscats originally imported from Italy.

ALEXANDER VALLEY VINEYARDS ★ *Sonoma County*

8644 Hwy. 128, Healdsburg, CA 95448
(707) 433-7209 Founded: 1975
Storage: Oak barrels, stainless steel.
Owner: The Wetzel Family. Winemaster: Harry H. Wetzel, III.

Purchased acreage in 1963 on original homestead of Cyrus Alexander who homesteaded the land in 1842. 240 acre vineyard is located at winery in Alexander Valley.

100% varietal, vintage-dated, estate bottled wines produced are Chardonnay, Johannisberg Riesling, Gewurztraminer, Chenin Blanc, Cabernet Sauvignon (80-90%, balance Merlot).

The winemaker's favorite wines are Johannisberg Riesling and Chardonnay.

['81 OC] (S) '78 CA, (B) '80 WR; ['82 OC] (S) '79 CA, (G) '80 C; ['82 SJP&C] (B) '80 C, (P) (B) '79 CA.

ALEXANDER'S CROWN

Souverain. Vineyard: 60 acres.

ALFONSO (*See* Bisceglia Bros.)

Alicante Bouschet

A prolific grape rarely used as a red table wine. Predominantly used in Burgundy blends for color. Heavily planted in San Joaquin Valley. Originally came from Spain. Produced as a varietal by very few.

Award winning wines to look for: Monterey Peninsula, Papagni.

ALMADEN ★ *Santa Clara, San Benito, Monterey Counties*

1530 Blossom Hill Road, San Jose, CA 95118
(408) 269-1312 Founded: 1852
Storage: White oak, French oak, Hungarian oak, redwood, stainless steel.
Owner: National Distillers and Chemical Corp., Inc. Winemaker: Klaus Mathes.

The vineyards are spread over three counties. 4,281 acres in San Benito Co., 2,105 acres in Monterey Co. and 16 acres in Santa Clara Co. Varietal wines all show appellation-of-origin and vintage. The varietal wines produced are: Chardonnay, Sauvignon Blanc, Johannisberg Riesling, Gewurztraminer, Grey Riesling, Chenin Blanc, French Colombard, Pinot Noir, Cabernet Sauvignon, Gamay Beaujolais, Gamay Zinfandel, Gamay Rose and Grenache Rosé.

Also produced are Monterey Chablis, Monterey Burgundy, Light Chablis, Light Rhine, Light Rosé, Sweet and Pale-Triple-Dry Vermouth, Solera Flor Fino, Solera Cocktail, Solera Golden and Solera Cream Sherry, Tinta Ruby and Solera Tinta Tawny Port.

The Almaden "Mountain" wines are Mountain Red Claret, Red Burgundy, Red Chianti, White Chablis, White Sauterne, Rhine and Nectar Vin Rosé.

The sparkling wines are Vintage Brut and Extra Dry Champagnes, Eye Of The Partridge, Chardonnay Nature and Blanc de Blancs all carry a cuvee date.

Bag-in-Box wines include Almaden Carafe Chablis, Rose and Burgundy in 10 and 18-liter containers and Le Domaine Crown Chablis, Rhine, Rosé and Burgundy in the 4-liter size.

The Le Domaine Champagnes are Brut, Extra Dry and Pink. Also Sparkling Burgundy and Select Cold Duck.

The label bearing the name and appellation, Charles Lefranc Founder's Wines are: Late Harvest Johannisberg Riesling, Chardonnay, Carbernet Sauvignon, Pinot St. George, Founders Port, Maison Rouge, Maison Blanc, Late Harvest Gewurztraminer, Fume Blanc and Zinfandel Royale.

Under the Laurent-Perrier label, a joint venture between Almaden's parent company and the French producer Laurent-Perrier, is the vintage California Chardonnay Blanc de Blancs.

['80 OC] (G) '78 CA; ['81 OC] (B) '78 SB, (G) '78 CA, (B) NVP, (G) NV TP; ['82 OC] (B) '80 G, (B) '77 JR, (B) '79 JR, (S) '80 Z LHS; ['82 SJC] (S) '79 LHJR, (B) '80 R.

ALTA VINEYARD CELLAR ★ *Napa County*

1311 Schramsberg Road, Calistoga, CA 94515
(707) 942 6708 Founded: 1878
Owners: Benjamin and Rose Falk. Winemaker: Jon P. Axhelm.

Alta was founded by Colin T. McEachran. In 1880 Robert Louis Stevenson visited Alta and his visit was described in his chapter on Napa wine in "Silverado Squatters". In 1970 the Falks bought Alta and replanted the 10 acre vineyard in Chardonnay. Varietal, vintage-dated estate bottled Chardonnay is produced.

['81 OC] (B) '79 C; ['82 OC] (S) '78 GA; ['82 SJC] (B) '80 C.

ALTA VISTA (*See* Grand Pacific Vineyards.)

AMADOR COUNTY *Sierra Foothills*

Appellations: Shenandoah Valley, Fiddletown.

AMADOR WINERY *Amador County*

P.O. Box 65, Highway 49 & O'Neill Alley, Amador City, CA 95601
(209) 267-5320
Storage: French and Spanish Oak.

Owner: Harry Ahrendt. Winemaker: Harry Ahrendt.

Wines produced are Sutters Gold, Spiced Mountain Jubilee, Sauterne, Chablis, Mountain Rhine, Burgundy, and Madame Pink Chablis.

AMADOR, CALAVERAS, EL DORADO, SACRAMENTO, TUOLUMNE

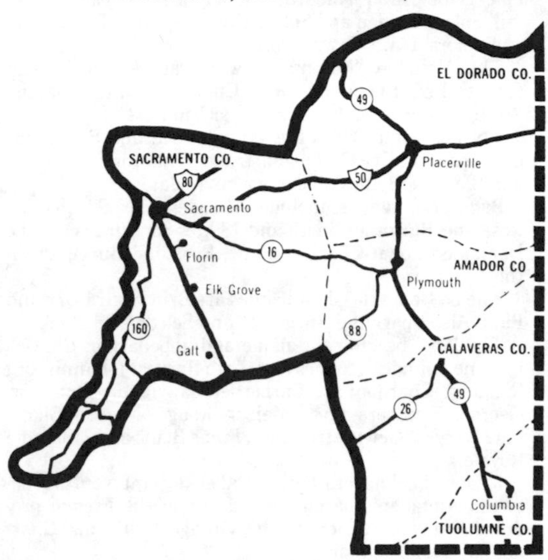

AMADOR FOOTHILL WINERY *Amador County*

12500 Steiner Rd., Shenandoah Valley, Plymouth, CA 95669

(209) 245-6307 Founded: 1980

Owners: Ben Zeitman & Joan Sieber. Winemaker: Ben Zeitman. Vineyards: 8 acres of Cabernet Sauvignon & Sauvignon Blanc; 2½ acres of Semillon.

Ben is a former NASA chemist and his wife Joan is a professor at Cal State, Hayward.

Label indicates vineyard and/or appellation. Vineyard in Shenandoah Valley. Varietal, vintage-dated wines produced are Zinfandel, White Zinfandel, Dry Chenin Blanc, Sauvignon Blanc and Semillon.

AMBASSADOR (*See* Perelli-Minetti.)

Americans for Wine

A nationwide organization to bank together wine consumers interested in the wellbeing of wine in the United States.

Americans for Wine, a voluntary grassroots network, will provide a forum for consumers, growers, restaurants, retailers, wholesalers and wineries as a cohesive, independent group to express a collective view on public policy issues that affect wine. Members receive periodic newsletters and bulletins.

To join send $1 to: Wine Institute (the Trade Association of the California Wine Industry), 165 Post St., San Francisco, CA 94108.

ANDERSON VALLEY—Vineyard district in Mendocino County.

S. ANDERSON VINEYARD *Napa County*
1473 Yountville Crossroad, Napa, CA 94558
(707) 944-8642 Founded: 1974
Storage: Small French cooperage, stainless steel.
Owners: Stanley and Carol Anderson. Winemaker: Stanley Anderson. Vineyard: 49 acres at winery.

Varietal, vintage-dated, estate bottled wines produced are 100% Chardonnay, Sparkling Cuvee de Noir and Sparkling Cuvee de Chardonnay made by the Methode Champenoise.

ANDERSON WINE CELLARS *Tulare County*
20147 Ave. 306, Exeter, CA 93221
(209) 592-4682 Founded: 1980
Storage: Oak and stainless steel.
Owners: Don and Cathy Anderson. Winemaker: Don Anderson. Vineyards: 15 acres near the winery.

Varietal, vintage-dated wines produced are Chenin Blanc and Ruby Cabernet.

ANDRE (*See* E. & J. Gallo.)

Angelica

A white dessert wine, traditionally one of the sweetest wine types. It is either straw or amber-colored and mild and fruity. Angelica originated in California and is produced from a number of grape varieties, including Grenache and Mission. Good with or following dessert, and with between-meals refreshments. Serve chilled or at room temperature. Most common sacramental wine.

Aperitif Wine

French word from the medieval Latin "Aperire," meaning "to open," and refers to wine and other drinks taken before meals to stimulate the appetite. In the strictest sense, it applies to vermouths and other wines flavored with herbs and other aromatic substances, but in general usage, any wine when served before a meal may be referred to as an "aperitif."

Appellation

Term which signifies the geographical origin of a wine. When the appellation of origin appears on the label, 75% of the wine must come from grapes grown in that region.

Appellations

The following appellations are approved American Viticultural Areas according to the Code of Federal Regulations #27 CFR part 9 in effect January 1, 1983 where 75% of the fruit grown in the wine is from these areas: Guenoc Valley, McDowell Valley, Napa Valley, Santa Cruz Mountains, San Pasqual Valley, Santa Maria Valley and Sonoma Valley.

Appetizer Wines

Wines enjoyed before the meal. Sherry and Vermouth,

the main appetizer wines, range from extra dry to sweet in taste.

Appleness

A frequent characteristic of fine white wine.

ARGONAUT WINERY *Amador County*

13675 Mt. Echo Drive, Ione, CA 95640

(209) 274-2882 Founded: 1976

Storage: Oak and stainless steel.

Owners: W. M. Bilbo, Harly Harty, Paul Loyd, Neal Overboe and Jim Payne. Winemaker: Neal Overboe.

Varietal, vintage-dated wines produced are Zinfandel and Barbera.

Argols

The tartrate deposited by wines during ageing.

Aroma

That part of the fragrance of wine which originates from the grapes used, as distinguished from "bouquet."

ARRATA'S VINEYARD—Santa Clara County vineyard.

ARROYO SECO VINEYARD—Salinas Valley, Monterey County vineyard.

ARROYO SONOMA (*See* Bandiera Winery.)

ASSUMPTION ABBEY (*See* Brookside.)

Astringency

The quality of causing the mouth to pucker. The degree of astringency of a wine depends primarily upon the amount of tannin it has absorbed from the skins and seeds of the grapes. Moderate astringency is a desirable quality in many red wine types. Not to be confused with dryness. Never call an astringent wine "sour".

Atmosphere

The unit of measure for pressure of wine in a bottle of sparkling wine or Champagne. Air pressure at sea level is equal to 1 Atmosphere. At 50 degrees F, sparkling wines have 1.5 Atmopsheres. It increases to 2.8 Atmospheres at 80 degrees F. This is why the bottles have metal cork retaining wires. Always open away from another individual.

Auslese

The German word for "selection". Refers to selecting only ripe grape bunches and discarding unripe berries.

B

WILLIAM BACCALA WINERY *Mendocino County*

10400 S. Hwy. 101, Ukiah, CA 95482

(707) 468-8936 Founded: 1981

Storage: American, French oak, stainless steel.

Owner: William Baccala.

Grapes are purchased on a select vineyard basis. Label indicates vineyard and/or appellation. Varietal, vintage-dated wines produced are Zinfandel, Sauvignon Blanc, Chardonnay and Cabernet Sauvignon.

BACIGALUP VINEYARD—Chardonnay vineyard near Healdsburg.

BACIGALUPI ★—*See* Belvedere Wine Co.
['82 OC] (G) '79 PN.

Balance
Denoting complete harmony in the principal constituents of the wine. Excessive amounts of one over another causes disharmony of palate impression and wines so constituted are described as "poorly balanced" or "unbalanced."

BALDINELLI VINEYARDS ★ *Amador County*
Route 2, Box 7A, Plymouth, CA 95669
(415) 339-8253 Founded: 1979
Storage: French and American 50-60 gallon barrels.
Owners: John Miller and Edward Baldinelli. Winemaker: Edward Baldinelli. 70 acre vineyard in the Shenandoah Valley.

Varietal, vintage-dated, estate bottled wines produced are: White Zinfandel, Zinfandel and Cabernet Sauvignon.
['81 OC] (S) '79 Z.

BALE MILL CELLARS (*See* Charles Shaw.)

BALI HAI (*See* Heublein.)

Balling
The system for measuring soluble solids in grape juice, which are mostly sugars. Balling degrees indicate sugar content. Similar to Brix.

BALLARD CANYON WINERY ★ *Santa Barbara Cty.*
1825 Ballard Canyon Road, Solvang, CA 93463
(805) 688-7585 Founded: 1978
Owners: the Hallock family. Winemakers: Gene Hallock and Fred Halloway.

The 45 acre vineyard is located at winery 3½ miles north of Solvang. 100% varietal, vintage-dated, estate bottled wines produced are Cabernet Sauvignon, Johannisberg Riesling, Cabernet Sauvignon Blanc, Chardonnay, Muscat-Santa Ynez, Johannisberg Riesling Reserve (botrytised) and Fume Blanc.
['82 OC] (G) '81 C, (B) '81 MC, (S) '81 JR, (G) '81 JR; ['82 SJP&C] (B) '81 C, (S&S) '81 JR, (P) (S) '81 SJR.

BALTO VINEYARD—Cabernet Sauvignon vineyard in Sonoma Valley.

BALVERNE WINERY & VINEYARDS *Sonoma County*
P.O. Box 70, 10810 Hillview Road, Windsor, CA 95492
(707) 433 6913
President and Cellarmaster: Bill Bird. Winegrowers: Glen Whitmire, Baltazar Mendez. Winemakers: John Kongsgaard, Doug Nalle.

A 710 acre estate includes winery and 250 acres of vineyards. Label indicates wineyard and/or appellation.

Varietal, vintage-dated, estate bottled wines produced are Chardonnay, Dry Gewurztraminer, Johannisberg Riesling, Sauvignon Blanc, Zinfandel, Scheurebe and Cabernet Sauvignon. Also produced is Healdsburger a Sonoma County white wine.

BANDIERA WINERY ★ *Sonoma County*
155 Cherry Creek Road, Cloverdale, CA 95425
(707) 894-4295
Owner: California Wine. Co., Winemaker: John B. Merritt,

Jr. Vineyards: Potter Valley (Mendocino County), Dry Creek Valley (Sonoma County), Chiles Valley (Napa Valley), Los Carneros (Sonoma Valley).

Label indicates vineyard and/or appellation.

Varietal, vintage-dated wines produced are Cabernet Sauvignon, Pinot Noir, Zinfandel, Chardonnay, Sauvignon Blanc and Johannisberg Riesling.

Produced under the John B. Merritt label are varietal, vintage-dated Chardonnay, Sauvignon Blanc and Cabernet Sauvignon.

['82 SJP] (B) '79 CA.

Barbera

(Red Table Wine)

A varietal grape. Produces red, full-bodied, dry and tannic wine. Will age up to 10 years. Excellent accompaniment to pasta, sea food and fish stews, when young. Aged Barbera is excellent with game. Originally from the Piedmont district of Italy.

Award winning wines to look for: Borra's Cellar, East-Side, Estrella River, Fortino, Gemello, Giumarra, Monterey Peninsula, Papagni, Ridge, Sebastiani, Walker.

BARBERONE

Generic type of wine. Barbera grapes from San Joaquin. Dry.

BARENGO *San Joaquin County*

3125 East Orange Street, Acampo, CA 95220

(209) 369-2746 (*See* Lost Hills) Founded: 1934

BARGETTO WINERY ★ *Santa Cruz County*

3535 North Main Street, Soquel, CA 95073

(408) 475-2258 Founded: 1933

Storage: Oak barrels, redwood, stainless steel.

Owner: Beverly Bargetto. Winemaker: Jeff Elliott.

Four other members of the family also work at the winery. Grapes are purchased on a select district basis. Primary sources are San Luis Obispo and Santa Barbara counties.

The varietal, vintage-dated wines are Chardonnay, Zinfandel, Zinfandel Rosé, Cabernet Sauvignon, Chenin Blanc, Merlot, Johannisberg Riesling, Select Late Harvest Johannisberg Riesling and Gewurztraminer.

The other varietal is Chaucers Mead. Also Chablis, Burgundy, and a selection of fruit and berry wines.

The winemaker's favorites are Chardonnay, Johannisberg Riesling and Cabernet Sauvignon.

['81 OC] (G) '80 CH, (B) '77 PS, (S) '80 WR, (S) '78 VP, (S) '65 P; ['82 OC] (S) '80 C, (B) '81 CH, (S) '81 JR, (B) '81 JR, (G) '81 JR, (B) '80 Z; ['82 SJP] (B) '80 C, (B) '81 G, (S) '81 R.

Barrel Fermented

Wine fermented in barrel instead of stainless steel or large wood tanks.

LOUIS BARTOLUCCI CELLARS (*See* Mont St. John Cellars.)

BATES RANCH—Cabernet Sauvignon vineyard in Santa Cruz Mountains, Santa Clara County.

Baume
The measure of the sugar content of the grape. One Baume is equal to approximately 1.75% of sugar content.

BAY CELLARS *Alameda County*
Winery: 1401 Stanford Avenue, Emeryville, CA 94608
Office: 1675 Tacoma Avenue, Berkeley, CA 94707
(415) 526-0469
Storage: French oak, stainless steel.
Owner, Winemaker: Richard L. Rotblatt.
Grapes are purchased on a selected vineyard basis. Varietal, vintage-dated wines produced are Pinot Noir, Merlot, Cabernet Sauvignon and Chardonnay.

BEAR MOUNTAIN WINERY (*See* LaMont Winery.)

BEATTY RANCH—Cabernet and Zinfandel vineyard near St. Helena in Napa Hills.

BEAUJOLAIS (*See* Gamay.)

BEAULIEU VINEYARD ★ *Napa County*
1960 St. Helena Highway, Rutherford, CA 94573
(707) 963-1451 Founded: 1900
President: Legh F. Knowles, Jr. Vice President, General Manager & Winemaker: Thomas B. Selfridge. Technical Director: Dimitri Tchelistcheff.
The 1500 acre vineyards are near the winery in central Napa Valley, while grapes for BV Pinot Noir and Pinot Chardonnay are grown in the Carneros region of southern Napa.
The varietal, estate bottled wines produced are Cabernet Sauvignon, Pinot Noir, Gamay Beaujolais, Pinot Chardonnay, Johannisberg Riesling, Muscat Blanc, Sauvignon Blanc and Muscat de Frontignan.
Generic wines are Chablis, Burgundy, Brut Champagne and Champagne de Chardonnay.
['81 OC] (B) '77 CA, (G) '78 PN, (S) '79 SB, (S) '74 SW; ['82 OC] (B) '77 CA, (B) '79 CA.

BEAU VAL WINES *Amador County*
Star Route #2, Box 8D, 10671 Valley Drive, Plymouth, CA 95669
(209) 245-3281 Founded: 1979
Storage: Small Oak cooperage.
Owners: Vernon and Jean Gilman, Nan and Robert Francis. Winemaker: Vernon Gilman.
7.5 acres of vineyards in Shenandoah Valley of Amador County. 100% varietal vintage-dated wines produced are Zinfandel, Zinfandel Blanc and Special Selection Zinfandel.

JOHN B. BECKETT CELLARS (*See* Diamond Oaks Vineyard.)

Beerenauslese
The German word for "berry selection". A special Auslese made from specially selected grapes that have been affected by Botrytis.

BEL ARBRES ★ *Mendocino County*
Downtown Hopland, S. Hwy. 101, (P.O. Box 339), Hopland, CA 95449
(707) 744-1146 Founded: 1975
Storage: Oak and stainless steel.

Owners: Limited Partnership. Consulting Winemakers: Diane Fetzer and Paul Dolan.

Bel Arbres has its own unique wines both from the standpoint of appellation and style. Grapes are purchased on a selected vineyard basis. Label indicates vineyard and/or appellation.

Varietal, vintage-dated wines produced are White Zinfandel, Sauvignon Blanc, Chardonnay, Cabernet Sauvignon, Dry Chenin Blanc, Merlot, Zinfandel and White Riesling. Also produced is Blanc de Blancs and Vin Rouge.

['81 OC] (S) '78 CA, (S) '80 CH, (B) '78 Z; ['82 OC] (G) '79 CA, (G) '81 CH; ['82 SJP&C] (S) '81 C, (S) '81 ZB, (B) '81 C, (C) (B) '81 SB, (C) (B) '79 M, (P&C) (S&B) '81 WZ.

BELL CANYON (*See* Burgess Cellars.)

BELLA NAPOLI WINERY *San Joaquin County*
21128 So. Austin Road, Manteca, CA 95336
(209) 599-3885 Founded: 1934
Storage: Wood and stainless steel.
Owner: Estate of Tony R. Hat. Vineyard: 60 acres.

Brands—Vine Flow, Family Vineyard, Ala Sante.

BELL HILL VINEYARD—Cabernet Sauvignon vineyard in Lake County.

BELLE TERRE VINEYARD—Cabernet Sauvignon, Chardonnay, and Johannisberg Riesling vineyard in Alexander Valley.

BELLEROSE VINEYARD *Sonoma County*
435 W. Dry Creek Road, Healdsburg, CA 95448
(707) 433-1637 Founded: 1979
Owners: Charles and Nancy Richard. Winemaker: Charles Richard. Vineyard: 52 acres.

Bellerose Vineyard was established in 1979, but grapes have been grown and wine made on the property since 1887, when Captain Everett Wise had stones hauled by wagon from nearby Mill Creek to build the original winery. That structure burnt in the late Thirties; the same stones now form the walls, two feet thick, of the present cellars, located on the site and incorporating part of the older building.

The 52 acre estate vineyard is located in the lower end of Dry Creek Valley. The vineyard produces Cabernet Sauvignon, Merlot, Cabernet Franc, Petite Verdot and Malbec. Bellerose specializes in a "Medoc" style wine, Cuvee Bellerose Cabernet Sauvignon, which combines the five varieties mentioned above. In certain years, a Rosé is produced, primarily of Merlot, "Rosé du Val" and "Rouge du Val", a blend primarily of Cabernet Sauvignon and Merlot, both wines produced from younger vines.

BELTANE VINEYARD—Cabernet Sauvignon and Chardonnay vineyard in Sonoma Valley.

BELVEDERE WINE CO. *Sonoma County*
4035 Westside Road, Healdsburg, CA 95448
(707) 433-8113 Founded: 1979
Storage: Oak and stainless steel.
Peter S. Friedman, Gen. Partner. Winemaker: Donald H. Frazer.

BERGSTROM VINEYARD—Cabernet Sauvignon vineyard of Ranchita Oaks Winery.

BERINGER VINEYARDS ★ *Napa, Sonoma Counties*
2000 Main St., St. Helena, CA 94574
(707) 963-7115 Founded: 1876
Storage: Nevers, Limousin, Yugoslavian and American oak; redwood, stainless steel.
Owner: Jean-Pierre Labruyere of France. Winemaker: Myron S. Nightingale.

The 2000 acres of vineyards are in the Napa and Knights Valleys. Each vineyard has been planted to grow specific grapes. The vineyards are Knights Valley, Gasser, St. Helena, DeCarle, Gamble, Yountville, Big Ranch Road, Lemmon Ranch, Marolf and Salvador.

Label indicates vineyard and/or appellation. The Beringer-labeled varietal vintage-dated wines are Cabernet Sauvignon (Estate and Private Reserve), Pinot Noir, Zinfandel, Chardonnay (Estate and Private Reserve), Johannisberg Riesling, Fumé Blanc, Chenin Blanc, Gamay Rose, Gamay Beaujolais, Gewurztraminer, Malvasia-Amabile, Cabernet Sauvignon Port, Malvasia Bianca and Dry French Colombard.

The Los Hermanos-labeled wines are Chablis, Burgundy, Vin Rosé, Rhine, Gamay Beaujolais, French Colombard, Chenin Blanc and Cabernet Sauvignon. Light wines include Chablis, Rosé, French Colombard, Rhine and Chenin Blanc.

The winemaker's favorites are: "Beringer" Cabernet Sauvignon, Chardonnay, Fumé Blanc, Cabernet Sauvignon and Port.

['81 OC] (S) '80 WR, (B) '80 G, (S) '79 C, (G) '77 CA, (G) '78 C, (B) NVP; ['82 OC] (G) '81 CH, (S) '80 G, (B) '80 SB, (S) '80 JR, (B) '78 PN, (G) '77 PS, (B) '78 PN, (S) '81 SB.

BERKELEY WINE CELLARS ★ *Alameda County*
907 University Ave., Berkeley, CA 94710
(415) 549-1266 Founded: 1970
Founder and Winemaker: Peter R. Brehm.

Varietal, vintage-dated wines produced are a specialty Zinfandel Port, Zinfandel, Chardonnay and Cabernet Sauvignon. Also imports and deals in winemaking equipment and supplies for wineries.

['81 OC] (S) '78 Z, (G) '78 VP.

BERNARDO WINERY, INC. *San Diego County*
13330 Paseo del Verano Norte, San Diego, CA 92128
(619) 487-1886 Founded: 1889
Storage: Redwood vats.
Owner and Winemaker: Ross Rizzo.

Ross Rizzo is a fifth generation winemaker. 75 acres of vineyards are in San Diego County. Grapes grown are Zinfandel, Muscat, Tokay, Carignane, Mission and Rosa Peru.

BERNSTEIN VINEYARD—Cabernet Sauvignon vineyard of Mt. Veeder Winery.

BERTERO WINERY *Santa Clara County*
3920 Hecker Pass Highway, Gilroy, CA 95020
(208) 842-3032 Founded: 1906
Storage: Redwood tanks, oak casks.

Owner, Winemaker: Angelo C. Bertero.

The 150 acre vineyard is located near the winery. The original 1906 planted vineyard is still producing Cabernet Sauvignon. Label indicates vineyard and/or appellation. 100% varietal, vintage-dated wines produced are: Grignolino, Barbera, Cabernet Sauvignon and Grenache Rose.

Other wines produced are: Burgundy (Grenache, Carignane and Barbera), Chablis (100% French Colombard) and Zinfandel. The Winemaker's favorite wines are: Barbera and Grignolino.

BIANCHI WINERY *Fresno County*

5806 N. Modoc Ave., Kerman, CA 93630

(209) 846-7356 Founded: 1974

Museum & Tasting Room, 2045 S. Harbor Blvd., Anaheim, CA 92802

(714) 750-4503

Owner: Joseph Bianchi.

Vineyards are located near the winery.

Varietal wines produced are Zinfandel, Grenache Rosé, Cabernet Sauvignon and French Colombard.

Also produced is a Red Lite Wine and White Wine Cooler: 5% alcohol and canned regular and light wines, 6-3 oz. "canteens" Villa Bianchi Chablis, Vin Rosé and Burgundy.

BIG RANCH ROAD VINEYARD—Chardonnay vineyard in Napa County.

BIG SUR (*See* Monterey Peninsula Winery.)

Big Wine

A tasting term to express body and fullness and apparent fruitiness.

Binning

Bottle-ageing of newly bottled wines, usually in bins, before release for sale.

BIRKMYER VINEYARD—Johannisberg Riesling vineyard in Napa County.

BISCEGLIA BROTHERS WINE CO. *Madera County*

25427 Avenue 13, Madera, CA 93637

(209) 673-3594 Founded: 1880

Subsidiary of Canandaigua Wine Co.

Wines produced under the Bisceglia label are Chablis, Rhine, Chenin Blanc, Vin Rosé, Burgundy and Cabernet Sauvignon.

BLACK MOUNTAIN VINEYARD—Chardonnay, Zinfandel, and Cabernet Sauvignon Blanc vineyard in Alexander Valley.

Black Muscat

A dessert wine made from one of the Muscat grapes. Sweet and high in alcohol content (12% - 20%). A Ruby Port type taste medium to deep red, rich fruity and full-bodied. Produced only by Novitiate. (*See* Muscatel.)

Blanc de Blancs

White wine made from white grapes.

Blanc de Noir

White wine made from black grapes, by fermenting must without the presence of skins. The excellent Domaine Chandon Champagne is made in this manner, and the label indicates this.

Award winning wines to look for: Baldinelli/Shenandoah, Richard Carey, Congress Springs, DeLoach, Edmeades, Franciscan, Geyser Peak, Grand Cru, Hacienda, Johnson's, Kenwood, Konocti, Mill Creek, Ross-Kellerei, San Antonio, Santa Ynez Valley, Stevenot, Stony Ridge, Trader Joe's, Valley of the Moon, Weibel, Mark West, Whitehall Lane, Zaca Mesa.

Blending

The art of mixing wines of various qualities and characteristics to make a better quality wine and insure uniformity from year to year.

BLUE HERON WINERY *Sonoma County*

P.O. Box 1053, 71 West North St., Unit J, Healdsburg, CA 95448

(707) 433-8164 Founded: 1980

Body

Consistency, thickness or substance of a wine, as opposed to the lack of body in a thin wine. Body of a wine reflects the quantity of solid matter, or "extract," in solution in the liquid and, more particularly, the alcohol content.

BOEGER WINERY, INC. ★ *El Dorado County*

1709 Carson Road, Placerville, CA 95667

(916) 622-8094 Founded: 1973

Storage: Small oak cooperage, stainless steel.

Owners: Greg and Susan Boeger, Dr. & Mrs. George Babbin. Winemaker: Greg Boeger.

Gold miners settled El Dorado County in late 1840's. When gold became scarce, miners turned to making wine. In 1860 the county had more vineyards than Napa or Sonoma. In 1890, there were more than 100 wineries in the Sierra Foothills. The stone cellar at Boeger was built during this period.

The 20 acre vineyard is located at the winery. Grapes are also purchased on a select district basis. Label indicates vineyard and/or appellation. Varietal vintage-dated wines produced are: Chardonnay, Sauvignon Blanc, Chenin Blanc, Johannisberg Riesling, Zinfandel, Cabernet Sauvignon. Also estate bottled Merlot.

"Hangtown Red," a blended red wine and Sierra Blanc are also produced.

['81 OC] (B) '80 CH, (G) '80 WR; ['82 OC] (B) '79 CA; ['82 SJC] (B) '81 SB, (B&B) '81 JR.

BOGLE VINEYARDS ★ *Yolo County*

Rt. 1, Box 276, Clarksburg, CA 95612

(916) 744-1139 Founded: 1979

Storage: Small Oak, stainless steel.

President: Warren Bogle. Winemaker: Richard Vierra.

The 350 acre estate vineyard is located at the winery and grows Chenin Blanc, Grey Riesling, Semillon, Sauvignon Blanc, Zinfandel and Petite Sirah.

Varietal, vintage-dated, estate bottled wines produced are Petite Sirah, Chenin Blanc and Merritt Island Rosé (100% Petite Sirah).

['82 OC] (B) '81 CA, (B) '81 CH; ['82 SJP] (B) '81 PSR.

JACQUES BONET (*See* United Vintners.)

BOONE'S FARMS (*See* E. & J. Gallo.)

CIRIACO BORELLI WINERY *San Joaquin County*
5471 North Jack Tone Rd., Stockton, CA 95205
(209) 931-2447 (by appointment only) Founded: 1975
Storage: Oak

BORRA'S CELLAR ★ *San Joaquin County*
1301 E. Armstrong Road, Lodi, CA 95240
(209) 368-5082 Founded: 1975
Storage: Oak barrels.
Owners: Stephen and Beverly Borra. Manager/Winemaker: Stephen Borra. Vineyards: 30 acres at winery.

Varietal, vintage-dated, estate bottled wines produced are Barbera and Carignane.

['82 OC] (B) '78 B.

BOSCHE—Cabernet Sauvignon vineyard in Napa Valley.

Botrytis

Called "Pourriture Noble" in France, "edel faule" in Germany, translated means "noble rot." Botrytis cinera when the white grapes become shrunken, pinkish raisins covered with grey mold. If nature infects the grapes with Botrytis at just the right time (after they have matured to around 17 degrees Brix), and if the humidity then alternates between high and low levels, and if it doesn't hail or rain too much, and if the temperature remains warm long enough for the mold to grow and concentrate sweetness in the grape cluster to levels approaching 30 degrees, then it is possibly a great year for a classic dessert wine that once only places like Barsac, Sauterne, Rhine and Mosel were capable of producing. But no longer is this true, California has its own fabulous Botrytis wines. Botrytis adds a "honey-like" flavor of its own, while concentrating the varietal character of the grape into the wine.

Bottled in Bond

A term used to indicate bottled under Government supervision on bonded premises.

Bottle Sizes

Half gallon: 64 oz., 1.75 liters, 59.2 oz.
Magnum: 51.2 oz., 1.50 liters, 50.72 oz.
Quart: 32 oz., 1.00 liters, 33.8 oz.
Fifth: 25.6 oz., 750 mil, 25.4 oz.
Pint: 16.0 oz., 500 mil, 16.9 oz.

BOUNTY (*See* California Growers Winery.)

Bouquet

That part of the fragrance of the wine which originates from fermentation and ageing, as distinguished from "aroma", the fragrance of the grape in the wine.

BOWMAN VINEYARD—Zinfandel vineyard in Shenandoah Valley of Amador County.

B. & R. VINEYARDS, INC. *Santa Clara County*
(dba Rapazzini Winery)
US Hwy. 101, P.O. Box 247, Gilroy, CA 95020
(408) 842-5649 Founded: 1962
President & Winemaker: John P. Rapazzini. Vice President: Sandra K. Rapazzini.

Brand names: Rapazzini, Los Altos, San Juan Bautista.

THE BRANDER VINEYARD ★ *Santa Barbara County*
P.O. Box 92, Los Olivos, CA 93441
(805) 688-2455 Founded: 1979
Storage: Stainless steel.
Owner/Winemaker: C. Frederic Brander. Vineyards: 40 acres.

All wines produced are estate-bottled.

['82 OC] (B) '81 SB; ['82 SJP] (B) '81 SB.

BRAREN PAULI WINERY *Mendocino County*
12507 Hawn Creek Rd., Potter Valley, CA 95469 or
1613 Spring Hill Road, Petaluma, CA 94952
(707) 743-1173 or (707) 778-0721 Founded: 1979
Storage: Oak, stainless steel.
Owners: Larry Braren & Bill Pauli.

Winery owns vineyards in Potter and Redwood Valley in Mendocino County. Varietal, vintage-dated wines produced are Zinfandel, Chardonnay and Sauvignon Blanc.

BRECKENRIDGE CELLARS (*See* Guimarra Vineyards.)

Brix

The system used for measuring the soluble solids in grape juice. A measure of sugar. Brix degrees range from zero degrees to about 40 degrees. Similar to Balling.

BRENNER CELLARS *Sonoma County*
P.O. Box 2785, Beverly Hills, CA 90213
(213) 768-4880 Founded: 1980
Owner/Winemaker: Allan Brenner.

Grapes are purchased on a select vineyard basis. Label indicates vineyard and/or appellation.

Varietal, vintage-dated wines are Zinfandel, Cabernet Sauvignon and Chardonnay.

J. F. J. BRONCO WINERY ★ *Stanislaus County*
6342 Bystrum Road, Ceres, CA 95307
(209) 538-3131 Founded: 1973
Storage: Stainless steel.
Owners: John Jr.; Joseph S.; and Fred T. Franzia. Winemaker: Robert Darby.

The three dynamic and knowledgeable Franzias grew up in the wine industry at the Franzia Brothers Winery. They founded the Bronco Wine Company in 1973.

Wines produced under the J.F.J. label are: Chablis, Ruby Rosé, Rich Burgundy, Pink Chablis, Rhinewine, Chablis Blanc, Sangria, Champagne, Pink Champagne and Cold Duck. Wines produced under the CC Vineyard label are: Chablis, Pink Chablis, Vin Rosé, Burgundy, Champagne, Pink Champagne, and Cold Duck.

['82 JC] (S) CHAB, (P) (B) BR.

BROOKSIDE ★ *San Bernardino County*
9900 Guasti Road, Guasti, CA 91743
(714) 983-2787 Founded: 1832
Storage: Oak, redwood, stainless steel.
Winemaker: Bill Wieland.

Brookside is the oldest continuing vineyard in business, having started in 1832.

['81 OC] (G) '79 PS, (B) '80 CH; ['82 OC] (B) '80 PS.

DAVID BRUCE WINERY ★ *Santa Cruz County*
P.O. Box 205, Saratoga, CA 95071
(408) 354-4214 Founded: 1964
Storage: Oak barrels, stainless steel.
President: David Bruce. Vineyard: 25 acres at the winery in the Santa Cruz Mountains.

Label indicates vineyard and/or appellation. Varietal, vintage-dated wines produced are: Chardonnay (estate bottled and non), Pinot Noir (estate bottled), Zinfandel, Petite Sirah, Cabernet Sauvignon and White Riesling. Also produced under Old Dog label are Red and White table wine.

The winemaker's favorite wines are the Chardonnay and Pinot Noir.

['81 OC] (S) '79 C, (G) '79 C, (S) '78 PN, (B) '78 Z; ['82 OC] (B) '80 C (B) '79 PN, (G) '79 Z; ['82 SJP&C] (S&B) '80 C, (P) (B) '79 CA.

Brut
The epitome of dryness, usually applied to Champagne, which means that little, or no, "dosage" has been added to the wine. Usually 0 to 0.5% residual sugar.

Brut
Dry Champagne. No sweetness.

BUEHLER VINEYARDS *Napa County*
820 Greenfield Road, St. Helena, CA 94574
(707) 963-2155 Founded: 1964
Storage: Oak barrels, stainless steel.
Owner: John P. Buehler, Sr. Winemaker: John Buehler, Jr. Vineyards: 60 acres.

100% varietal vintage-dated, estate bottled wines produced are Zinfandel, Cabernet Sauvignon and Pinot Blanc.

BUENA VISTA WINERY ★ *Sonoma County*
27000 Ramal Road, Sonoma, CA 95476
(707) 938-8504 Founded: 1857
Owner: A. Racke of Germany. Winemaker: Don Harrison.

The winery was founded in 1857 by Agòston Haraszthy who is considered to be the founder of the California wine industry. An apostle of experimentation and uncompromising quality for all California wines, he was a leader in efforts to adapt premium European grape varieties to New World conditions. His famous 1861 trip to all the wine producing regions of Europe resulted in the importation of over 100,000 cuttings of 300 varieties. Buena Vista Winery is a state historic landmark. New 620 acre estate vineyards and winemaking facility are located in the Carneros district.

Varietal, vintage-dated wines produced are: Chardonnay, Johannisberg Riesling, Gewurztraminer, Green Hungarian, Fumé Blanc, Cabernet Sauvignon, Gamay Beaujolais, Zinfandel and Pinot Noir. Those that are estate-bottled are indicated on the label. Also produced are Chablis and Burgundy. Winemakers favorite wines are: Chardonnay Special Selection and Cabernet Sauvignon Special Selection.

['81 OC] (G) '77 CA, (S) '79 G; ['82 OC] (B) '78 CA, (G)

'81 GA, (S) '79 PN; ['82 SJP] (B) '80 C (Sp.Sel.), (S) '81 Spiceling, (P) (B) '78 CA.

Bulk Wines

Wines which are stored, shipped or packaged in containers usually having a capacity of five gallons, or more.

BURGESS CELLARS ★ *Napa County*

P.O. Box 282, St. Helena, CA 94574

(707) 963-4766 Founded: 1889

Storage: Oak, stainless steel.

Owners: Tom, Linda, Steve and James Burgess. Winemaker: Bill Sorenson.

The vineyard is located at the winery, which was started by the original homesteaders, about 1880. Varietal, vintage-dated wines produced are: Chardonnay, Cabernet Sauvignon and Zinfandel.

['81 OC] (S) '77 CA, (G) '78 CA, (B) '79 C, (G) '78 Z; ['82 OC] (S) '80 C, (B) '79 Z; ['82 SJP] (B) '80 C, (P) (B) '79 Z.

Burgundy

The name used to describe generous, full-bodied, dry red dinner wines, with a pronounced flavor, body, and bouquet and a deep red color. California Burgundy is made from a number of different grape varieties, including Gamay, Petite Sirah, Pinot Noir, Carignane and Zinfandel.

Pinot Noir, Gamay, Petite Sirah, Pinot St. George, Burgundy-type wines, named for the grapes from which they are principally made, having the flavors and names of their respective grapes; California wine made from them has a velvety-soft body and a deep, rich bouquet.

Award winning wines to look for: Almaden, Buena Vista, Davis Bynum, CC Vineyards, Christian Brothers, Colony Wines, Concannon, Conn Creek, Diamond Oaks, East-Side, Fetzer, Franciscan, Gallo, Geyser Peak, Gibson, Giumarra, Hecker Pass, JFJ Bronco, Kenwood, Charles Krug, Mirassou, Parducci, Riverside Farm, Round Hill, San Martin, Sebastiani, Sonoma, Souverain, Stag's Leap, Weibel, Whitehall Lane.

BURGIO (*See* J. Carey Cellars.)

Butt

A wine cask with the capacity of 100 to 140 gallons.

DAVIS BYNUM WINERY ★ *Sonoma County*

8075 Westside Road, Healdsburg, CA 95448

(707) 433-7738 Founded: 1965

Storage: Oak, redwood, stainless steel.

Owner: Davis Bynum. Winemaker: Gary Farrell.

Grapes are purchased on a selective basis from vineyards predominantly in Sonoma County.

The varietal, vintage-dated wines produced are: Zinfandel, Late Harvest Zinfandel, Pinot Noir, Cabernet Sauvignon, Fumé Blanc and Chardonnay. Also, Sonoma Chablis.

The winemaker's favorite is Allen-Hafner Private Reserve Chardonnay.

['81 OC] (S) '79 C, (S) '79 Z; ['82 OC] (B) '79 CA, (S) '81 GB.

C

CACHE CELLARS *Solano County*

Rt. 2 Box 2780, Davis, CA 95616

(916) 756-6068 Founded: 1978

Owners: Charles and Elizabeth Lowe. Winemaker: Charles Lowe.

Grapes are purchased on a select vineyard basis. Label indicates vineyard and/or appellation. Varietal, vintage-dated wines include Chardonnay, Pinot Noir, Zinfandel, Cabernet Sauvignon, Sauvignon Blanc and Carnelian Nouveau.

Cabernet Franc

One of two Cabernet grape varieties. Franc is the leading variety of the St. Emilion District of Bordeaux. Small plantings in the north coastal counties of California. Franc yields a lighter quicker maturing wine than Sauvignon. Excellent in Rose's.

Cabernet Pfeffer

Named for vinegrower and breeder William Pfeffer who came to California in the 1860's. Highly popular until the turn of the century when it was destroyed by disease and drought. In 1908 California wine pioneer, Dr. Harold Ohrwall planted Cabernet Pfeffer in the Cienega Valley. The Charles Lefranc Cellars bottle a small amount from this rare stand of grapes from the San Benito County vineyard. Cabernet Pfeffer is a great curiosity that has been saved by the Charles Lefranc Cellars.

Cabernet Sauvignon

A varietal grape capable of producing prestigious wines. This wine is dry, full-bodied and capable of great complexity if allowed to age. When young, Cabernet Sauvignon has a dominant tannic characteristic. Originally from the Bordeaux region of France where it is one of the principal grapes for the great Chateaux Clarets. The intensive ruby-red color deepens with age. A classic accompaniment with beef, lamb or duck. Also enjoyable with fruit and cheese: Brie, Port Salut, Cheddar or Roquefort.

Award wines to look for: Ahlgren, Alexander Valley, Almaden, Arroyo Sonoma, Bandiera, Barengo, Beaulieu, Bel Arbres, Beringer, Boeger, David Bruce, Buena Vista, Burgess, Davis Bynum, Cakebread, Callaway, Cambiaso, J. Carey, Richard Carey, Carmel Bay, Cassayre-Forni, Caymus, Chateau Chevalier, Chateau Montelena, Chateau St. Jean, Christian Brothers, Clos du Bois, Clos du Val, Conn Creek, R. & J. Cook, Cordtz Brothers, Dehlinger, Diamond Creek, Diamond Oaks, Domaine Laurier, Dry Creek, Duckhorn, Durney, Edmeades, Estrella River, Fenestra, Fetzer, Fieldstone, Firestone, Fortino, Franciscan, Freemark Abbey, Gemello, Geyser Peak, Girard, Guimarra, Grand Cru, Gundlach-Bundschu, Hacienda, Harbor, Heitz, William Hill, HMR (Hoffman Mountain Ranch), Husch, Inglenook, Iron Horse, Jekel, Johnson's, Kenwood, Konocti, Charles Krug, Lambert Bridge, Landmark, Lawrence, Llords & Elwood, Lower Lake, Marietta, M. Marion & Co., Louis Martini, Matanzas Creek, Mayacamas, McDowell Valley, Milano, Mill Creek, Mirassou, Robert Mondavi, Montclair, Monterey, Monterey Peninsula, Montevina, Mount Eden, Napa Wine Cellars, Navarro, Novitiate, Obester, Olivina, Page Mill, Papagni, Parducci, J. Pedroncelli, Pellegrini, Pendleton, Perelli-Minetti, Pesenti (California Nouveau), Joseph Phelps, Pine Ridge, Pommeraie, Pope Valley, Ranchita Oaks, Rancho Yerba Buena, Raymond, Ridge, River Oaks, Rosenblum, Roudon-Smith, Round Hill, Rutherford Hill, Rutherford Ranch, Rutherford, San Antonio, San Martin, Santa Barbara, Santa Cruz Mountain, Sebastiani, Shafer, Sherrill, Shown & Sons, Sierra Vista, Silver Oak, Simi, Smith & Hook, Sommelier, Sonoma, Sotoyome, Souverain, Spring Mountain, Stag's Leap, Robert Stemmler, Sterling, Stonegate, Stony Ridge, Sunrise, Sycamore Creek, Taylor California Cellars, Toyon, Trader Joe's, Trefethen, Trentadue, Turner, Tyland, Veedercrest, Ventana, Verdugo, Villa Mt. Eden, William Wheeler, York Mountain, Zaca Mesa, ZD.

Cabernet White

Cabernet Sauvignon Blanc.

Cabernet Sauvignon Blanc

Award wines to look for: Ballard Canyon, Congress Springs, R. & J. Cook, Los Vineros, Montevina, Obester, River Oaks, Santa Ynez Valley, Stony Ridge, Veedercrest, Weibel.

CADENASSO WINERY *Solano County*

P.O. Box 22, Fairfield, CA 94553

(707) 425-5845 Founded: 1906

Storage: Oak, redwood, stainless steel.

President, Winemaker: Frank G. Cadenasso.

68 acres of vineyards in Suisun Valley managed by John F. Cadenasso. Varietal wines produced are Cabernet Sauvignon, Grey Riesling, Pinot Noir, Grignolino, Zinfandel and Chenin Blanc. Also Burgundy, Chablis, Rosé, Passionatta and Haut Sauterne.

CADLOLO WINERY *San Joaquin County*

1124 California Street, Escalon, CA 95320

(209) 838-2457 Founded: 1913 Storage: Oak, redwood, stainless steel.

Owner: Dorothy Walton, Winemaker: Consultants.

CAKEBREAD CELLARS ★ *Napa County*

8300 St. Helena Highway, Rutherford, CA 94573

(415) 832-8444 Founded: 1973

Storage: French oak barrels, stainless steel.

Owners: Jack and Dolores Cakebread. Winemaker: Bruce Cakebread. Vineyard: 22 acres at winery.

Grapes are also purchased from select Napa Valley vineyards. Label indicates vineyard and/or appellation. 100% varietal, vintage-dated wines produced are: Sauvignon Blanc, Chardonnay, Cabernet Sauvignon and Zinfandel.

['81 OC] (G) '78 CA; ['82 SJP] (S) '80 C (P) (B) '79 Z.

CALAFIA WINES ★ *Napa County*
629 Fulton Lane, St. Helena, CA 94574
(707) 944-2666 Founded: 1979
Label indicates vineyard and/or appellation. Varietal, vintage-dated wines produced are: Merlot (Pickle Canyon Vineyards), Zinfandel (Glen Ellen Vineyards), Cabernet Sauvignon (Kitty Hawk Vineyard) and Chardonnay (Foureeminette Vineyards).
['82 OC] (B) '79 M.

CALAVERAS CELLARS (*See* Stevenot Winery.)

CALAVERAS COUNTY
Sierra Foothills.

CALERA WINE COMPANY ★ *San Benito County*
11300 Cienega Road, Hollister, CA 95023
(408) 637-9170 Founded: 1975
Storage: Oak barrels, stainless steel.
Owners: Josh and Jeanne Jensen. Winemaker: Steve Doerner.
Winery is the first and only gravity-flow winery. Built on site of old limestone kiln (calera in Spanish). The vineyards are south of Hollister at 2200 feet elevation in the Gavilan Mountains. Zinfandel and Pinot Noir grapes are purchased on a select vineyard basis. Three estate bottled Pinot Noirs, named Selleck, Reed and Jensen from their own vineyards. Label indicates vineyard and/or appellation.
Varietal, vintage-dated wines produced are Zinfandel and Pinot Noir. Names indicate separate vineyard entities.
['81 OC] (G) '79 Z; ['82 SJC] (B) '79 Z, (S) '79 Z, (P&C) (B&B) '80 PN.

CALIFORNIA CELLAR MASTERS *San Joaquin County*
P.O. Box 478, Lodi, CA 95240
(209) 368-6681 Founded: 1974
President: Marlow E. Stark.
Wine is purchased on a selected winery basis. Varietal wines produced under the "Coloma Cellars" label are Gewurztraminer, Zinfandel, Gamay Beaujolais, Napa Gamay, and Cabernet Sauvignon. Also produced are Blanc, Rose, Rouge, Champagne, Sherry and Port. Under the "Gold Mine" label—Burgundy and fruit wines are produced. Mulled wine and Spiced Jubilee are produced under the "Mother Lode" label.

CALIFORNIA CELLARS, TAYLOR (*See* The Monterey Vineyard.)

CALIFORNIA GROWERS WINERY *Tulare County*
38558 Road 128, Cutler, CA 93615
(415) 398-1111 Founded: 1936
Storage: Oak barrels, stainless steel.
Owner: Setrakian family.
Family owned since 1936. Vineyard at winery and grapes are purchased from growers in selected districts. A major bulk producer, private labeler, with own label "Growers".
Varietal wines produced are: Chenin Blanc, French Colombard, Petite Sirah, Cabernet Sauvignon and Johannisberg Riesling. Also produced are: Chablis, Bur-

gundy, Vin Rosé, Emerald Riesling, Sherry, Cream Sherry, Port and Brandy.

CALIFORNIA MEADERY *Napa County*

P.O. Box 235, Napa, CA 94559

(707) 253-7280 Founded: 1981

Owner and Winemaker: Bruce H. Rector.

Produce mead (honey wine) from yellow star thistle, high desert blossom and orange blossom. Mead produced is Rather Dry, Nigh Sweet and Blossom Sweet.

Brands: Honeymoon Mead and Winery of the Roses.

California Wine

Wine produced 100% from grapes grown within California.

CALIFORNIA WINE COMPANY *San Francisco County*

2211-14th St., San Francisco, CA 94103

(415) 431-3533 Founded: 1937

Owner: Tony Di Bono. Produced under labels: Pride of California, Champagne, Louis 5th.

California Wine Trade Beginning

Commercial wine-grape growing was started about 1824 by Joseph Chapman, one of the first Americans to settle in California. At the Pueblo of Los Angeles, he set out about 4,000 vines. In 1831, Jean Louis Vignes, a Frenchman from the Bordeaux wine district, started a commercial vineyard approximately where the Los Angeles Union Station now stands, importing cuttings of different varieties of grapes direct from Europe. Other plantings soon followed, and within a generation wine-grape growing was the principal agricultural industry of the Los Angeles district.

By 1840, Vignes was chartering ships which he loaded at San Pedro with wines and brandies destined for Santa Barbara, Monterey and San Francisco. As early as 1860, California wine firms had established agencies in New York and shipped wines around Cape Horn to the Eastern States. The first transcontinental reailroad, in 1869, opened the remainder of the country to the wine firms. Soon California wine growers were shipping wines to Europe, Latin America and Australia. Records show that Germany, Denmark, England and Canada were buying California Port in 1867. *See* History of Early California.

CALLAWAY VINEYARD & WINERY ★ *Riverside County*

32720 Rancho California Road, Temecula, CA 92390

(714) 676-4001 Founded: 1974

Storage: American, French, German oak, stainless steel. Chairman: Ely Callaway. Winemaker/Manager: Steve O'Donnell. Vineyards: 150 acres at winery. Owner: Hiram Walker of Canada.

Wines are produced from grapes grown on vinifera root stock.

Wines produced are 100% varietal, estate bottled and vintage-dated. They are Fumé Blanc, Chardonnay, Chenin Blanc—Dry, Sauvignon Blanc—Dry, Zinfandel, Cabernet Sauvignon, Petite Sirah, "Sweet Nancy" (Chenin Blanc). Also Callaway Port (a blend of Petite Sirah, Zinfandel, Chardonnay, and Cabernet Sauvignon.)

['81 OC] (G) '78 CH; ['82 OC] (B) '80 SB.

CAMBIASO VINEYARDS ★ *Sonoma County*

1141 Grant Avenue, Healdsburg, CA 95448
(707) 433-5508 Founded: 1934
Storage: Oak, redwood, stainless steel.
Owner: the Four Seas Investment Co. Winemaker: Robert Fredson. General Mgr.: Somchai Likitprakong.

Old country house built in 1852 which later became residence of Cambiaso family still stands. The vineyard is located at the winery.

Varietal, vintage-dated wines produced are Chenin Blanc, Fumé Blanc, Chardonnay, Cabernet Sauvignon, Petite Sirah, Zinfandel and Barbera. Under the "1852 House Wine" label, Burgundy, Chablis and Vin Rosé are produced.

['81 OC] (B) '80 SB; ['82 OC] (B) '78 CA, (S) '81 CH, (B) '80 SB; ['82 SJP] (S) '81 CH (P) (B) '76 PS.

CAPARONE WINERY ★ *San Luis Obispo County*

Rt. 1, Box 176 G, Paso Robles, CA 93446
(805) 467-3827 Founded: 1980
Storage: Barrels.
Owners: David and Mary Caparone. Winemaker: Dave Caparone. Vineyards: 8 acres at winery.

Grapes are also purchased on a select vineyard basis. Label indicates vineyard and/or appellation.

Varietal, vintage-dated wines produced are Cabernet Sauvignon and Merlot.

['82 OC] (B) '80 M.

Carbonic Maceration

A very old method of fermentation most closely associated with the traditional "methode Beaujolais". The grapes after being picked, are placed whole, uncrushed and with stems, into tanks. In the tanks, the weight of the grapes releases the juice and fermentation occurs almost immediately in the grapes without oxygen. The carbon dioxide is released and macerates the grapes.

J. Carey Cellars ★ *Santa Barbara County*

1711 Alamo Pintado Road, Solvang, CA 93463
(805) 688-8554 Founded: 1978
Storage: French Limousin, Nevers, American oak; stainless steel.
Owners: the Carey family. Winemaker: Richard Longoria. Vineyards: 45 acres at winery in Santa Ynez Valley.

Varietal, vintage-dated, estate bottled wines produced are Cabernet Sauvignon, Merlot, Cabernet Blanc, Chardonnay and Sauvignon Blanc.

['81 OC] (B) '79 M, (G) '80 SB; ['82 OC] (S) '80 C; ['82 SJP] (B) '79 CA.

Carignane

(Red Table Wine) A varietal grape that is predominantly used for blending. Full of tannin and heavy bodied. Goes well with hearty meals. Originally from the Mediterranean region of Europe. Serve with hamburger, stews and Mediterranean foods.

Award wines to look for: Borra's, Cygnet, Fetzer, Fortino, Hecker Pass, Stony Ridge, Sycamore Creek,

Trentadue.

CARLO ROSSI (*See* E. & J. Gallo.)

CARMEL BAY WINERY ★ *Monterey County*

P.O. Box 2496, Carmel, CA 93921
(408) 375-2292 (Winery) Founded: 1977
(408) 659-2943 (Winery Information)
Storage: Oak barrels.
Owners, Winemakers: Fred Crummey, Bob Eyerman. Consultant: Kathy Eyerman.

['82 OC] (G) '78 CA, (S) '79 PN.

Carmine Grape

A new California grape that is the cross pollination of Ruby Cabernet and Merlot.

Carnelian

A new grape variety developed by University of California at Davis. A cross between Cabernet Sauvignon, Grenache and Carignane. Yields a zesty, robust wine with complex aroma. Produced by: Giumarra Vineyards.

CARNEROS CREEK WINERY ★ *Napa County*

1285 Dealy Lane, Napa, CA 94559
(707) 253-WINE Founded: 1972
Storage: American, French, German oak, stainless steel.
Owners: Balfour and Anita Gibson, Francis and Kathleen Mahoney. Winemaker: Francis Mahoney. Vineyards: 20 acres adjacent to winery.

Grapes are also purchased on a select vineyard basis. Label indicates vineyard and/or appellation. Varietal, vintage-dated wines produced are: Cabernet Sauvignon, Pinot Noir, Chardonnay and Sauvignon Blanc. The winemaker's favorite wines are Cabernet Sauvignon and Pinot Noir.

['81 OC] (S) OC '78 M, (S) '79 Z.

CASA de FRUTA *San Benito County*

6680 Pacheco Pass, Hollister, CA 95023
(408) 637-0051 Founded: 1908
Owners: the Zanger Families. Winemaker: Greg Bruni.

Located in the Historic Pacheco Pass Valley. Among wines produced are Zinfandel Rosé, Gewurztraminer, Chenin Blanc and Johannisberg Riesling. Also dessert wines Black Muscat, Apricot, Blackberry, Strawberry and Pomegranate.

CASA NUESTRA *Napa County*

3473 Silverado Trail N., St. Helena, CA 94574
(707) 963-4684 Founded: 1980
Owners: Gene & Cody Kirkham. Winemaker: Allen Price. Vineyards: 10 acres at winery.

Varietal, vintage-dated, estate bottled wine produced is Dry Chenin Blanc.

Cask

Any round, bulging wooden container for wine. Includes barrels, puncheons, pipes, butts, tuns, hogsheads, all which signify various specific measures of capacity in different countries and various products they may contain. A container used for fermenting wine usually is called a tank or vat. The two terms in the U.S. usually are applied to containers which stand upright and are straight sided rather than barrel shaped. A vat is an open container, while a tank is closed. In U.S. wineries its capacity is stenciled on its side.

CASSAYRE-FORNI CELLARS ★ *Napa County*
1271 Manley Lane, Rutherford, CA 94573
(707) 944-2165 Founded: 1976
Storage: Oak, stainless steel.
Owners: Jim and Paul Cassayre, Mike Forni. Winemaker: Mike Forni.

Grapes are purchased on a selected grower and district basis. Label indicates vineyard and/or appellation. Varietal, vintage-dated wines produced are Dry Chenin Blanc, Chardonnay, Cabernet Sauvignon and Zinfandel. Winemaker's favorite wine is Zinfandel.

['81 OC] (G) '78 CA.

CAVALCADE (*See* Emilio Guglielmo Winery.)

C.C. VINEYARD (*See* J.F.J. Bronco Winery.)

CAYMUS VINEYARDS ★ *Napa County*
P.O. Box 268, Rutherford, CA 94573
(707) 963-4204, 963-5683 Founded: 1971
Storage: Oak, redwood.
Owners: Charles Wagner II and son Chuck. Winemaster: Charles Wagner II. Winemakers: Chuck and Randy Dunn.

Original land was purchased in 1906 by Charles I to produce grapes and prunes. Charles Wagner and son Chuck founded Caymus in 1971. Caymus refers to a tribe of Indians around in the area during the first land grants in California. The second label Liberty School refers to the school that existed on the property and where some of the early Wagners went to school.

Varietal, vintage-dated, estate bottled wines produced are Pinot Noir, Pinot Noir Blanc (Oeil de Perdrix), Cabernet Sauvignon and Chardonnay. Grapes are also purchased on a select vineyard basis. Label indicates vineyard and/or appellation. Varietal, vintage-dated wines produced are Zinfandel, Cabernet Sauvignon and Sauvignon Blanc. Many of these wines are also produced under the Liberty School label.

['81 OC] (G) '75 PS.

Centurion Grape
Developed in California. A cross pollination of Carignane, Cabernet Sauvignon and Grenache. Produces a more full bodied and darker wine than the Carnelian grape. Grown in the Central Valley.

Chablis
A dry, white dinner or table wine, Chablis has a fruity flavor, but less tart than Rhine. It is delicate, light to medium straw in color and light to medium bodied. Good with white meats and seafood.

Award wines to look for: Brookside, Buena Vista, CC Vineyards, Christian Brothers, Concannon, Delicato, East-Side, Fetzer, Geyser Peak, Giumarra, JFJ Bronco, Charles Krug, Paul Masson, Parducci, Perelli-Minetti, Riverside Farm, San Antonio, Sonoma, Souverain, Stone Creek, Weibel.

CHALK HILL VINEYARD—Chardonnay vineyard in Russian River Valley of Sonoma.

CHALONE VINEYARD *Monterey County*
P.O. Box 855, Soledad, CA 93960
(415) 441-8975 Founded: 1920
Storage: Limousin oak, stainless steel.
Owner: Gavilan Vineyards. Winemaker: Peter Watson-Graff.

The winery was established in 1960. The 110 acre vineyard is near the Pinnacles National Monument at 2,000 feet elevation. Varietal, vintage-dated, estate bottled wines produced are: Pinot Noir, Chardonnay, Pinot Blanc, and Chenin Blanc.

New appellation—Chalone.

CHAMISAL VINEYARD ★ *San Luis Obispo County*
7525 Orcutt Rd., San Luis Obispo, CA 93401
(805) 544-3576 Founded: 1972
Storage: Limousin & Nevers oak, stainless steel.
Owner: Norman L. Goss. Winemaker: Scott Campbell Boyd. Vineyards: 52 acres Chardonnay, 5 acres Cabernet Sauvignon at winery.

The first commercial vineyard in the Edna Valley. Son, son-in-law and daughter are all in the business.

Label indicates vineyard and/or appellation. Varietal, vintage-dated, estate bottled wines produced are Chardonnay and Cabernet Sauvignon.

['81 OC] (B) '79 C.

Champagne Bottle Sizes

"Split": 187 ml or 6.4 oz, single serving, convenient for Champagne Cocktails.

"Tenth": 375 ml or 12.8 oz, serves two.

"Fifth": 750 ml or 25.4 oz, four to five servings.

"Magnum": 1.5 liters or 51 oz.

"Double Magnum": 3 liters for celebrations.

Champagne, "Bulk Process" Method

"Bulk Process" involves fermenting wine in large tanks and filtering and bottling in the same manner as the transfer process. This product must carry the designation "Charmat" or "Bulk Process" on the label. Less expensive California sparkling wines are produced by this method.

Champagne Production "Naturally Fermented in This Bottle" French: Methode Champenoise

The individual bottle-fermented method in which every stage of production takes place in the individual bottle, and the resulting product reaches the consumer in its original container. This process is referred to as the "Traditional Method." By law, only Champagne produced by this method may bear the inscription "NATURALLY FERMENTED IN THIS BOTTLE."

The first fermentation in the bottle is the art of the Champagne Cellarmaster or Winemaker. Before bottling the blended wines that are destined for Champagne, it is necessary to add the exact amount of sugar in order to produce—supported by addition of a very active, pure cultured yeast—6 atmospheres of carbon dioxide at a temperature of 50 degrees. The carbon dioxide makes the wine sparkling as soon as the fermentation in the bottle has finished.

The bottles are stacked in cool cellars of equitable temperature, where they await ripening and bottle-ageing. At regular intervals the bottles are removed and shaken in order to avoid having the sediment—produced by the fermentation—stick to the sides of the bottles.

After storage and ageing of several years, the Champagne is placed on racks with holes for the necks of the bottles, which are always directed downward. Each bottle is shaken and turned, alternately, in the right and left direction, at regular intervals during a period of 8-10 weeks, until the sediment has settled on the cork of the downwardly-directed bottle, and the wine is absolutely transparent.

Only 3-6 months before shipment takes place, the Champagne is freed from the sediment. For this purpose, the bottles with their heads placed downwards, are brought into a freezing solution and cooled below 12 degrees F. A few minutes of this immersion are sufficient to freeze the sediment and a small amount of the wine onto the cork. It is now possible to turn the bottle upright, and to get the cork out of the bottle, which is blown out of the neck, together with the sediment, with force. The pressure forces the cork out carrying the frozen sediment with it.

Before the second finishing cork is put into the bottle, a small additional dosage is added. The finest cane sugar is dissoved in an excellent old, well-balanced wine, and the best quality of aged grape brandy makes this dosage perfect. This creation of the dosage and the amount is the art of the Winemaker. The "Style" reflects the individual Winemaker. The quantity of the dosage depends on the taste to suit the consumer. For "Natural" there is no addition of dosage.

Special heavy bottles made to withstand pressure of 6-8 atmospheres and only finest corks available are used. After being disgorged, the Champagne is stored for several months before being made available for shipment.

Champagne, "Transfer Method"

The "Transfer Method" is a variation on the traditional method, which involves fermenting the Champagne in the bottle, thus qualifying for a "FERMENTED IN THE BOTTLE" label designation. After fermenting in the bottle, however, the contents are removed under counter-pressure and placed in large pressurized tanks, mechanically filtered into another tank, and then refilled into empty bottles. Method used for medium priced Champagnes.

Award wines to look for: Almaden, Beaulieu, Christian Brothers, Cresta Blanca, Crystal Valley, Cucamonga, Domaine Chandon, Franciscan, Franzia Brothers, Geyser Peak, Gibson, JFJ Bronco, Korbel, Hans Kornell, Paul Masson, Mirassou, Papagni, Perelli-Minetti, Schramsberg, Shadow Creek, Sonoma, Stanford, Stony Ridge, Trader Joe's (Raymond Hill), Weibel.

CHANDON (*See* Domaine Chandon.)

CHAPPELLET VINEYARD ★ *Napa County*

1581 Sage Canyon Road, St. Helena, CA 94574
(707) 963-7136 Founded: 1969
Storage: Oak, stainless steel.
Owner: Donn Chappellet. Winemaker: Cathy Cotison. Vineyards: 110 acres.

Varietal vintage-dated wines produced are Cabernet Sauvignon, Chenin Blanc, Johannisberg Riesling and Chardonnay. Known for superb Cabernet.

['82 OC] (S) '78 M.

Chaptalizing

To increase alcohol content, a sugaring of the must before or during fermentation.

Character

The wine's "personality" as revealed by the senses of taste and smell. The combination of vinosity, balance and style.

Charbono

(Red Table Wine) A varietal grape that means a full-bodied, distinct tannic, robust, earthy wine. Very few acres planted in California. Originally from Italy. Fuller bodied than Barbera. Serve with stews and robust Italian foods. Ages very well. (Best at 4 to 6 years.)

Award wines to look for: Fortino, Franciscan, Inglenook, Papagni, Souverain.

Chardonnay

(White Table Wine) A varietal grape that produces a prestigious wine, whether it be in California or in one of the great white Burgundy wine-producing districts of France.

Full-bodied with medium acidity. A dry austere wine with a slight or faint flavor reminiscent of apples, mellons or figs. Bright, crisp and complex.

Magnificant with a wide range of "white" foods, including rich cream sauces, or enjoyed simply with fruit, crackers and cheese—Brie or Camembert. Currently California's most expensive wine grape.

Award wines to look for: Acacia, Ahern, Ahlgren, Alexander Valley, Alta, Ballard Canyon, Bargetto, Bel Arbres, Beringer, David Bruce, Buena Vista, Burgess Cellars, Cakebread Cellars, California Wine Co., Cambiaso, J. Carey, Carneros Creek, Chamisal, Chateau Chevalier, Chateau Montelena, Chateau St. Jean, Christian Brothers, Clos du Bois, Concannon, Conn Creek, Cordtz Brothers, Cresta Blanca, Cuvaison Delicato, De Loach, Domaine Laurier, Dona Maria, Dry Creek, Edmeades, Estrella River, Far Niente, Fetzer, Fieldstone, Firestone, Flora Springs, L. Foppiano, Franciscan, Gallo, Geyser Peak, Grgich Hills, Gundlach-Bundschu, Hacienda, J.J. Haraszthy & Son, Haywood, HMR (Hoffman Mountain Ranch), Husch, Iron Horse, Jekel, Robert Keenan, Kenwood, Kirigin, Charles Krug, La Crema Vinera, Lakespring, Landmark, Lawrence, Leeward, Louis M. Martini, Paul Masson, Matanzas Creek, McDowell Valley, Milano, Mill Creek, Mirassou, Robert Mondavi, Monterey, Monterey

Peninsula, MPM, Napa Wine Cellars, Navarro, Charles Ortman, Page Mill, Papagni, Parducci, Parsons Creek, J. Pedroncelli, Pendleton, Martin Ray, Raymond, River Oaks, River Road, Roudon-Smith, Round Hill, San Martin, Santa Ynez Valley, Sequoia Grove, Shafer, Sierra Vista, Simi, Smothers, Sommelier, Sonoma/Windsor, Souverain, Spring Mountain, St. Francis, Stags' Leap, Stevenot, Stonegate Stony Ridge, Sunrise, Sycamore Creek, Taylor, Trefethen, Turgeon & Lohr, Tyland, Veedercrest, Ventana, Villa Mt. Eden, Mark West, William Wheeler, Whitehall Lane, Zaca Mesa, ZD.

Charmat

The method of producing sparkling wine. Wine is fermented in glass lined tanks, filtered and bottled.

CHATEAU BOSWELL *Napa County*

3468 Silverado Trail, St. Helena, CA 94574
(707) 963-5472 Founded: 1979
Storage: Barrels.
Owner: Dr. Richard Thornton Boswell. Wine Consultant: Andre Tchelistcheff.

Founded in 1979, the winery is built as a traditional slate roof and hand hewn rock chateau. Grapes are purchased on a slected vineyard basis. Label indicates vineyard and/or appellation. Varietal, vintage-dated wine produced is Cabernet Sauvignon.

CHATEAU BOUCHAINE *Napa County*

1975 Buchli Station Rd., Napa, CA 94558
(707) 252-9065 Founded: 1924
Storage: Small oak, redwood, stainless steel.
Owner: David Pollak, Jr. President/Gen'l. Partner. Winemaker: Jerry E. Luper.

Chateau Bouchaine is located in the Carneros district.

The 30 acre Chardonnay vineyard located at the winery will be producing wines in 1984. Grapes are also purchased on a select vineyard basis. Label indicates vineyard and/or appellation. Varietal, vintage-dated wines to be released are Chardonnay and Pinot Noir.

CHATEAU CHEVALIER WINERY ★ *Napa County*

3101 Spring Mountain Road, St. Helena, CA 94574
(707) 963-2342 Founded: 1884
Storage: Oak, stainless steel.
Owners: Greg and Kathy Bissonette. Winemaker: Greg Bissonette.

The 57 acre vineyard was originally planted in the late 1870s. The vineyard is located at the winery on Spring Mountain Road. Varietal, vintage-dated, estate bottled wines produced under Chateau Chevalier label are: Cabernet Sauvignon, Chardonnay and Pinot Noir.

Favorite wine of the Winemaker is the Private Reserve Cabernet Sauvignon, vintage dated.

['81 OC] (G) '79 C, (G) '78 PN; ['82 OC] (S) '80 C; ['82 SJP] (B) '79 CA, (P&C) (B&B) '80 PN.

CHATEAU CHEVRE *Napa County*

2040 Hoffman Lane, Yountville, CA 94599
(707) 944-2184 Founded: 1979
Storage: Oak and stainless steel.

Owner/Winemaker: Gerald P. Hazen. Vineyard: 10 acres at winery.

Varietal, vintage-dated, estate bottled wine produced is Merlot.

CHATEAU DE LEU WINERY *Solano County*

1635 W. Mason Rd., Suisun, CA 94585

(707) 864-1517 Founded: 1981

Storage: Oak, stainless steel.

Owners: Ben A. Volkhardt, Jr. & III. Winemaker: Ben Volkhardt, III. The 80 acre vineyard was originally planted in the 1880's in Green Valley, West Solano County near the West Napa/Solano border.

Varietal, vintage-dated wines produced are Chardonnay, Fumé Blanc, Chenin Blanc, French Colombard, Gamay and Petite Sirah.

CHATEAU D'IVRESSE *Riverside County*

33685 Pathfinder Rd., Mountain Center, CA 92361

(213) 394-6342 Founded: 1979

Owner/Winemaker: John W. Schaeflein.

CHATEAU DU LAC, INC. *Lake County*

Adm. Office: 180 Park Road, P.O. Box 709, Burlingame, CA 95453

(415) 342-6364

Winery: 600 Matthews Road, Lakeport, CA 95253

(707) 263-9333

Jess S. Jackson, President.

Label indicates vineyard and/or appellation. Varietal, vintage-dated wines produced are Chardonnay, Johannisberg Reisling, Sauvignon Blanc and Cabernet Sauvignon.

CHATEAU FILIPPI (*See* J. Filippi.)

CHATEAU JULIEN *Monterey County*

8990 Carmel Valley Road, Carmel, CA 93923

(408) 624-2600 Founded: 1982

Owners: Robert S. and Patricia Brower. Manager/Winemaker: Scott Richert.

Varietal, vintage-dated wines produced are Chardonnay, Sauvignon Blanc, Merlot and Cabernet Sauvignon.

CHATEAU MARTIN (*See* The Martin Winery.)

CHATEAU MOREAU (*See* Gibson Wine Co.)

CHATEAU MONTELENA ★ *Napa County*

1429 Tubbs Lane, Calistoga, CA 94515

(707) 942-5105 Founded: 1882

Storage: French, American, Yugoslavian oak.

Gen'l. Partner: James L. Barrett. Limited Partners: Lee J. Paschich, Ernest W. Hahn and Laura G. Barrett. Vineyards: 90 acres at winery.

Founded by Alfred L. Tubbs, who was a state senator, builder and owner of a whaling fleet, the Chateau was designed by a French architect and built of local and imported stone. The current owners took over in 1972. The most significant award that set the wine world on its ear took place at the "Paris Tasting," in 1976. Chateau Montelena's 1973 Chardonnay was awarded first place over nine other top French White Burgundies, and California Chardonnays in a blind tasting. The tasting panel was comprised of nine of France's "Who's Who" of the wine world.

Label indicates appellation. The 100% varietal, vintage-dated wines produced are: Cabernet Sauvignon (estate bottled), Chardonnay, Zinfandel (estate bottled) and Johannisberg Riesling (JR for sale only at winery). The Winemaker's favorite is Cabernet Sauvignon.

['81 OC] (B) '77 CA, (B) '79 C; ['82 OC] (S) '78 CA.

CHATEAU NAPOLEON (*See* Weibel Champagne Vineyards.)

CHATEAU NOUVEAU ★ *Napa County*

377 McCormick, St. Helena, CA 94574

Owner/Winemaker: Jack Clark

['82 OC] (B) '81 GB

CHATEAU RUTHERFORD (*See* Rutherford Vintners.)

CHATEAU ST. JEAN ★ *Sonoma County*

8555 Sonoma Highway, Kenwood, CA 95452

(707) 833-4134 Founded: 1974

Storage: American, French oak, stainless steel.

Owners: Robert and Edward Merzoian, W. Kenneth Sheffield. President: Allan J. Hemphill. Vice President & Winemaker: Richard L. Arrowood. Winemaker Sparkling Wines: Edgar Downs.

The vineyards are located at the winery. Grapes are also purchased on a select vineyard basis. Label indicates vineyard and/or appellation.

Varietal, vintage-dated wines produced are: Johannisberg Riesling, Chardonnay, Muscat Canelli, Gewurztraminer and Sauvignon Blanc. In 1980, the first grapes were crushed for the 1983 release of champagne at their new sparkling wine facility located 25 miles from the Chateau. This is an entirely separate facility, managed by Edgar "Pete" Downs, St. Jean Winemaker, Sparkling Wines.

['81 OC] (G) '79 C, (S) '79 C, (G) '80 G, (B) '80 G, (G) '80 SB, (S) '80 SB, (B) '80 WR, (S) '80 WR; ['82 OC] (G) '80 C, (S) '80 C, (G) '81 SB, (S) '81 JR, (G) '80 JR, (B) '80 WR, (B) '81 JR, (B) '80 C, (B) '81 G, (S) '81 G, (G) '80 G, (B) '81 MC, (S) '80 MC.

CHAUVET VINEYARD—Zinfandel vineyard in Sonoma Valley.

Chenin Blanc

A widely planted white grape essential to the popular jug, white wines now consumed as cocktails. It yields a variety of different types and quality of wine subject to where it is grown and the intention of the winemaker. Usually associated with a lovely, fruity, aromatic "feminine" wine with slight residual sweetness. Usually drank as a social wine rather than a dinner wine but it is quite appropriate with Chinese or Polynesian food. There are some dry versions that are more suitable table wines.

Award wines to look for: Alexander Valley, Almaden, Bargetto, Bel Arbres, Beringer, Boeger, Bogle, Brookside, Burgess, California Hillside, Callaway, Cambiaso, Richard Carey, Cassayre-Forni, Christian Brothers, Colony, Concannon, Congress Springs, R. & J. Cook, Cresta Blanca, Delicato, Dry Creek, Durney, East-Side, Felton-Empire,

Fenestra, Fetzer, Fieldstone, Foppiano, Franciscan, Franzia Brothers, Gallo, Girard, Geyser Peak, Giumarra, Grand Cru, Hacienda, HMR (Hoffman Mountain Ranch), Inglenook, Johnson's, Kenwood, Charles Krug, Ronald Lamb, Landmark, Lawrence, Lost Hills, Martin Brothers, Paul Masson, McDowell Valley, Milano, Robert Mondavi, Monterey Vineyard, Mount Palomar, Mount Veeder, North Coast Cellars, Novitiate, Page Mill, Parducci, Pedroncelli, Pine Ridge, Pope Valley, Preston, Raymond, San Antonio-Maddalena, San Martin, San Pasqual, Sebastiani, Shown & Sons, Sierra Vista, Simi, Sonoma, Souverain, Stag's Leap, Stevenot, Taylor, Trader Joe's, Turgeon & Lohr, Turner, Ventana, Weibel, Wente, Yverdon.

Chianti Wine

A generic full bodied, ruby red wine, strongly flavored, fruity with a medium tartness. Traditionally made from Sangiovese grapes, but other grapes are often used. Especially good with red meats and pastas. Serve at room temperature or slightly chilled.

Chilling Wine

Chilling is one thing and cold is another factor when it comes to wines. Many wines taste better chilled. Rose's and light-bodied reds, such as Gamay, taste fruitier and more refreshing when chilled. The crispness and character of dry and off-dry white wines is enhanced with chilling. Dry and off-dry white wines and rosés should be served at between 50 and 55 degrees F. Lightbodied red should be served at between 55 and 60 degrees F.

The length of time it takes to properly chill wine in a refrigerator that the temperature is 42 degrees F is:

Time	Wine Temp.
0	65
1/2 hr.	59
1 hr.	55
1-1/2 hr.	52
2 hr.	49

CHISPA CELLARS *Calaveras County*

P.O. Box 255, Murphys, CA 95247
(209) 728-3492 Founded: 1976
Owner, Winemaker: Robert Bliss.

Grapes are purchased on a select vineyard basis. Wines produced are Ruby Cabernet and Zinfandel.

THE CHRISTIAN BROTHERS ★ *Napa County*

4411 Redwood Road, Napa, CA 94558
(707) 226-5566 Founded: 1882
Storage: Oak, redwood, stainless steel.
Owner: The Christian Brothers. President: Brother David Brennan, F.S.C. Winemaker: Brother Timothy Diener, F.S.C.

The Christian Brothers is a Catholic order of men devoted to teaching. About 10,000 Christian Brothers teach in over 1600 schools in 80 countries. Profits from the wines are used to support the schools of the San Francisco Province. 1298 acres of vineyards are in the Napa Valley and 100 acres in the San Joaquin Valley.

Label indicates vineyard and/or appellation.

Varietal, vintage-dated, Napa Valley wines produced are Pinot St. George, Chenin Blanc, Cabernet Sauvignon, Gewurztraminer and Chardonnay. Varietal wines produced are Grey Riesling, Johannisberg Riesling, Riesling, Chenin Blanc, Napa Fumé Blanc, Sauvignon Blanc, Gamay Noir, Zinfandel, Pinot Noir, Cabernet Sauvignon and Chardonnay. Also produced are Claret, Burgundy, Chablis, Rhine, Sauterne, Napa Rosé, La Salle Rosé, Vin Rosé, vintage-dated 1975 Cream Sherry, Centennial Private Reserve Sherry, Meloso Cream Sherry, Cream, Golden, Dry and Cocktail Sherry. Vintage-dated 1969 and 1973 Port, Tinta Cream Port, Ruby, Treasure and Tawny Port. Amber Tokay and Golden Muscatel. Also Brut, Extra Dry, Champagne Rosé and Extra Cold Duck.

['81 OC] (S) '79 CH, (S) NVP, (G) NV SB, (B) NV SB, (S) '69 VTP; ['82 OC] (B) '79 C, (B) PN, (G) SB, (B) SB, (B) '80 JR, (G) Z, (B) CHA; ['82 SJP] (B) FB, (B) SB, (B) (C) '80 G, (P&C) (B&B) Z.

CILURZO VINEYARD AND WINERY ★ *Riverside County*

41220 Calle Contento, Temecula, CA 92390
(714) 676-5250 Founded: 1968
Storage: Oak barrels, stainless steel.
President & Winemaker: Vincenzo Cilurzo, Vice President: Audrey Cilurzo. Vineyard: 10 acres in Temecula.

The varietal wines produced are: Fumé Blanc, Cabernet Sauvignon, Gamay Beaujolais, Chenin Blanc (dry), Chardonnay and estate bottled Petite Sirah. The winemaker's favorite is Petite Sirah.

['81 OC] (B) '79 PS; ['82 OC] (S) '79 PS.

Claret

Claret applies to any dry pleasantly-tart, light and medium-bodied dinner wine of ruby-red color. Originated by the British to describe acceptable Bordeaux wines. This is the most widely-used mealtime wine in the world. In California, Clarets are made from one, or more, of a number of grape varieties, such as Cabernet Sauvignon, Zinfandel and Merlot.

Award wines to look for: Christian Brothers, Clos du Bois, Guglielmo, Navarro.

Clean

A well made wine, with no alien tastes, well stored.

Climates and Wine

European vineyardists have known for centuries that "cool climate loving" varieties like Riesling, Gewurztraminer and Pinot Noir must be planted in naturally cool climates, like Germany, Alsace and Burgundy. Those varieties are never planted in warmer places like Bordeaux. Neither do the Burgundians or Germans plant Cabernet Sauvignon in their cool areas. There is no simple answer to all the questions. However, when we consider the fact that the Europeans can reach back for hundreds, if not thousands, of years and the Californians have just begun so to speak, the progress in California has been proven since the early seventy's based upon the results. The greatest discovery in the field of climates has been the fact that no one region has a uniform climate and that each region has a multitude of "microclimates", small, local areas which are usually warmer, cooler, wetter or drier than the general areas surrounding them. This is a very complicated matter and takes a considerable number of years to match land and grape variety.

As a general rule of thumb, the best quality wines will usually match up as follows:

Coldest Climates: Upper Monterey, Sonoma, Santa Maria, Santa Cruz, Oregon and Washington

Grape Varieties: Pinot Noir, Pinot Blanc, Johannisberg Reisling, Gewurztraminer and Grey Riesling

Medium Cool: Monterey, Napa-Carneros, Sonoma, Santa Barbara

Grape Varieties: Pinot Blanc, Chardonnay, Sylvaner, Grenache, Grey Riesling, Johannisberg Riesling, Petite Sirah

Medium Warm: Upper Napa Valley, San Luis Obispo, Lower Monterey

Grape Varieties: Semillon, Sauvignon Blanc, Chenin Blanc, Zinfandel, Cabernet Sauvignon, Petite Sirah, Grenache, Napa Gamay and French Colombard

Hot Climates: Central Valley, Modesto, Fresno, Lodi, Bakersfield

Grape Varieties: French Colombard, Ruby Cabernet, Barbera, Carignane, Palomino, Tinta Madera and Grenache

It is also important to keep in mind that a unique microclimate can be the exception and is often the case.

CLOS DU BOIS ★ *Sonoma County*

5 Fitch Street, Healdsburg, CA 95448
(707) 433-5576 Founded: 1974
Storage: American and French oak, stainless steel.
Owner: Frank Montgomery Woods. Winemaker: John Hawley. Winery Manager: Tom Hobart.

The 650 acre vineyards are located in Dry Creek Valley and Alexander Valley. The first vintage wines were released in 1976.

Varietal, estate bottled, vintage-dated wines produced are: Chardonnay, Sauvignon Blanc, Gewurztraminer, Johannisberg Riesling, Pinot Noir, Merlot, and Cabernet Sauvignon. Also produced are Marlstone (Cabernet, Merlot blend), Flintwood (barrel fermented Chardonnay), Woodleaf (Cabernet Sauvignon), Cherry Hill (Pinot Noir), and Calcaire (Chardonnay). Recommended: Cabernet Sauvignon, Proprietor's Reserve.

['81 OC] (B) '78 CA, (S) '79 C, (B) '79 G; ['82 OC] (B) '79 G, (B) '79 M, (S) '78 CA, (S) '80 C, (B) '81 G, (B) '78 CA, (G) '80 C; ['82 SJP&C] (S&B) '81 EH, G (P&C) (B&B) '79 LH,G.

CLOS DU VAL ★ *Napa County*

5330 Silverado Trail, Napa, CA 94558
(707) 252-6711 Founded: 1972
Storage: Oak tanks and barrels. Winemaker: Bernard M. Portet.

The 120 acre vineyard is located near the winery. Bernard Portet was raised in Pauillac, France, and is the son of the former Regisseur of Chateau Lafite Rothschild.

The vintage-dated varietal wines produced under the Clos du Val and Granval labels are: Cabernet Sauvignon, Zinfandel, Merlot, Chardonnay and Pinot Noir.

['81 OC] (G) '78 M, (B) '78 CA; ['82 OC] (B) '79 M; ['82 SJP] (B) '79 CA, (P) (S) '79 M, (P) (S) '79 Z.

CLOUDSTONE VINEYARDS *Santa Clara County*
27345 Deer Springs Way, Los Altos Hills, CA 94022
(415) 948-8621 Founded :1981

Label indicates vineyard and/or appellation. Varietal, vintage-dated wines produced in 1982 are Cabernet Sauvignon and Chardonnay.

Cloudy
An imperfect wine containing sediment.

Coarse
A young wine lacking breed and without finesse.

COAST RANGE NEGOCIANTS
c/o Grape Empire
1132 Beecher St., San Leandro, CA 94577

Coast Range offers three releases: 100% varietal, vintage dated 1981 Sonoma Chardonnay, 1979 Napa Cabernet, 1979 Alexander Valley Zinfandel.

Cold Duck
A blend of White Champagne and Sparkling Burgundy and a little Concord grape wine. Cold Duck is semi-sweet to sweet and is ruby-red in color. It is a light and festive wine, traditional in Germany and enjoying success recently during the "Pop Wine" trend in the U.S.

Award wines to look for: Almaden, Christian Brothers, Perelli-Minetti, Weibel.

COLE RANCH VINEYARD—a Johannisberg Riesling vineyard in Mendocino County.

COLOMA CELLARS *San Joaquin County*
(*See* California Cellar Masters.)
McHenery Ave., Escalon, CA 95320
(209) 838-7060 Founded: 1860

Coloma Cellars was established in 1860, less than a mile from Old Sutters Mill, site of the original California gold strike. The winery's first owner, joined the gold rush in 1849 and soon after planted the first vines. By 1867 Coloma Cellar wines were in demand in Virginia City, Nevada. The following years saw the Vineyard House Hotel built, additional cellars constructed and from around 1875 until recent years when the property was acquired by California Cellar Masters the winery has continued to produce wines.

Varietal wines produced are Gamay Beaujolais, Zinfandel, Cabernet Sauvignon, Chardonnay and Gewurztraminer.

Also produced are Champagne, Sherry, Port, Chablis, Blanc, Rouge and Rhine.

COLONY (Italian Swiss) ★ *Sonoma County*
(*See* Heublein.)
P.O. Box One, Asti, California 95413

(707) 894-2280 Founded: 1881
Owners: United Vintners. Winemaker: Ed Rossi, Jr.

Formerly known as Italian Swiss Colony which was formed as a mutual Association, in 1881. United Vintners purchased the property in the late 1960s. Varietal wines produced are: French Colombard, Chenin Blanc, Rhine, Riesling, Cabernet Sauvignon, Pinot Noir, Zinfandel, Barbera and Ruby Cabernet. Also produced are: Chablis, Rhine, Sauterne Blanc, Rhineskeller, Moselle, Grenache Vin Rosé, Burgundy, Chianti, Sherry and Port.

['82 OC] (S) NV CH; ['82 SJP] (S) FC (P&C) (B&B) BR.

COLUMBIA CELLARS (*See* Yankee Hill Winery.)

CONCANNON VINEYARD ★ *Alameda County*
4590 Tesla Road, Livermore, CA 94550
(415) 447-3760 Founded: 1883
Storage: Oak, stainless steel.
Owner: Augustin Huneeus. Winemaker: Sergio Traverso.

Founded by James Concannon. Jim Concannon is the winery's third generation president. The 222 acre vineyard is located in the Livermore Valley. The first winery in America to produce Petite Sirah. Varietal, vintage-dated wines produced are: Chenin Blanc, Sauvignon Blanc, Johannisberg Riesling, Petite Sirah, Chardonnay, Cabernet Sauvignon, Zinfandel Rosé, Livermore-Riesling and vintage-dated Burgundy and Chablis.

The winemaker's favorite wines are: Petite Sirah and Sauvignon Blanc.

['81 OC] (S) '80 CH, (G) '79 WR, (B) '80 JR; ['82 OC] (B) '81 MC (B) '78 PS, (B) '81 SB, (B) '81 JR; ['82 SJP] (S) '81 Es. Bot. SB, (S) '81 Cal. SB, (P&C) (B&B) '78 PS.

Condition
A wine's clarity or soundness.

CONGRESS SPRINGS VINEYARDS ★ *Santa Clara County*
23600 Congress Springs Road, Saratoga, CA 95070
(408) 867-1409 Founded: 1892
Storage: Oak, stainless steel.
Owners: Vic Ericson, Dan Gehrs. Winemaker: Dan Gehrs.

The winery was founded in 1892 by a French immigrant Pierre C. Pourroy. The current owners first crush was in 1976. The 60 acre vineyard is in the Santa Cruz Mountains of Santa Clara County.

Varietal, vintage-dated wines produced are Pinot Blanc, Fumé Blanc, Semillon, Chenin Blanc, Chardonnay, Cabernet Sauvignon, Pinot Blanc and Pinot Noir. The winemaker's favorite wines are Pinot Noir and Chardonnay.

['82 OC] (G) '80 CH, (S) '81 CH, (S) '81 CH, (B) '80 PB; ['82 SJP] (B) '79 Z.

CONN CREEK WINERY ★ *Napa County*
8711 Silverado Trail, St. Helena, CA 94574
(707) 963-9100 Founded: 1974
Storage: French oak, stainless steel.
Owners: Conn Creek Vineyards, CCW Investments, Inc., Croft Winery Ltd. Winemaker: Daryl Eklund.

There are two vineyards of 120 acres in the Napa Valley. Label indicates vineyards and/or appellation.

Varietal wines produced are: Cabernet Sauvignon, Zinfandel (estate bottled), Chardonnay and Chateau Maja Chardonnay. The winemaker's favorites are: Cabernet Sauvignon and Chardonnay.

['81 OC] (G) '77 CA, (B) '78 C; ['82 OC] (S) '78 CA, (S) '79 C (B) '79 C, (S) '80 C, (S) '79 JR, (S) '78 Z.

CONROTTO WINERY *Santa Clara County*
1690 Hecker Pass Highway, Gilroy, CA 95020
(408) 842-3053 Founded: 1933
Owner: Chinto Conrotto. Winemaker: James Burr.

CONSUMERS RIVER VINEYARD (*See* Story Vineyards.)

CONTI ROYALE (*See* East-Side Winery.)

CONTRA COSTA COUNTY
Inland North Central Coast.

Controlled Fermentation
The most common method is refrigeration. The aim is to speed up or slow down the process, as needed and prevent excessive heat which might cause oxidation or damage to the delicate flavors of the wine.

R. & J. COOK ★ *Yolo County*
Netherlands Road, P.O. Box 227, Clarksburg, CA 95612
(916) 775-1234 Founded: 1979
Storage: American, French oak; stainless steel.
Owners: Roger and Joanne Cook. Winemaker: Janos Radyanyi, Jr.

The 130 acre vineyards are in regions unknown to most people and is another unique microclimate region. The vineyards are in Clarksburg and Solano. Varietal, estate bottled, vintage-dated wines produced are: Chenin Blanc Extra Dry, Very Dry and Semi-Dry, Rosé of Petite Sirah, Cabernet Blanc, Cabernet Sauvignon, Semillon, Merlot Blanc and Napa Gamay. Also estate bottled Varietal Red and White table wine.

['81 OC] (G) '80 CH, (S) '80 CH; ['82 OC] (G) '80 CH, (G) '79 PS; ['82 SJP&C] (B) '81 FB, (P) (B) '80 CH, (P) (B) '81 MB, (B) '81 SB.

COOK-ELLIS WINERY, INC. *Santa Cruz County*
2900 Buzzard Lagoon Rd., Corralitos, CA 95076
Mail: P.O. Box 66586, Scotts Valley, CA 95066
(408) 688-7208 Founded: 1981
Owners: Wm. J. (Jim) Ellis and Rebecca Cook. Winemaker: Jim Ellis.

8 acre vineyard to be planted in 1984. Grapes are purchased on a selected vineyard basis. Label indicates vineyard and/or appellation. Varietal, vintage-dated wines produced are Chardonnay and Pinot Noir. Also produced is Strawberry Wine.

Cooperage
The general term used to designate containers in which wines are stored and aged. It includes casks and wooden or stainless steel ageing tanks. The term derives from the occupation of cooper—one who makes or repairs wooden containers. The cooper's art has recently been revived in Northern California where several small shops assemble, repair and shave fine oak barrels from Europe. The

actual manufacture of small American Oak barrels is still limited to Missouri and Arkansas.

COPENHAGEN CELLARS—
VIKINGS FOUR *Santa Barbara County*
448 Alisal Road, Solvang, CA 93463
(805) 688-4218 Founded: 1965
Owners: Douglas & Candace Scott. Manager: Fred Golin.

A comprehensive list of over 40 different wines are available for tasting daily.

CORDTZ BROTHERS CELLARS ★ *Sonoma County*
28237 River Rd., Cloverdale, CA 95425
(707) 894-5245 Founded: 1979
Storage: French & American Oak.
General Manager/Winemaker: David Cordtz.

Winery located on old Musalacon landgrant in upper Alexander Valley, Cloverdale. The bonded winery number 328 dates back to 1906. Re-opened and completely refurbished in 1980. Grapes are also purchased on select vineyard basis. Label indicates vineyard and/or appellation.

Varietal, vintage-dated wines produced are Gewurztraminer, Chardonnay and Sauvignon Blanc. Also produced are varietal, vintage-dated Zinfandel and Cabernet Sauvignon.

['82 OC] (B) '80 CA, (B) '80 C, (G) '80 Z; ['82 SJP] (B) '81 SB, (P) (B) '80 Z.

Corky or Corked
When the wine has been affected by an inferior or leaky cork.

CORTI BROTHERS *Sacramento County*
5770 Freeport Blvd., Sacramento, CA 95822

Highly regarded retailers who select and have wines finished to their specifications. Stony Hill Semillon de Soleil is produced exclusively for Corti Bros. The strip label indicates this. Various vintages Amador County Zinfandel and Edmeades Cabernet Sauvignon.

H. COTURRI & SON LTD. *Sonoma County*
6725 Enterprise Rd. P.O. Box 396, Glen Ellen, CA 95442
(707) 996-6247 Founded: 1979
Storage: Small oak.
Owners: H. Coturri & Sons, Ltd. Winemaker: Tony Coturri. Vineyard Manager: Phillip Coturri.

Phillip is also a vineyard developer by profession. Grapes are purchased on a select vineyard basis. Label indicates vineyard and/or appellation. Varietal wines produced are Semillon, Riesling, Chardonnay, Zinfandel, Pinot Noir and Cabernet Sauvignon.

Cremant
Champagne that is about one-half the standard effervescence.

CRESCINI WINES *Santa Cruz County*
P.O. Box 216, 2621 Old San Jose Rd., Soquel, CA 95073
(408) 462-1466 Founded: 1980
Owner/Winemaker: Richard and Paule Crescini.

Grapes are purchased on a select vineyard basis from Napa Valley and Monterey County. Varietal, vintage-dated wines produced are Cabernet Sauvignon, Petite Sirah and Chenin Blanc.

CRESTA BELLA (*See* Gibson Wine Co.)

CRESTA BLANCA VINEYARDS ★ *Mendocino County*
2399 North State St, Ukiah, CA 95482
(707) 462-2985 Founded : 1882
Storage: Limousin and American oak, stainless steel.
Owner: Guild Wineries & Distilleries. Manager & Winemaker: Mark Gabrielli.

Cresta Blanca was founded in 1882 by one of California's pioneering winemakers, Charles Wetmore, whose wines were the first California wines to win an International Competition: the 1889 Paris Exposition with 17,000 entrants.

Vineyards are located in Mendocino County and in the Santa Maria Valley. Label indicates vineyard and/or appellation.

Cresta Blanca produces the following vintage varietal wines: Pinot Chardonnay, Grey Riesling, French Colombard, Chablis, Johannisberg Riesling, Gewurztraminer, Chenin Blanc, Blanc de Blanc, Gamay Rosé, Cabernet Sauvignon, Pinot Noir, Petite Sirah, Zinfandel and Gamay Beaujolais. Also produced are vintage-dated Chablis, and non-vintage Burgundy. Also Champagne, Sherry, Fin de Nuit and vintage-dated Port.

['82 OC] (B) '80 CH, (S) '78 Z, (B) CHA.

CRESTON MANOR VINEYARD
San Luis Obispo County
Indian Creek Ranch, 17 Mile Post, Hwy #58, Creston, CA 93432
(805) 238-7398 Founded: 1982
Owners: Koontz and Rosenbloom families. Winemaker: Victor Hugo Roberts.

The vineyard and winery are part of the 479 acre Indian Creek Ranch. There are presently 44 acres of vineyard planted. An additional 106 acres will be planted in the next three years. At the present time grapes are purchased on a selected vineyard basis.

Varietal, vintage-dated wines produced are Chardonnay, Sauvignon Blanc and Cabernet Sauvignon.

CRIBARI & SONS WINERY ★ *Fresno County*
3223 East Church Ave., Fresno, CA 93714
(209) 485-6080 Founded: 1904
Storage: Redwood, stainless steel.
Owner: Guild Wineries & Distilleries. Manager: Richard Huber. Winemaker: Albert B. Cribari.

Vineyards are located in the San Joaquin Valley. Label indicates vineyard and/or appellation.

Varietal wines produced are Cabernet Sauvignon, Zinfandel, Pinot Chardonnay, Chenin Blanc and French Colombard. Also produced are Mendocino Burgundy, Mello Burgundy, Mountain Burgundy, Chianti, Vino Rosso, Chablis Blanc, Mountain Chablis, Mountain Rhine, Vino Bianco, Light Chablis, Mountain Vin Rosé, Vino Fiamma, Marsala, Madeira, Sherry, Champagne, Cold Duck, Pink Champagne and Spumante.

['82 OC] (S) Z.

CRONIN VINEYARDS *San Mateo County*
11 Old LaHonda Rd., Woodside, CA 94062
(415) 851-1452 Founded: 1980
Owner/Winemaker: Duane Mansell Cronin. Vineyard: 1 acre at winery.

Grapes are also purchased on a select vineyard basis. Label indicates vineyard and/or appellation. Varietal, vintage-dated wines produced are: Chardonnay, Pinot Noir, Cabernet Sauvignon and Zinfandel.

Cru
A vineyard or growth.

Crush
The process of stemming and crushing grapes for wine at harvest time. The purpose is to break the skins and release the juice. Not to be confused with pressing which comes later.

Crust
Deposit of sediment by wine while aging in the bottle; the deposit adheres to the inside of the bottle as a crust. Crusted wines are old, bottle-aged.

CRYSTAL VALLEY CELLARS/CONSENTINO WINE COMPANY *Stanislaus County*
P.O. Box 4751, Modesto, CA 95352
(209) 526-5513 Founded: 1981
Storage: French & American oak, stainless steel.
Owner and Winemaker: Mitch Cosentino.

The 20 acre vineyard is located in Stanislaus County. Grapes are also purchased on a select vineyard basis. Varietal wines produced are Cabernet Sauvignon, Chardonnay and Merlot.

Proprietary wines produced are Robin's Glow (R) (Brut Sparkling Blanc de Noir) and Crystal Fumé (R) (Sauvignon Blanc). Also produced are Spumante, Champagne Rosé, Extra Dry Champagne and occasional Limited Reserve wines under the name Cosentino Selections.

Winemakers favorite wines are Robin's Glow, Chardonnay, Merlot and Cabernet Sauvignon.

['82 OC] (S) BDN, CHA, SM.

CUCAMONGA VINEYARDS *San Bernardino County*
10013-8th Street, Rancho Cucamonga, CA 91730
(714) 980-7987
Storage: Oak, redwood, stainless steel.
Owner/Manager: Philo Pierre Biane. Winemaker: Prino F. Scorsatto.

The Biane family is a sixth-generation California winemaking family. Wines produced are: Limited Edition Brut and Extra Dry Champagne, Moscato Spumante, Cuvée d'Or Extra Dry Champagne, Pink Champagne, Sparkling Burgundy, Cold Duck, Chablis, Rosé, Burgundy, Cabernet Sauvignon, Chenin Blanc, Petite Sirah, Johannisberg Riesling, Moscato de Primo and generic wines.

The winemaker's favorite wines are: the Limited Edition Champagnes and Moscato Spumante.

JOHN CULBERTSON WINERY *San Diego County*
2608 Via Rancheros, Fallbrook, CA 92028
(714) 728-0398 Founded: 1981
Storage: Stainless steel.
Owners: John C. and Martha Culbertson. Winemaker: John C. Culbertson.

The ranch is 60 acres of which 5 acres is planted in Chardonnay. The only wine to be produced will be Champagne.

Cutting
In viticulture a segment of the cane or branch of a grapevine cut during the dormant season and used for propogation of new vines. Most new grapevines are planted as cuttings—rarely as seeds.

CUVAISON *Napa County*
4550 Silverado Trail, Calistoga, CA 94515
(707) 942-6266 Founded: 1970
Storage: French oak, stainless steel.
Owner: Stefan Schmideiny. Winemaker: John Thacher.

The vineyard is at Carneros on a hillside in the Napa Valley.

Varietal, vintage-dated wines produced are: Chardonnay, Cabernet Sauvignon and Zinfandel.

The winemaker's favorite wine is Cabernet Sauvignon.

Cuvee
Literally, the contents of a cask of wine—usually refers to an especially prepared blend of wines such as a blend of still wines before secondary fermentation, to produce Champagne.

CUVEE d'OR (*See* Cucamonga Vineyard Co.)

CYGNET CELLARS *San Benito County*
Winery: 11736 Cienega Road, Hollister, CA 95023
(408) 733-4276 Founded: 1977
Office: 1024 Lupine Dr., Sunnyvale, CA 94086
Storage: Oak barrels.
Owners: Jim Johnson and Bob Lane, 2 general partners. Winemaker: Jim Johnson.

The grapes are purchased from vineyards in San Luis Obispo County. Varietal, vintage-dated wines produced are: Zinfandel, Chardonnay, Cabernet Sauvignon, Petite Sirah, Pinot Noir, Pinot St. George and Carignane. Also Palomino (Palomono and French Colombard).

The winemaker's favorite wine is Zinfandel.

D

DACH VINEYARDS *Mendocino County*
9200 Highway 128, Philo, CA 95466
Owners: John and Sandi Dach. Winemaker: John Dach.

The 20 acre vineyard is located at the winery.

The wines, as they become available, will be sold at the Dach fruit stand. Wines to be produced are Pinot Chardonnay, Gewurztraminer, Pinot Noir, and Apple.

D'AGOSTINI WINERY *Amador County*
Shenandoah Road, Plymouth, CA 95669

(209) 245-6612 Founded: 1856
Storage: Oak, redwood.
Owners: Michele J., Tulio, Armenio, and Henry D'Agostini. Winemaker: Tulio D'Agostini.

Varietal, estate-bottled wine produced is Zinfandel. Also produced are Claret, Sauterne, Burgundy and Dry Muscat.

Decant

To pour wine gently from the bottle in which crust or sediment has been deposited, for the purpose of obtaining clear wine for serving. The container into which the wine is poured is called a decanter. Decant also means to pour wine from a large container into a small container for more convenient handling.

DEAVER RANCH VINEYARD—Zinfandel vineyard in Shenandoah Valley of Amador County.

DEER PARK WINERY *Napa County*
1000 Deer Park Road, Deer Park, CA 94576
(707) 963-5411 Founded: 1979
Storage: French oak, stainless steel.
Managing Partner and Winemaker: David Clark. Vineyard: 7 acres.

Varietal, vintage-dated wines produced are Zinfandel, Chardonnay and Sauvignon Blanc.

Degree Days (*See* Heat, Heat Summation.)

DEHLINGER WINERY *Sonoma County*
6300 Guerneville Road, Sebastopol, CA 95472
(707) 823-2378 Founded: 1976
Storage: Oak, stainless steel.
Owner/Winemaker: Tom Dehlinger. Vineyard: 14 acres.

Wines produced are Chardonnay, Pinot Noir, Cabernet Sauvignon and Zinfandel.

Delicate

A light wine, usually white, young and fresh.

DELICATO VINEYARDS ★ *San Joaquin County*
12001 So. Highway 99, Manteca, CA 95336
(209) 239-1215 Founded: 1924
Storage: Oak, redwood, stainless steel.
Owners: Anthony, Frank, and Vincent Indelicato. Winemaker: Hector Castro.

The 365 acre vineyards were planted in 1924 by two brothers-in-law, Gaspare Indelicato and Sebastiano Luppino. The winery was started in 1935. The vineyards are located at the winery in the Clements area.

Varietal, vintage-dated wines produced are: Green Hungarian, Pinot Chardonnay, Grenache Rosé, Chenin Blanc, French Colombard, Zinfandel, Cabernet Sauvignon, Sauvignon Blanc, and Petite Sirah. Varietal non-vintage wine produced is Mountain Zinfandel.

Also produced are Mtn. Chablis, Chablis Blanc, Mtn. Rhine, Mtn. Vin Rosé, Mtn. Burgundy, Mtn. Chianti, Mtn. Sauterne, Barberone, Claret, Sangria, Burgundy, Vin Rosé, Champagne, Pink Champagne, Cold Duck, Sherry, and Port. The winemaker's favorites are Green Hungarian, Franch Colombard, Petite Sirah, Cabernet Sauvignon, and Grenache Rosé.

['82 SJC] (B) '80 C, (C) (S) '80 CH, (P) (B) '79 PS.

DE LOACH VINEYARDS ★ *Sonoma County*

1791 Olivet Road, Santa Rosa, CA 95401
(707) 526-9111 Founded: 1975
Storage: Oak, stainless steel.
Owners: Cecil and Christine De Loach. Winemaker: Cecil De Loach. Associate Winemaker: James R. Ullom. Vineyard Manager: John De Loach.

The 140 acre vineyard is located at the winery in the Russian River Valley. 100% varietal, vintage-dated, estate bottled wines produced are White Zinfandel, Zinfandel, and Pinot Noir.

Also produced are vintage-dated, varietal Chardonnay, Fumé Blanc and Gewurztraminer.

['81 OC] (S) '79 PN, (S) '79 Z; ['82 OC] (S) '80 C, (B) '81 SB; ['82 SJP] (B) '81 FB, (B&S) '81 G, (C) (B) '80 PN.

Demi-sec

Half-dry. A term to describe a fairly sweet Champagne with a residual sugar of over 2.5%. Often seen in Latin American Nations.

Dessert Wines

Sweet, full-bodied wines served with desserts or as refreshments, are called dessert wines. Their alcohol content is 18% - 21%. They range from medium-sweet to sweet and from pale gold to red. The three distinct popular types, in addition to Sherry, are: Port, Muscatel and Tokay. Dessert Wines: Angelica, Madeira, Marsala, Muscatel, Port, Sherry and Tokay.

Dessert Wines

Award wines to look for: Barengo, Brookside, Callaway, Christian Brothers, Rapazzini, San Antonio, Quady.

DEVLIN WINE CELLARS ★ *Santa Cruz County*

P.O. Box 723, Soquel, CA 95073
(408) 476-7288 Founded: 1978
Storage: American and French oak, stainless steel.
Owner, Winemaker: Charles Devlin.

The grapes are purchased on a selected region basis.

Varietal, vintage-dated wines produced are Chardonnay, Cabernet Sauvignon, Merlot and Chenin Blanc.

['81 OC] (B) '78 Z.

DIABLO VISTA WINERY *Solano County*

674 E. "H" St., Benicia, CA 94510
(707) 433-8534 Founded: 1977
Owner: Robert E. Polson.

Grapes grown at Polson Vineyards, Dry Creek Valley. Varietal wines produced are Cabernet Sauvignon, Merlot, Zinfandel, Chardonnay and Chenin Blanc.

DIAMOND CREEK VINEYARDS ★ *Napa County*

1500 Diamond Mountain Road, Calistoga, CA 94515
(707) 942-6926 Founded: 1972
Storage: Nevers oak barrels.
Owner/Winemaker: Al Brounstein. Vineyard: 20 acres at winery.

Label indicates vineyard: i.e., Volcanic Hill, Red Rock Terrace or Gravelly Meadow. Diamond Creek produces only Cabernet Sauvignon.

['81 OC] (B) '78 CA.

DIAMOND OAKS VINEYARDS ★ *Napa County*
26700 Dutcher Creek Road, Cloverdale, CA 95425
Mailing Address: P.O. Box 2703, So. San Francisco, CA 94080
(415) 873-9463 Founded: 1978
Storage: French oak barrels and stainless steel.
Owner: Dinesh Maniar. Winemaker: Jeff Libarle. Vineyards: 53 acres in Napa Valley, Calistoga. 100 acres in Wild Horse Valley.

Grapes are also purchased from selected vineyards in Napa and Sonoma Counties.

Varietal, vintage-dated wines produced are Chardonnay, Fumé Blanc and Cabernet Sauvignon. Also produced are Thomas Knight Red (a blend of Cabernet Sauvignon and Merlot) and Thomas Knight White (a blend of Sauvignon Blanc, Semillon and Gewurztraminer.)

['82 SJP] (B) '76 CA, (P) (B) RT.

J. E. DIGARDI WINERY *Contra Costa County*
3785 Pacheco Blvd., Martinez, CA 94553
Owner: Francis J. Digardi. Vineyard: 1 acre. Founded: 1886

Dinner Wine (*See* Table Wine.)

DOLAN VINEYARDS *Mendocino County*
1482 Inez Way, Redwood Valley, CA 95470
(707) 485-7250 Founded: 1980
Storage: Oak, stainless steel.
Owners: Paul and Lynne Dolan. Winemaker: Paul Dolan.

Wines produced are varietal, vintage-dated, Chardonnay and Cabernet Sauvignon.

DOMAINE CHANDON ★ *Napa County*
California Drive, Yountville, CA 94599
(707) 944-8844 Founded: 1973
Storage: Stainless steel, aging in bottles.
President: John Wright. Winemakers: Edmond Maudiere (Moet and Chandon, France) and Dawnine Sample Dyer.

Domaine Chandon is a wholly-owned subsidiary of Moet-Hennessy, a French Company that owns Champagne Moet and Chandon, Hennessy Cognac and Dior Perfumes—the first French-owned vineyards in America. The vineyards are located on Mt. Veeder, Carneros district and at the winery. They specialize in sparkling wines.

Two sparkling wines are produced: Chandon Napa Valley Brut (Pinot Noir, Chardonnay and Pinot Blanc) and Chandon Blanc de Noirs (Pinot Noir).

The winemaker's favorite wines are Napa Valley Brut and Blanc de Noirs. They also produce an interesting aperitif made of Pinot Noir called "Panache."

['81 OC] (S) '79 C, (G) NV SW; ['82 OC] (B) CHA.

DOMAINE HANS (*See* Gemello Winery.)

DOMAINE LAURIER ★ *Sonoma County*
8075 Martinelli Rd., Forestville, CA 95436
(707) 887-2176 Founded: 1978
Storage: Oak, stainless steel.
Owners: Jacob and Barbara Shilo. Winemaker: Steve

Test. Wine Consultant: Mary Ann Graff.

The 30 acre vineyard is located at the winery in the Russian River Valley area. Varietal, vintage-dated, estate bottled wines produced are Pinot Noir, Cabernet Sauvignon, Sauvignon Blanc and Chardonnay. Varietal, vintage-dated Chardonnay. We purchase grapes from selected vineyards in a 3 mile radius. All our varietals are 100% varietals.

The winemaker's favorite wines are Pinot Noir and Chardonnay.

['81 OC] (B) '78 CA; ['82 SJP] (S) '79 CA, (P) (B) '79 PN.

DONATONI WINERY *Los Angeles County*

10620 So. La Cienega Blvd., Unit D, Inglewood, CA 90304
(213) 645-5445 Founded: 1980
Owners: Hank & Judy Donatoni. Winemaker: Hank Donatoni.

Grapes are purchased on a select vineyard basis. Label indicates vineyard and/or appellation.

Varietal, vintage-dated wines produced are Cabernet Sauvignon and Chardonnay.

DONNA MARIA VINEYARDS ★ *Sonoma County*

10286 Chalk Hill Rd., Healdsburg, CA 95448
(707) 838-2807 Founded: 1980
Storage: Oak, stainless steel.
Owner: Frederick Furth. General Manager: Gary Chesak. Winemaker: Larry Wara. Vineyards: 150 acres.

Vineyards are at Sonoma Chalk Hill.

Varietal, vintage-dated wines produced are Chardonnay, Gewurztraminer, Pinot Noir, Sauvignon Blanc and Cabernet Sauvignon.

['82 OC] (S) '81 G; ['82 SJP] (B) '80 C, (P) (B) '81 SG, (B) '81 G.

Dosage

The addition of sugared wine and brandy to another wine in order to make it conform to established standards of dryness. Only used for Champagne and sparkling wines.

Dry

The opposite of sweet; free of sugar. Fermentation converts the natural sugar of the grape into wine alcohol and carbon dioxide gas. A wine becomes dry when all the sugar has been consumed by fermentation. Dryness should not be confused with astringency, acidity, tartness or sourness; it simply means lacking in sweetness. The wines, which uninformed individuals are apt to call "sour", are dry or tart, made with these flavor characteristics especially to blend with the flavors of main course foods. (A Champagne or Sherry labeled "dry" is actually semi-dry, and even an "extra-dry" Champagne may be slightly sweet). Really dry Champagne is labeled "Brut" or "Nature"; the driest Sherries are labeled "Extra Dry."

DRY CREEK VINEYARD ★ *Sonoma County*

3770 Lambert Bridge Road, Healdsburg, CA 95448
(707) 433-1000 Founded: 1972
Storage: Oak, stainless steel.
Owner: David S. Stare. Vineyard: 45 acres at winery in the Dry Creek Valley.

Grapes are also purchased on a select vineyard basis. Label indicates vineyard and/or appellation.

The winery specializes in 100% varietal, vintage-dated wines. The wines produced are Zinfandel, Cabernet Sauvignon, Chenin Blanc, Fumé Blanc, and Chardonnay.

['81 OC] (G) '80 G, (G), '80 SB, (S) '79 Z; ['82 OC] (B) '79 CA, (S) '81 SB, (S) '79 Z, (G) '80 C, (B) '80 C; ['82 SJP] (S) '81 FB, (C) (B) '79 CA, (P&C) (B&B) '79 Z.

Dry Semillon Wine

A varietal dry wine produced from Semillon grapes. Light golden in color, flowery bouquet, medium bodied with a rich dry flavor. Serve well chilled with fresh poultry and light entrees with cream sauces.

GEORGES DUBOEUF & SON *Sonoma County*

476 Moore Lane, (P.O. Box 1056), Healdsburg, CA 95488
(707) 433-7619 Founded: 1980
Owner: George Duboeuf, President. Winemaker: Guy Marion. Enologist: Patrick Leon.

Founded in 1980 by Georges Duboeuf, a negociant in Beaujolais. Grapes are purchased on a selected vineyard basis. Label indicates vineyard and/or appellation. All reds made by traditional "methode Beaujolais" using carbonic maceration. No oak used in reds.

Varietal, vintage-dated wines produced are Gamay Beaujolais and French Colombard.

DUCKHORN VINEYARDS ★ *Napa County*

3027 Silverado Trail, St. Helena, CA 94574
(707) 963-7108 Founded: 1978
Storage: French oak, stainless steel.
Owner: closely held corporation. President: Daniel J. Duckhorn. Winemaker: Thomas Rinaldi. Vineyard: 6.5 acres at the winery.

Varietal, vintage-dated wines produced are Merlot, Sauvignon Blanc and Cabernet Sauvignon.

['81 OC] (S) '78 CA; ['82 OC] (S) '79 M.

DUDENHOEFER (*See* Barengo Vineyards.)

DUNN VINEYARDS *Napa County*

805 White Cottage Road, Angwin, CA 94508
(707) 965-3642 Founded: 1982
Storage: French oak.
Owners: Lori and Randall Dunn. Winemaker: Randall Dunn.

The six acre vineyard is in the Howell Mountain area of the Napa Valley. Varietal, vintage-dated wine produced is Cabernet Sauvignon.

DU PRATT VINEYARD—Zinfandel vineyard in Anderson Valley.

DURNEY VINEYARD ★ *Monterey County*

P.O. Box 222016, Carmel, CA 93922
(408) 625-5433 Founded: 1968
Storage: Oak barrels, stainless steel.
Owners: W. W. and D. K. Durney. Manager: David Armanasco. Winemaker: John Estell.

Durney Vineyards is a 128 acre wine estate located high in the Santa Lucia Coastal Mountain Range at the upper end of the Carmel Valley in Monterey County.

Begun in 1968 with a 20 acre planting, Durney Vineyards is now the only vineyard and winery in the Carmel Valley which has an appellation.

Varietal, vintage-dated, estate bottled wines produced are Cabernet Sauvignon, Johannisberg Riesling, Chenin Blanc, and Gamay Beaujolais.

['81 OC] (G) '78 CA, (S) '80 CH, (S) '80 WR; ['82 SJC] (S) '81 CH, (P) (B) '81 JR, (B) (P) '79 CA.

DUSI RANCH—Zinfandel vineyard in San Luis Obispo County.

DUTCHER CREEK (*See* Rege Wine Co.)

DUTTON VINEYARD—Chardonnay vineyard in Russian River Valley.

E

EAGLE POINT VINEYARD—Zinfandel vineyard in Mendocino County.

Early Harvest

The equivalent to the Trocken & Halb-Trocken wines of Germany. Early harvest wines are generally Johannisberg Rieslings and are produced only in the coolest years. Wines produced from these grapes will usually contain low levels of alcohol and residual sugar coupled with high total acidity.

EAST-SIDE WINERY *San Joaquin County*

6100 E. Highway 12, Lodi, CA 95240

(209) 369-4768 Founded: 1934

Owner: A Corporate Cooperative. Winemaker: Lee Eichelel.

Varietal wines produced under the Conti-Royale label are Gamay Rosé, Barbera, Zinfandel, French Colombard, Cabernet Sauvignon, Ruby Cabernet, Dry Semillon, Grey Riesling, Emerald Riesling, Chenin Blanc, Tinta Madeira, Port, and Petite Sirah.

Also produced are Cocktail Sherry, Marsala, Chablis, Sauterne, and Burgundy.

Edelwein

A varietal sweet wine produced by Freemark Abbey from Johannisberg Riesling by a process similar to German Beerenauslese or Trochenberenauslese.

Edelzwicker

A white wine from a blend of Gewurztraminer and White Riesling grapes. ("Edel"—Noble, "Zwicker"—mixture or blend.)

EDMEADES VINEYARDS ★ *Mendocino County*

5500 California State Highway #128, Philo, CA 95466

(707) 895-3232 Founded: 1972

Storage: American and French oak, stainless steel.

Owners: Edmeades, Inc. Wine Consultant: Jed Steele.

The 37 acre vineyard is located at the winery in the Anderson Valley 3 miles north of Philo on Hwy. 128. Varietal, vintage-dated wines produced are Cabernet Sauvignon, Zinfandel, Chardonnay and Gewurztraminer.

Also produced are Rain Wine (Generic White), Whale

Wine (Generic White), and Opal (Pinot Noir Blanc).

The winemaker's favorite wines are Rain Wine, Zinfandel, Pinot Noir, and Gewurztraminer.

['81 OC] (B) '78 CA, (S) '79 Z; ['82 OC] (B) '80 C, (S) '80 PN, (S) '80 Z, (B) '80 Z.

EDNA VALLEY VINEYARD *San Luis Obispo County*
Rt. 3, Box 155, San Luis Obispo, CA 93401
(805) 544-9594 Founded: 1980
Storage: Oak.
Winemaker: Gary Mosby. Vineyards: 600 acres near San Luis Obispo.

Varietal, vintage-dated, estate bottled wines produced are Chardonnay and Pinot Noir.

EISLE VINEYARD—Cabernet Sauvignon vineyard in Napa Valley.

VOLKEN EISLE VINEYARD—Zinfandel vineyard in Chiles Valley of Napa.

EL DORADO COUNTY
Sierra Foothills.

EL DORADO VINEYARDS *El Dorado County*
3551 Carson Road, Camino, CA 95709
(916) 644-3773 Founded: 1975
Storage: Oak.
Owners: Earl & Jo Anne McGuire and John & Margaret Mirande. Winemaker: Earl McGuire.

Varietal wines produced are Zinfandel, Chenin Blanc, Cabernet Sauvignon, Chardonnay, Merlot, and Apple.

EL PASO DE ROBLES WINERY & VINEYARDS *San Luis Obispo County*
Rt. 1, Box 101, Willow Creek Rd., Paso Robles, CA 93446
(805) 238-6986 Founded: 1981

Emerald Riesling
(White Table Wine) A varietal grape developed at the University of California, Davis. It is the child of Johannisberg Riesling and Muscadelle—one of the Muscat family. A light, fruity, slightly sweet wine. Excellent with poultry and shellfish.

EMILE'S (*See* Emilio Guglielmo Winery.)

Enology
The science of the study of winemaking; related to viticulture, which is the science of grape culture. The University of California, Davis, is the leading center in the United States.

ENZ VINEYARDS *San Benito County*
Lime Kiln Valley, P.O. Box 1435, Hollister, CA 95023
(408) 637-3956 Founded: 1973
Storage: Oak, stainless steel.
Owners: Robert and Susan Enz. Winemaker: Robert Enz.

The 30 acre vineyards were planted in 1895 and are still producing. They are located at the winery.

Varietal, vintage-dated wines produced are Pinot St. George, Zinfandel, White Zinfandel, Golden Chasselas, and Fumé Blanc.

ESCHAN VINEYARD—Zinfandel vineyard in Shenandoah Valley of Amador County.

ESHCOL (*See* Trefethen Vineyards.)
ESOLA VINEYARD—Zinfandel vineyard in Shenandoah Valley of Amador County.
ESPIRIT (*See* Heublein.)
ESTANCIA (*See* Hacienda Wine Cellars.)
Estate Bottled
For "estate bottled" to be used on a label, both the winery and the vineyards which are the source of the grapes must be located in the same "Viticultural Area", the "Viticultural Area" appellation must be used, and the winery must own or control the vineyards. Also, all winemaking processes, from crushing to bottling, must be done at the single winery facility.
Esters
Aromatic substances brought about by the reactions of alcohols and acids in wine, which contribute to bouquet.
ESTRELLA RIVER WINERY ★ *San Luis Obispo County*
Shandon Star Route, P.O. Box 30496, Paso Robles, CA 93446
(805) 238-6300 Founded: 1972
Storage: American and French oak, stainless steel.
Owners: Cliff & Sally Giacobine. Manager: Clifford R. Giacobine. Winemaker: Tom Myers.
The 710 acre vineyard is located at the winery. Estate bottled, varietal, vintage-dated wines produced are: Chenin Blanc, Sauvignon Blanc, Chardonnay, Johannisberg Riesling, Muscat Canelli, Cabernet Sauvignon, Zinfandel, Barbera, and Sirah.
['81 OC] (B) '78 CA, (B) '80 MC, (B) '79 MC, (S) '79 PS, (S) '81 JR; ['81 SJC] (B) '80 FB, (C) (S) '78 CA.
EVENSEN VINEYARDS ★ *Napa County*
8254 St. Helena Highway, Oakville, CA 94562
(707) 944-2396 Founded: 1979
Storage: Stainless steel.
Owners: Richard and Sharon Evensen. Winemaker: Richard Evensen.
All are descendants of pioneer Sonoma and Napa county families dating back to the 1800's. Vineyard is located at winery in Napa Valley.
Varietal, vintage-dated, estate-bottled wine produced is Gewurztraminer.
['81 OC] (B) '80 G.
Extra Dry
In Champagne, slightly less dry than Brut. In Sherry, the driest.

F

FAMILY VINEYARD (*See* Bella Napoli Winery.)
FAR NIENTE WINERY ★ *Napa County*
P.O. Box 327, Oakville, CA 94562
(707) 944-2861 Founded: 1885 by Capt. John Benson
Storage: French oak.
Owners: Gil Nickel, Douglas Stelling, and Robert Lieff. Winemaker: Gil Nickel. Vineyard: 120 acres.

The winery, located in Napa Valley near Oakville, has been renovated. Vineyards are in Napa Valley. Its first crush was in 1979. The 100% varietal, vintage-dated wine produced in Chardonnay.

['81 OC] (B) '79 C.

FARNESI WINERY *Fresno County*
2426 Almond Ave., Sanger, CA 93657
(209) 875-3004 Founded: 1936
Owner: Danny C. Farnesi.

FARVIEW FARM VINEYARD ★ *San Luis Obispo County*
Rt. 2, Box 40, Templeton, CA 93465
(805) 434-1247 Founded: 1972
Owner: Dan Roy. Ray Krause is a partner in sales and marketing.

The vineyard was planted in 1972 with 36 acres of Zinfandel and 14 acres of Merlot. Varietal, vintage-dated wines include White Zinfandel, Zinfandel and Merlot.

['82 OC] (B) '79 M; ['82 SJC] (S) '79 Z.

FAY VINEYARD—Cabernet Sauvignon vineyard in Napa Valley.

FBF WINERY *El Dorado County*
Fairplay Rd., Somerset, CA 95684
(209) 245-3248 Founded: 1980
Storage: Oak, stainless steel.
Owners: Michael Fitzpatrick, Bill Betram and Brian Fitzpatrick.

Varietal, vintage-dated wines produced are Chardonnay, Sauvignon Blanc, Cabernet Sauvignon, Zinfandel, Zinfandel Blanc and Chenin Blanc.

FELTA SPRINGS (*See* Mill Creek Vineyards.)

FELTON-EMPIRE VINEYARDS ★ *Santa Cruz County*
379 Felton Empire Road, Felton, CA 95018
(408) 335-3939 Founded: 1976
Storage: American and French oak, stainless steel.
Owners: A corporation with 12 stockholders, major shareholders are J. Pollard, L. McCloskey and W. Gibbs.

Vineyards are in three parts of Santa Cruz County, one at the winery and two in the Bonny Doon district. Vineyards are on the California Coast. Blends are made under U.S. Patent/California copyright protected Maritime Series. The wine single-vineyard bottles other wines including Tepusquet vineyards.

Varietal, vintage-dated wines produced are Cabernet Sauvignon, Riesling, Gewurztraminer, "Botrytized" Late Harvest White Riesling, Chenin Blanc, Pinot Noir, Chardonnay and Zinfandel.

['81 OC] (B) '79 PN, (G) '79 WR; ['82 OC] (B) '81 G, (B) '81 JR, (S) '81 JR; ['82 SJC] (S) '80 G, (B) '81 CH (P&C) (S&B) '81 LHJ.

FENESTRA WINERY ★ *Alameda County*
83 E. Vallecitos Road, Livermore, CA 94550
(408) 258-1092 Founded: 1976
Storage: French & American oak, stainless steel.
Owners: Lanny & Frances Replogle. Winemaker: Lanny Replogle.

Lanny is a professor of chemistry at San Jose State teaching organic chemistry and the chemistry of wine.

Grapes are purchased on a select vineyard basis. Label indicates vineyard and/or appellation.

Varietal, vintage-dated wines produced are Chardonnay, Dry Chenin Blanc, Late Harvest Chenin Blanc, Sauvignon Blanc, Cabernet Sauvignon, Petite Sirah and Zinfandel. Occasionally Late Harvest White Riesling.

['81 OC] (G) '80 SB; ['82 OC] (S) '79 CA, (B) '81 CH, (B) '81 CH, (G) '79 PS; ['82 SJP] (B) '81 CHD, (P) (B) '79 CA.

FENTON ACRES WINERY *Sonoma County*
6192 Westside Road, Healdsburg, CA 95448
(709) 433-2305 Founded: 1976
Storage: Oak barrels.
Owners: Joe Rochioli, Jr.; Gerry O'Conner; John Broschofsky.

Varietal wines produced are Chardonnay and Pinot Noir.

Fermentation
The chemical process whereby sugars are broken down into alcohol, carbonic acid gas, and other by-products.

FERRARA WINERY *San Diego County*
1120 West 15th Avenue, Escondido, CA 92025
(714) 480-8991 Founded: 1932
Owner: Gasper D. Ferrara. Winemaker: George Ferrara.

The family is a third-generation winemaking family.

FERREIRA WINES *Sacramento County*
5990 Wine Road, Newcastle, CA 95658
(714) 745-7632 Founded: 1977
President: Alex Ferreira.

FERRERO VINEYARD—Zinfandel vineyard in Shenandoah Valley of Amador County.

FETZER VINEYARDS ★ *Mendocino County*
1150 Bel Arbres Road, Box 227, Redwood Valley, CA 95470
(707) 485-7634 Founded: 1968
Storage: Oak, stainless steel.
President: John Fetzer. Winemaker: Paul Dolan III.

Ten members of the Fetzer family work at the vineyards. Parts of the original vineyard were planted in the late 1880s. The vineyard is located near the headwaters of the Russian River. Label indicates vineyard and/or appellation. Estate vineyards are both in Mendocino County, one in Redwood Valley, North of Ukiah, and one in Sanel Valley near Hopland. Mendocino appellation.

The varietal, vintage-dated wines produced are Cabernet Sauvignon, Petite Sirah, Zinfandel, Gamay Beaujolais, Johannisberg Riesling, Sauvignon Blanc, Gewurztraminer, Chenin Blanc, Pinot Blanc, Chardonnay, French Colombard, Muscat Canelli and Pinot Noir. Winemaker's favorites are 1979 Cole Ranch Mendocino Cabernet Sauvignon and 1980 Special Reserve Mendocino Pinot Noir.

['81 OC] (S) '78 PS, (B) '78 CA, (B) '80 C, (G) '80 CH, (S) '80 G, (G) '77 PS, (B) '80 SB, (S) '80 WR, (S) '79 Z, (B) '78 Z; ['82 OC] (B) '79 CA, (B) '80 CA, (B) '80 C, (B) '81 C, (G) '81

GB, (B) '81 G, (S) '80 PS, (S) '78 PN, (B) '81 JR, (B) '80 Z; ['82 SJP] (B) '80 PB, (S&G) (P&C) '81 SG, (P&C) (S&B) '79 Z.

FICKLIN VINEYARDS ★ *Madera County*
30246 Avenue 7½, Madera, CA 93637
(209) 674-4598 Founded: 1948
Owners: the Ficklin family. Winemaker: David B. Ficklin and Peter Ficklin. Vineyardist: Walter C. Ficklin, Jr.

David's son, Peter, is also Winemaker. Walter's son, Steve, is also Vineyardist. The vineyard is located at the winery. Ficklin specializes in one wine—Ficklin Tinta Port.

['81 OC] (S) NV P.

FIELDBROOK VALLEY WINERY *Humboldt County*
4241 Fieldbrook Road, Fieldbrook, CA 95521
(707) 839-4140 Founded: 1976
Owner, Winemaker: Robert Hodgson.

The varietal, vintage-dated wines produced are Dry Chenin Blanc, Zinfandel, Petite Sirah and Merlot. Also produced is Trinity River Blanc (a blend of Sauvignon Blanc and Semillon).

FIELD STONE WINERY ★ *Sonoma County*
(dba Redwood Ranch & Vineyard, Inc.)
10075 Highway 128, Healdsburg, CA 95448
(707) 433-7266 Founded: 1966
Storage: American, French and German oak, stainless steel.
Owner: Family Owned Corporation. Winemaker: James Thopson. Consulting Enologist & Advisor: Andre Tchelistcheff. Vineyard: 800 acres at winery in the Alexander Valley.

The estate bottled, 100% varietal wines produced are Johannisberg Riesling, Chenin Blanc, Gewurztraminer, Cabernet Sauvignon, Petite Sirah, Rosé of Petite Sirah, and Spring-Cabernet (Rosé of Cabernet).

The winemaker's favorite wines are Cabernet Sauvignon, Johannisberg Riesling, Gewurztraminer, Chenin Blanc and Petite Sirah.

['81 OC] (B) '78 CA, (S) '78 PS; ['82 OC] (G) '78 CA, (S) '81 JR.

J. FILIPPI VINTAGE CO. *San Bernardino County*
P.O. Box 2, Mira Loma, CA 91752
(714) 984-4514 Founded: 1934
Storage: Oak, redwood, stainless steel.
Owners: the Joseph Filippi Family. Winemaker: Joseph A. Filippi.

The family has been making wine for generations. The 300 acre vineyard is in the Cucamonga Valley. Wine is sold direct to the consumer through sales and tasting rooms. Varietal wines produced are Barbera, Gamay Beaujolais, Pinot Noir, Johannisberg Riesling, Gewurztraminer, Riesling, Chenin Blanc, Green Hungarian, Pinot Chardonnay, and Cabernet Sauvignon. Also, Sherries, Ports, Champagnes, Cold Duck, Moscato Spumante, Marsala, fruit wines, Mead, vermouths, and dry and mellow table wines are produced.

FILSINGER VINEYARDS & WINERY ★ *Riverside County*
39050 DePortola Rd., Temecula, CA 92390
(714) 676-4594 Founded: 1980
Storage: Oak, stainless steel.
Owners: William & Kathy Filsinger. Winemaker: Greg Hahn. Vineyards: 55 acres at winery.

Grapes are also purchased on a select vineyard basis. Label indicates vineyard and/or appellation.

Varietal, vintage-dated, estate bottled wines produced are Sauvignon (Fumé) Blanc, Emerald Riesling, Chardonnay and Zinfandel. Also, Cabernet Sauvignon, Gamay Beaujolais, Petite Sirah and Johannisberg Riesling.

['82 OC] (G) '80 C, (S) '80 SB.

Fine
Fining, the process of clearing young wines by adding beaten egg, lactic acid, heavy gelatin, etc.

Finish
The very last impression of the tasting mouthful.

Fino
Denoting the qualities of dryness and lightness in Sherry.

FIRESTONE VINEYARD ★ *Santa Barbara County*
P.O. Box 244, Los Olivos, CA 93441
(805) 688-3940 Founded: 1974
Storage: Oak and stainless steel.
President: Brooks Firestone. General Manager: Allen Russell. Winemaker: Alison Green. Vineyard: 253 acres at the winery in the Santa Ynez Valley.

Vintage-dated, varietal estate bottled wines produced are: Gewurztraminer, Chardonnay, Rosé of Cabernet, Sauvignon Blanc, Cabernet Sauvignon, Pinot Noir, Johannisberg Riesling, and Merlot.

Special harvest varietals, vintage-dated are Gewurztraminer and Johannisberg Riesling.

The winemaker's favorite wine is Cabernet Sauvignon (Vintage Reserve).

['81 OC] (B) '77 CA, (G) '79 WR; ['82 OC] (B) '78 PN; ['82 SJP] (B) '81 SB, (P) (B) '81 CAR.

FIRPO WINERY *Contra Costa County*
Box 175 Sellers Ave., Oakley, CA 94561
(415) 625-1514

FISHER VINEYARDS *Sonoma County*
6200 St. Helena Road, Santa Rosa, CA 95404
(707) 539-7511
Storage: French and German oak, stainless steel.
Owners: Fred J. Fisher and Juelle L. Fisher. Consulting Enologist: Charles Ortman. Winemaker: Fred Fisher.

The 75 acres of vineyards are located in Napa Valley and the Mayacamas Mountains, Sonoma.

Varietal wines produced are Cabernet Sauvignon and Chardonnay.

FITCH MOUNTAIN VINEYARDS (*See* Richert & Sons Winery.)

FITZPATRICK WINERY (*See* FBF Winery.)

Flat
Lacking acidity; with sparkling wines, without effer-

vescence.

Flinty

Often used to describe wine that is dry, clean, sharp.

Flor

A selected yeast culture which, under suitable conditions, grows on the surface of wine and produces the flavor characteristic in Sherries, so named.

FLORA SPRINGS WINE CO. ★ *Napa County*

1978 W. Zinfandel Lane, St. Helena, CA 94574
(707) 963-5711 Founded: 1979
Storage: American and French oak, stainless steel.
Owners: John and Carrie Komes; Jerome, Flora, Michael, and Rosalie Komes; Julie and Pat Garvey. Winemaker: Ken Deis.

The 4 vineyards totalling 300 acres are located in Napa Valley. Varietal, vintage-dated, estate-bottled wines produced are Cabernet Sauvignon, Chardonnay and Sauvignon Blanc.

['82 OC] (S) '80 C; ['82 SJP] (B) '80 C (Special Selection).

Flora Wine

A varietal semi-sweet wine produced from Flora grapes. Developed by the University of California. It is a descendant of the Traminer grape. Flowery aroma and slightly sweet. Serve chilled with light lunch or picnics.

THOMAS FOGARTY WINERY *San Mateo County*

5937 Alpine Road, Portola Valley, CA 94025
(415) 851-1946 Founded: 1982
Storage: French oak, stainless steel.
Owner: Thomas Fogarty. Winemaker: Michael J. Martella.

12 acres of vineyard are located in the Santa Cruz Mountains. Grapes are also purchased on a selected vineyard basis. Label indicates vineyard and/or appellation.

Varietal, vintage-dated wines produced are Chardonnay, Pinot Noir and Cabernet Sauvignon.

Folle Blanche

(White Table Wine) A varietal grape that produces a dry, tart, fruity and fresh tasting wine with a mild aroma that is both apple and grapey. Goes well with fish, poultry and casseroles.

Originally from France where it once was the Cognac grape. Produced in California only by Louis Martini.

FOPPIANO WINE COMPANY ★ *Sonoma County*

12707 Old Redwood Highway, Healdsburg, CA 95448
(707) 433-7272 Founded: 1896
Storage: Oak, redwood, stainless steel.
Owned, operated, and managed by the Foppiano family. President: Louis J., grandson of John. Manager: Louis M. Winemaker: Rod A. Foppiano. Vineyards: 200 acres adjoin winery.

Under the Louis J. Foppiano label the varietal, vintage-dated wines are Sonoma Fumé (100%), Dry Chenin Blanc (100%), Chardonnay (100%), Dry Chenin Blanc, Chardonnay, Pinot Noir, Zinfandel (100%), Petite Sirah (100%) and Cabernet Sauvignon.

Also produced is vintage-dated Sonoma County White Burgundy.

Under the Riverside Farm label the dry, barrel aged generics include Premium Dry White, Red and Rosé, Zinfandel, French Colombard and Chenin Blanc.

The winemaker's favorite wines are Petite Sirah and Sonoma Fumé.

['81 OC] (B) '80 CH, (B) '77 PN, (B) '78 PS, (B) '79 SB; ['82 OC] (B) '80 CH, (S) '80 SB, (B) '78 Z, ['82 SJC] (B) '79 C, SJP (B) '80 FB, (P) (B) '78 Z.

FORT ROSS (*See* Seaview Winery.)

Fortification

In the early days of Sherry, the Spanish helped Sherries to stand up to sea voyages in casks by adding grape spirit to all except the lightest natural finos. Fortification can also help to develop different styles.

Fortified

Wines whose natural alcoholic strength is increased by the addition of brandy.

FORTINO WINERY ★ *Santa Clara County*

4525 Hecker Pass Highway, Gilroy, CA 95020
(408) 842-3305 Founded: 1970
Storage: Oak and redwood.
Owners: Ernest and Marie Fortino. Winemaker: Ernest Fortino.

The vineyard is located at the winery. As of 1970, in the first 10 years since the winery was founded, it had won 32 medals in tasting competitons.

The varietal wines produced are Zinfandel "Blanc," Cabernet Sauvignon "Blanc," Johannisberg Riesling, Carignane, Zinfandel, Ruby Cabernet, Petite Sirah, Charbono, Cabernet Sauvignon, Grenache Ruby, Rose of Cabernet Sauvignon, Sauvignon Vert and White Grenache. The other wines produced are Chablis, Haut Sauterne, Vin Rosé Reserve, Chianti, and Burgundy Reserve.

['81 OC] (B) '78 PS, (B) '77 Z; ['82 OC] (B) '78 CA, (B) '78 PS, (B) '78 CB.

FOUNTAIN GROVE (*See* Martini & Prati Wines.)

Foxiness

An unpleasant characteristic of some native Eastern American grape species—the Vitis Labrusca.

FRANCISCAN VINEYARDS ★ *Napa County*

1178 Galleron Road, Rutherford, CA 94573
(707) 963-7111 Founded: 1972
Storage: Stainless steel.
Owner: Peter Eckes Co. President: Thomas Wigginton. Vice President & Winemaker: Thomas A. Ferrell.

The winery has about 500 acres of vineyards. About 250 acres are in Oakville, Napa Valley, Napa County and 250 acres are in Northern Alexander Valley, Sonoma County. Label indicates vineyard and/or appellation.

Estate bottled wines are produced from both Napa and Alexander Valleys. Estate bottled Napa Valley varietals include Private Reserve Cabernet Sauvignon, Cabernet Sauvignon, Merlot, Zinfandel, Charbono, Riesling and Chardonnay. Estate bottled Alexander Valley wines include Private Reserve Cabernet Sauvignon, Cabernet Sauvignon, Sauvignon Blanc and Chardonnay.

Winemaker's favorites are Napa Valley Cabernet Sauvignon, Merlot, and Chardonnay, Alexander Valley Cabernet and Sauvignon Blanc.

['81 OC] (S) '78 CA, (S) '79 C; ['82 SJC] (B) '81 R, (P&C) (B&B) '77 CA.

Franken Riesling

Not a true Riesling (*See* Sylvaner.)

FRANZIA WINERY ★ *San Joaquin County*

1700 E. Hwy. 120, Ripon, CA 95366

(209) 599-4111

Storage: Stainless steel.

Owner: Private. Winemaker: Jim Walls.

The vineyards are located in the San Joaquin Valley. Varietal wines produced are Zinfandel, Chenin Blanc, French Colombard, Cabernet Sauvignon and Grenache Rosé.

Also produced are Chablis, Rhine, Pink Chablis, Vin Rosé, Burgundy, Sparkling Rosé, Champagne and Pink Champagne.

['82 OC] (B) CHA; ['82 SJP] (B) CH, (C) (S) GER.

FRASINETTI WINERY *Sacramento County*

7395 Frasinetti Road, Sacramento, CA 95828

(916) 383-2444 Founded: 1897

Owners: Howard and Gary Frasinetti. Manager: John Czech. Winemaker: Gary Frasinetti.

The grapes are purchased thru brokers. This is the oldest family winery in Sacramento, started in 1897 by James Frasinetti.

Varietal wines produced are Chenin Blanc, Johannisberg Riesling, French Colombard, Gamay Beaujolais, Zinfandel, Cabernet Sauvignon and Petite Sirah. Also produced are Angelica, Marsala, Cream Sherry, Port, Burgundy, Chablis and Rose.

CHRIS A. FREDSON WINERY *Sonoma County*

18521 Redwood Hwy., Geyserville, CA 95441

(707) 433-1290 Founded: 1911

Storage: Redwood and oak.

Owners: Leonard, Jane, Donald & Josephine Fredson. Winemakers: Leonard & Donald Fredson. Vineyards: 70 acres in Alexander Valley.

All wines are produced for and distributed by Krug Winery, St. Helena.

Wines produced are Burgundy, Zinfandel and Chablis.

FREEMARK ABBEY WINERY *Napa County*

3020 St. Helena Hwy. North, St. Helena, CA 94574

(707) 963-9694 Founded: 1887

Storage: French oak, stainless steel.

Owner: Limited Partnership. Winemaker: Larry Langbehn. Managers: Chas. Carpy & William Jaeger.

Winemaking at the Freemark Abbey dates back to 1887. The vineyards are located primarily in the Rutherford area, in the Napa Valley. Grapes are also purchased on a select vineyard basis.

Varietal, vintage-dated wines produced are Chardonnay,

Johannisberg Riesling, Edelwein (Sweet Johannisberg Riesling), Cabernet Bosche and Cabernet Sauvignon.

FRED'S FRIENDS (*See* Domaine Chandon.)

FREI BROTHERS WINERY *Sonoma County*
3387 Dry Creek Rd., Healdsburg, CA 95448
(707) 433-4849

French Colombard
The second most widely planted white wine grape in California (after Thompson Seedless). It is grown in virtually all areas and is most prolific in the San Joaquin Valley where it is relied on heavily to provide acid for blending the dry white wines, for distillation into Brandy, and Champagne production. It is the more reliable of the dry white jug wines and still a good value.

Award wines to look for: Alamaden, Beringer, Chateau de Leu, Colony, East-Side, Fetzer, Filippi, Foppiano, Gallo, Giumarra, LaMont, Lawrence, Livermore Valley, McDowell Valley, Parsons Creek, Pedroncelli, Perelli-Minetti, River Oaks, San Antonio, Sebastiani, Sonoma, Souverain, Taylor California Cellars, Villa Armando, Villa Baccala.

FRESNO COUNTY
Central San Joaquin Valley

FRESNO, KERN, MADERA, MERCED, TULARE

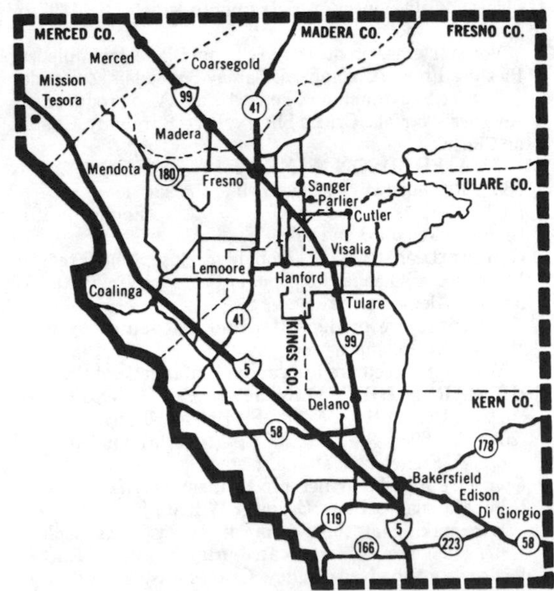

FRETTER WINE CELLARS, INC. *Alameda County*
805 Camelia Street, Berkeley, CA 94710
(415) 525-3232 Founded: 1977
Storage: Small oak.
Owner/Winemaker: Travis Fretter.

Grapes are purchased on a select vineyard basis from Napa and Mendocino.

Varietal wines produced are Chardonnay, Cabernet Sauvignon, estate-bottled Pinot Noir, Gamay, Gamay Rosé and Merlot.

FREY VINEYARDS *Mendocino County*
14000 Tomki Rd., Redwood Valley, CA 95470
(707) 485-5177 Founded: 1980
Storage: American oak, stainless steel.
Owner: Frey Vineyards, Inc. Winemaker: Jonathan Frey.
Vineyards: 10 acres Cabernet Sauvignon, 5 acres Grey Riesling, 10 acres Sauvignon Blanc and 2 acres Chardonnay.

Grapes are also purchased on a select vineyard basis. Label indicates vineyard and/or appellation.

Varietal, vintage-dated, estate bottled wines produced are Grey Riesling, Sauvignon Blanc and Cabernet Sauvignon. Also produced are varietal, vintage-dated French Colombard, Gewurztraminer, Zinfandel and Chardonnay.

FRICK WINERY ★ *Santa Cruz County*
303 Potrero St. #39, Santa Cruz, CA 95060
(408) 426-8623 Founded: 1976
Storage: Oak and stainless steel.
Owners, winemakers: Bill & Judith Frick.

Grapes are purchased on a select vineyard basis.

100% varietal, vintage-dated wines produced are Pinot Noir, Chardonnay, Petite Sirah and Zinfandel.

The winemaker's favorite wines are Pinot Noir, Petite Sirah, and Chardonnay.

['82 OC] (S) '79 PN.

FRITZ CELLARS *Sonoma County*
24691 Dutcher Creek Rd., Cloverdale, CA 95425
(707) 433-7268 Founded: 1981
Proprietor: A. J. Fritz. Winemaker: Paul Brasset. Christopher Stone, General Manager.

Varietal, vintage-dated wines produced are Chardonnay, Sauvignon Blanc and Zinfandel.

FROG'S LEAP WINERY *Napa County*
3358 St. Helena Hwy., St. Helena, CA 94574
(707) 963-4704 Founded: 1981
Storage: Wood, stainless steel.
Larry Turley & John T. Williams, Partners.

Fruit and Berry Wines
Award wines to look for: Bargetto, Brookside, California Fruit & Berry, Gibson, San Benito, Summerhill, Verdugo.

Fruity
With pronounced flavor and/or fragrance of the constituent fruit.

Having the fragrance and flavor of the grape.

Fumé Blanc (*See* Sauvignon Blanc.)
This term has become more popular to describe this increasingly consumed dry, crisp white wine.

G

GALLEANO WINERY *Riverside County*
4231 Wineville Road, Mira Loma, CA 91752
(714) 685-5376 Founded: 1933
Storage: Oak, redwood, concrete.
Owner: The Galleano family (Three Generations). Winemaker: B. D. "Nino" Galleano.

The vineyard dates back 80 years to General Cantu, former governor of Baja, California. Domenico Galleano purchased the vineyard in 1918. The 400 acre vineyard is in the Cucamonga district.

Wines produced are mostly generic and some vintage-dating. Galleano wines are not sold outside the state.

The winemaker's favorite is Zinfandel.

THE WINE CELLARS OF ERNEST AND JULIO GALLO ★ *Stanislaus County*
P.O. Box 1130, Modesto, CA 95353
(209) 521-3111 Founded: 1933
Storage: Oak and stainless steel.
Owners: Ernest and Julio Gallo. Winemaker: Julio Gallo.

The Gallos began in 1933, have been, and continue to be, the pace and trend-setters in the California wine industry. They are the leading wine producers in the world, with the kind of demand for quality that is sought and desired by a great classic Chateau. They are on a constant search for viticultural improvement—the art of creating varietal and generic wines of the highest quality still has the personal attention of Ernest and Julio and their immediate family. The Gallo vineyards are located in Mendocino, Sonoma, Napa, Lodi, Monterey, Modesto, Livingston and Fresno.

Under the label "The Wine Cellars of Ernest and Julio Gallo" the varietal wines produced are: Cabernet Sauvignon, Chardonnay, Sauvignon Blanc, Chenin Blanc, Johannisberg Riesling, Gewurztraminer, French Colombard and Zinfandel. Also produced is Rosé.

Under the "Gallo" label the wines produced are: Burgundy, Hearty Burgundy, Rhine, Chablis Blanc, Pink Chablis, Red Rosé, Vin Rosé and Chianti of California. Also Andre Brut California Champagne and Andre Dry Champagne.

['81 OC] (G) NV SB, (G) NV WR; ['82 OC] (S) NV CH, (S) SB; ['82 SJP&C] (B&B) G (P) (S) Hearty BR.

GAMBARELLI AND DAVITTO (*See* Heublein.)

Gamay

(Red Table Wine) A varietal light, fruity, fresh and slightly tart wine. Originally from the Burgundy region of France where it is the dominant grape in Beaujolais. Also referred to as Napa Gamay. Should be drunk when still young—one or two years old. Some enjoy this red wine slightly chilled.

Award wines to look for: Alta, Buena Vista, Christian Brothers, R. & J. Cook, Hop Kiln, Lawrence, J. Lohr (Turgeon & Lohr), North Coast Cellars, Preston, Richardson, San Pasqual, Charles Shaw, Stevenot, Trentadue.

Gamay Beaujolais

(Red Table Wine) A varietal grape that produces a light, fresh wine very much in the style of Gamay. The Gamay Beaujolais is a sub-variety of Pinot Noir.

Award wines to look for: Almaden, Beringer, Buena Vista, Davis Bynum, Chateau Noveau, Cilurzo, Fetzer, Giumarra, Hop Kiln, Inglenook, Lawrence, Louis Martini, Paul Masson, Mill Creek, Parducci, Robert Pecota, Pedroncelli, Preston, Rapazzini, Round Hill, San Martin, Sonoma, Souverain, Tyland.

Gamay Noir

(Red Table Wine) A red varietal wine made from the Gamay.

Gamay Rosé

(Pink Table Wine) A varietal pink table wine that is fresh, fruity and slightly sweet, made from the Gamay.

GARDEN CREEK RANCH—Gewurztraminer vineyard in Alexander Valley.

GAUTHIER & CLEVENGE LTD. (*See* Vikings Four.)

PAUL GARRETTS VINTNERS CHOICE (*See* Guild Wineries.)

GAVILAN (*See* Chalone Vineyard.)

GEMELLO WINERY ★ *Santa Clara County*

2003 El Camino Real, Mountain View, CA 94040

(415) 948-7723 Founded: 1934

Storage: Oak, redwood, stainless steel.

Owners: the Gemello family and Paul A. Obester. Winemaker: Sandy Obester.

Label indicates vineyard and/or appellation. Varietal wines produced are Petite Sirah, Cabernet Sauvignon, Barbara and Zinfandel.

Winemakers favorites are Cabernet Sauvignon and Zinfandel.

['82 SJP] (B) '75 CA (P) (B) Z, (P&C) (B&S) '77 PS.

Generic

Wine-type names which stand for definite type characteristics are called "generic" or "semi-generic"—generic names of geographic origin originally applied to the wines of specific Old World viticultural districts; as those wines became famous, their names, through the centuries, came to designate any wines with similar characteristics, wherever grown. Burgundy, Champagne, Claret, Port, Rhine Wine, Sauterne and Sherry are the best-known semi-generic wine-type names of geographic origin. Vermouth is a generic name without geographic significance.

J. H. GENTILI WINES *San Mateo County*

60 Lowell St., Redwood City, CA 94062

(415) 368-4740 Founded: 1981

Storage: Wood, stainless steel.

Jim H. Anderson, Owner/Winemaker.

Gewurztraminer

(White Table Wine) A varietal grape that produces an aromatic, medium-bodied, spicy-in-character wine with the slightest touch of sweetness. In German "gewurz" means spicy—and that actually describes the wine. It has a unique floral spiciness like that of carnation—rather than that of cinnamon or ginger. Mostly preferred before dinner with appetizers. Gewurztraminer also goes well with salmon, pork, poultry and sausages. Serve chilled. There are a few produced dry in the "Alsace" style.

Award wines to look for: Adler Fels, Almaden (Charles LeFranc), Bargetto, Beringer, Buena Vista (Gewurztraminer/Johannisberg Riesling blend), Richard Carey, Chateau St. Jean, Christian Brothers, Clos du Bois, DeLoach, Donna Maria, Evensen, Felton-Empire, Fetzer, Firestone, Gallo, Geyser Peak, Grand Cru, Gundlach-Bundschu, Hacienda, Hop Kiln, Husch, Inglenook, Landmark, Lost Hills, Louis Martini, Milano, Mirassou, Monterey, Monticello, Navarro, Parsons Creek, Pedroncelli, Joseph Phelps, Pine Ridge, River Oaks, Round Hill, Rutherford Hill, San Martin, Santa Ynez Valley, Sebastiani, Smothers, Sonoma, Souverain, St. Francis, Toyon, Tyland, Veedercrest, Wente, Mark West, Yverdon.

Gewurztraminer—Late, Early and Select Harvest
Award wines to look for: (Late)—Almaden, Chateau St. Jean, Clos du Bois, Dry Creek, Felton-Empire, Fetzer, Grand Cru, Monterey, Navarro, Smothers, Veedercrest; (Early)—Clos du Bois; (Select)—Firestone, Hacienda.

GEYSER PEAK WINERY ★ *Sonoma County*
22280 Geyserville Ave., Geyserville, CA 95441
(707) 433-6585 Founded: 1880
Storage: Oak, redwood, stainless steel.
Owners: Victor and Mark Trione. Chmn. of Board: Henry Tirone. President: John C. Senkevich.

The 1100 acre vineyards are located in Sonoma County. Varietal, vintage-dated wines produced are Cabernet Sauvignon, Chardonnay, Chenin Blanc, Soft Johannisberg Riesling (estate bottled), Fumé Blanc (estate bottled), Dry Gewurztraminer, Pinot Noir, Pinot Noir Blanc, Zinfandel, Rosé Cabernet Sauvignon and Gewurztraminer. Also produced are vintage-dated Chablis and Burgundy. Also Brut California Champagne. Also under the Summit label are Chablis, Rhine, Winterchill, Vin Rosé, Cabernet Sauvignon and Burgundy.

['81 OC] (B) '80 CH, (B) '76 PS, (S) '80 SB, (S) '80 WR; ['82 OC] (G) '77 CA (G) '80 C, (S) '77 PN; ['82 SJC] (B) '81 FB, (P) (B) '78 Z.

GIBSON WINE CO. *Fresno County*
1720 Academy St., Sanger, CA 93657
(209) 875-2505 Founded: 1934
Second Winery: *Sacramento County*
9750 Kent Street, Elk Grove, Sacramento, CA 95624
Owner: a cooperative of about 150 growers. Winemaker: Alex Farafontoff in Elk Grove, Gerald D. Homulka in Sanger. V.P. and Gen'l. Mgr.: Thomas P. Kelley. Vineyards in Fresno, Tulare, and Kings Counties.

The wines produced under the Gibson Vineyards label are Chablis, Rhine, Vin Rosé, Burgundy, Chanti, Chablis Blanc, Sauterne, Pink Chablis and Zinfandel. Also California Villages Light Chablis, Light Rhine and Light Rosé. Also produced as "Gibson Vineyards" are Sherry,

Port, Muscatel, Tokay and Marsala.

Under the Oreon label Retsina and Kokinelli Greek-style wines are produced.

The winemaker's favorite is Chablis.

GILES VINEYARD—Chardonnay vineyard in Sonoma County.

GIRARD WINERY ★ *Napa County*
7717 Silverado Trail, Oakville, CA 94562
(707) 944-8577 Founded: 1980
Storage: Oak.
Owner: the Girard family. Winemaker/Vineyard Mgr.: Fred Payne. Vineyards: 44 acres at winery. 200 acres under development.

Label indicates vineyard and/or appellation.

Varietal, vintage-dated, estate bottled wines produced are Dry Chenin Blanc, Chardonnay and Cabernet Sauvignon.

['82 OC] (B) '80 CA.

GIUMARRA VINEYARDS ★ *Kern County*
Edison Road and Edison Highway, Edison, CA 93303
(805) 366-5511 Founded: 1946
Storage: Stainless steel, oak barrels.
Owners: the Giumarra and Corsaro families. Chairman of the Board: Joe Giumarra. President: Sal Giumarra. Manager: John Giumarra, Jr. Winemakers: Dale Anderson and Bill Nakata.

Three generations oversee the winery and vineyards. It all started with "Papa" Joe when he bought his first land in the San Joaquin Valley in 1922. The approximately 3000 acres of vineyards are on foothills of Sierra Nevada Mountains at the beginning of San Joaquin Valley.

The varietal, vintage-dated wines produced are Cabernet Sauvignon, Gamay Beaujolais Nouveau, Zinfandel, Johannisberg Riesling, Chenin Blanc, French Colombard, Green Hungarian and Chardonnay. Varietal, non-vintage wines produced are Gamay Beaujolais, Carnelian Rosé, Cabernet Sauvignon Rose, Grenache Rosé, Petite Sirah, Pinot Noir, Carnelian. Also produced are vintage-dated Mountain Burgundy, Vin Rosé, Chablis and Rhine.

['81 OC] (B) '79 PS, (B) NV PN, (G) '80 Z; ['82 OC] (B) '81 CH, (B) '81 GB, (B) '79 PS.

GLEN ELLEN WINERY *Sonoma County*
1883 London Ranch Rd., Glen Ellen, CA 95442
(707) 996-1066 Founded: 1968
M. Benziger, Gen. Partner. Joseph B. Benziger & Katherine Williamson, Ltd. Partners.

The 41 acre vineyard is located at the winery in Glen Ellen, Sonoma Valley.

Varietal, vintage-dated, estate bottled wines produced are Sauvignon Blanc, Chardonnay and Cabernet Sauvignon. Also a Proprietor's Reserve Red and White.

GLENOAK HILLS WINERY
Hugo's Cellar *Riverside County*
40607 Los Ranchos Circle, Temecula, CA 92390
(714) 676-5831 Founded: 1978
Storage: Oak barrels, stainless steel.

Owner, winemaker: Hugo Woerdemann.

The grapes are purchased on a selected vineyard district basis. Varietal, vintage-dated wines produced are Cabernet Sauvignon, Zinfandel, Chardonnay, Sauvignon Blanc, Gamay Beaujolais and White Riesling.

GOLD BELL (*See* East-Side Winery.)

GOLD MINE WINERY *Tuolumne County*
Parrott's Ferry Rd., Columbia State Park, Columbia, CA 95310
(209) 532-3089 Founded: 1970
Storage: Stainless steel.

GOLD NUGGETT (*See* Amador Winery.)

GOLDEN BONANZA (*See* Yankee Hill Winery.)

GRAND CRU VINEYARDS ★ *Sonoma County*
#1 Vintage Lane, Glen Ellen, CA 95442
(707) 996-8100 Founded: 1970
Storage: Oak, stainless steel.
General Manager: Allen Ferrera. Winemaker: Robert Magnani.

Grapes are purchased on a select vineyard basis. Label indicates vineyard and/or appellation. Wines produced are 100% varietal Chenin Blanc, Zinfandel, Sauvignon Blanc, Gewurztraminer, and Cabernet Sauvignon. "Induced Botrytis" Gewurztraminer is produced occasionally.

['82 OC] (G) '78 CA, (S) '80 CH, (B) '80 G, (S) '78 G, (B) '78 Z; ['81 OC] (B) '80 CA, (B) '81 G, (B) '81 SB; ['82 SJP] (S) '81 CH, (P&C) (S&B) '81 SG.

GRAND PACIFIC VINEYARD *Marin County*
134 Paul Drive, #9, San Rafael, CA 94960
(415) 479-WINE Founded: 1974
Storage: Oak barrels, stainless steel.
Owner, winemaker: Richard B. Dye.

The grapes are purchased on a selected district vineyard basis.

Varietal wines produced are Cabernet Sauvignon, Merlot, Chardonnay and White Riesling.

GRANITE SPRINGS WINERY *El Dorado County*
6060 Granite Springs Rd., Somerset, CA 95684
(209) 245-6395 Founded: 1981
Storage: Oak and stainless steel.
Owners: Lester & Lynne Russell. Winemaker: Les Russell. Vineyards: 23 acres at winery.

Grapes ae also purchased on a select vineyard basis. Label indicates vineyard and/or appellation. Vineyard at winery is 2,400 ft. elevation in upper Sierra Foothills.

Varietal, vintage-dated wines produced are Chenin Blanc, White Zinfandel, Sauvignon Blanc, Petite Sirah, Zinfandel and Cabernet Sauvignon.

GRAN VAL (*See* Clos du Val.)

GRAVELLY MEADOW (*See* Diamond Creek Vineyards.)

Green
Disagreeable acidity—usually in young wine.

Green Hungarian
(White Table Wine) A varietal grape that produces a light, neutral fresh and semi-dry wine; drink young.

Award wines to look for: Buena Vista, Delicato, Parducci, Weibel.

GREEN & RED VINEYARD *Napa County*
3208 Chiles Pope Valley Road, St. Helena, CA 94574
(707) 965-2346 Founded: 1977
Storage: Oak, stainless steel.
Owner, winemaker: Jay Hemingway.
16 acre vineyard is at Chiles Canyon hillside, Napa Valley. The varietal, vintage-dated, estate bottled wine produced is Zinfandel. Chardonnay will be produced in 1984.

ANNIE GREEN SPRINGS (*See* United Vintners.)

GREEN VALLEY (*See* Galleano Winery.)

GREENSTONE WINERY ★ *Amador County*
Hwy. 88 & Jackson Valley Rd., P.O. Box 1164, Ione, CA 95640
(209) 274-2238 Founded: 1981
Storage: Oak, stainless steel.
Owners: Stan & Karen Van Spanje and Durward & Jane Fowler. Located at the gateway to California's "Gold Country" and the Sierra Nevadas.
Wines produced are Zinfandel, Colombard, White Zinfandel, Zinfandel Rosé and Cream Sherry.
['82 SJP] (B) '81 SWZ.

GREENWOOD RIDGE VINEYARDS ★ *Mendocino County*
Box 1090 Star Route, Philo, CA 95466
(707) 877-3262 Founded: 1980
Storage: French oak, stainless steel.
Winemaker: Allan Green. Vineyard: 8 acres at winery.
Varietal, vintage-dated, estate bottled wines produced include White Riesling and Cabernet Sauvignon.
['81 OC] (G) '80 WR; ['82 SJP] (B) '81 WR.

Grenache
(Red Table Wine) A varietal grape that is predominantly used for Rosé, because of its pale color and strong flavor.

Grenache Rosé
(Pink Table Wine) A varietal grape that is mainly used for Rosé. When used for Rosé, the grapes' strong character is much tempered. A fruity, light, tart wine that has a noticeable sweetness. Originally from the Tavel region of France. Serve with ham, turkey, picnics and luncheon.

Grey Riesling
(White Table Wine) A varietal grape that produces a light, fresh, slightly sweet, but delicate, wine. Originally from France under the name Chauche gris. Serves well with poultry, fish and picnics.

Greystone
(*See* Perelli-Minetti Winery) Also used by insiders at Christian Bros. to describe the historic old stone winery in St. Helena purchased in 1950 and used for ageing.

GRGICH HILLS CELLAR ★ *Napa County*
1829 St. Helena Highway, Rutherford, CA 94573
(707) 963-2784 Founded: 1977
Storage: French oak.
Owners: Miljenko (Mike) Grgich and Austin Hills. Wine-

maker: Miljenko (Mike) Grgich.

Formerly of Chateau Montelena, Miljenko Grgich created the Chardonnay which stormed Paris in 1976. The vineyards are in Rutherford and Napa, all Napa Valley. Label indicates vineyard and/or appellation.

Varietal, vintage-dated wines produced are Late Harvest Johannisberg Riesling, Johannisberg Riesling, Zinfandel (Alexander Valley), Fumé Blanc and Chardonnay.

['81 OC] (S) '78 C, (S) '79 SB, (B) '78 Z; ['82 SJP] (S) '79 C.

GRIFFIN VINEYARD (*See* Hop Kiln Winery.)

Grignolino

(Red Table Wine) A varietal grape that produces a tart, sharp wine with an orange pigment character. Should be drunk two to five years old. Originally from Northern Italy. Excellent with rich meat dishes. A relatively rare variety, something of a curiosity.

GROVER GULCH WINERY *Santa Cruz County*

7880 Glen Haven Road, Soquel, CA 95073

(408) 475-0568 Founded: 1979

Storage: Oak barrels.

Owners, Winemakers: Dennis Bassano and Reinhold Banek.

The grapes are purchased on a select region basis. Varietal wines produced are Cabernet Sauvignon, Carignane, Zinfandel, and Petite Sirah.

GROWERS (*See* California Growers Winery.)

GUASTI (*See* Perelli-Minetti.)

GUENOC WINERY *Lake County*

21000 Butts Canyon Rd., Middleton, CA 95461

(707) 987-2385 Founded: 1981

Owner: Chateau Magoon Lambert, Orville T. Magoon, proprietor. Winemaker: Walter Raymond. Vineyard: 270 acres overlooking Guenoc Valley in south east Lake County.

Varietal, vintage-dated wines produced are Cabernet Sauvignon, Cabernet Franc, Petite Verdot, Malbec, Merlot, Petite Sirah, Zinfandel, Chardonnay, Chenin BLanc, Sauvignon Blanc and Semillon.

EMILIO GUGLIELMO WINERY ★ *Santa Clara County*

1480 East Main Ave., Morgan Hill, CA 95037

(408) 779-2145 Founded: 1925

Storage: Oak, redwood and stainless steel.

Owner: the George W. Guglielmo family. Winemaker: George E. Guglielmo.

Founded by Emilio, owned by his son, George, and operated by his grandsons, George E. and Eugene, the 150 acre vineyard is located at the winery in the Santa Clara Valley.

Under the Emilio Guglielmo label the varietal, vintage-dated, estate bottled wines produced are: Dry Semillon, Dry Chenin Blanc, Johannisberg Riesling, Gamay Beaujolais, Zinfandel, Barbera, Petite Sirah, Cabernet Sauvignon and Zinfandel. Also produced are Chablis Blanc, Santa Clara Claret, and Burgundy.

Under the Emile's label the premium jug wines

produced are: Chablis, Blanc Sec, Vin Rosé, Mellow Burgundy, Grignolino Rosé (100%) and Santa Clara Valley Burgundy. Also produced are Champagne, Sherry and Port.

['81 OC] (S) '77 PS; ['82 OC] (B) '77 PS.

GUILD WINERIES *San Joaquin County*

One Winemasters' Way, Lodi, CA 95240
(209) 368-5151
Owner: The Guild Corporation. President: Robert M. Ivie. Winemaker: Albert B. Cribari. Wineries: Fresno, Lodi, Woodbridge, Del Rio, Delano, Sanger, and Ukiah. Tasting rooms: Lodi, Fresno and Ukiah.

Guild was started in 1948 and is now the nation's largest grower-owned cooperative wine company. The wineries produce Cresta Blanca in Ukiah, Mendocino County and Cribari in Fresno. Other Guild labels are Guild Vino da Tavola, Paul Garrett Vintners Choice, Roma di California, Roma D'Uva and Winemasters. Label indicates vineyard and/or appellation.

At the Cresta Blanca Winery in Ukiah, the vintage wines produced are Blanc de Blanc, Cabernet Sauvignon, Chablis, Chardonnay, Chenin Blanc, French Colombard, Gamy Rosé, Gamay Beaujolais, Gewurztraminer, Grey Riesling, Johannisberg Riesling, Petite Sirah, Pinot Noir, Zinfandel. Also produced are three Sherries, Tinta Port, Extra Dry Champagne, Brut Champagne and Chardonnay Champagne.

Guild produces a number of good brandies under the Cribari, Ceremony, Directors Choice, St. Mark and Guild labels, as well as Cresta Blanca Vintage-dated Brandy. Also a unique product is Silverado Vodka, the only one made 100% from grapes.

GUNDLACH-BUNDSCHU WINERY ★ *Sonoma County*

3775 Thornberry Road, Sonoma, CA 95487
(707) 938-5277 Founded: 1858
Storage: Oak barrels, stainless steel.
Owner: James T. Bundschu. Winemaker: Lance Cutler.

Founded by Jacob Gundlach, a few years later its name was changed to its current one when James' great-grandfather became a partner in the business. The winery still maintains its original Bonded Winery Number 64 from the United States Government. The 350 aces of vineyards are located in the Sonoma Valley.

Label indicates vineyard and/or appellation. Varietal, vintage-dated, estate bottled wines produced are Pinot Noir, Riesling, Zinfandel, Gewurztraminer, Chardonnay, Cabernet Sauvignon and Merlot.

Varietal, vintage-dated wines produced are Late Harvest Johannisberg Riesling, Johannisberg Riesling, Gewurztraminer, Riesling and Chardonnay.

Also produced is estate bottled and vintage-dated Sonoma Valley Kleinberger (White wine).

The winemaker's favorites are Merlot and Gewurztraminer.

['81 OC] (B) '79 G, (B) '79 CA, (B) '78 M, (OS) '80 WR; ['82 OC] (B) '80 G, (G) '79 M; ['82 SJP&C] (B&S) '81 R, (P) (S) '79 M.

H

HACIENDA VINEYARD—Chardonnay vineyard in Salinas Valley.

HACIENDA WINE CELLARS ★ *Sonoma County*
1000 Vineyard Lane, P.O. Box 416, Sonoma, CA 95476
(707) 938-3220 Founded: 1973
Storage: Oak, redwood, stainless steel.
Owners: F. H. Bartholomew, A. Crawford Cooley and Steven W. MacRostie. Winemaker: Steven W. MacRostie.

Bartholomew owned Buena Vista for years. Hacienda is located in the midst of the historic Buena Vista Vineyard originally founded by Agoston Haraszthy in 1862. The vineyard was purchased by F. H. Bartholomew in 1941. The Buena Vista vineyard is 50 acres and the Oat Valley Farm vineyard in Cloverdale is 60 acres.

Varietal, vintage-dated wines produced are Chardonnay, Cabernet Sauvignon (estate grown), Gewurztraminer, Dry Chenin Blanc, Johannisberg Riesling (estate grown), Zinfandel (estate grown) and Pinot Noir (estate grown).

The winemaker's favorite wines are Cabernet Sauvignon and Gewurztraminer.

['81 OC] (G) '78 CA, (B) '79 C, (B) '80 CH; ['82 OC] (B) '80 C, (B) '81 G, (S) '79 PN, (B) '79 Z; ['82 SJP] (S) '80 C, (B) '81 G.

HAGAFEN CELLARS *Napa County*
P.O. Box 3035, Napa, CA 94558
(707) 252-0781 Founded: 1979
Owners: Zachary D. Berkowitz, Norman M. Miller, Norman E. Weir and René DiRosa. Winemakers: Zachary Berkowitz and Ernie Weir.

Founded to produce premium varietal Napa Valley wines that are also Kosher. Kashrut supervision by Orthodox Rabbinical Council of San Francisco, Rabbi Jacob Traub, Chmn. Grapes are purchased on a select vineyard basis. Label indicates vineyard and/or appellation.

Varietal, vintage-dated wines produced are Johannisberg Riesling, Chardonnay and Cabernet Sauvignon.

HALE CELLARS/LOS ALAMOS VINEYARD *Santa Barbara County*
P.O. Box 5, Los Alamos, CA 93440
(805) 344-2391 Founded: 1974
Owners: Sam and Dona Hale.

HANZELL VINEYARDS *Sonoma County*
18596 Lomita Ave., Sonoma, CA 95476
(707) 996-3860 Founded: 1957
Storage: French oak, stainless steel.
Owner: Barbara de Brye. Winemaker: Robert Sessions.

The 32 acre vineyard is located at the winery in Sonoma Valley. It was founded by the late Ambassador Zellerbach.

Varietal, vintage-dated, estate bottled wines produced are Pinot Noir and Chardonnay, in the tradition of the great Burgundian winemakers.

HARASZTHY CELLARS (*See* Buena Vista Winery.)

J. J. HARASZTHY & SON *Sonoma County*
14301 Arnold Drive, Glen Ellen, CA 95442
(707) 996-3040 Founded: 1978
Storage: Stainless steel.
Owners: Jan and Vallejo Haraszthy. Winemaker: Val Haraszthy.
Varietal wines produced are Zinfandel, Chardonnay and Sauvignon Blanc.

HARBOR WINERY *Yolo County*
610 Harbor Blvd., West Sacramento, CA 95831
(916) 371-6776 Founded: 1972
Storage: Oak, stainless steel.
Owner, Winemaker: Charles H. Myers.
Wines produced are Cabernet Sauvignon, Chardonnay, and Mission del Sol.

HART WINERY *Riverside County*
41300 Avenida Biona, Temecula, CA 92390
(714) 676-6300 Founded: 1980
Storage: Oak, stainless steel.
Owner/Winemaker: Joe Hart. Vineyards: 11 acres.
Wines produced are varietal, vintage-dated Petite Sirah, Cabernet Sauvignon, Merlot, Sauvignon Blanc and Chenin Blanc.

WILLIAM M. HATCH & SON *Sonoma County*
12154 Occidental Road, Sebastopol, CA 95472
(707) 874-2287
Owners: Bill & Ann McKeever. Cidermaker: Bill McKeever.
Hatch Hard Cider is made at the Hatch orchard from Red Gravenstein and Jonathan apples.

HAVELOCK GORDON NEGOCIANTS *San Francisco County*
Stanford Wine Co., 1488 San Mateo Ave., S. San Francisco, CA 94080
Havelock Gordon Negociants program is very much like the traditional Burgundian Negociant. Paul Draper Selection is indicated. Regularly offered are Chardonnay, Cabernet Sauvignon and Zinfandel. Occasionally other varietals and generics.

HAWK CREST (*See* Stag's Leap Wine Cellars.)

HAYWOOD WINERY ★ *Sonoma County*
18701 Gehricke Rd., Sonoma, CA 95476
(707) 996-4298 Founded: 1974
Storage: French oak and stainless steel.
Owner: Peter Haywood. Winemaker: Charles Tolbert. Vineyards: 95 acres in Chamizal Valley in center of Sonoma Valley viticultural area.
Chardonnay is planted high on valley ridge, Cabernet Sauvignon on valley floor, Zinfandel on rocky terraces and White Riesling on steep slopes.
Varietal, vintage-dated, estate bottled wines produced are Cabernet Sauvignon, Merlot, Zinfandel, White Riesling, and Chardonnay.
['81 OC] (G) '80 WR; ['82 OC] (G) '81 JR; ['82 SJP] (S) '80 C, (S) '81 WR.

HECKER PASS WINERY *Santa Clara County*
4605 Hecker Pass Highway, Gilroy, CA 95020
(408) 842-8755 Founded: 1972
Storage: Oak, redwood.
Owner, winemaker: Mario Fortino.

The vineyard is located at the winery. The varietal wines produced are Ruby Cabernet, Carignane, Zinfandel, Petite Sirah, and Chenin Blanc. Other wines produced are Chablis, Vin Rosé, Vino Rosso, Petite Sirah Select, Grenache Nouveau, Cream Sherry, Medium Dry Sherry and Port.

HEITZ WINE CELLARS ★ *Napa County*
436 St. Helena Hwy. So., St. Helena, CA 94574
(707) 963-3542 Founded: 1961
Storage: Oak, redwood, stainless steel.
Owner: the Heitz family. Winemakers: Joseph E. Heitz and son, David T. Heitz.

Grapes are purchased on a select vineyard basis. The most famous Heitz wine is the Martha's Vineyard Cabernet Sauvignon, which comes from Tom and Martha May's vineyard near Oakville.

Label indicates vineyard and/or appellation. Varietal, vintage-dated wines produced are Cabernet Sauvignon, Grignolino Rosé, Chardonnay, Sweet Johannisberg Riesling, Johannisberg Riesling, Grignolino, Barbera, and Gewurztraminer.

Also produced are Burgundy, Chablis, Champagne. "Cellar Treasure" Sherry, Port.

The winemaker's favorite wines are Cabernet Sauvignon and Chardonnay.

['81-OC] (S) '76 CA; ['82 OC] (S) '77 CA.

CARL HELMHOLZ VINEYARD—Cabernet Sauvignon vineyard in Alexander Valley.

HERBERT VINEYARDS *Amador County*
P.O. Box 438, Somerset, CA 95684
(916) 626-0548
Owners: Mr. & Mrs. Frank Herbert. Winemaker: John MacCready.

A new vineyard. Currently 6 acres Zinfandel and 6 acres Sauvignon Blanc.

HEUBLEIN WINES
601 4th St., San Francisco, CA 94107
President: Robert M. Furek. Includes Inglenook and Colony Wineries. Inglenook Estates Winemaker: John Richburg. Colony Winemaker: Edmund Ross, Jr.

Wines produced are: Inglenook Estate Bottled Wines, Inglenook Vintage Wines and Navalle Wines; Colony Classic, Generic and Varietal Wines, Petri Table Wines, Jacare and Lejon Champagne.

Inglenook Estates winemaker recommends: Cabernet Sauvignon, Cask Cabernet, Charbono, Fumé Blanc and Pinot Chardonnay.

HIDDEN CELLARS *Mendocino County*
4901 Mill Creek Road, P.O. Box 1, Talmage, CA 95481
(707) 462-0301 Founded: 1981
Storage: French, American oak, stainless steel.

Owners: Dennis Patton & Joseph Rawitzer. Winemaker: D. Patton.

Varietal, vintage-dated wines produced are: Gewurztraminer, Sauvignon Blanc, Late Harvest Johannisberg Riesling, Cabernet Sauvignon and Petite Sirah.

WILLIAM HILL WINERY ★ *Napa County*

P.O. Box 3989, Napa, CA 94558

(707) 224-6565 Founded: 1976

Owner/Manager/Winemaker: William Hill.

The 1000 acres of vineyards are located in the Mount Veeder and Atlas Peak areas of Napa County. Varietal, vintage-dated, estate bottled wines produced are Cabernet Sauvignon and Chardonnay.

['81 OC] (S) '78 CA.

History of Early California

The Jesuit Fathers carried Spanish colonization and winegrowing up the Western Coast into the Mexican Peninsula of Baja, California. Their successors, the Franciscans, advanced into what is now the State of California. As each new settlement or mission was established, vines were planted as one of the first steps in transforming wilderness into civilization.

The Franciscans and their leader, Padre Junipero Serra, established Mission San Diego, in 1769, and planted wine grapes there. Thus, it was discovered that California was a land especially favored for wine-growing. In Northern Mexico and Baja California these pioneers of western wine-growing suffered many hardships in cultivating the arrid lands and in trying to supply themselves with wines needed for sacramental and table use. At San Diego, the grapevines thrived and the wines were better.

As the Franciscans moved northward, establishing new missions, they found the same results. They had discovered a new wine-growing region. More than a century later, it was destined to become one of the premier wine regions of the world.

Eventually, Padre Serra's missionaries built a chain of 21 missions, from San Diego to Sonoma. Sonoma was the northernmost point of their El Camino Real or "Kings Highway." They planted vineyards and made wine at nearly all of the missions. San Gabriel Mission, near Los Angeles, was the site of their largest winery. There they had three wine presses. Mission San Diego and its vineyards were established six years before the American Revolution.

H.M.S. FROST (*See* Heublein.)

Hock

A dry, white table wine usually made with Riesling grapes, in which, as with other white wines, the fermentation takes place after the skins have been separated. Hock was originally a term used by the English in reference to wine shipped from Hockheim, Germany.

HMR (HOFFMAN MOUNTAIN RANCH) VINEYARDS ★ *San Luis Obispo County*

Adelaide Road, Star Route, Paso Robles, CA 93446

(805) 238-4945 Founded: 1972
Owners: HMR, Ltd. Operated by: Dr. Stanley Hoffman and sons, David and Michael. Winemaker: Michael Hoffman.

The vineyards are in the foothills of Santa Lucia mountains 10 miles west of Paso Robles. Altitude 1400'-1800'. The 100% estate bottled, vintage-dated varietal wines produced are: Chardonnay, Franken Riesling, Sauvignon Blanc, Cabernet Sauvignon and Pinot Noir. The vintage-dated varietal wines are Zinfandel, Chenin BLanc and Cabernet Sauvignon.

The winemaker's favorites are Cabernet Sauvignon, Chardonnay and Pinot Noir.

['81 OC] (S) '75 CA, (B) '77 CA, (B) '78 CA; ['82 OC] (S) '79 CA, (B) '79 JR; ['82 SJP] (S) '79 LHJ (P&C) (B&B) '77 PN.

HNW VINEYARDS ★ *Napa County*
P.O. Box 153, 850 Rutherford Rd., Rutherford, CA 94573
(707) 963-5618

The 67 acre vineyard is located at the winery. Varietal, vintage-dated, estate bottled Sauvignon Blanc is produced.

['82 OC] (G) '81 SB.

HOLDENREID VINEYARD—Cabernet Sauvignon vineyard in Kelseyville, Lake County.

HOP KILN WINERY ★ *Sonoma County*
6050 Westside Road, Healdsburg, CA 95448
(707) 433-6491 Founded: 1975
Storage: Oak, stainless steel.
Owner: L. Martin Griffin, Jr. Winemakers: L. Martin Griffin and Jack Fitzgerald. Vineyard: 65 acres at the winery.

Because some vines were planted in 1880 and are still in production, the winery and vineyard have been designated a California Historical Landmark. The name derives from the hop-drying barn on the ranch, as this was previously a prime hop-growing area.

The 100% varietal, estate bottled wines are: Napa Gamay, Petite Sirah, Johannisberg Riesling, Late Harvest Riesling, and a limited-production Sparkling Johannisberg Riesling, Verveux. Other 100% varietals are Zinfandel, Chardonnay, Gewurztraminer and Primitivo Zinfandel. The winery also produces "A Thousand Flowers" (a blend of Johannisberg Riesling, French Colombard and Gewurztraminer) and Marty Griffin's Big Red, a dry table wine.

The winemaker's favorite wines are Zinfandel and Gewurztraminer.

['82 OC] (B) '80 GA, (G) '79 PS.

HOPPER CREEK WINERY (*See* Silkwood Cellars.)

HORIZON WINER *Sonoma County*
2594 Athena Court, Santa Rosa, CA 95401
(707) 544-2961 Founded: 1977
Storage: Oak.
Owner, Winemaker: Paul D. Gardner.

The vineyard is in Sonoma County. Label indicates vineyard and/or appellation. Varietal, vintage-dated wines produced are Zinfandel, Zinfandel Essence and Petite Sirah.

HUGO'S CELLAR (*See* Glenoak Hills Winery.)

HULTGREN & SAMPERTON ★ *Sonoma County*
P.O. Box 1026, Healdsburg, CA 95448
(707) 433-5120 Founded: 1979
Storage: French oak.
Owners: J. Leonard Hultgren and Edward Samperton. Winemaker: Edward Samperton.

14 acre vineyards are in Dry Creek and Alexander Valleys. Varietal, vintage-dated wines produced are Cabernet Sauvignon, Chardonnay, and Gamay Beaujolais.

['81 OC] (S) '79 PS.

HUMBOLDT COUNTY
NORTHERNMOST COASTAL.

HUNTER FARMS—Chardonnay vineyard in Sonoma Valley.

HUSCH VINEYARDS ★ *Mendocino County*
4900 Star Route, Philo, CA 95466
(707) 895-3216 Founded: 1971
Storage: Oak, stainless steel.
Owner, Winemaker: Hugo A. Oswald.

The 23 acre vineyard is in the Anderson Valley and the 180 acre vineyard is in the Ukiah Valley. Varietal, vintage-dated wines produced are Pinot Noir, Cabernet Sauvignon, Chardonnay, Gewurztraminer and Sauvignon Blanc.

['81 OC] (B) '79 C, (B) '80 G; ['82 OC] (S) '80 C, (G) '81 G, (S) '79 PN, (G) '80 SB; ['82 SJP] (B) '80 C, (P) (B) '81 SG.

I

Ice Wine
Wine that has been made from grapes that have been allowed to freeze and are harvested and pressed when frozen. A very sweet wine.

INDIAN CREEK (*See* Navarro Vineyards.)

INGLENOOK VINEYARDS ★ *Napa County*
P.O. Box 19, Rutherford, CA 94573
(707) 963-2616 Founded: 1879 by Capt. Neibaum.
Owner: Heublein Company (United Vinters). President/General Manager: Robert Furek. Winemaker: John Richburg.

The vineyards are in three wine growing areas, Napa Valley and North Coast Counties. Label indicates vineyard and/or appellation.

Varietal, vintage-dated, estate bottled and "Cask Limited" wines are Chenin Blanc, Cabernet Sauvignon, Fumé Blanc, Merlot, Muscat Blanc, Charbono, Zinfandel, Petite Sirah, Pinot Chardonnay, Gewurztraminer, Johannisberg Riesling, Cabernet Sauvignon, Chardonnay, Pinot Noir, Gamay Beaujolais and Gamay Rosé. Also produced are vintage-dated Burgundy, Chablis, Rhine and Cabernet Rosé.

The Navalle line of wines produced are Zinfandel,

Chablis, Burgundy, Rhine, Vin Rosé, Riesling, French Colombard, Chenin Blanc and Ruby Cabernet.

Recommended: Charbono and Cabernet Sauvignon.

['81 OC] (S) '77 PS; ['82 SJP&C] (B&B) '78 CA, (P) (B) '77 CA, (P&C) (B&B) '76 CB.

IRON HORSE VINEYARDS *Sonoma County*

9786 Ross Station Road, Sebastopol, CA 95472

(707) 887-2913 Founded: 1976

Storage: Oak, stainless steel.

Owners: Barry & Audrey Sterling, and Forrest & Kate Tancer. Winemaker: Forrest Tancer.

Pinot Noir and Chardonnay are grown at the 110 acre Iron Horse Vineyards, and Cabernet Sauvignon and Sauvignon Blanc are grown at the 30 acre vineyard in the Alexander Valley.

The varietal, vintage-dated, estate bottled wines produced are Chardonnay, Blanc de Pinot Noir, Cabernet Sauvignon, Pinot Noir, Sauvignon Blanc Sparkling Wine.

ITALIAN SWISS COLONY (*See* Colony.)

J

JACABEL CELLARS (*See* Whitehall Lane Winery.)

JACARÉ (*See* Heublein.)

JADE (*See* Turgeon & Lohr.)

JADE MOUNTAIN WINERY *Sonoma County*

1335 Hiatt Road, Cloverdale, CA 95425

(707) 894-5579 Founded: 1975

Owner: Douglas Sebastian Cartwright MD. Vineyard: 26 acres.

JEKEL VINEYARD ★ *Monterey County*

40155 Walnut Ave., Greenfield, CA 93927

(408) 674-5522 Founded: 1978

Storage: Oak, stainless steel.

Owners: Bill and Gus Jekel. Winemaker: Daniel Lee. Asst: Rick Jekel. Vineyard: 140 acres at the winery.

The varietal, vintage-dated, estate bottled wines produced are Chardonnay, Pinot Blanc, Johannisberg Riesling, Pinot Noir, and Cabernet Sauvignon.

['81 OC] (B) '77 CA, (G) '79 C, (S) '79 C, (B) '79 WR, (S) '79 WR; ['82 OC] (B) '78 CA, (S) '80 C, (G) '81 PB, (S) '81 JR, (B) '81 JR, (G) '80 PB, (S) '80 JR; ['82 SJP&C] (B) '80 C Pvt. Res., (S) '81 JR (Prop.), (P) (G) '80 LHJ, (P) (S) '81 MCS.

J.F.J. WINERY (*See* J.F.J. Bronco Winery.)

Johannisberg Riesling

(White Riesling) A varietal grape that produces a fruity-floral, slight-greenish tinge, slightly tart piquant wine, with a touch of sweetness. The ideal wine for clams, crabs and seafood. Its botanic name in California is White Riesling. This is the premier grape of the great vineyards of Germany. The late harvest versions are made from over-ripe grapes, are thick, sweet and long lasting social wines comparable with German Ausleses.

Johannisberg Riesling (*See* Riesling for Award Wines.)

Johannisberg Late Harvest Riesling

Award wines to look for: Almaden (Charles LeFranc), Bargetto, Chateau St. Jean, HMR (Hoffman Mt. Ranch), Jekel, Monterey Peninsula, Joseph Phelps, Raymond, San Martin, Sonoma, Stony Ridge.

JOHNSON'S ALEXANDER VALLEY ★ *Sonoma County*

8333 Hwy. 128, Healdsburg, CA 95448
(707) 433-2319 Founded: 1975
Storage: Oak, stainless steel.
Owners: Jay, Tom and Will Johnson. Winemaker: Tom Johnson.

Purchased in 1952 by James Johnson and sold to his sons in 1971, the vineyard located at southern end of Alexander Valley. 100% varietal, vintage-dated, estate bottled wines produced are Chenin Blanc, Chardonnay, Gewurztraminer, Johannisberg Riesling, Pinot Noir, Cabernet Sauvignon and Zinfandel. Also Pear wine. Also produced under J.D. Martin label is Alexander Valley Red.

The winemaker's favorite wines are Late Harvest Zinfandel, Chenin Blanc and Zinfandel.

['81 OC] (G) '79 WR.

JOHNSON-TURNBULL VINEYARDS (*See* Turnbull.)

JORDAN VINEYARD AND WINERY *Sonoma County*

1474 Alexander Valley Road, Healdsburg, CA 95448
(707) 433-6955 Founded: 1976
Storage: American, French oak, stainless steel.
Owner: Thomas N. Jordan, Jr. Winemaker: Rob Davis.

The 240 acre vineyard is located at the winery in the Alexander Valley. The new winery and "Chateau" are architecturally exquisite.

The varietal, vintage-dated, estate bottled wine produced is Cabernet Sauvignon (8% Merlot). Chardonnay will be the only other wine produced by Jordan.

Jug Wines

The dictionary definition of jug is "a vessel in various forms for holding liquids commonly having a handle, often a lip or spout, sometimes with a narrow neck stopped by a cork." My definition is a fair to excellent table wine selling at a moderate price in 1.5, 3 and 4 liter bottles. Homage must be paid to E. & J. Gallo for their outstanding contribution in making Jug Wines far superior to the general inferior European "vin ordinaire." Today we find not only generic but also varietals and often vintage dated "Jugs." No telling what 1990 will bring.

K

KALIN CELLARS *Marin County*

61 Galli Dr., Novato, CA 94947
(415) 883-3543 Founded: 1977
Storage: Oak.
Owners: T. J. Leighton and Frances Leighton. Winemaker: T. J. Leighton.

Grapes are purchased on a select vineyard basis. Label

indicates vineyard and/or appellation. Varietal, vintage-dated wines produced are Cabernet Sauvignon, Semillon, Gewurztraminer, Riesling, Merlot, Pinot Noir, Zinfandel, and Chardonnay.

KARLY WINES *Amador County*
P.O. Box 721, Plymouth, CA 95669
(209) 245-3922 Founded: 1980
Storage: Oak and stainless steel.
General Partner/Winemaker: Lawrence L. Cobb. Vineyards: 18 new acres at winery mostly Sauvignon Blanc.

Grapes are also purchased on a select vineyard basis. Label indicates vineyard and/or appellation.

Varietal, vintage-dated wines produced are Zinfandel, Chardonnay and Sauvignon Blanc (dry).

ROBERT KEENAN WINERY ★ *Napa County*
3660 Spring Mountain Road, St. Helena, CA 94574
(707) 963-9177 Founded: 1977
Storage: French oak, stainless steel.
Owner: Robert Keenan. Winemaker: Joe Cafaro. Vineyard: 45 acres at the winery.

The winery was built in 1904 and remodeled in 1977. Robert Keenan purchased the property in 1974.

The wines produced are varietal, vintage-dated Cabernet Sauvignon and Chardonnay. Label indicates vineyard and/or appellation.

['82 OC] (B) '80 C, (S) '79 M.

KELLEY CREEK VINEYARD—Zinfandel vineyard in Dry Creek Valley.

KENDALL CELLARS (*See* Kalin Cellars.)

KATHRYN KENNEDY WINERY *Santa Clara County*
13180 Pierce Road, Saratoga, CA 95070
(408) 867-4170 Founded: 1979
Storage: French, American oak.
Owner: Kathryn Kennedy. Manager: Martin T. Mathis. Winemaker: Bill Anderson. Vineyard: 8 acres at the winery of Cabernet Sauvignon.

Varietal, vintage-dated, estate bottled wines produced under the Kathryn Kennedy label are Cabernet Sauvignon and Pinot Noir Blanc. Also produced is vintage-dated Monterey Pinot Noir Vin Gris, Pinot Noir Blanc and Chenin Blanc under the Saratoga Cellars label.

KENWOOD VINEYARDS ★ *Sonoma County*
9592 Sonoma Hwy., Kenwood, CA 95452
(707) 833-5891 Founded: 1906
Storage: American and French oak, stainless steel.
Owner: a corporation of which John Sheela is President and Martin Lee is Vice-President. Winemaker: Mike Lee.

Grapes are purchased from selected vineyards. Label indicates vineyard and/or appellation. Varietal, vintage-dated wines produced are Pinot Noir, Zinfandel, Cabernet Sauvignon, Chardonnay, Pinot Noir Blanc, Dry Chenin Blanc, Johannisberg Riesling, Gewurztraminer, and Sauvignon Blanc. Also generic, vintage-dated Red and White.

The winemaker's favorite wine is "Jack London" Cabernet Sauvignon.

['81 OC] (B) '78 CA, (G) '79 C, (G) '80 CH, (B) '80 G, (B)

'78 PN, (G) '80 SB, (B) '80 WR, (B) '78 Z; ['82 OC] (S) '79 CA, (B) '81 SB, (S) '80 C; ['82 SJP] (S) '79 CA.

KENWORTHY VINEYARDS ★ *Amador County*
Route 2, Box 2, Plymouth, CA 95669
(209) 245-3198 Founded: 1979
Storage: Oak, stainless steel.
Owner, Winemaker: John Kenworthy.

The 7 acre vineyards are in Shenandoah Valley of Amador County. Varietal wines produced are Zinfandel, Cabernet Sauvignon and Chardonnay.

['82 OC] (G) '79 Z.

KERN COUNTY
Southern San Joaquin Valley.

KIKKOMAN MANSO HON-MIRIN (*See* Ozeki San Benito.)

KIRIGIN CELLARS *Santa Clara County*
11550 Watsonville Road, Gilroy, CA 95020
(408) 847-8827 Founded: 1916
19500 Monterey Rd., Morgan Hill, CA 95037
(408) 779-5478—Tasting Rooms
Storage: Oak, redwood, stainless steel.
Owner: Nikola Kirigin Chargin.

Nikola Sr. is a fourth generation winemaker from Croatia where he started in his family vineyard. The 50 acre vineyard is located at the winery in the Uvas Valley.

The varietal, vintage-dated wines produced are White Riesling, Pinot Chardonnay, Sauvignon Vert, Malvasia Bianca, Gewurztraminer, Chenin Blanc, Pinot Noir, Zinfandel and Cabernet Sauvignon.

Also produced are Opol Rosé, Champagne, Rhine, Rosé, Burgundy, and Vino de Mocca.

KIRKPATRICK CELLAR WINERY *Humboldt County*
3801 H Street, Eureka, CA 95501
(707) 433-4474 Founded: 1980
Owner, Winemaker: Robert G. Kirkpatrick.

Producer of Apple and Pear wines.

KIRKWOOD (*See* Barengo Vineyards.)

KISTLER VINEYARDS *Sonoma County*
997 Madrone Road, Glen Ellen, CA 95442
(707) 833-4662 Founded: 1978
Winery: Nelligan Road, Glen Ellen, CA 95442
(707) 996-5117
Storage: French oak.
Winemaker: Stephen Kistler. Vineyard: 35 acres at winery.

Varietal wines produced are Chardonnay, Cabernet Sauvignon and Pinot Noir. Vines not bearing yet. Grapes are purchased from Napa and Sonoma Counties. Label indicates vineyard and/or appellation.

Kleinberger Riesling
(White Table Wine) A varietal grape which produces a light and delicate wine.

THOMAS KNIGHT (*See* Diamond Oaks Vineyard.)

KONOCTI WINERY ★ *Lake County*
P.O. Box 927—Highway 29 at Thomas Drive, Kelseyville, CA 95451

(707) 279-8861 Founded: 1974
Storage: Oak, stainless steel.
Owners: a cooperative of Lake County vintners. Winemaker: Wm. T. Pease. Marketing Manager: Paul Hessinger.

27 small family owned vineyards are located in Lake County. Average size 15 acres. Varietal, vintage-dated, estate bottled wines produced are Cabernet Sauvignon, Fumé Blanc, Johannisberg Riesling, Zinfandel, Cabernet Sauvignon Blanc, Sauvignon Blanc, Zinfandel and Gamay Blanc. Also Lake County White and Red.

['81 OC] (S) '80 WR; ['82 OC] (S) '81 SB, (S) '80 SB; ['82 SJP&C] (S) '81 FB.

F. KORBEL AND BROS. ★ *Sonoma County*
13250 River Road, Guerneville, CA 95446
(707) 887-2294 Founded: 1880
Storage: Oak, stainless steel.
Chrm. Bd.: Adolf L. Heck. President: Gary B. Heck. Winemaker: Bob Stashak.

The vineyards are located in western Sonoma County. The first section of the present winery was built in 1880 by the Korbel Bros. First champagne produced in 1882, first brandy in 1889. First vineyards planted in the late 1870's. In 1954, the Heck family bought the winery. Adolph had been a Champagne maker and was president of Italian Swiss Colony. The Champagnes produced are Blanc de Blancs, Natural, Blanc de Noirs, Brut, Extra Dry, Sec, Rouge and Rosé. Also known for their Brandy. Recommended: Blanc de Noirs Champagne.

['81 OC] (G) NV SW, (S) NV SW, (B) NV SW; ['82 OC] (S) CHA, (S) CHA.

HANNS KORNELL CHAMPAGNE CELLARS ★ *Napa County* 1091 Larkmead Lane, St. Helena, CA 94574
(707) 963-2334 Founded: 1952
Storage: Bottle storage.
Owner, Champagne Master: Hanns Kornell.

A third generation Champagne Master, Hanns Kornell came from Germany in 1940 and started his cellars in 1952. The historic ageing vaults or cellars originally built in 1906 were designated as a historic site in the National Register. The original Victorian cupola still graces the roof of the cellars. Grapes are purchased on a selected vineyard basis.

The Champagnes produced are bottle fermented and aged in the original bottle. They are Extra-dry, Brut, Demi-sec, Rosé, Rouge and Muscat Alexandria and the internationally award winning Sehr Trocken.

['81 OC] (S) NV SW, (B) NV SW.

KOSROF ★ (*See* Barengo Cellars)
['81 OC] (G) NV P.

CHARLES KRUG WINERY ★ *Napa County*
P.O. Box 191, 200 Main St., St. Helena, CA 94574
(707) 963-2761 Founded: 1861
Owner/Manager/Winemaker: Peter Mondavi.

Vineyards are located in the Napa Valley. The oldest operating winery in the valley, established by Charles

Krug in 1861.

The only wine produced under the Charles Krug "Vintage Selection" is Cabernet Sauvignon. Under the Charles Krug label Fumé Blanc and Chardonnay are produced. Other varietal wines produced are Cabernet Sauvignon, Zinfandel, Gamay Beaujolais, Pinot Noir, Johannisberg Riesling, Blanc Fumé, Chardonnay, Gewurztraminer and Muscat Canelli. Also produced are vintage-dated Burgundy, Claret, Sherry and Port.

The wines produced under the C.K. Mondavi label (jug wines) are Chablis, Rhine, Vin Rosé, Burgundy, Barberone, Fortissimo, Bravissimo, Chianti and Zinfandel.

The winemaker's favorite wines are Charles Krug Chardonnay, Johannisberg Riesling, and Cabernet Sauvignon (Vintage Select).

['81 OC] (B) '79 C, (S) NV CH, (S) '79 WR; ['82 OC] (B) '77 CA.

THOMAS KRUSE WINERY *Santa Clara County*

4390 Hecker Pass Road, Gilroy, CA 95020
(408) 842-7016
Storage: Oak, stainless steel.
Owner/Winemaker: Thomas Kruse.

Varietal wines produced are Cabernet Sauvignon, Chardonnay and Zinfandel. Also produced is a methode champenoise Champagne.

L

Label Reading

Vintage Date: To carry a vintage date, a wine must be made from 95% of the grapes harvested during that year.

Appellation of Origin: At least 75% of the grapes used in the wine were grown in the named region (either state or county). If the label indicates a specific "viticultural area" (i.e. vineyard or ranch name) the wine must contain 95% of the grapes from that area.

Wine Type: The name of the grape that inspired the wine except in the case of generic wines. The wine must have been made from at least 51% of that particular grape. (In 1983, the requirement rises to 75%). Any other wine other than a varietal name (Burgundy, Rhine, etc.) has no regulations as to what grape is used.

LA CREMA VINERA ★ *Sonoma County*

P.O. Box 976, Petaluma, CA 94953
(707) 762-0393 Founded: 1979
Storage: French oak, stainless steel.
Owners: Rod Berglund, Bob Goyette, John Bessey, and Rick Burmester. Winemaker: Rod Berglund.

Grapes purchased on a select vineyard basis. Label indicates vineyard and/or appellation. Varietal, vintage-dated wines produced are Pinot Noir, Cabernet Sauvignon and Chardonnay.

['81 OC] (S) '79 PN.

LA CROIX (*See* Bisceglia Bros.)

LA ESTANCIA VINEYARD—Chardonnay and Pinot

Noir vineyard in Salinas Valley.

LAKE COUNTY

North of Napa County.

LAKESPRING WINERY ★ *Napa County*

2055 Hoffman Lane, Napa, CA 94558

(707) 944-2475 Founded: 1980

Owners: Frank, Harry and Ralph Battat. Winemaker: Randy Mason. Vineyard: 7 acres at the winery.

Grapes are also purchased on a select vineyard basis. Label indicates vineyard and/or appellation.

Varietal, vintage-dated wines produced are: Chenin Blanc, Merlot, Sauvignon Blanc, Chardonnay and Cabernet Sauvignon.

['82 OC] (B) '80 C.

RONALD LAMB WINERY ★ *Santa Clara County*

17785 Casa Lane, Morgan Hill, CA 95037

(408) 779-4268

Storage: Oak barrels, stainless steel.

Owners: Ronald and Aldrene Lamb. Winemaker: Ronald Lamb.

The Chardonnay vineyard is located in Santa Clara County. Grapes are also purchased on a select vineyard basis.

Label indicates vineyard and/or appellation. Varietal, vintage-dated wines produced are Johannisberg Riesling, Zinfandel, Gamay Beaujolais, Dry Chenin Blanc and Chardonnay.

Winemaker's favorite wine is Chardonnay.

['82 OC] (G) '81 CH.

LAMBERT BRIDGE *Sonoma County*

4085 West Dry Creek Road, Healdsburg, CA 95448

(707) 433-5855 Founded: 1975

Storage: Oak, stainless steel.

Owner: Gerard B. Lambert. Winemaker: Edward Killian.

The 76 acre vineyards are located in the Central Dry Creek Valley.

Varietal, vintage-dated, estate bottled wines produced are Chardonnay and Cabernet Sauvignon.

LAMONT WINERY, INC. *Kern County*

#1 Bear Mountain Winery Road, DiGiorgio, CA 93217

(805) 327-2200

Storage: Oak, stainless steel.

Owner: John Labatt, Ltd. Breweries of Canada. Chief Winemaker: Charles R. Feaver.

Purchases grapes on a selected regional basis and south coast areas. Varietal wines produced are French Colombard, Chenin Blanc, Ruby Cabernet, Zinfandel, Cabernet Sauvignon and Chardonnay.

LA MONTANA (*See* Martin Ray Vineyard.)

LANDMARK VINEYARDS ★ *Sonoma County*

9150 Los Amigos Road, Windsor, CA 95492

(707) 838-9466 Founded: 1974

Storage: Limousin, stainless steel.

Owner: the William R. Mabry family. Winemaker: William R. Mabry III.

The home of Landmark vineyards which the Mabry

family calls "Home Ranch" was originally a Spanish land grant. The Spanish style home that was built in 1800's is now winery office and tasting room. The cypress trees shown on the label were planted over 100 years ago. The Mabry's acquired "Home Ranch" in 1974. Vineyards are located in Alexander Valley 60 acres, Sonoma Valley 20 acres and Windsor 10 acres.

Label indicates vineyard and/or appellation. The 100% varietal, vintage-dated wines produced are Chardonnay, Cabernet Sauvignon and Zinfandel.

['81 OC] (B) '78 CA; ['82 SJP] (B) '80 C, (C) (B) '78 CA.

MAMO LANZA (*See* Wooden Valley Winery.)

LA LOMA VINEYARD—Louis Martini vineyard in Carneros, Napa Valley.

LA PURISMA WINERY *Santa Clara County*
970 B. O'Brien Dr., Menlo Park, CA 94025
(415) 326-9860 Founded: 1976
Owner, Winemaker: Bob Grant

LAS TABLAS WINERY *San Luis Obispo County*
P.O. Box 697, Winery Road, Templeton, CA 93465
(805) 434-1389 Founded: 1856
Owners: John and Della Mertens. Manager: Della Mertens. Winemaker: John Mertens.

The Mertens are the third family to own Las Tablas since it was started in 1856. The vineyard is located at the winery.

Wines produced are Zinfandel, Rosé and White Table Wine.

LA QUESTA (*See* Woodside Vineyards.)

LAS AMIGAS VINEYARD—Louis Martini vineyard in Carneros, Napa Valley.

Late Harvest
Equivalent to the Spatlese and Auslese wines of Germany. Johannisberg Riesling or Gewurztraminer grapes are picked in an over-ripe condition with some incidence of Botrytis. The German word Spatlese means "late picking" thus the term Late Harvest.

LAUREL GLEN VINEYARD *Sonoma County*
P.O. Box 548, Glen Ellen, CA 95442
(707) 526-3914 Founded: 1968
Storage: Barrels.
Owner/Winemaker: Patrick Campbell. Vineyards: 30 acres, of Cabernet Sauvignon, Cabernet Franc, Malbec and Petite Verdot on 6 various hillsides within 1/4 mile of winery on north-east slope of Sonoma Mountain at an elevation of 1000 ft.

Varietal, vintage-dated, estate bottled blended Cabernet Sauvignon is the only wine produced.

LAWRENCE WINERY ★ *San Luis Obispo County*
P.O. Box 3159, San Louis Obispo, CA 93406
(805) 543-5800 Founded: 1978
Storage: Oak, stainless steel.
Owner: Glenmore Distilleries Co. General Manager: Jeff Maiken. Winemaker: Barry Douglas.

Grapes are selected from San Luis Obispo and Santa Barbara Counties. Vintage-dated wines produced are

Gamay Beaujolais, Merlot, Gewurztraminer, Gewurztraminer-Rosé, Johannisberg Riesling, Pinot Noir, Zinfandel, Chenin Blanc, Cabernet Sauvignon, French Colombard and Fumé Blanc. Also produced are Red Table Wine, White Table Wine, Rosé Table Wine, Chablis and Burgundy.

['81 OC] (S) '80 M, (S) '80 PN; ['82 OC] (B) '80 CH, (S) '81 GA, (G) '81 M, (S) '81 M; ['82 SJC] (B) '80 PN.

LAZY CREEK VINEYARD ★ *Mendocino County*

4610 Hwy. 128, Philo, CA 95466

(707) 895-3623 Founded: 1975

Storage: Oak, stainless steel.

Owners: Johann J. and Theresia Kobler. Manager-Winemaker: Johann Kobler. Vineyards: 20 acres.

Varietal, vintage-dated wines produced are: Pinot Chardonnay, Pinot Noir and Gewurztraminer.

['82 OC] (G) '79 PN.

LE BARON VINEYARD—White Riesling vineyard near Healdsburg.

LE BAY CELLARS *Sonoma County*

26900 Dutcher Creek Rd., Cloverdale, CA 95425

(707) 894-3191 Founded: 1939

Storage: Oak, stainless steel.

Owners: Douglas Bay Shaffer & Helen Dauphiney. Winemaker: Douglas Shaffer. Vineyards: 45 acres at winery.

Original vineyards were planted in the 1930's. LeBay Cellars bought the winery in 1980. Doug is a chemist and plant pathologist. Helen has been a farmland owner and manager for many years.

Label indicates vineyard and/or appellation. Varietal, vintage-dated, estate bottled wines produced are Zinfandel, Sirah and Sauvignon Blanc. Also produced is "Russian River Red."

LE BLANC (*See* California Growers Winery.)

L. LE BLANC VINEYARDS (*See* California Growers Winery.)

LE DOMAINE (*See* Almaden Vineyards.)

LeFleuron (*See* Joseph Phelps.)

LE FLEURON (*See* Joseph Phelps Vineyards.)

Lees

Yeast sediment deposited by wine in the cooperage after fermentation.

LEEWARD WINERY ★ *Ventura County*

2784 Johnson Dr., Ventura, CA 93003

(805) 656-5054 Founded: 1978

Storage: American and French oak, stainless steel.

Owners/Winemakers: Chuck Brigham and Chuck Gardner.

Grapes are purchased on a select vineyard basis. Label indicates vineyard and/or appellation. Varietal, vintage-dated wines produced are Zinfandel, Chardonnay, Sauvignon Blanc, Cabernet Sauvignon and Pinot Noir Blanc.

['81 OC] (G) '79 C, (S) '79 C.

CHARLES LEFRANC ★ (*See* Almaden Vineyards.)

['81 OC] (S) '79 G, (B) '79 SB, (B) NV P; ['82 SJC&P] (B&B) P, (P&C) (S&S) '79 Sel. LHR.

LEJON
Champagne and Vermouth brand; (*See* Heublein.)

LEMON RANCH—Cabernet Sauvignon vineyard near St. Helena.

LERAXA WINERY *Merced County*
18000 W. River Rd., Livingston, CA 95334

LIBERTY (*See* Rubidoux Winery.)

LIBERTY SCHOOL (*See* Caymus Vineyards.)

Liquid Measurements

Ounces difference		Ounces difference
	Miniature 100 ml. —3 oz.	3.4 oz.
	Split—187 ml. —6.4 oz.	6.3 oz.
	Tenth—375 ml. —12.8 oz.	12.7 oz.
	Fifth—750 ml. —25.6 oz.	25.4 oz.
	Quart—1 liter —32 oz.	33.8 oz.
	Magnum 1.5 liter —51.2 oz.	50.7 oz.
	Jeroboam 3 liter —102.4 oz.	101.4 oz.
	Gallon—4 liters —120 oz.	135.0 oz.

LIVE OAKS WINERY *Santa Clara County*
3875 Hecker Pass Hwy., Gilroy, CA 95020
(408) 842-2401 Founded: 1974
Storage: Oak, redwood, stainless steel.
Owner: Peter Scagliotti. Winemaker: Mitsuo Takemoto.

The 69 acres of vineyards are located at the winery in the Santa Clara Valley. The vineyard was planted by Peter's father Eduardo in 1912. Grapes are also purchased on a select vineyard basis.

Wines produced are "Premium Quality" Burgundy (aged 65 months), Sauterne, Haut Sauterne, Grenache Rosé and Chenin Blanc (extra dry, sweet and medium).

LIVERMORE VALLEY CELLARS *Alameda County*
1508 Wetmore Road, Livermore, CA 94550
(415) 447-1751 Founded: 1978
Storage: Oak.
Owner, winemaker: Chris Lagiss.

The 34-acre vineyard is in Livermore Valley.

Varietal, estate bottled, vintage-dated wines produced are Pinot Blanc, Grey Riesling, French Colombard. Also produced are Servant Blanc, Golden Seco and Chardonnay.

LLORDS & ELWOOD WINERY ★ *Alameda County*
P.O. Box 3397, Fremont, CA 94539
(213) 716-7794 (Business Office) Founded: 1955
Storage: Oak and outdoors Sherry solera.
Owner: The Elwood family. Winemaker: Richard H. Elwood.

Grapes are purchased on a select vineyard basis. The first in California to develop a commercially successful

Spanish type Solera for ageing sherries. Also pioneered Rosé made from Cabernet Sauvignon grapes and late-harvest style Johannisberg Riesling.

The varietal, vintage-dated wines produced are The Rare Chardonnay, Castle Magic Johannisberg Riesling, Rosé of Cabernet, Velvet Hill Pinot Noir and Cabernet Sauvignon. Also produced are Great Day D-r-ry Sherry, Dry Wit Sherry, The Judge's Secret Cream Sherry and Ancient Proverb Port.

['81 OC] (B) NV P; ['82 SJP] (B) '81 CAR, (P) (S) P.

J. LOHR (*See* Turgeon-Lohr Winery.)

LOLINIS VINEYARD—Zinfandel vineyard in Redwood Valley Mendocino.

JACK LONDON VINEYARD—Cabernet Sauvignon and Pinot Noir vineyard west of Sonoma Valley.

LONG VINEYARDS ★ *Napa County*

P.O. Box 50, St. Helena, CA 94574

(707) 963-2496 Founded: 1978

Storage: Oak, stainless steel.

Owners: Robert and Zelma Long. Winemaker: Zelma Long.

The vineyard is located at the winery. Varietal, vintage-dated, estate bottled wines produced are Johannisberg Riesling and Chardonnay. Wines sold from waiting list.

['81 OC] (S) '79 WR.

JASPER LONG VINEYARD—Merlot vineyard in Dry Creek Valley.

LOS ANGELES COUNTY

Southern California.

LOS ANGELES, ORANGE

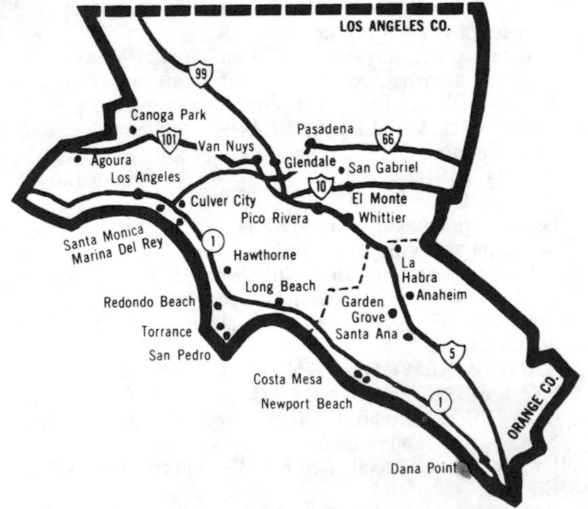

LOS ALTOS (*See* B & R Vineyards.)
LOS COCHES CELLARS (*See* Beringer Vineyards.)
LOS HERMANOS (*See* Beringer Vineyards.)
LOS NINOS VINEYARD—Chardonnay vineyard in Napa Valley.
LOS OLIVOS VINEYARD—Chardonnay vineyard near Santa Ynez.

LOS VINEROS WINERY ★ *Santa Barbara County*
618 Hanson Way, Santa Maria, CA 93456
(805) 928-5917 Founded: 1981
Storage: Stainless steel, wood.
Owners: Corporation. President: Edwin N. Woods. Winemaker: Kurt Lorenzi.

Label indicates vineyard and/or appellation. Varietal, vintage-dated wines produced are Pinot Noir, Cabernet Sauvignon, Pinot Noir Blanc, Cabernet Sauvignon Blanc, Chenin Blanc, Chardonnay and Sauvignon Blanc.

['82 SJP] (B) PN BL.

LOST HILLS VINEYARDS ★ *San Joaquin County*
P.O. Box C, Acampo, CA 95220
(209) 369-2746
Owner: Herbert R. Benham, Jr.; President of Berrenda Mesa Farming. General Manager: Albert Luongo. Prod. Mgr.: Bill Jiron. Winemakers: Philip Loechler, Eric Striocker, John Smiderle.

Lost Hills Vineyards is only a 1500-acre part in a complex 26,000 acre farming operation. Grapes are also purchased on a select vineyard basis. Label indicates vineyard and/or appellation.

Varietal, vintage-dated wines produced are Chenin Blanc, French Colombard, Muscat Pantelleria, Zinfandel, Cabernet Sauvignon, Chenin Blanc Light, Zinfandel Light, Zinfandel Rosé, Pinot Noir Blanc, Pinot Noir Rosé, Grey Riesling and Sauvignon Blanc. Generic wines produced are Lost Hills Cremocha, Ambermint, Creme Marsala, Dudenhoeffer May and Spiced Wine.

['82 OC] (B) '81 CH, (B) '80 G, (B) '80 JR.

Louis 5th (*See* California Wine Co.)

LOWER LAKE WINERY ★ *Lake County*
P.O. Box 950, Hwy. 29, Lower Lake, CA 95457
(707) 994-4069 Founded: 1977
Storage: French oak, stainless steel.
Owners: Family Partnership. Winemaker: Daniel H. Stuermer, PhD.

Grapes are purchased from select Lake County Vineyards. Label indicates vineyard and/or appellation. 100% varietal, vintage-dated wines produced are Cabernet Sauvignon and Fumé Blanc.

['82 SJP&C] (B&B) '78 CA.

THE LUCAS WINERY *San Joaquin County*
18196 N. Davis, Lodi, CA 95240
(309) 368-2006 Founded: 1978
Storage: French, American oak.
Owners: David and Tamara Lucas. Winemaker: David Lucas. Manager: T. Lucas. Vineyard: 30 acres.

Varietal, estate bottled, vintage-dated wine produced is

Zinfandel.

LYETH VINEYARD & WINERY *Sonoma County*
24625 Chianti Road, P.O. Box 558, Geyserville, CA 95441
(707) 857-3745
Owner: Munro L. Lyeth, Jr. Winemaker: William L. Arbios.

The 100 acre vineyard is in the Alexander Valley. It was originally purchased in 1973 and was known as the Brignole Ranch. The three wines that are produced are Lyeth (a blend of Cabernet Sauvignon, Merlot, Malbec and Cabernet Franc), Lyeth Blanc (a blend of Sauvignon Blanc and Semillon) and Port.

LYTTON SPRINGS WINERY ★ *Sonoma County*
650 Lytton Springs Road, Healdsburg, CA 95448
(707) 433-7701 Founded: 1977
Storage: Oak, stainless steel.
Owners: Walt Walters and Dee Sindt.

Grapes are purchased on a select vineyard basis. Valley Vista vineyard is located at the winery. Label indicates vineyard and/or appellation.

Varietal, vintage-dated wine produced is Zinfandel. Recommended: Zinfandel.

['81 OC] (G) '80 Z.

M

Madeira
A rich fortified wine of the Sherry class, originally from the island of Madeira. It is made from white grapes and has additional sugar added for sweetening. Addition of sugar is not permitted when produced in California.

MADERA COUNTY
Mid San Joaquin Valley.

Maderise
When referring to Madeiras, true to type. When referring to other wines past their prime with an acquired brownish color.

MADRIA-MADRIA (*See* E. & J. Gallo.)

MADRONA VINEYARDS ★ *El Dorado County*
P.O. Box 454, Gatlin Road, Camino, CA 95709
(916) 644-5948 Founded: 1973
Storage: Oak, stainless steel.
Owners: Richard & Leslie Bush. Winemaker: Richard Bush. Vineyard 3,000 ft. elevation near Placerville in Sierra Foothills.

Varietal, vintage-dated, estate bottled wines produced are Cabernet Sauvignon, Merlot, Zinfandel, Chardonnay, White Riesling and Gewurztraminer.

['82 OC] (G) '80 Z; ['82 SJC] (B) '80 JR.

Malbec
One of the three great Bordeaux grapes. Long lasting and tannic. Usually blended with Cabernet Sauvignon.

Malvasia Bianca
(White Table and Dessert Wine) A varietal grape that because of its sweetness is used for dessert wines or

sweet table wine. Also used for Asti-Spumante style sparkling wines. Originally imported from the Asti region of Italy.

Award wines to look for: Beringer, Brookside, Monterey Peninsula, Novitiate.

MANIAR VINEYARDS (*See* Diamond Oaks.)

MARIETTA CELLARS ★ *Sonoma County*

P.O. Box 1260, Healdsburg, CA 95448
(707) 433-2747
Owner, Winemaker: Chris Bilbro.

Varietal, vintage-dated wines produced are Zinfandel and Cabernet Sauvignon.

['82 OC] (B) '78 CA.

MARIN COUNTY

North Central Coast.

M. MARION & CO. *Santa Clara County*

14573 2B Big Basin Way, P.O. Box 265, Saratoga, CA 95070
(408) 867-6055 Founded: 1981
M. Dennis Marion, President. Negociants of California Wines.

M. Marion & Company wines are selected from varietal stocks originating from high quality producing regions of California. Since they are not a winery with the enormous expenses of a winery operation, they are able to offer high quality wines at extremely reasonable prices. They simply locate and contract for batch wines that meet their standards and offer them on a direct basis.

MARKHAM VINEYARD *Napa County*

2812 North St. Helena Hwy., St. Helena, CA 94574
(707) 963-5292 Founded: 1978
Storage: Limousin oak, stainless steel.
Owners: H. Bruce and Kate F. Markham. Manager: Bryan A. DelBondio. Winemaker: Robert D. Foley. Vineyards: 300 acres in Napa Valley.

100% varietal, vintage-dated, estate bottled wines produced are Chenin Blanc, Muscat de Frontignan, Gamay Blanc, Chardonnay, Cabernet Sauvignon, Merlot, and Johannisberg Riesling.

MARK WEST VINEYARDS ★ *Sonoma County*

7000 Trenton-Healdsburg Road, Forestville, CA 95436
(707) 544-4813 Founded: 1972
Storage: Stainless steel.
Owners: Robert and Joan Ellis. Winemaker: Joan Ellis.

The 60 acre vineyard is located at the winery in the Russian River Valley. All wines are estate bottled with the exception of Zinfandel and some Chardonnays.

The 100% varietal, vintage-dated, estate bottled wines produced are: Gewurztraminer, Johannisberg Riesling, Chardonnay, Pinot Noir and Pinot Noir Blanc.

['82 SJP&C] (B) '79 C, (P&C) (S&B) '81 SG.

Marsala wine

A generic sweet dessert wine. Mission and Grenache grapes are predominantly used. Dark amber in color with strong raisin flavor.

Award wines to look for: Brookside, Cucamonga, J.

Filippi, Perelli-Minetti, Verdugo.

MARTIN BROS. WINERY ★ *San Luis Obispo County*
P.O. Box 2597, Paso Robles, CA 93446
(805) 238-2520 or (805) 239-1640 Founded: 1981
Storage: Oak, stainless steel.
Owner: Martin & McFarlane, Inc. President: Tom Martin. Winemaker: Dominic Martin. Vineyards: 20 acres at winery planted in 1982, 50 acres in 1983.

Premium grapes are purchased on a select vineyard basis from central coast counties. Label indicates vineyard and/or appellation.

Varietal, vintage-dated wines produced are Chenin Blanc, Sauvignon Blanc, Chardonnay appellation and Zinfandel, all scheduled for their first release in 1982.

['82 OC] (B) '81 CH; ['82 SJP&C] (B&B) '81 CH.

MARTIN RAY VINEYARDS *Santa Clara County*
2060 Louis Rd., Palo Alto, CA 94303
(415) 321-6489 Founded: 1943
Storage: Oak.
Owner: Martin Ray Vineyards. President: Kenton Brooks.

Grapes are estate grown and purchased on a select vineyard basis. Label indicates vineyard and/or appellation. 100% varietal, vintage-dated wines produced are Pinot Noir, Chardonnay, Cabernet Sauvignon and Merlot. Methode Champenoise Champagne is also produced.

MARTIN WINERY *Los Angeles County*
11800 West Jefferson Blvd., Culver City, CA 90230
(213) 390-5736 Founded: 1970
Owners, Winemakers: Chuck Martin, Jim Umphries.

Owns no vineyards. Varietal wines produced are Cabernet Sauvignon, Merlot, Sauvignon Blanc and Chardonnay. Wines under label names: Martin, Chateau Martin and St. Martin. Also Champagne and Brandy. No connection with San Martin Winery.

LOUIS M. MARTINI ★ *Napa County*
P.O. Box 112, St. Helena, CA 94574
(707) 963-2736 Founded: 1922
Storage: American oak, redwood, stainless steel.
Owners: the Martini family. Winemakers: Louis P., Michael R. Martini, son and grandson of the founder.

Four vineyards in Napa County, two in the Carneros Region, one in Pope Valley and one in Chiles Valley. New vineyard in Southern Lake County. Two vineyards in Sonoma County are on Mayacamas Mountains and near Healdsburg. The varietal wines produced are Cabernet Sauvignon, Pinto Noir, Merlot, Barbera, Zinfandel, Gamay Beaujolais, Chardonnay, Johannisberg Riesling, Gewurztraminer, Folle Blanche, Dry Chenin Blanc and Moscato Amabile.

The generics produced are Burgundy, Claret, Chianti, Chablis, Mountain Red, Mountain White, Mountain Vin Rosé, Pale Dry and Cream Sherry. Occasionally limited amounts of Private Reserve and Special Selection wines are produced.

Winemaker's favorites are the Special Selection Cabernet Sauvignon, Chardonnay and Merlot.

['81 OC] (B) '79 G, (B) NV TP; ['82 OC] (B) '80 G, (S) '76 PN; ['82 SJP] (B) '80 G, (P) '78 CA.

MARTINI & PRATI WINES *Sonoma County*

2191 Laguana Rd., Santa Rosa, CA 95401
(707) 823-2404 Founded: 1951
Storage: Oak, redwood, cement.
Owners: Elmo Martini, Edward Prati. Winemaker: Frank J. Vannucci.

Originally founded in the early 1900s when their Fountain Grove label became famous. The winery is operated once again by members of the original family.

Varietal wines produced are Zinfandel, Gamay Beaujolais, Pinot Noir, Petite Sirah, Merlot, Chenin Blanc, Grey Riesling and French Colombard. Also produced are Sparkling Burgundy and Champagne.

PAUL MASSON VINEYARDS ★ *Santa Clara, Monterey Counties*

13150 Saratoga Avenue, Saratoga, CA 95070
(408) 257-7800 Founded: 1852
Storage: Oak, redwood, stainless steel. Winemaker: Joseph Stillman.

Paul Masson is a subsidiary of the House of Seagram. The history of Paul Masson begins in 1852, when Etienne Thee, a vigneron from Bordeaux, came to California and planted a vineyard south of San Jose, thus pioneering winegrowing in the Santa Clara Valley. He was succeeded by his son-in-law, Charles Le Franc, who was succeeded in turn by his son-in-law, Paul Masson, a native of Beaune in the Burgundy district of France. Masson's "Vineyard in the Sky" in the Santa Cruz Mountains is still in operation and is a State Historical Landmark. Masson retired in 1936. Seagrams acquired the vineyards in 1943. Paul Masson vineyard holdings total 4500 acres.

Varietal, vintage-dated, estate bottled "Pinnacles" wines are Gewurztraminer, Johannisberg Riesling, Chardonnay and Fumé Blanc, all from Monterey County.

Varietal, vintage-dated wines produced are Johannisberg Riesling, Sauvignon Blanc, Pinot Blanc, Zinfandel, Chenin Blanc, Pinot Chardonnay, Cabernet Sauvignon, Pinot Noir, Gamay Beaujolais, Petite Sirah, Riesling, French Colombard and Gamay Rosé. Also produced are Burgundy, Chablis, Rosé, Rhine, Vine Rosé Sec, Rhine Castle, Emerald Dry, Light Chablis, Light Rosé, Light Rhine, Sangria, Tawny, Rich Ruby, and Rare Souzao Port, Pale Dry, Medium Dry, Cocktail, Golden Cream and Rare Cream Sherry, Madiera, Vermouth. Sparkling wines produced are Crackling Rosé, Crackling Chablis, Sparkling Burgundy, Very Cold Duck, and Brut (vintage), Extra Dry (vintage) and Pink Champagnes.

The winemaker's favorite wines are the varietal, estate bottled "Pinnacles."

['81 OC] (B) NV P; ['82 OC] (B) '80 GB, (B) '80 Z, (S) '79 PS.

MASTANTUONO WINERY ★ *San Luis Obispo County*

101-3/4 Willow Creek Road, Paso Robles, CA 93446
(805) 238-1078 Founded: 1977

Storage: American oak, stainless steel.
Owners: Pasquale and Leona Mastan. Winemaker: Pasquale A. Mastan.
The 14 acre vineyard is in the hills west of Templeton. Wines produced are varietal, vintage-dated Zinfandel, Cabernet Sauvignon, Chardonnay and Sauvignon Blanc. New tasting room at Hwy. 46 and Vineyard Drive in Templeton opens March 1983.
['81 OC] (B) '79 Z; ['82 OC] (G) '80 Z; ['82 SJP&C] (B) '80 SB, (P) (S) '80 Z.

MATANZAS CREEK WINERY ★ *Sonoma County*
P.O. Box 9083, Santa Rosa, CA 95405
(707) 542-8242 Founded: 1978
Storage: French oak, stainless steel.
Owner: Sandra P. MacIver. Winemaker/Manager: Merry Edwards.
42 acres of vineyards are at the base of Bennett Peak in Bennett Valley. Some grapes are also purchased on a select vineyard basis. Label indicates vineyard and/or appellation.
Varietal, vintage-dated, estate bottled wines produced are Chardonnay, Pinot Noir, Merlot, Cabernet Sauvignon and Sauvignon Blanc.
['81 OC] (B) '78 CA.

MATHEWS NAPA VALLEY WINERY *Napa County*
Owners: Kenneth & Barbara Nelson. Winemaker: Kenneth Nelson.
Varietal wines produced are Cabernet Sauvignon, Chardonnay, Zinfandel, Chenin Blanc. Also produced are Tokay, Tawny Port and Sherries.

May Wine
An aromatic wine flavored with woodruff herbs. Light and fruity, with a scented bouquet and fruity, sweet flavor. Serve very cold with baked and barbecued meats or between meals.

MAYACAMAS VINEYARDS ★ *Napa County*
1155 Lokoya Road, Napa, CA 94558
(707) 224-4030 Founded: 1889
Storage: Oak.
Owners: Robert B. and Elinor D. Travers. Winemaker: Robert B. Travers. Vineyards: 47 acres at the winery.
The original winery was built in 1889 and was located at and named after the mountain range that separates the Napa and Sonoma Valleys.
The estate bottled, vintage-dated varietal wines produced are Chardonnay and Cabernet Sauvignon. Also produced are varietal Late-Harvest Zinfandel, Pinot Noir and Sauvignon Blanc.
['81 OC] (B) '79 SB.

MCDOWELL VALLEY VINEYARDS ★ *Mendocino County*
dba McDowell Cellars
P.O. Box 449, 3811 Hwy. 175, Hopland, CA 95449
(707) 744-1053 Founded: 1978
Storage: Oak barrels.
Owners: Rich and Karen Keehn. Winemaker: George

Bursick.

The original ranch was homesteaded by Paxton McDowell in the mid-1800s. The first grape plantings were in 1890. Today there are 700 acres, 360 owned by McDowell Vineyards. The winery is solar integrated; vineyard is located at the winery.

100% varietal, vintage-dated, estate bottled wines produced are Chardonnay, Chenin Blanc, Fumé Blanc, French Colombard, Cabernet Sauvignon, Petite Sirah and Zinfandel. Also Grenache (not 100%).

['81 OC] (G) '78 CA, (G) '79 Z, ['82 OC] (S) '79 CA, (B) '80 C, (G) '79 PS.

McLESTER WINERY ★ *Los Angeles County*
10670 South La Cienega, Unit D, Inglewood, CA 90304
(213) 641-9686 Founded: 1979
Storage: Oak and stainless steel.
Owner, Winemaker: Cecil McLester.

Grapes are purchased on a select vineyard basis. Label indicates vineyard and/or appellation. 100% varietal, vintage-dated wines produced are Zinfandel, Cabernet Sauvignon, Merlot, French Colombard and Cabernet Sauvignon Rosé.

['81 OC] (B) '80 Z.

McFADDEN RANCH—Sauvignon Blanc vineyard in Mendocino's Potter Valley.

McHENRY VINEYARDS *Santa Cruz County*
Bonny Doon Rd., Santa Cruz, CA 95060
(916) 756-3202 Founded: 1980
Storage: French oak.
Owners: Henry, Linda, Dean & Jane McHenry. Winemaker: Henry McHenry. Vineyards: 3.5 acres at winery.

Label indicates vineyard and/or appellation. Varietal, vintage-dated wines produced are Pinot Noir, Chardonnay and Pinot Blanc.

MEAD RANCH—Zinfandel vineyard on Atlas Peak near city of Napa.

Medium
As applied to Sherry, it means slightly sweet, in the middle range between dry and sweet.

Mellow
Soft in taste, term used to describe "Vino Rosso" red dinner wines. Also sometimes used to designate well-matured Sherries, wines containing some sweetness.

MENDOCINO COUNTY
(Northern Coast) Appellations: Anderson Valley and Redwood Valley.

Merlot
(A Red Table Wine) A varietal grape that produces a distinctive aromatic, spicy, medium red in color wine with some of the green olive and herbaceous odor of Cabernet Sauvignon. Originally from the Bordeaux region of France where it is a major factor in the wines of Pommard and St. Emilion.

Award wines to look for: Boeger, Calafia Cellars, Caparone, J. Carey, Carneros Creek, Chappellet, Chateau Chevre, Chateau St. Jean, Clos du Bois, Clos du Val, R. &

J. Cook (Merlot Blanc), Devlin, Duckhorn, Farview Farm, Franciscan, Gundlach-Bundschu, Inglenook, Robert Keenan, Lawrence, Markham, Mill Creek, Monterey Peninsula, Parducci, Ridgewood, Rutherford Hill, Souverain, St. Francis, Stag's Leap, Sterling, Trentadue, Turner, Veedercrest, York Mountain, Zaca Mesa.

Metallic

A defect in wine. A hint of bitterness, a hard finish.

Microclimates and Quality

This is no end of facts. For the most part, the grapes have the best love affairs in these regions. Like all love affairs, there are exceptions.

Coldest Climates: Santa Cruz, Santa Maria, Sonoma, Upper Monterey, Pinot Noir, Pinot Blanc, Johannisberg Riesling, Gewurztraminer, Grey Riesling.

Medium Cool: Monterey, Napa Carneros, Santa Barbara, Sonoma: Pinot Blanc, Chardonnay, Sylvaner, Grenache, Grey Riesling, Johannisberg Riesling, Petite Sirah, Zinfandel (sometimes).

Medium Warm: Lower Monterey, San Luis Obispo, Upper Napa Valley: Semillon, Sauvignon Blanc, Chenin Blanc, Zinfandel, Cabernet Sauvignon, Petite Sirah, Grenache, Napa Gamay, French Colombard, Chardonnay (sometimes).

Hot Climates: (Central Valley) Bakersfield, Fresno, Lodi, Modesto: French Colombard, Ruby Cabernet, Barbera, Carignane, Palomino, Tinta Madera, Grenache.

MENDOCINO, SONOMA

LOUIS K. MIHALY VINEYARDS *Napa County*
3103 Silverado Trail, Napa, CA 94558
(707) 253-9306
Chairman: Louis K. Mihaly. Winemaker: John D. Nemeth.

34 acres of vineyards are located at the winery. 100% varietal, estate bottled, vintage-dated wines produced are Pinot Noir, Chardonnay and Sauvignon Blanc.

MILANO WINERY ★ *Mendocino County*
14594 South Hwy. 101, Hopland, CA 95449
(707) 744-1396 Founded: 1977
Storage: Oak, redwood, stainless steel.
President and Winemaster: Jim Milone.

The family vineyards go back to the early 1900s. Grapes are purchased from select vineyards in Mendocino County.

Varietal, vintage-dated wines produced are Chardonnay, Sauvignon Blanc, Pinot Noir, Cabernet Sauvignon, Zinfandel, Gewurztraminer, and Late Harvest Riesling.

The winemaker's favorite wines are Chardonnay and Cabernet Sauvignon.

['81 OC] (S) '78 CA, (B) '80 CH, (S) '79 Z; ['82 OC] (G) '80 C, (B) '81 G, (G) '81 JR; ['82 SJP] (B) '80 C, (B) '81 G, (P) (G) '81 LHJ.

MILL CREEK VINEYARDS ★ *Sonoma County*
1401 Westside Road, Healdsburg, CA 95448
(707) 433-5098
Storage: American and French oak, stainless steel.
Owners: Charles, William, and James Kreck. Winemaker: James Kreck.

The 65 acre vineyard is located at winery in Dry Creek Valley. Varietal, vintage-dated, estate bottled wines produced are Cabernet Sauvignon, Cabernet Blush (Rosé—100% Cabernet Sauvignon), Chardonnay (100%), Gewurztraminer, Pinor Noir (100%), Merlot and Gamay Beaujolais (100%).

The winemaker's favorite wines are the Cabernet Sauvignon, Chardonnay and Cabernet Blush.

['81 OC] (G) '79 C; ['82 OC] (B) '80 C, (B), '80 PN; ['82 SJP] (B) '78 CA, (P) (B) '80 M, (P&C) (S&B) '81 CAR.

F. J. MILLER *Napa County*
8329 St. Helena Hwy., Napa, CA 94558
(707) 963-4252
Owner, Winemaker: F. Justin Miller.

The winery was established in 1960 in order to demonstrate his "Millerway" method of carbonating a still wine, in the bottle, without recourse to fermentation of sugar added to the wine. Wines produced are effervescent.

MIRASSOU ★ *Santa Clara, Monterey Counties*
3000 Aborn Road, San Jose, CA 95135
(408) 274-4000 Founded: 1854
Storage: Oak, redwood, stainless steel.
Owners: James, Peter, Daniel, Steve Mirassou and Don Alexander. Winemaker: Don Alexander.

1300 acres of vineyards are in Monterey County and Santa Clara Valley. Twenty-two acres of Cabernet

Sauvignon surround the winery. This Cabernet is referred to as "Home Vineyards" Cabernet Sauvignon. The Mirassou family is America's oldest wine making family. Varietal, vintage-dated wines produced are Chardonnay, Chenin Blanc, Johannisberg Riesling, Monterey Riesling, White Burgundy (Pinot Blanc), Cabernet Sauvignon, Gamay Beaujolais, and Monterey Zinfandel. Also produced are Dry Chablis, Burgundy and L.D. (Late Disgorged), Au Naturel, Blanc de Noir and Brut Champagne. Recommended: 1981 Johannisberg Riesling, 1981 Monterey Fumé and 1978 'H' Zinfandel. The Harvest Selections (full bodied, limited production) are Chardonnay, Monterey Fumé, Zinfandel, Pinot Noir and Cabernet Sauvignon.

['81 OC] (S) '77 PS, (S) '80 WR, (B) '78 Z, (S) '74 SW, (G) '78 SW; ['82 OC] (B) '79 CA, (S) '78 PS, (S) '81 PB, (B) '78 Z, (G) '78 CHA, (B) '79 CHA; ['82 SJP] (B) '81 Hvst. Res. FB, (B&S) (P&C) '81 R.

Mission Grape

The first vinifera grape planted in California by the Franiscan Fathers. Today grown in the warm districts and is mainly used to produce cheap Port and Angelica, though many better grapes abound.

C. K. MONDAVI (*See* Charles Krug Winery.)

ROBERT MONDAVI WINERY ★ *Napa County*

7801 St. Helena Hwy., Oakville, CA 94562
(707) 963-9611 Founded: 1966
Storage: Oak, stainless steel.
Owner: Robert Mondavi and his family. President: Michael Mondavi. Winemakers: Robert and Tim Mondavi.

Tim is in charge of production. The two vineyards TO-KALON and OAK KNOLL are located at the winery and on Silverado Trail. To-Kalon dates to 1886. 593 acres are at foot of Mayacamas Mountains on western side of Napa Valley. 398 acres of Oak Knoll are along the Silverado Trail.

Varietal, vintage-dated wines produced are Fumé Blanc, Chardonnay, Johannisberg Riesling, Chenin Blanc, Gamay Rosé, Napa Gamay, Pinot Noir, Cabernet Sauvignon, Zinfandel and Moscato D'Oro.

Also produced is R.M. vintage Red, White and Rosé.

['81 OC] (G) '80 WR, (B) '75 CA, (G), '78 C, (S) '79 C, (G) '80 CH, (B) '79 SB; ['82 OC] (B) '77 CA, (B) '77 PN, (B) '80 SB, (B) '80 JR, (S) '80 C; ['82 SJP] (B) '81 RO.

R. MONTALI WINERY *Alameda County*

719 Allston Way, Berkeley, CA 94710
(415) 834-5513
Owner: Ralph Montali, Gen'l. Partner. Winemaker: Dr. Richard Carey.

Dr. Richard Carey previously owned his own winery. He has won numerous medals for award winning wines. Ralph Montali and associates purchased the Carey winery and have formed this new winery.

Grapes are purchased on a selected vineyard basis. Label indicates vineyard and/or appellation. Varietal, vintage-dated wines produced are Cabernet Sauvignon, Zinfandel, Gamay Beaujolais, Blanc Fumé, Chardonnay and Gewurztraminer. Also produced is La Belle Blanc.

MONTCLAIR WINERY ★ *Alameda County*

180 Maxwelton Road, Peidmont, CA 94618
(415) 658-1014 Founded: 1975
Storage: Oak.
Owners: R. K. Dove, L. A. Dorie, and J. H. Burkhard.
Winemaker: R. K. Dove.

Varietal, vintage-dated type wines produced are Zinfandel, Petite Sirah and French Colombard.

['82 SJP] (S) '80 Z, (P&C) (B&B) '80 Z.

MONT D'EDE L'ESCANTE (*See* Endgate Vineyards.)

MONTEAGLE WINERY (*See* Vichon Winery.)

MONTEREY CELLARS (*See* Monterey Peninsula.)

MONTEREY COUNTY

Central Coast. Appellations: Carmel Valley, Soledad and Arroyo Seco.

MONTEREY, SAN BENITO, SANTA CLARA, SANTA CRUZ

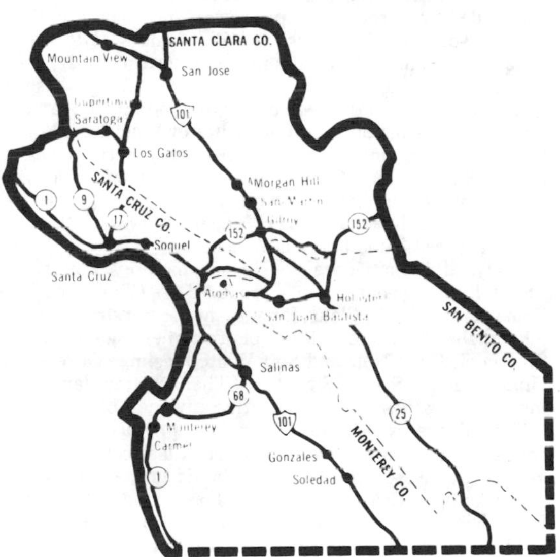

MONTEREY PENINSULA WINERY ★ *Monterey County*

2999 Monterey Salinas Hwy., Monterey, CA 93940
(408) 372-4949 Founded: 1974
Storage: American and French oak.
Owners: Drs. Roy Thomas and Deryck Nuckton. Winemaker: Mark Theis. Winemaster: Roy Thomas.

The winery has won over 90 awards at competitive wine tastings. Grapes are purchased on a select vineyard basis. Label indicates vineyard and/or appellation.

100% varietal, vintage-dated wines produced are Zinfandel, Barbera, Pinot St. George, Chardonnay, Pinot Noir, Cabernet Sauvignon, Petite Sirah, Sauvignon Blanc, Johannisberg Riesling and Muscat Canelli.

Wines produced under the Monterey Cellars label are Dry Chablis, Emerald Riesling and California Rosé. Produced under the Big Sur label are Big Sur White and Red.

The winemaker's favorite wines are Chardonnay, Cabernet Sauvignon and Zinfandel.

['81 OC] (S) '79 C; ['82 OC] (S) '79 B, (G) '79 CA, (S) '81 PB, (B) '78 Z, (B) '77 Z, (B) '80 Z LHS; ['82 SJP] (B) '81 PB, (P) (B) '79 CA, (P) (S) '79 CA, (P) (S) '79 Z.

THE MONTEREY VINEYARD ★ *Monterey County*
800 South Alta St., Gonzales, CA 93926
(408) 675-2481 Founded: 1973
Storage: Oak, redwood, stainless steel.
Owner: The Wine Spectrum (The Coca-Cola Co. of Atlanta, GA.). President and Winemaster: Richard G. Peterson. Ph.D. Winemaker: Linda O'Brien.

Founded by a group of grape growers, purchased by R. G. Peterson and D. A. Lucas in 1976, and sold to the Coca-Cola Co. in 1977, The Monterey Vineyards produces Taylor California Cellars for The Taylor Wine Co. (also owned by the Wine Spectrum). Only production and quality control are done by The Monterey Vineyards. Not the marketing. Only winery to produce generic wines from 100% Coastal County grapes. Peterson is also responsible for producing several wines that were never produced in California before, "January Harvest," "December Harvest," and Botrytis Wines.

Vineyard is in Gonzales. Upper Monterey County. Varietal, vintage-dated wines produced are Chardonnay, Fumé Blanc, Chenin Blanc, Pinot Blanc, Gewurztraminer, Johannisberg Riesling, Rosé of Cabernet Sauvignon, Zinfandel, Pinot Noir and Soft White Riesling. Varietal, vintage-dated, "Special Signature" Thanksgiving Harvest Johannisberg Riesling and Botrytis Sauvignon Blanc.

The Monterey Vineyard does not produce generic wines in the commonly used sense. Classic Red, Dry White, and Rosé are blends of classic grape varieties grown only in Coastal vineyards. For example: Classic Red is 65% Cabernet, 20% Zinfandel, and 15% Pinot Noir.

The winemaker's favorite wines are Gewurztraminer, Johannisberg Riesling and Chardonnay.

['81 OC] (G) '78 CA, (B) '80 CH, (S) '79 WR; ['82 OC] (B) '79 C, (B) '81 G, (G) '79 PB; ['82 SJP] (S) '81 G.

MONTE ROSSO VINEYARD—Louis Martin vineyard in Sonoma.

MONTEVINA WINES ★ *Amador County*
Shenandoah School Road, Plymouth, CA 95669
(209) 245-6942 Founded: 1973
Storage: American, Yugoslavian and French oak, stainless steel.
President: W. H. Field. Winery Manager: Alan Johansen. Winemakers: Jeff Runquist and Jeffrey Meyers.

Portions of the 175 acre vineyrd in the Shenandoah Valley were originally established in the early 1900's. Estate bottled, vintage-dated 100% varietal wines produced are Sauvignon Blanc, Barbera, Cabernet Sauvignon and Zinfandel. Recently Chardonnay from Tepusquet vineyards.

The winemaker's favorite wines are Zinfandel and Sauvignon Blanc.

['81 OC] (S) '80 SB, (S) '79 Z; ['82 OC] (B) '79 CA, (G) '81 SB, (S) '78 Z, (S) '79 Z, (G) '80 Z; ['82 SJP] (S) (C) '81 SB, (P) (S) '79 Z Sp. Sel.

MONTICELLO CELLARS ★

P.O. Box 2500, Yountville, CA 94599
(707) 944-8863
Owner: Jay Corley. Winemaker: Alan Phillips.

['82 OC] (B) '81 G, (B) '81 SB.

MONT LA SALLE (*See*Christian Bros.)

MONT ST. JOHN CELLARS *Napa County*

5400 Old Sonoma Rd., Napa, CA 94558
(707) 255-8864 Founded: 1979
Owner: Louis Bartolucci. Winemaker: Son, Andrea Bartolucci.

The Bartolucci family were founders of Madonna Winery dating back to 1934. Mont St. John Cellars and Madonna Vineyards are located in the Carneros Region of Napa Valley.

Varietal, vintage-dated, estate bottled wines produced are Chardonnay, Pinot Noir, Johannisberg Riesling, Gewurztraminer, and Muscat Di Canelli. Also Napa Valley vintage dated Cabernet Sauvignon, Zinfandel, and Petite Sirah.

MORGAN HILL CELLARS (*See* Pedrizzetti.)

J. W. MORRIS WINERIES ★ *Contra Costa County*

4060 Pike Lane, Concord, CA 94520
(415) 680-1122 Founded: 1975
Storage: American, French oak, stainless steel.
Owners: James W. Morris, James L. Olsen, Terrill M. Olsen. Winemaker: James L. Olsen.

Grapes are purchased on a select vineyard basis. Label indicates vineyard and/or appellation. The wines produced are Founders Port, White & Red Private Reserve, Vintage Port.

"California Selects" varietal, vintage-dated wines produced are Chardonnay, Sauvignon Blanc, Zinfandel, Pinot Noir and Cabernet Sauvignon. The winemaker's favorite wines are Vintage Port and Chardonnay.

['81 OC] (B) '78 VP, (G) NVP; ['82 OC] (B) '80 Z.

MOSCATO CANELLI

A varietal grape, the Moscato produces a rich, fruity wine with a delicate muscat character. Sweet enough to be a dessert wine also. Will age very well.

MOSELLE WINE

A generic semi-dry wine. Usually produced from Chenin Blanc and Riesling grapes. Semi-dry, mildly sweet, pale straw in color and fruity. Serve chilled with light meats and seafood.

MOTHER LODE (*See* California Cellar Masters.)

MOUNT EDEN VINEYARDS ★ *Santa Clara County*

22020 Mt. Eden Road, Saratoga, CA 95070
(408) 867-5832 Founded: 1972
Owner: the M.E.V. Corporation. Winemaker and Manager: Jeffrey Patterson.

35 acres of vineyard are in Santa Cruz Mountains at approximately 2000 ft. elevation. Estate bottled, vintage-dated, varietal wines produced are Cabernet Sauvignon, Pinot Noir and Chardonnay. A varietal produced under the MEV label from Monterey grapes is a Chardonnay.

['82 OC] (B) '78 CA, (B) '79 PN.

Mount Madonna (*See* Emilio Guglielmo Winery.)

MOUNT PALOMAR WINERY ★ *Riverside County*

33820 Rancho California Road, Temecula, CA 92390
(714) 676-5047 Founded: 1975
Storage: Oak, stainless steel.
Owner: John H. Poole. Winemaker: Joseph E. Cherpin.

The 150 acre vineyard is at the winery in the high country close to Palomar Mountain. Wines produced under the Mount Palomar label are Sauvignon Blanc, White Riesling, Chenin Blanc, Zinfandel, Chardonnay, Rosé de Petite Sirah, Cabernet Sauvignon, Petite Sirah, White Zinfandel, Shiraz, and Chateau Mt. Palomar (medium dry Sauvignon Blanc). Mount Palomar dessert wines are Cocktail Sherry (dry), Golden Sherry (medium), Cream Sherry and Limited Reserve Port.

['81 OC] (B) '80 CH, (B) '79 SB, (G) '79 WR.

MOUNT VEEDER WINERY *Napa County*

1999 Mt. Veeder Road, Napa, CA 94558
(707) 224-4039 Founded: 1972
Storage: Oak and stainless steel.
Owners: Henry & Lisille Mathison. Consultant: Michael Bernstein. Winemaker: Peter Franus.

The 22-acre vineyard is located on the slopes of Mount Veeder in the Napa Valley. Planted are French Bordeau blending varieties—Merlot, Cabernet Franc, Petite Verdot and Malbec. Wine produced is varietal, vintage-dated Cabernet Sauvignon blended with grapes from their own vineyards. Also Late Harvest Zinfandel.

Mountain Gold (*See* La Mont Winery.)

MOUNTAIN HOUSE WINERY *Mendocino County*

38999 Hwy. 128, Cloverdale, CA 95425
(707) 894-3074 Founded: 1979
Owners: Ron Lipp and partners. Winemaker: Ron Lipp.

Mountain House was an inn and stagecoach stop in the late 1800's. The winery was established in 1979 by Ron Lipp and several partners. It is situated in the Mendocino Mountains at a 1200 foot elevation. Grapes are purchased on a select vineyard basis. Mountain House produces Chardonnay, Cabernet Sauvignon and Late Harvest Zinfandel. It also produces two proprietary wines, Mendocino Gold and Vermillion.

MOUNTAIN RED CHIANTI

A generic dry wine. Robust and tart, with berry-like bouquet.

MOUNTAIN RED WINE
A generic red table wine made in the same way and from the same grapes as "Burgundy." Just another name for generic Burgundy.

THE MOUNTAIN VIEW WINERY *Santa Clara County*
2263 Old Middlefield Way, Mountain View, CA 94043
(415) 964-5398 Founded: 1980
Storage: French oak.
Owner/Winemaker: Patrick Ferguson.

Grapes are purchased on a select vineyard basis. Label indicates vineyard and/or appellation.

Varietal, vintage-dated wines produced are Chardonnay, Zinfandel, and Cabernet Sauvignon.

Mountain White Wine
A generic white table wine. Made in the same way and from the same grapes as generic "Chablis." Just another name for Chablis.

Mountain Peak (*See* La Mont Winery.)

Mountain View (*See* Gemello Winery.)

MOUNTAINSIDE VINEYARDS (*See* Chateau Chevalier Winery.)

Muscatel
A rich, flavorful, sweet dessert wine made from Muscat grapes and having their unmistakable flavor and aroma. Its color ranges from golden or dark amber to red. While most Muscatel is made from the Muscat of Alexandria grape and is golden in color, several other varieties are used in California to make Muscatels of varying flavor.

Red Muscatel, Black Muscatel: Muscatels which are red or dark red and are sometimes made from black Muscat grapes. Black Muscat is produced only by Novitiate Winery.

Muscat de Frontignan, Muscat Canelli: Muscatel made from the Muscat Blanc variety of Muscat grapes. Both names refer to the same grape.

Muscat
Award wines to look for: Brookside, Inglenook, Papagni, Sutter Home, Veedercrest.

Muscat Canelli
Award wines to look for: Ballard Canyon, Beringer, Chateau St. Jean, Concannon, Estrella River, Inglenook, Jekel, Charles Krug, Monterey Peninsula, Mount St. John, Papagni, Parducci, Pat Paulsen, Rapazzini, San Martin, San Pasqual, Souverain.

Muscat de Frontignan (*See* Moscato Canelli.)

Muscatel
Award wines to look for: Brookside, Concannon, Ferrara, Novitiate, Shenandoah.

Must
Unfermented grape juice, with or without the skins and seeds.

N

NAPA COUNTY *(Northern Coast)*
Appellations: Carneros, Yountville, Oakville, Rutherford,

Calistoga, Stags' Leap, Pritchard Hill, Mount Veeder, Spring Mountain, St. Helena.

NAPA, SOLANO

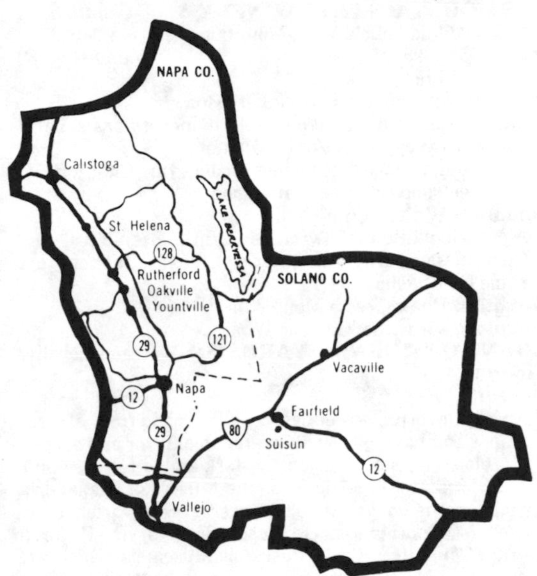

NAPA CREEK WINERY ★ *Napa County*
1001 Silverado Trail, St. Helena, CA 94574
(707) 963-9456 Founded: 1980
Storage: Oak, stainless steel.
General Partner: Jack Schulze. Winemaker: Eric Peterson. Vineyards: 20 acres at winery.

Label indicates vineyard and/or appellation.

Varietal, vintage-dated wines produced are Cabernet Sauvignon, Chardonnay, Johannisberg Riesling, Gewurztraminer, Sauvignon Blanc, and Dry Chenin Blanc '81V.

['82 SJC] (S) '81 FB, (C) (B) '81 SJR.

Napa Deluxe (*See* Matthews Napa Valley Winery.)
Napa Gamay (*See* Gamay.)
NAPA VINTNERS (*See* Don Charles Ross Winery.)

NAPA WINE CELLARS ★ *Napa County*
7481 St. Helena Hwy., Oakville, CA 94562
(707) 944-2565 Founded: 1976
Owner: Small Investor Group. Winemaker: Aaron Mosley.

Label indicates vineyard and/or appellation. Varietal, vintage-dated wines produced are Cabernet Sauvignon, Zinfandel and Chardonnay.

['81 OC] (S) '79 Z, (S) '78 CA, (G) '79 C; ['82 OC] (S) '80 C, (G) '81 SB; ['82 SJC] (B) '80 C, (P) (B) '79 CA.

Natural
The designation for absolutely dry champagne.

NAVARRO VINEYARDS ★ *Mendocino County*
5601 Hwy. 128, Philo, CA 95466
(707) 895-3683 Founded: 1974
Storage: Oak, stainless steel.
Owners: Edward Bennett and Deborah Cahn. Winemaker: Edward Bennett.

Vineyards are in Anderson Valley: grapes are also purchased on a select vineyard basis. Label indicates appellation. Varietal, vintage-dated, estate bottled wines produced are Pinot Noir, Gewurztraminer, Chardonnay, White Riesling and Cabernet Sauvignon. Also produced are Vin Rouge, Edelzwicker and Blanc de Noir.

['81 OC] (S) '80 G; ['82 OC] (S) '80 G, (G) '81 G; ['82 SJP] (B) '80 C Pvt. Res., (B&B) (P&C) '81 G, (P) (S) '81 LHG, (P&C) (B&B) '81 SWR.

NEBBIOLO
(Red Table Wine) A varietal grape producing a dry, fruity and tart wine. Originally from Italy where it is used to produce Barolo and Gattinara.

NEVADA CITY WINERY *Nevada County*
321 Spring Street, Nevada City, CA 95959
(916) 265-WINE
Storage: Oak and stainless steel.
Owner: Ltd. Partnership. President: Allan Haley. Winemaker: Tony Norskog. Vineyards: 80 acres to be planted in 1983.

The first winery in Nevada County since before Prohibition. Grapes are purchased on a select vineyard basis in Sierra Foothill counties. Label indicates vineyard and/or appellation.

Varietal, vintage-dated wines produced are Pinot Noir, Cabernet Sauvignon, Zinfandel, Douce Noir (Charbono), Petite Sirah, Chardonnay and Sauvignon Blanc.

NERVO WINERY *Sonoma County*
19550 Geyserville Ave., Geyserville, CA 95441
(707) 857-3417
Owner: Geyser Peak.

NEWLAN VINEYARDS & WINERY *Napa County*
5225 St. Helena Hwy., Napa, CA 94562
(707) 944-2914
Storage: Oak and stainless steel.
Owner, Winemaker: Bruce M. Newlan.

60 acres of vineyards are located at or near winery. Varietal, vintage-dated, estate bottled wines produced are Cabernet Sauvignon, Pinot Noir, Sauvignon Blanc and Chardonnay. Late Harvest Johannisberg Riesling is produced when possible.

NEWTON WINERY *Napa County*
2555 Madrona Ave., St. Helena, CA 94574
(707) 963-4613
Storage: French oak barrels, stainless steel.
Owners: P. L. Newton and R. W. Forman. Winemaker: R. W. Forman. 60 acre vineyard on Spring Mountain.

Label indicates vintage and/or appellation. Varietal,

vintage-dated wines produced are Cabernet Sauvignon, Merlot, Chardonnay and Sauvignon Blanc.

NICASIO VINEYARDS *Santa Cruz County*

14300 Nicasio Way, Soquel, CA 95073
(408) 423-1073
Owner, Winemaker: Dan Wheeler.

Grapes are purchased on a select vineyard basis. Varietal, vintage-dated wines produced under the "Wines by Wheeler" label are White Riesling, Chardonnay, Zinfandel Rosé, Zinfandel and Cabernet Sauvignon. Also produced is Champagne (Natural).

NICHELINI VINEYARD *Napa County*

2349 Lower Chiles Road, St. Helena, CA 94574
(707) 963-3357 Founded: 1890
Storage: Wood and stainless steel.
Owner, Winemaker: Jim Nichelini.

Established by Anton and Catrina Nichelini and still carried on by grandson, Jim. 200 acre vineyard is east of Rutherford. Varietal wines produced are Petite Sirah, Gamay, Chenin Blanc (vintage-dated), Sauvignon Vert, Cabernet Sauvignon (vintage-dated), Semillon and Zinfandel (vintage-dated).

The winemaker's favorite wines are Petite Sirah and Chenin Blanc.

NIEBAUM-COPPOLA ESTATE *Napa County*

1460 Niebaum Lane, Rutherford, CA 94573
(707) 963-9435 Founded: 1978
Owner: Francis Ford Coppola. Winemaker: Russ Turner. Vineyards: 110 acres.

Premium red table wine (blend of Cabernet Sauvignon, Cabernet Franc and Merlot). First release—spring 1984, vintage 1978.

Noble Rot (*See* Botrytis.)

NOBLE VINEYARDS *Kern County*

P.O. Box 31, Kerman, CA 93630
(209) 846-7361 Founded: 1973
Storage: Stainless steel.
Owner: Pacific Land & Viticulture. Winemaker: Richard de los Reyes. Vineyards: 3000 acres.

Varietal wines produced are French Colombard, Chenin Blanc, Semillon, Emerald Riesling, Ruby Cabernet and Barbera. Also produced are Dry White and Dry Red.

A. NONINI WINERY *Fresno County*

2640 Dickenson Ave., Fresno, CA 93711
(209) 275-1936 Founded: 1936
Storage: Wood.
Owner: Geno H. Nonini. Vineyards: 200 acres.

Wines produced are red and white table wines.

Non-Vintage

Wines blended from several vintages in order to obtain a wine of higher quality. The purpose of this blending is to maintain consistency of quality and taste from year to year, without change in color, character, bouquet, etc.

Nose

Refers mainly to the qualities of bouquet and aroma.

Nouveau

Literally "New" wine. In the tradition of Beaujolais, wine is bottled and released in late November, a few days after fermentation is finished. It is fresh, yeasty; a wine that captures the full fresh essence of the grape. Usually made from Gamay.

NORTH COAST CELLARS (*See* Souverain.)

NOVITIATE WINES ★ *Santa Clara County*

300 College Avenue, Los Gatos, CA 95030
(408) 354-6471 Founded: 1888
Storage: Oak and redwood.
Owner: The Society of Jesus. Winemaker: Brother Lee Williams, S.J.

The vineyards are located at the winery in the foothills of the Santa Cruz Mountains. Grapes are purchased from North Coast and Manteca Vineyards. The wines produced are Chablis, Pinot Blanc, Chenin Blanc, Johannisberg Riesling, Cabernet Sauvignon, Dry Malvasia, Burgundy, Petite Sirah and Sherry. Black Muscat (unique), Tinta Port, Novitiate Angelica and Muscat Frontignan. The producer of eight varieties of Sacramental wines.

The winemaker's favorite is Cabernet Sauvignon.

['82 SJP] (B) '78 CA, (P) (B) P.

NUMANO SAKE COMPANY *Alameda County*

708 Addison St., Berkeley, CA 94710
(415) 540-8250 Founded: 1977
Storage: Stainless steel.
Owners: Takara Shuzo Company, Ltd., Japan. Mutual Trading Company, Los Angeles, and David Banliff. Sakemaker: S. Kawano.

Numano was formed when Japanese sake became more expensive to import, and it was determined that sake could be more economically produced in California utilizing locally grown rice and water. Sake is a rice wine. Its alcohol content is usually 16-17%. Sake has been a major beverage for over 1,000 years in Japan, Korea and other countries in Asia.

Numano sake is made from special strains of California rice, called Tsuru Mai, developed at PIRMI's rice research center in the Sacramento Valley. Seed is given to farmers in the spring and they deliver their crop to PIRMI's mill upon the harvest in the fall. The rice is then milled, brewed and fermented. After fermentation it is pasteurized, filtered and returned to an aging tank until the sakemaster decides it is ready. At that point, it is pasteurized, filtered and bottled.

Wines produced are Numano California Sake, Koshu White Rice Wine and Koshu Masamune Sake. Also Numano Plum Elite, Koshu Plum Supreme and Senryo Mirin.

Nutty

Term denoting the characteristic flavor of Sherry; not desirable in table wines.

O

OAK BARREL *Alameda County*
1201 University Ave., Berkeley, CA 94702
(415) 849-0400 Founded: 1959
Owner and Winemaker: John Bank.
Leaving Hungary in 1956 where he was a winemaker, John Bank started the winery in 1959. Grapes are purchased on a select vineyard basis. Label indicates vineyard and/or appellation.
The varietal wines produced are Moscato Secco, Pinot Noir, Zinfandel and Cabernet Sauvignon. Also produced are Chateau Oak Barrel (white wine), Light Muscat, Chablis and Vino Bianco.

OAK GLEN WINERY *San Bernardino County*
P.O. Box 381, Yucaipa, CA 92399
(714) 797-3724 Founded: 1977
Storage: Wood.
Owners: Charles Colby, Frank Rivers. Winemaker: Charles Colby.
Table wine, fruit and berry wine.

OAK VALLEY WINERY *Stanislaus County*
P.O. Box 399, Oakdale, CA 95361
(209) 847-5907 Founded: 1978
Owner/Winemaker: Cutting B. Favour, M.D.

OBESTER WINERY ★ *San Mateo County*
Route 1, Box 2Q, Half Moon Bay, CA 94019
(415) 726-9463 Founded: 1977
Owners: Paul and Sandy Obester. Winemaker: Paul Obester.
Grapes are purchased on a select vineyard basis. Label indicates vineyard and/or appellation. Varietal, vintage-dated wines produced are Sauvignon Blanc, Johannisberg Riesling and Cabernet Sauvignon.
The winemaker's favorite wine is Sauvignon Blanc.
['81 OC] (G) '80 WR; ['82 OC] (B) '79 CA, (G) '81 JR, (B) '79 Z; ['82 SJP&C] (B&S) '81 SB, (P&S) '81 JR, (P&C) (B&S) '79 CA.

Oeil de Perdrix
A pale wine made from the free-run juice of Pinot Noir grapes. The French Translation is "eye of the partridge." The same color as the bird's pink iris.

OLD CASTEEL VINEYARDS *San Luis Obispo County*
Rt. 1, Box 93, Jensen Rd., Paso Robles, CA 93446
(805) 239-0860 Founded: 1980
Storage: Oak.
Owners: John Wyatt & Clifford Hight. Winemaker: Clifford Hight. Vineyards: 30 acres at winery.
Grapes are also purchased on a select vineyard basis. Label indicates vineyard and/or appellation.
Varietal, vintage-dated estate bottled wines produced are Zinfandel, Carignane, Grenache, Cabernet Sauvignon, Petite Sirah and Merlot.

OLD CREEK RANCH WINERY *Ventura County*
10024 Old Creek Rd., P.O. Box 173, Oakview, CA 93022

(805) 482-2452 Founded: 1981
Storage: French & American oak, stainless steel.
Principal: Charles Branham.

Grapes are purchased on a select vineyard basis. Varietal, vintage-dated wines produced are Merlot, Gamay Beaujolais, Cabernet Sauvignon, Dry Sauvignon Blanc and Johannisberg Riesling.

OLD GUASTI (*See* Brookside.)

OLD RANCH (*See* Thomas Vineyards.)

OLD ROSE (*See* Bisceglia Bros.)

Oloroso
A sweet Sherry of medium type, darker and richer than Amontillado.

OLSON VINEYARDS *Mendocino County*
3620 Road B, Redwood Valley, CA 95470
(707) 485-7523 Founded: 1982
Storage: Stainless steel, oak barrels.
Owners: Donald and Nancy Olson. Winemaker: Don Olson.

Even though the winery was recently built, the 23 acre vineyard was purchased in 1971.

Varietal, vintage-dated, estate bottled wines produced are Gamay, French Colombard and two styles of Zinfandel.

On the Yeast
Period during secondary fermentation when wine and yeast cells are allowed to remain in contact contributing to traditional "yeasty" nose of Champagne. This "yeastiness" may remain from one month to several years depending on producer.

OPICI WINERY *San Bernardino County*
Highland & Hermosa Ave., Alta Loma, CA 91701
(714) 987-2710 Founded: 1944
Owners: Mary Opici Nimmergut and Kurt Nimmergut.

Produce table and sparkling wines.

ORLEANS HILL VINICULTURAL ASSOC. *Yolo County*
625 Second St., Woodland, CA 95695
(916) 662-1928 Founded: 1980
Storage: Wood.
Owners: James & Carol Lapsley. Winemaker: James Lapsley.

CHARLES ORTMAN WINES ★ —Winemaker releasing wines under his own name. Edna Valley Chardonnay and Napa Valley Sauvignon Blanc. ['82 OC] (B) '80 C.

Oreon (*See* Gibson Winery.)

Oxidation
The effect of air upon wine. The character of a wine can be substantially altered in proportion to its exposure to air. Partially filled bottles will quickly oxidize if not refrigerated. White wines not carefully made or stored will take on a brownish color and "burnt sugar" taste. The production of Sherry and Madiera requires slow oxidation.

OZEKI SAN BENITO, INC. *San Benito County*
249 Hillcrest Rd., Hollister, CA 95023

(408) 637-9217 Founded: 1979
Storage: Oak, stainless steel.
Owners: A joint venture between 2 American and 2 Japanese companies. Chm. of Bd.: Bunjiro Osabe. President: Rodney W. Ballard. Brewmaster: Takao Fujii.

The first joint venture sake brewing company in America. Rice comes from the Sacramento Valley. Sake is labeled Ozeki Sake.

P

PACHECO RANCH WINERY *Marin County*
5495 Redwood Hwy., Ignacio, CA 94947
(415) 456-4099 Founded: 1979
Owner: the Rowland family. Winemaker: Jamie Meves. Vineyard: 5-1/2 acres at the winery.

Winery on original Spanish land grant of Pacheco Rowland family. The only winery producing from grapes grown in Marin County.

Varietal, vintage-dated, estate bottled wine produced is Cabernet Rosé. Also varietal, vintage-dated Cabernet Sauvignon. Varietal, vintage-dated Chardonnay in 1983.

PAGE MILL WINERY ★ *Santa Clara County*
13686 Page Mill Road, Los Altos Hills, CA 94022
(415) 948-0958 Founded: 1976
Owners: Richard and Ome Stark. Winemaker: Richard Stark.

Grapes are purchased on a select vineyard basis. Label indicates vineyard and/or appellation. Varietal, vintage-dated wines produced are Cabernet Sauvignon, Zinfandel, Dry Chenin Blanc and Chardonnay.

['81 OC] (B) '79 Z; ['82 SJP] (B) '81 C, (C) (S) '82 CHD, (C) (B) '80 CA.

Paisano (*See* E. & J. Gallo.)

PALACE HILL RANCH—Zinfandel vineyard in Dry Creek Valley.

PALO CEDRO CELLARS *Shasta County*
1500 Deschutes Rd., Palo Cedro, CA 96073
(916) 574-4389 Founded: 1981

Palomino
(Aperitif wine) The varietal grape produces a Sherry that is rather dry. Dominant Sherry grape grown in Central Valley area.

Panache
Aperitif. (*See* Domaine Chandon.)

PAPAGNI VINEYARDS ★ *Madera County*
31754 Avenue 9, Madera, CA 93637
(209) 674-5652 Founded: 1973
Storage: Oak, stainless steel.
Owner: Angelo Papagni. Winemaker: John Daddino.

Founded by Demetrio Papagni who was a wine grape grower in Bari, Italy and came to California as a young man in 1912. In 1920, he planted his first 20 acres in the San Joaquin Valley. In the 1940's, Angelo planted vineyards in Madera County.

The varietal, vintage-dated, estate bottled wines produced are Chenin Blanc, Muscat Alexandria, Moscato D'Angelo, Late Harvest Emerald Riesling, Chardonnay, Fumé Blanc, Alicante Bouschet, Barbera, Zinfandel, Charbono, Chardonnay Au Naturel, Sparkling Chenin Blanc, Madera Rosé and Late Harvest Zinfandel.

Also produced are Bianca Di Madera (estate bottled), Spumante D'Angelo (estate bottled), Brut Champagne, Extra Dry Champagne, Madera Rosé (estate bottled), Finest Hour, Cream and Dry Sherry.

The winemaker's favorite wines are Alicante Bouschet, Sparkling Chenin Blanc and Chardonnay.

['81 OC] (B) '79 SB, (S) '79 SB; ['82 OC] (S) NV MC, (B) '79 CHA, (S) CHA; ['82 SJC] (B) '80 GER.

Paradise (*See* Bisceglia Bros.)

PARDUCCI WINE CELLARS ★ *Mendocino County*
501 Parducci Rd., Ukiah, CA 95482
(707) 462-3828 Founded: 1931
Storage: Oak, redwood, stainless steel.
Owner: The TMI Corp. Gen'l. Mgr. and Winemaster: John A. Parducci. Winemakers: Joe Monostori and Tom Monostori.

The vineyards are located in Ukiah. Four generations of Parducci's now work at the winery. 100% varietal, vintage-dated wines produced are Gamay Beaujolais, Zinfandel, Green Hungarian, Gewurztraminer, Barbera, Flora, Charbono, Carignane, Petite Sirah, Pinot Noir, Cabernet Sauvignon, Chenin Blanc, French Colombard, Mendocino Riesling, Chardonnay, Muscat Canelli, and Sauvignon Blanc. Also vintage Red, White and May Wine.

['81 OC] (S) '80 C, (S) '80 CH; ['82 OC] (B) '77, (B) '80 C, (S) '81 CH, (B) '81 GB, (B) '81 MC, (G) '78 PS, (S) '78 PS, (S) '81 C, (S) '81 G, (S) '81 JR, (S) '79 PN, (G) '81 SB, (S) '80 Z; ['82 SJP] (B) '80 C, (S) '81 CH, (P) (B) '78 PS.

PARSONS CREEK WINERY ★ *Mendocino County*
3001 S. State St., Ukiah, CA 95482
(707) 462-8900 Founded: 1979
Owners: Jesse Tidwell and Hal Doran. Winemaker: Jesse Tidwell.

Grapes are purchased on a select vineyard basis. Label indicates vineyard and/or appellation. Varietal, vintage-dated wines produced are Chardonnay, Johannisberg Riesling and Zinfandel.

['81 OC] (B) '80 C; ['82 OC] (S) '80 C, (S) '81 C, (S) '81 G, (S) '81 JR; ['82 SJP] (S) '81 SG.

MICHAEL T. PARSONS WINERY *Santa Cruz County*
170 Hidden Valley Road, Soquel, CA 95073
(408) 867-6070 Founded: 1976
Owner/Winemaker: Michael T. Parsons.
Vineyards located in Santa Cruz Mountains. Varietal, vintage-dated wines produced are Cabernet Sauvignon and Pinot Noir.

PASTORI WINERY *Sonoma County*
23189 Geyserville Ave., Cloverdale, CA 95425
(707) 857-3418 Founded: 1914

Owner: Frank Pastori. Vineyard: 60 acres.

PAT PAULSEN VINEYARDS ★ *Sonoma County*
25510 River Rd., Cloverdale, CA 95425
(707) 894-3197 Founded: 1970
Storage: Oak & Stainless Steel.
Owners: Jane & Pat Paulsen. Winemaker: T. James Meves. Vineyards: 40 acres.

The ranch was bought in 1970 and the vineyards were planted in 1970, 1973 and 1978. Winery was built in 1980. Label indicates vineyard and/or appellation.

Varietal, vintage-dated, estate bottled wines produced are Sauvignon Blanc, Cabernet Sauvignon and Muscat Canelli (slightly dry style). First crush of Chardonnay in 1981.

['82 OC] (S) '81 MC; ['82 SJP] (S) '81 MC.

PEACOCK HILL (*See* Mark West Vineyards.)

PECK RANCH—Sauvignon Blanc vineyard in San Luis Obispo county.

ROBERT PECOTA WINERY ★ *Napa County*
3299 Bennett Lane, Calistoga, CA 94515
(707) 942-6625 Founded: 1978
Storage: Oak, stainless steel.
Owner, Winemaker: Robert Pecota.

40 acre vineyard is at foot of Mt. St. Helena at the end of Napa Valley. Varietal, vintage-dated, estate bottled wines produced are Cabernet Sauvignon, Colombard, Sauvignon Blanc and Gamay Beaujolais.

['82 OC] (S) '81 GB.

PEDRIZZETTI WINERY ★ *Santa Clara County*
1645 San Pedro Ave., Morgan Hill, CA 95037
(408) 779-7389 Founded: 1938
Storage: Redwood, stainless steel.
Owners: Ed and Phyllis Pedrizzetti. Winemaker/Manager: Ed Pedrizzetti.

Grapes are purchased on a select vineyard basis. The winery is now operated by three generations of the family. Label indicates vineyard and/or appellation. Varietal, vintage-dated wines produced.

['81 OC] (B) '77 PS; ['82 OC] (B) '77 PS; ['82 SJP] (B) '77 PS, (P) (S) '81 ZR.

PEDRO XIMINEZ
(Dessert Wine) A varietal grape; produces a sweet dessert Sherry. Limited plantings in Central San Joaquin Valley.

J. PEDRONCELLI WINERY ★ *Sonoma County*
1220 Canyon Road, Geyserville, CA 95441
(707) 857-3531 Founded: 1904
Storage: Stainless steel, oak and redwood.
Owners: John and James Pedroncelli. Winemaker: John Pedroncelli.

The winery was acquired by John Sr. in 1927. It is now owned and operated by his sons. The 135 acre vineyards are located at the winery and in Dry Creek Valley. Grapes are also purchased on a select vineyard basis. Label indicates vineyard and/or appellation.

100% varietal, vintage-dated wines produced are Zinfandel Rosé, Gamay Beaujolais, Zinfandel, Cabernet Sauvignon, Johannisberg Riesling, Gewurztraminer, Sauvignon Blanc, Chenin Blanc, French Colombard, Chardonnay, and Pinot Noir. Three jug wines, Sonoma Red, Sonoma Rosé, and Sonoma White are produced.

['81 OC] (B) '78 CA, (G) '80 CH, (B) '77 PN, (S) '77 Z, (G) '78 Z; ['82 OC] (B) '78 CA, (S) '79 CA, (B) '80 C, (S) '81 G, (G) '79 PN, (B) '80 SB, (B) '79 Z; ['82 SJP] (B) '81 SB, (P) (B) '81 SG, (P) (B) '77 Z, (P) (S) '81 ZR.

PELLEGRINI BROS. WINERY ★ *Sonoma County*
4055 West Olivet Rd., Santa Rosa, CA 95401
(415) 761-2811 Founded: 1934
Owner: Pellegrini Brothers Wines Inc. Winemaker: Bob Fredson. Vineyard: 90 acres in Sonoma.

Label indicates vineyard and/or appellation. Produces a unique "Clos du Merle." A field blend of Zinfandel, Petite Sirah, Cabernet Sauvignon and Gamay. Varietal wines produced are Cabernet Sauvignon, Chenin Blanc, Chardonnay, French Colombard, Fumé Blanc, and Zinfandel. Also produces La Collina, Russian River Red, Dry Red, White and Rosé.

['82 SJC] (S) '79 CA.

PENDLETON WINERY ★ *Santa Clara County*
499 Aldo Avenue, Santa Clara, CA 95050
(408) 280-1300 Founded: 1977 as Arroyo Wines
Owners: R. Brian Pendleton, Mary Ann Anderson, Scott & Kathi McGraw. Winemaker: R. Brian Pendleton.

Grapes are purchased on a select vineyard basis. Label indicates vineyard and/or appellation. Varietal, vintage-dated wines produced are Johannisberg Riesling, Chardonnay, Zinfandel, Select Harvest Johannisberg Riesling, Sauvignon Blanc, Dry Chenin Blanc, Pinot Noir and Cabernet Sauvignon.

['81 OC] (B) '78 CA; ['82 OC] (G) PN; ['82 SJC] (B) '80 C, (P&C) (S&B) '79 CA.

ROBERT PEPI WINERY *Napa County*
P.O. Box 421, Oakville, CA 94562
(707) 944-2807 Founded: 1981
Gen. Partners: Robert A. & Robert L. Pepi

Predominantly a Sauvignon Blanc Winery. Produce small amounts of Chardonnay and Cabernet Sauvignon.

PERELLI-MINETTI WINERY ★ *Kern County*
Pond Road & Hwy. 99, Delano, CA 93216
(805) 792-3162 Founded: 1933
Owner: the Perelli-Minetti family (also known as California Wine Association).

The vineyards are located at the winery and were planted by Antonio Perelli-Minetti, who was active in the winery until he was 94 years old. He was known for his viticultural expertise.

Label indicates vineyard and/or appellation. The Perelli-Minetti label varietal, vintage-dated wines are Cabernet Sauvignon, Zinfandel, Fumé Blanc, Chardonnay and Johannsiberg Riesling.

Under the Guasti Ambassador and Greystone labels are vintage-dated, varietal Cabernet Sauvignon, Zinfandel, Colombard Rosé, Chenin Blanc and French Colombard.

Vintage-dated Generic wines are Burgundy, Vin Rosé, Chablis, Sauterne, Rhine, Brut, Extra Dry and Pink Champagne, Cold Duck and Spumante. Also produced are Vermouth, A. R. Morrow Brandy, and Marsala.

['81 OC] (G) '74 PN.

PESENTI WINERY *San Luis Obispo County*

2900 Vineyard Drive, Templeton, CA 93465

(805) 434-1030 Founded: 1934

Owner: the Pesenti family and Nerelli family. Winemaker: Frank Nerelli.

The vineyard was first planted in 1923. The winery was founded in 1934 by Frank Pesenti.

Varietal wines produced are Zinfandel, Zinfandel Blanc, Rosé of Ruby Cabernet, Ruby Cabernet, Zinfandel Rosé and Cabernet Sauvignon Blanc.

The winemaker's favorite wines are Zinfandel and Zinfandel Blanc.

PETALUMA CELLARS (*See* La Crema Vinera.)

Petillant

Slightly sparkling.

Petite Sirah

(Red Table Wine) A varietal grape that produces a dry, full-bodied, tannic wine. Believed to originate in the Middle East as the shiraz grape prior to being planted in France. The California Sirah is more of the French Duriff and is not the same as the famous Rhone Valley grape. Ages well. Excellent for big and well seasoned meals.

Award wines to look for: Bargetto, Bel Arbres, Beringer, Brookside, David Bruce, Burgess, Cambiaso, Caymus, Cilurzo, Concannon, R. & J. Cook, Cresta Blanca, Delicato, Dry Creek, East-Side, Estrella River, Fenestra, Fetzer, Fieldstone, Foppiano, Fortino, Freemark Abbey, Gemello, Geyser Peak, Giumarra, Guglielmo, Hecker Pass, Hop Kiln, Hultgren-Samperton, Inglenook, Turgeon & Lohr, Paul Masson, McDowell Valley, Mirassou, Parducci, Pedrizzetti, Ranchita Oaks, Rosenblum, Roudon-Smith, Round Hill, Setrakian, Sonoma, Sotoyome, Souverain, Stags' Leap, Topolos, Trentadue, Veedercrest, Ventana, Vache, Villa Armando, Walker Wines, Wente Brothers, Woodbury.

Petri (*See* Heublein.)

JOSEPH PHELPS VINEYARDS ★ *Napa County*

200 Taplin Road, St. Helena, CA 94574

(707) 963-2745 Founded: 1973

Storage: French and German oak.

Owner: Joseph F. Phelps. Winemaker: Walter Schug.

The 175 acre vineyard is located at the winery. Grapes are also purchased on a select vineyard basis. Label indicates vineyard and/or appellation.

Varietal, vintage-dated wines produced under the "Joseph Phelps Vineyard" label are Chardonnay, Sauvignon Blanc, Gewurztraminer, Johannisberg Riesling (Early Harvest, Late Harvest, Selected Late Harvest), Cabernet Sauvignon, Pinot Noir, Sirah, Zinfandel, Scheurebe, Vin Blanc, and Insignia (blend of Cabernet Sauvignon, Merlot and Cabernet Franc).

['81 OC] (S) '79 G, (S) '79 SB, (S) '79 WR; ['82 OC] (S) '78 CA, (B) '80 G.

Phenols (*See* Tannin.)

PICKLE CANYON VINEYARD

Mt. Veeder Road, Napa, CA 94558

PICONI WINERY LTD. *Riverside County*

33410 Rancho California Rd., Temecula, CA 92390

(714) 676-5400 Founded: 1981

Owner: Dr. John R. Piconi & Family. Winemaker: Dr. J. Piconi.

The five acre vineyard is located at the winery. Grapes are also purchased on a selected vineyard basis. Label indicates wines that are estate bottled, vineyard and/or appellation.

Varietal, vintage-dated wines produced are Petite Sirah, Cabernet Sauvignon, Chardonnay, Sauvignon Blanc and Chenin Blanc.

PIEDMONT CELLARS *Alameda County*

468 66th Street, Oakland, CA 94609

(415) 654-5549 Founded: 1981

PINE RIDGE ★ *Napa County*

5901 Silverado Trail, Napa, CA 94558

(707) 253-7500 Founded: 1978

Storage: Stainless steel and oak.

Owners: Gary Andrus and Mike Klassen. Winemaker: Gary Andrus.

A 51 acre vineyard is located at the winery. 30 acres in Carneros, 7 acres in Rutherford, 6 acres in Stags' Leap, and 10 acres in the Oak Knoll. Grapes are also purchased on a select vineyard basis. 100% varietal, vintage dated wines produced are Cabernet Sauvignon, Chenin Blanc, Chardonnay and Merlot.

['81 OC] (B) '78 CA; ['82 OC] (S) '79 CA; ['82 SJP] (S) '81 SG, (A&C) (B&B) '79 CA.

Pink Champagne

Pinot Noir or another dark-skinned grape is used to make the base wine. The pink color results from letting the juice remain with the grape skins during fermentation until the desired hue is obtained.

Pinot Blanc

(White Table Wine) A varietal grape that produces a light, dry, medium-bodied, moderately tart wine with a pronounced grape flavor and aroma. The better ones are rich and full and age well for 2-3 years.

Award wines to look for: Congress Springs, Fetzer, Iron Horse, Jekel, Mirassou, Monterey, Monterey Peninsula, Novitiate, Turgeon & Lohr, Ventana, Wente Bros., Whitehall Lane.

Pinot Chardonnay (*See* Chardonnay.)

Pineau de la Loire

(Christian Brothers Special Chenin Blanc.)

Pinot Noir

(Red Table Wine) A varietal grape that produces clear, brilliant medium to deep red color. Rich, with just a hint of violets, velvety and full of flavor. Originally from France where it is used in all of the great red Burgundies:

Beaune, Pommard and Cote D'Or. Serve with beef, lamb, fowl, veal and egg dishes. Also with fruit, nuts and cheese; Brie, Cheddar, Munster. Age 3-7 years.

Award wines to look for: Alatera, Bacigalupi, Belvedere, Beringer, Berkeley, Bonny Doon, David Bruce, Buena Vista, Burgess, Davis Bynum Calera, Richard Carey, Carmel Bay, Caymus, Chateau Chevalier, Christian Brothers, Clos du Bois, Cresta Blanca, Dehlinger, DeLoach, Domaine Laurier, Edmeades, Felton-Empire, Fenton Acres, Fetzer, Firestone, Foppiano, Fortino, Frick, Geyser Peak, Giumarra, Gundlach-Bundschu, Hacienda, Hoffman Mt. Ranch (HMR), Husch, Inglenook, Iron Horse, Jekel, Johnson's, Kenwood, Kirigin, LaCreama Vinera, Lawrence, Lazy Creek, Louis Martini, Mill Creek, Mirassou, Robert Mondavi, Monterey, Monterey Peninsula, J. W. Morris, Mount Eden, Navarro, North Coast Cellars, Parducci, J. Pedroncelli, Pendleton, Perelli-Minetti, Pope Valley, Martin Ray, Raymond, Round Hill, Rutherford Hill, Santa Cruz Mountain, Sebastiani, Smith-Madrone, Sonoma, Souverain, Stony Ridge, Sunrise, Topolos, Trefethen, Tulocay, Turgeon & Lohr, Valley of the Moon, Veedercrest, Ventana, Villa Mt. Eden, Weibel, Whitehall Lane, York Mountain, Zaca Mesa, ZD.

Pinot Noir Blanc

White wine made from Pinot Noir grapes by removing juice from skins immediately after grapes are crushed.

Pinot St. George

(Red Dinner Wine) A varietal grape that produces a robust, earthy, fruity wine similar to the California Gamay. A good accompaniment to red meats. Relatively rare.

Award wines to look for: Almaden, Brookside, ENZ (late harvest), J. Filippi, Giumarra (late harvest), Monterey Peninsula.

PIPER-SONOMA *Sonoma County*

P.O. Box K, Windsor, CA 95492

(707) 433-3090 Founded: 1980

Owners: Piper-Heidsieck Sonoma vineyrds (French based), and Renfield Importers. Winemakers: Rodney D. Strong of Sonoma and Michel La Criox, Piper-Heidsieck's winemaster.

Joint venture founded 1980 to produce French style premium champagne in Sonoma County.

Varietal, vintage-dated, bottle fermented (Methode-Champanoise) sparkling wines produced will be Brut, Blanc de Noir and a Tete de Cuveé.

PIRRONE WINE CELLARS *Stanislaus County*

Pirrone Road, Salida, CA 95368

(209) 545-0704 Founded: 1936

Owner: Alfred F. Pirrone. Vineyards: 425 acres.

POINT LOMA WINERY *San Diego County*

3655 Poe St., San Diego, CA 92106

(714) 224-1674 Founded: 1980

Storage: Stainless steel.

Owners/Winemakers: Ron McClendon & Kurt Mengel. Vineyard: 4 acres experimental in Ramona.

Grapes are purchased on a select vineyard basis. Label indicates vineyard and/or appellation.

Varietal, vintage-dated wines produced are Gamay Beaujolais Cabernet Sauvignon, Sauvignon Blanc and White Gamay.

Pomace

The pulp, skins and seeds of grapes remaining after the juice or newly fermented wine has been drawn off or pressed out.

POMMERAIE VINEYARDS ★ *Sonoma County*

10541 Cherry Ridge Road, Sebastopol, CA 95472
(707) 823-9463 Founded: 1979
Storage: American & French oak, stainless steel.
Owners: Ken & Arlene Dalton and Bob & Norma Wiltermood. Winemaker: Ken Dalton.

5 acre vineyard is at the winery. 100% varietal, vintage-dated wines produced are Cabernet Sauvignon and Chardonnay.

['82 OC] (B) '79 CA.

POPE VALLEY WINERY ★ *Napa County*

6613 Pope Valley Road, Pope Valley, CA 94567
(707) 965-2192 Founded: 1972
Owner: the James M. Devitt family. Winemaker: Steve Devitt.

Ed Haus, a German Blacksmith, built what was known as the "Burgundy Winery." When the Devitts purchased the property in 1972, it needed total restoration and they have been successful at retaining the natural beauty of the winery. Grapes are purchased on a select vineyard basis. Label indicates vineyard appellation.

Varietal, vintage-dated wines produced are Chardonnay, Sauvignon Blanc, Cabernet Sauvignon, Zinfandel and Pinot Noir.

The winemaker's favorite wines are Chardonnay, Cabernet Sauvignon and Zinfandel.

['81 OC] (G) '80 SB, (G) '78 Z.

PHILIP POSSON (*See* Sierra Wine Co.)

Poplar Vineyards (*See* Bouchaine.)

Port

Port is a fortified, rich, fruity, heavy bodied, sweet wine, usually deep red. However, there is a lighter-colored, lighter-bodied Port called Tawny Port, and also a white Port which is straw colored. Port originated in Portugal. Many grape varieties can be used in making Port, including Carignane, Petite Sirah, Tinta Cao, Tinta Madeira and Zinfandel. Port is not baked (as Madera and some Sherries), influenced by yeast (as 'Flor' Sherry) nor flavored as Marsala. The alcohol content is usually 18-21%.

Award wines to look for: Almaden, Barengo, Bargetto, Beringer, Berkeley, Brookside, Buena Vista, Richard Carey, Channing Rudd, Christian Brothers, East-Side, Ferrara, Fetzer, Ficklin, J. Filippi, Kosrof, Charles LeFranc, Llords & Elwood, Louis Martini, Paul Masson, R. W. Morris, Novitiate, Papagni, Perelli-Minetti, Quady, Richert & Sons, Sebastiani, Shenandoah, Sonoma/Windsor, Sunrise, Verdugo, Woodbury.

Port Tinta Wine
A varietal fortified Port produced from Tinta Madeira grapes.

POTTER VALLEY (*See* California Wine Co.)

POUR LE GOURMET (*See* Louis Cherpin Winery.)

Pourriture Noble
A state overripeness which concentrates the sugar content of grapes (*see* Botrytis).

PRAGER WINERY & PORT WORKS *Napa County*
1281 Lowelling Lane, St. Helena, CA 94574
(707) 963-3720 Founded: 1979
Storage: Oak, stainless steel.
Owners: Jim and Imogene Prager. Winemaker: Jim Prager.

Grapes are purchased on a selected vineyard basis. Varietal, vintage-dated wines produced are Cabernet Sauvignon, Chardonnay and Zinfandel. Also produced is 100% Cabernet Sauvignon Port.

PRESTIGE VINEYARDS
9355 El Cajon Bl., Ste. 2B, La Mesa, CA 92041

PRESTON VINEYARDS ★ *Sonoma County*
9282 West Dry Creek Road, Healdsburg, CA 95448
(707) 433-3977 Founded: 1975
Storage: French & American oak, stainless steel.
Owner, Winemaker: Louis D. Preston.

The 120 acre vineyards are in Dry Creek Valley. Varietal, vintage-dated, estate bottled wines produced are Sauvignon Blanc, Zinfandel, Dry Chenin Blanc, and Cabernet Sauvignon. Also Red Table Wine.

['81 OC] (B) '80 CH, (B) '78 Z; ['82 OC] (S) '81 GA; ['82 SJP] (B) '81 TB, (P) (B) '81 GA, (S) '80 C.

PRIDE OF CALIFORNIA (*See* California Wine Co.)

PRIVATE CELLAR STOCK (*See* James Frasinetti's & sons.)

Purchasing Wine—Store or Restaurant
The following are pointers to look for in a store or restaurant:

Name of producer.

Special labeling—indicating limited bottling, cask number, special reserve, etc.

Geographic origin—North Coast, Napa, Sonoma, etc. (Keep in mind that to indicate this 75% of the grapes must come from that region.)

Vintage—to indicate a date means that 95% of the wine must be harvested and fermented in the year shown.

Estate bottled—the grapes were grown and crushed on the estate of the winery and it was also bottled at the winery.

Q

QUADY WINERY ★ *Madera County*
13181 Road 24, Madera, CA 93637
(209) 673-8608 Founded: 1977
Storage: American & French oak, stainless steel.

Owner, Winemaker: Andrew Quady.

Label indicates vineyard and/or appellation. The wines produced are Zinfandel Port, Vintage Port, Essensia (a dessert wine) and Zinfandel Ports in various types.

['81 OC] (G) '78 VP, (S) '78 P, (S) '77 VP; ['82 SJP] (S) '79 VP, (B) '78 VP, (S) Lot 2 VP '78, (P) (S) '81 Essensia.

QUAIL RIDGE *Napa County*
1055 Atlas Peak Rd., Napa, CA 94558
(707) 944-8128 Founded: 1978
Owner/Winemaker: Elaine Wellesley. Gen'l. Mgr./Co-winemaker: Leon Santoro.

20 acre vineyard is located at 3230 Mt. Veeder Rd. Varietal, vintage-dated wines produced are Chardonnay and French Colombard. Label indicates vineyard and/or appellation.

QUERCUS VINEYARD—Cabernet Sauvignon vineyard in Lake County.

R

Racking
The drawing of wine from a storage cask into a fresh cask.

A. RAFANELLI *Sonoma County*
4685 West Dry Creek Road, Healdsburg, CA 95448
(707) 433-1385 Founded: 1974
Owner, Winemaker: Americo Rafanelli.

Vineyard is in Dry Creek Valley. Varietal, vintage-dated, estate bottled wines produced are Zinfandel and Gamay Beaujolais.

RANCHITA OAKS WINERY, INC. ★ *San Luis Obispo County*
Box 4790, Estrella Rt., San Miguel, CA 93451
(805) 467-3422 Founded: 1979
Storage: French and American oak.
Owners: Ron and Mae Bergstrom.

The 46 acre vineyard is in the foothills. Estate bottled wines are labeled Bergstrom Vineyards. 100% varietal wines produced are Cabernet Sauvignon, Petite Sirah, Chardonnay and Zinfandel.

['81 OC] (S) '79 PS, (G) '79 Z; ['82 SJP&C] (B&B) '79 CA.

RANCHO DE PHILO *San Bernardino County*
10050 Wilson Ave., Alta Loma, CA 91701
(714) 987-4208 Founded: 1975
Storage: Oak, stainless steel, redwood.
Owner, Winemaker: Philo Biane.

Wine produced is Cream Sherry.

RANCHO DOS AMIGOS—Barbera vineyard in San Luis Obispo County.

RANCHO SISQUOC WINERY *Santa Barbara County*
Rt. 1, Box 147, Santa Maria, CA 93454
(805) 937-3616 Founded: 1977
Storage: Oak and stainless steel.
Owner: Flood Ranch Co. Winemaker: Harold Pfeiffer.

The 200 acre vineyard is in the Santa Maria Valley.

The varietal, vintage-dated, estate bottled wines produced are Franken Riesling, Johannisberg Riesling, Merlot, Cabernet Sauvignon, Sauvignon Blanc, Chardonnay and Cabernet Sauvignon Blanc.

RANCHO TEMECULA (*See* Mt. Palomar Winery.)

RANCHO YERBA BUENA (*See* Papagni Vineyards.)
['81 OC] (G) '78 CA.

RAPAZZINI WINERY *Santa Clara County*
P.O. Box 247, Gilroy, CA 95020
(408) 842-5649 Founded: 1962
Storage: Oak, stainless steel.
Owners/Winemakers: Jon P. Rapazzini and Sandra K. Rapazzini.

Co-owners and winemakers, Jon and Sandra represent 37 years of winemaking in Santa Clara Valley. Their original historical winery burned to the ground in October 1980, however, they have spent two years building the all new modern Rapazzini Winery and tasting room. Feature a wide range of wines from varietal, specialty, fruit wines, dessert wines and champagnes.

RAVENSWOOD *Sonoma County*
2145 Broadway, Sonoma, CA 95476
(707) 938-1960 Founded: 1976
Storage: French oak.
Owners: Joel E. Peterson & W. Reed Foster. Winemaker: Joel Peterson.

Grapes are purchased on a select vineyard basis. Label indicates vineyard and/or appellation.

Varietal, vintage-dated wines produced are Zinfandel and Cabernet Sauvignon.

RAYMOND VINEYARD & CELLAR ★ *Napa County*
849 Zinfandel Lane, St. Helena, CA 94574
(707) 963-3141 Founded: 1974
Storage: Oak, stainless steel.
Owners: Roy Raymond Jr. & Sr. and Walter Raymond. Winemaker: Walter Raymond.

The family has been involved in viticulture since the 1870's. The 90 acre vineyard is in the Napa Valley. Varietal, vintage-dated, estate bottled wines produced are Napa Valley Cabernet Sauvignon, Zinfandel, Chardonnay, Johannisberg Riesling, and Chenin Blanc.

['81 OC] (S) '78 CA, (S) '78 PN, (G) '80 WR, (G) '78 Z; ['82 OC] (B) '79 CA, (G) '80 CH, (B) '81 JR, (G) '79 Z, (G) '80 C; ['82 SJP] (S) '80 C, (C) (S) '81 SJR, (P&C) (B&B) '79 CA.

Red Pinot (*See* Pinot St. George.)

Red Rock Terrace (*See* Diamond Creek Vineyards.)

Red Table Wines

Dinner or table wines are usually dry, suited to accompany main course dishes. Dry means most or all of the grape sugar was fermented out, and thus the opposite of dry is sweet. Most red dinner wines are dry. Some red dinner wines are soft and mellow (i.e., slightly sweet) while others impart a robust astringence which results from tannin, the same substance that in tea makes your mouth slightly puckery. Most red dinner wines fall into two general types. Burgundy and Claret. There are also some semi-sweet red dinner wines sometimes known as "mellow red wines" or Vino Rossos. Alcochol content is from 10.5 to 14 percent, usually about 12 percent by volume. Red Dinner Wines—Generic: Burgundy, Claret, Chianti, Vino Rosso. Red Table Wines—Varietal: Barbera, Cabernet Franc, Cabernet Sauvignon, Charbono, Gamay (Napa Gamay), Gamay Beaujolais, Grenache, Grignolino, Merlot, Petite Sirah, Pinot Noir, Pinot Red (Pinot St. George), Ruby Cabernet, Zinfandel.

Award wines to look for: Barengo, Boeger, Brookside, CC Vineyards, Clos du Bois, Colony, R & J Cook, Diamond Oaks, Domaine Laurier, Estrella, Giumarra, Hecker Pass, Hop Kiln, Inglenook, Novitiate, Perelli-Minetti, River Oaks, San Antonio, Souverain, Veedercrest, Villa Armando, Zaca Mesa. Also look for dry Red Table Wines: Brookside, R & J Cook, Fortino, Hop Kiln, Inglenook, Monterey Peninsula, Newland, Pellegrini, Joseph Phelps, Sonoma, Turgeon & Lohr.

REDWOOD VALLEY CELLARS (*See* Weibel Champagne Vineyards.)

RENAISSANCE VINEYARD AND WINERY *Yuba County*
P.O. Box 1000, Renaissance, CA 95962
(916) 692-2222 Founded: 1978
President: Karl Werner. Vineyards: 370 acres.

RHINE WINE
A white dinner or table wine, thoroughly dry, pleasantly tart, pale golden or slightly green gold in color. Medium bodied, fresh and fruity. Good with white meats and seafood.

Award wines to look for: Geyser Peak, Gibson, Giumarra.

RICHARDSON VINEYARDS *Sonoma County*
2711 Knob Hill Rd., Sonoma, CA 95476

RICHERT CELLARS *Santa Cruz County*
P.O. Box 1049, Soquel, CA 95073
(408) 475-1670 Founded: 1954
Storage: Oak.
Owners: Richert and Sons, Inc. Winemaker: Kelly Richert.

Grapes are purchased on a select vineyard basis. Wines produced are table, dessert, fruit and berry wines.

RICHERT & SONS WINERY ★ *Santa Clara County*
18980 Monterey Road, Morgan Hill, CA 95037
(408) 779-5100 Founded in 1954 by Walter F. Richert
Winemaker: Scott Richert.

Wines produced are primarily Sherry and Port. Recently has begun producing Alexander Valley Cabernet Sauvignon and Triple Cream Sherry.

['81 OC] (S) '67 VP, (B) NV TP; ['82 SJP&C] (B&B) '68 SHD, (P&C) (S&G) Triple Cream SH.

RIDGECREST (*See* Giumarra Vineyards.)

RIDGE VINEYARDS ★ *Santa Clara County*
17100 Monte Bello Road, P.O. Box AI, Cupertino, CA 95015
(408) 867-3233 Founded: 1962

Storage: Oak.
Owners: the Bennions, Cranes, Rosens, Paul Draper and others. Winemaker: Paul Draper.

The 50 acre vineyard is on the Monte Bello Ridge of the Santa Cruz Mountains. Grapes are also purchased on a select vineyard basis. Label indicates vineyards and/or appellation. Varietal wines produced are Petite Sirah, Zinfandel, and Cabernet Sauvignon.

The winemaker's favorites are the Cabernet Sauvignons from the estate vineyards at Monte Bello.

['81 OC] (S) '78 CA, (B) '79 Z, (B) '78 Z.

Riesling

Award wines to look for: Alexander, Almaden, Ballard Canyon, Balverne, Bargetto, Bel Arbres, Beringer, Berkeley, Boeger, Brookside, Buena Vista, Chateau St. Jean, Christian Brothers, Clos du Bois, Concannon, Conn Creek, Durney, Edmeades, Estrella River, Felton-Empire, Fetzer, Fieldstone, Firestone, Flora Springs, Franciscan, Freemark Abbey, Gallo, Geyser Peak, Greenwood Ridge, Gundlach-Bundschu, Hacienda, Haywood, Herrera, Hoffman Mt. Ranch (HMR), Hop Kiln, Jekel, Johnson's, Kenwood, Konocti, Charles Krug, Llords & Elwood, Long, Lost Hills, Madrona, Markham, Paul Masson, Milano, Mirassou, Robert Mondavi, Monterey, Monterey Peninsula, Mount Palomar, Napa Creek, Navarro, North Coast, Obester, Parson's Creek, Perelli-Minetti, Joseph Phelps, Potter Valley, Raymond, River Oaks, Round Hill, Rutherford, Rutherford Hill, San Antonio-Maddalena, San Martin, Santa Ynez Valley, Sarah's Vineyard, Shown & Sons, Smothers, Sonoma, Souverain, St. Francis, Stony Ridge, Sycamore Creek, Taylor California, Trefethen, Turgeon & Lohr, Vache, Veedercrest, Vega, Ventana, Villa Armando, Weibel, Wente Bros., Zaca Creek, Zaca Mesa.

Ripe

The term used to describe a wine which has attained maturity, mellowness, perfection. When the term "ripe for bottling," is used, it means the wine has improved in the cask to the highest point possible.

Ripple (*See* E. & J. Gallo.)

RITCHIE CREEK VINEYARDS *Napa County*

4024 Spring Mountain Road, St. Helena, CA 94574
(707) 963-4661 Founded: 1974
Owner/Winemaker: R. P. Minor

The 8 acres that are currently planted are in the Napa Valley, Spring Mountain District at the 2000 ft. elevation.

Label indicates vineyard and/or appellation. Varietal, vintage-dated wines produced are Cabernet Sauvignon and Chardonnay.

RIVER EAST VINEYARD

Owner: Sonoma Vineyards.

Johannisberg Riesling vineyard near Healdsburg.

RIVER OAKS VINEYARDS ★ *Sonoma County*

Lytton Station Road, Healdsburg, CA 95448
(415) 456-7310 Founded: 1964
Storage: American oak, stainless steel.

Owner: River Oaks Vineyard Corp. Winery Mgr.: Tom Hobart.

The vineyards are located in Alexander Valley. Varietal, vintage-dated, estate bottled wines produced are Chardonnay, Zinfandel, Pinot Noir, Pinot Noir Blanc, Gamay Beaujolais, Johannisberg Riesling, Gewurztraminer and Cabernet Sauvignon. Also produced are Soft Zinfandel (an aperitif wine), Zinfandel Rosé, Pinot Noir Rosé, Premium White Table Wine (Johannisberg Riesling, Gewurztraminer, French Colombard and Sauvignon Vert), Premium Dry White, Premium Red Table Wine, and Premium Rosé Table Wine. Both table wines produced from Alexander Valley Vineyards. Also produced are French Colombard, Zinfandel Dinner and Cabernet Sauvignon Blanc.

['82 OC] (B) '79 CA, (B) '81 C, (S) '80 G; ['82 SJP&C] (S&S) '80 G, (B) '81 TB.

RIVER ROAD VINEYARDS ★ *Sonoma County*
7145 River Road, Forestville, CA 95436
(707) 887-7890 Founded: 1979
Owner/Winemaker: Gary Mills. Vineyards: 70 acres in Forestville. 45 acres in Alexander Valley and Russian River Valley.

Varietal, vintage-dated wines produced are Chardonnay, Johannisberg Riesling, Fumé Blanc and Zinfandel.

['82 SJP] (B) '80 C.

RIVER RUN VINTNERS *Santa Cruz County*
65 Rogge Lane, Watsonville, CA 95076
(408) 726-3112 Founded: 1978
Owner: Kristine Arneson. Winemaker: J. P. Pawloski.

Grapes are purchased on a select vineyard basis. Label indicates vineyard and/or appellation. Wines produced are Chardonnay, Cabernet Sauvignon, Zinfandel and Petite Sirah.

The winemaker's favorites are '82 "Ventana Vineyards" Chardonnay and '80 "Shardon Valley Vineyards" Cabernet Sauvignon.

RIVERSIDE COUNTY
Southern California.

RIVERSIDE FARM (*See* Foppiano.)

RMS CELLARS (*See* Pacheco Ranch.)

RODDIS CELLARS *Napa County*
1510 Diamond Mtn. Rd., Calistoga, CA 94515
(707) 942-5868 Founded: 1979
Owner, Winemaker: William H. Roddis.

The vineyard is on Diamond Mountain in Napa. Only wine produced is varietal, vintage-dated, estate bottled Cabernet Sauvignon.

ROLLING HILLS VINEYARDS *Ventura County*
167 Aviador, Camarillo, CA 93010
(805) 495-7275 Founded: 1981
Storage: Oak & stainless steel.
Owner: the Pragor family. Winemaker: Edward Pragor.
Vineyards: 5acres at Rancho California.

Grapes are also purchased on a select vineyard basis. Label indicates vineyard and/or appellation.

Varietal, vintage-dated wines produced are: Cabernet Sauvignon, Zinfandel, Merlot, Chardonnay and White Riesling. First release in 1982 the '81 White Riesling.

RIVERSIDE, SAN BERNARDINO, SAN DIEGO

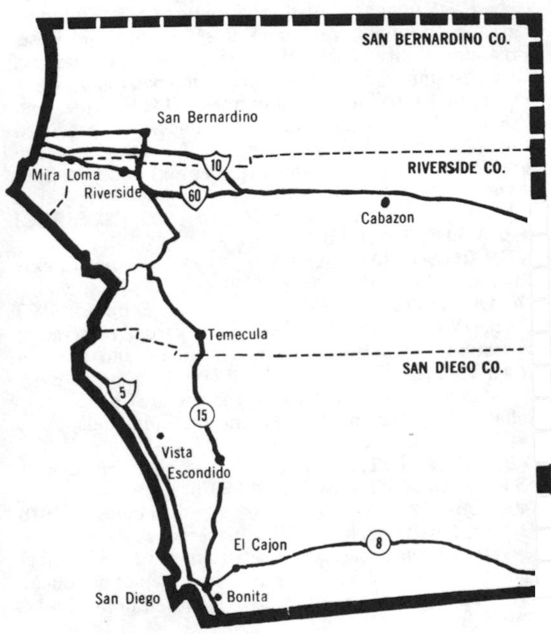

Roma (*See* Guild Wineries.)

Room Temperature

The temperature at which red wines are usually served, between 60 degrees and 65 degrees F. Older and great wines are better at room temperature. Other red wines (particularly young ones) are often preferred slightly cool. Wine is never brought to room temperature by abrupt "warming," which would spoil it, but it is left to stand for a few hours before serving. There are other opinions which indicate that half an hour is sufficient.

Rosa (*See* Sebastiani Vineyards.)

Rosé

A pink dinner wine, sometimes called a luncheon wine. Rosés range from dry to slightly sweet and are usually fruity-flavored light-bodied and made from Cabernet, Gamay, Grenache, Grignolino or Zinfandel grapes. Alcohol content is 10 to 14 percent, usually about 12 percent by volume. The pink or pale red color is obtained by removing the grape skins as soon as the required amount of color has been attained by the wine.

Rosé, Varietal table wines: Cabernet Sauvignon Rosé,

Gamay Rosé, Grenache Rosé, Grignolino Ro
Sirah Rosé, Pinot Noir Rosé, Zinfandel Rosé.

Award wines to look for: Baldinelli, Bargetto, Brookside, Buena Vista, Davis Bynum, Cambiaso, Ri Carey (sweet), Cilurzo, Concannon, R. & J. Cook, E Side, Estrella River, Fetzer, Fieldstone, Fortino (swee Giumarra, Hecker Pass, Inglenook, JFJ Bronco, Konoct Lawrence, Lejon, McDowell Valley, Robert Mondavi, Monterey, Papagni, Pedroncelli, Perelli-Minetti, Pesenti, San Martin, Sebastiani, Sonoma, Souverain, Taylor California, Turgeon & Lohr.

Rosé of Cabernet

Award wines to look for: Bargetto, Fieldstone, Firestone, Fortino, Geyser Peak, Llords & Elwood, Mill Creek, Pacheco Ranch, Ross-Kellerei, Santa Ynez Valley, Simi, Turner, Weibel.

Rosé of Pinot Noir

Award wines to look for: Brookside, Souverain.

Rosé of Gamay

Award wines to look for: Almaden, East-Side, Inglenook, San Pasqual, Sebastiani.

Rosé of Grenache

Award wines to look for: Brookside, Fortino, Franzia, Giumarra, McDowell Valley, Papagni.

Rosé of Petite Sirah

Award wines to look for: Bogle, Ventana.

Rosé of Zinfandel

Award wines to look for: Bargetto, Concannon, Konocti, Pedrizzetti, Pedroncelli, Santa Barbara.

ROSENBLUM CELLARS ★ *Alameda County*

1775 Sixteenth St., Oakland CA 94612

(415) 834-6067 Founded: 1978

Storage: Oak, stainless steel.

Owners: the Rosenblums and the Hanleys and Mike Sirna, Cindy Rice, Roger Rosenblum, Susan Rupert. Winemaker: Kent Rosenblum.

Grapes are purchased on a select vineyard basis. Label indicates vineyard and/or appellation.

Varietal, vintage-dated wines produced are Chardonnay, Johannisberg Riesling, White Zinfandel, Petite Sirah, Cabernet Sauvignon and Zinfandel.

The winemaker's favorite wine is Johannisberg Riesling.
['81 OC] (G) 79 Z; ['82 OC] (S) 80 PS.

DON CHARLES ROSS WINERY *Napa County*

Box 2502, 1721C Action Ave., Napa, CA 94558

(707) 255-9463 Founded: 1978

Owner, Winemaker: Don Charles Ross.

Grapes are purchased on select district basis. Label indicates vineyard and/or appellation. 100% varietal wines produced are Cabernet Sauvignon, Zinfandel, Chardonnay and Sauvignon Blanc (dry).

The winemaker's favorite wine is Sauvignon Blanc.

ROSS-KELLEREI WINERY *San Luis Obispo County*

895 Orchard Road, Nipomo, CA 93444

(805) 929-3928 Founded: 1980

Storage: Oak & stainless steel.

…: Howard & Jackie Tanner. Winemaker: Jim … Jr.

…e smallest winery in the Santa Ynez Valley where …se farms and vineyards are famous. The winery name …mes from the German: Ross (horse) and Keller (Cellar). …rapes are also purchased on a select vineyard basis. Label indicates vineyard and/or appellation.

Varietal, vintage-dated wines produced are Chardonnay, Cabernet Sauvignon, White Riesling, Pinot Noir Blanc, Pinot Noir and Johannsiberg Riesling.

CARLO ROSSI (*See* E. & J. Gallo.)

Rosso/Vino Rosso

Award wines to look for: Brookside, Christian Brothers, Pesenti, Rapazzini, Villa Armando.

Rotta(*See* Las Tablas Winery.)

ROUDON-SMITH VINEYARDS, INC. ★ *Santa Cruz County*

2364 Bean Creek Road, Santa Cruz, CA 95066
(408) 438-1244 Founded: 1972
Storage: French and American oak.
Owners: Robert & Anna Maria Roudon and James & June Smith. Winemaker: Robert Roudon.

Label indicates vineyard and/or appellation. Varietal, vintage-dated wines produced are Zinfandel, Chardonnay, Cabernet Sauvignon and Petite Sirah.

Favorite wine of winemaker is vintage Zinfandel.

['81 OC] (B) '78 CA; ['82 SJC] (B) '80 C, (P&C) (B&B) '79 CA.

ROUND HILL CELLARS ★ *Napa County*

1097 Lodi Lane, St. Helena, CA 94574
(707) 963-5251 Founded: 1977
Storage: Oak, stainless steel.
President: Charles A. Abela.

Grapes are purchased on a select vineyard basis. Label indicates vineyard and/or appellation. Varietal, vintage-dated wines produced are Chardonnay, Chenin Blanc, Johannisberg Riesling, Gewurztraminer, Cabernet Sauvignon, Pinot Noir, Zinfandel, Petite Sirah, Fumé Blanc, Gamay Beaujolais and Vin Rosé.

Also produced are Chablis and Burgundy.

['81 OC] (B) '78 CA, (G) '79 C; ['82 OC] (B) '81 GB, (B) '78 PS, (B) '79 Z; ['82 SJC] (S) '81 SJR, (P) (B) '79 CA, (P) (S) '79 Z.

Rounded

A wine with all the vinous elements well balanced.

ROWAN VINEYARDS—Chardonnay vineyard in Santa Barbara County near Santa Maria.

Royal Host (*See* East-Side Winery.)

Royalty

A varietal grape that was developed at University of California to grow in San Joaquin Valley as a base for Port-type wines.

RUBEDOUX WINERY *Riverside County*

3477 Arlington Avenue, Riverside, CA 92506
(714) 686-5771 Founded: 1976
Owners: Joe Tavaglione and Sons.

Ruby

A port of very deep-red color, usually quite yo opposed to one which has been aged for some ti wood and has become "tawny" which is pale in through repeated finings.

Ruby Cabernet

(Red Table Wine) A varietal grape developed by the University of California to grow under the warm conditions of the San Joaquin Valley. It is the child of the Cabernet Sauvignon and the Carignane. The wine is dry, a Cabernet-like aroma with good acidity and a fruity flavor. A red meat wine.

Award wines to look for: Barengo, Boeger, Edmeades, Fortino, Giumarra, Hecker Pass, LaMont, Montevina, Novitiate.

RUBY HILL (*See* Stony Ridge.)

CHANNING RUDD CELLARS *Lake County*

P.O. Box 426, Middletown, CA 95461
(415) 523-1544 Founded: 1976
Storage: Oak.
Owner, Winemaker: Channing Rudd.

The 56 acre property currently has 12 acres of land cleared for vineyard. Vineyard is Mt. St. Claire. Varietal, vintage-dated wines produced are Merlot and Cabernet Sauvignon.

RUSSIAN RIVER VINEYARDS (*See* Toplos at Russian River.)

RUTHERFORD CELLARS (*See* Rutherford Vintners.)

RUTHERFORD HILL WINERY ★ *Napa County*

Rutherford Hill Road, Rutherford, CA 94574
(707) 963-9694 Founded: 1976
Storage: Oak, stainless steel.
Managing Partners: William Jaeger and Charles Carpy.
Winemaker: Phil Baxter.

Over 700 acres of vineyards are located in Rutherford and St. Helena. The varietal, estate bottled, vintage-dated wines produced are Cabernet Sauvignon, Zinfandel, Merlot, Pinot Noir, Chardonnay, Johannisberg Riesling, Gewurztraminer, and Sauvignon Blanc.

['81 OC] (S) '79 G, (G) '78 CA, (G) '78 M, (S) '80 WR, (S) '77 Z; ['82 OC] (B) '78 CS, (B) '80 CH, (G) '79 M; ['82 SJP] (B) '80 C, (B&B) '80 G, (P) (B) '78 CA, (P) (B) '79 M.

RUTHERFORD RANCH BRAND ★ (*See* Round Hill Cellars.)

Rutherford Ranch is an exlusive label solely produced and marketed by Round Hill Cellars. Chardonnay, Sauvignon, Blanc, Zinfandel, and Cabernet Sauvignon are produced under this label.

['81 OC] (G) '78 Z, (G) '78 CA.

RUTHERFORD VINTNERS ★ *Napa County*

P.O. Box 238, Rutherford, CA 94573
1673 St. Helena Hwy. South, Rutherford, CA 94573
(707) 963-4117 Founded: 1977
Storage: American, Yugoslavian, German and French casks and barrels.
Owners: Bernard L. and Evelyn Skoda. Winemaker:

d L. Skoda.
ablished in 1976 after Skoda retired from Louis M. tini. The 30 acre vineyard is located at winery in pa Valley. Varietal, vintage-dated Napa Valley appellaon wines produced are Cabernet Sauvignon, Johannisberg Riesling, Merlot, Pinot Noir and Alexander Valley Chardonnay. A Special Reserve Cabernet Sauvignon is also produced under Chateau Rutherford label. Varietal, vintage Muscat of Alexandria is also produced.

The winemaker's favorite wines are Cabernet Sauvignon and Johannisberg Riesling.

['81 OC] (S) '80 JR; ['82 OC] (B) '78 CA, (G) '79 M, (B) '80 C; ['82 SJP&C] (B&S) '80 SJR, (P&C) (B&B) '78 CA.

S

SACRAMENTO COUNTY
Northern San Joaquin Valley.

SAGE CANYON WINERY *Napa County*
Box 458, Rutherford, CA 94573
(707) 963-1491
Owners: Gordon and Eugenia Millar. Wine Consultant: Charles Ortman.

Grapes are purchased on a select vineyard basis. Label indicates vineyard and/or appellation. Varietal, vintage-dated wine produced is Chenin Blanc.

SAN ANTONIO WINERY ★ *Los Angeles County*
737 Lamar St., Los Angeles, CA 90031
(213) 223-1401 Founded: 1917
Owner: the Riboli family.

In 1917 the winery was founded by Santo Cambianica. His first vines were planted near Lamar Street in Los Angeles and his first winery was an empty boxcar. Today there are no vineyards and only the winery remains. Classified as a Historical Landmark in 1963 and designated Cultural Historical Monument #42.

The founder's nephew Steve Riboli is president of the winery.

Grapes are purchased on a select vineyard basis. Varietal, vintage-dated wines are produced. Also generic wines.

['82 OC] (G) '81 CH, (S) '81 JR, (B) '81 SB.

SAN BENITO COUNTY
Central Coast—Inland.
Appellations: Paicines.

SAN BENITO VINEYARDS ★ *San Benito County*
251 Hillcrest Road, Hollister, CA 95023
(408) 637-4447 Founded: 1970
Storage: Redwood, stainless steel.
Owner: Dr. Rodney Ballard, Sandra and Robert Ballard.
Winemaker: Kirby Anderson.

Wines produced are pure fruit and berry—Apricot, Pomegranate, Pineapple Strawberry, Plum, Blackberry, Peach and Raspberry.

['82 SJP&C] 2 Awards, (S) NV Fruit.

SAN BERNARDINO COUNTY
Southern California.

SAN DIEGO COUNTY
Appellations: Rancho California and Temecula.

SANFORD AND BENEDICT *Santa Barbara County*
Santa Rosa Road, Lompoc, CA 93436
(805) 688-8314 Founded: 1970
Owner: Michael Benedict. Winemaker: Michael Benedict.
Vineyard: 110 acres at the winery.

Varietal, vintage-dated, estate bottled wines produced are Pinot Noir, Chardonnay and Cabernet Sauvignon.

SANFORD WINERY ★ *Santa Barbara County*
Office: 1730 Lasuen Road, Santa Barbara, CA 93103
(805) 966-5100
Owner/Winemaker: J. Richard Sanford.

Formerly one of the partners in the Sanford and Benedict Winery, Richard Sanford has started his own winery and will plant a vineyard in the Santa Ynez Valley. Grapes are purchased on a selected vineyard basis. Label indicates vineyard and/or appellation.

Varietal, vintage-dated wines produced are Chardonnay, Sauvignon Blanc, Pinot Noir and Pinot Noir Vin Gris (light Pinot Noir).

['82 OC] (B) SW.

SAN CARLOS DE JONATA (*See* Ross-Kellerei.)

Sangrole (*See* Heublein.)

SAN JOAQUIN COUNTY
Central Valley.

SAN JOAQUIN, STANISLAUS

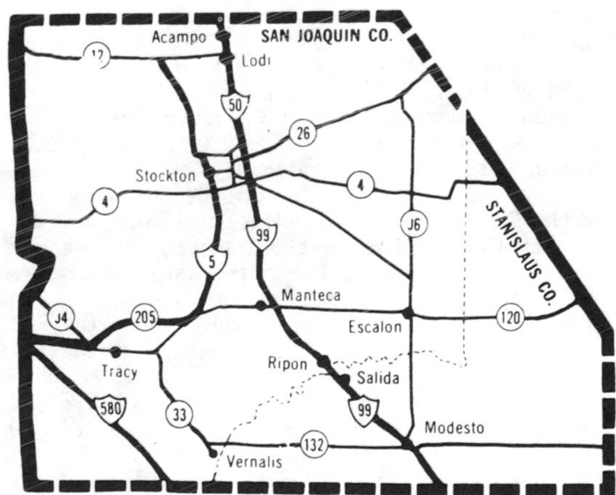

SAN JUAN BAUTISTA (*See* B & R Vineyards.)

SAN LUIS OBISPO COUNTY
Central Coast.
Appellation: Paso Robles.

SAN LUIS OBISPO, SANTA BARBARA, VENTURA

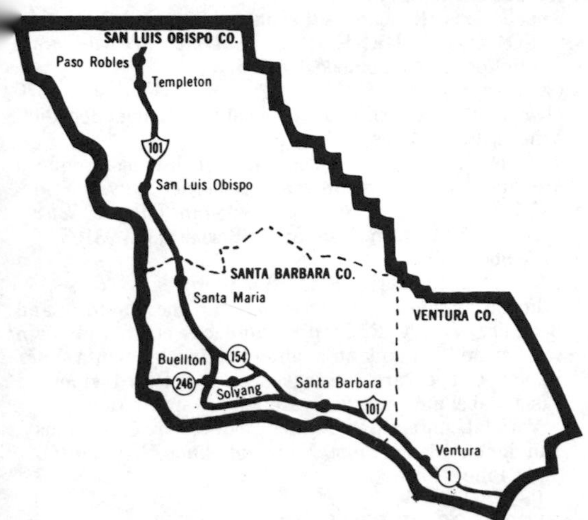

SAN MARTIN WINERY ★ *Santa Clara County*
P.O. Box 53, San Martin, CA 95046
(408) 683-4000 Founded: 1906
Storage: Oak, redwood, stainless steel.
Owner: Somerset Wine Co., a Division of Norton Simon, Inc. Winemaster: Greg Bruni.

Grapes are purchased on a selected vineyard basis. Label indicates appellation. Vintage-dated, varietal wines produced are Chardonnay, Fumé Blanc, Johannisberg Riesling, Emerald Riesling, Chenin Blanc, Gewurztraminer, Zinfandel, Cabernet Sauvignon, Gamay Beaujolais. Also under "Special Reserve" are Cabernet Sauvignon, Fume Blanc and Chardonnay.

Under the label of San Martin, the soft wines (low alcohol 7-10%) the varietal, vintage-dated wines produced are Soft Chenin Blanc, Soft Johannsiberg Riesling, and Soft Gamay Beaujolais. The vintage-dated table wines are Chablis, Rhine, Rosé and Burgundy.

The winemaker's most interesting wine is the Soft Johannisberg Riesling which was pioneered as the first California table wine released with less than 10% alcohol.

['81 OC] (G) '79 C, (B) '79 SB, (S) '79 WR, (S) '78 Z; ['82 OC] (S) '80 C, (B) '80 SB, (B) '80 JR, (S) '79 Z; ['82 SJC] (B) '80 C, (P) (S) '80 SJR, (P&C) (B&B) '78 CA.

SAN PASQUAL VINEYARDS ★ *San Diego County*
13455 San Pasqual Road, San Diego, CA 92025
(714) 741-0855 Founded: 1973
Storage: Oak, stainless steel.
Owners: a corporation. Winemaker/Manager: Kerry Damskey.

The 110 acre vineyard is in the San Pasqual Valley.

The varietal, vintage-dated, estate bottled wines produce are Chenin Blanc, Dry Chenin Blanc, Fumé Blanc Muscat Canelli and Napa Gamay. Also produced is Red Table Wine.

The winemaker's favorite wines are Gamay, Dry Chenin Blanc, and Fumé Blanc.

['81 OC] (S) '80 CH, (B) '80 CH; ['82 OC] (S) '79 G, (G) '81 Dry CB.

SANTA BARBARA COUNTY
South Central Coast.
Apellations: Santa Maria and Santa Ynez.

SANTA BARBARA WINERY ★ *Santa Barbara County*
202 Anacapa Street, Santa Barbara, CA 93101
(805) 963-8924 Founded: 1972 by Pierre LaFond

The 42 acre vineyard is in the Santa Ynez Valley. Wines produced are a 100% varietal vintage-dated, estate bottled Chenin Blanc, Johannisberg Riesling, Cabernet Sauvignon and Zinfandel. Also Dry, Medium and Cream Sherry, and Champagne. Fruit wines are produced under the Solvang label.

['82 SJP] (S) '81 LHZ.

SANTA CLARA COUNTY
Central Coast.
Appellations: Santa Clara Valley, Santa Cruz Mountains and Gilroy-Hecker Pass.

SANTA CRUZ CELLARS (*See* Bargetto's.)

SANTA CRUZ COUNTY
Central Coast.

SANTA CRUZ MOUNTAIN VINEYARD ★ *Santa Cruz County*
2300 Jarvis Road, Santa Cruz, CA 95065
(408) 426-6209 Founded: 1975
Storage: Small oak.
Owner, Winemaker: Ken D. Burnap.

The 15-acre vineyard is located at the winery. Varietal, vintage-dated, estate bottled wines produced are Pinot Noir and Cabernet Sauvignon.

['81 OC] (G) '78 CA, (G) '77 PN.

Santa Fe (*See* Heublein.)

SAN MATEO COUNTY
San Francisco Bay—Central Coast.

SANTA YNEZ VALLEY WINERY ★ *Santa Barbara County*
365 North Refugio Road, Santa Ynez, CA 93460
(805) 688-8381 Founded: 1976
Owners: the Bettencourt, Davidge and Brander families.
Winemaker: C. Fredric Brander.

The vineyards are in the valley which is 35 miles north of Santa Barbara. The estate bottled, varietal, vintage-dated wines produced are Sauvignon Blanc, Chardonnay Reserve de Cave, Blanc de Cabernet Sauvignon, White Riesling, Cabernet Sauvignon and Gewurztraminer.

The winemaker's favorites are the Sauvignon Blanc and the Chardonnay Reserve de Cave.

['81 OC] (B) '79 C, (B) '80 SB, (S) '80 WR; ['82 OC] (S) '80 C, (S) '81 JR; ['82 SJP] (S) '80 C, (B) (C) '81 G, (P&C) (B&S)

'81 SWR, (C) (S) '81 CAR.

SANTINO WINES ★ *Amador County*
Rt. 2 Box 21-A Steiner Road, Plymouth, CA 95669
(209) 245-3555 Founded: 1979
Storage: French oak and stainless steel.
Owners: Mathew and Nancy Santino. Winemaker: Scott Harvey.

Grapes are purchased on a select vineyard basis. Label indicates vineyard and/or appellation. Varietal wines produced are Special Selection Zinfandel, Zinfandel, Sauvignon Blanc, Cabernet Sauvignon, and White Harvest Zinfandel.

['82 OC] (S) '79 Z, (B) '79 Z, (B) '80 Z; ['82 SJP] (B) '79 Z.

SARAH'S VINEYARD ★ *Santa Clara County*
4005 Hecker Pass Hwy., Gilroy, CA 95020
(408) 842-4278 Founded: 1978
Storage: Oak, stainless steel.
Owners: Marilyn and John Otteman. Winemaker: Marilyn Otteman. Vineyards: 7 acres.

Varietal wines produced are Chardonnay, Riesling and Cabernet Sauvignon.

['82 OC] (G) '81 JR, (S) '80 Z, (B) '80 Z.

SARATOGA CELLRS (*See* Kathryn Kennedy Winery.)

SATIETY *Yolo County*
1027 Maple Lane, Davis, CA 95616
(916) 753-5812
Owners: Sterling and Elaine Chaykin. Winemaker: Sterling Chaykin.

25 acre vineyard located at winery. Label indicates vineyard and/or appellation. Varietal, vintage-dated wines produced are Chenin Blanc, Cabernet Sauvignon and French Colombard.

V. SATTUI WINERY *Napa County*
White Lane/Hwy. 29, 1/2 mi. S. of St. Helena, St. Helena, CA 94574
(707) 963-7774 Founded: 1885
Owner, Winemaker: Daryl Sattui.

Daryl is the great-grandson of the original owner Vittorio who started the winery in 1885. The vineyard is 2 miles south of St. Helena. Grapes are also purchased on a select vineyard basis. Label indicates vineyard and/or appellation.

Vintage-dated, varietal wines produced are Cabernet Sauvignon, Zinfandel, Chardonnay and a dry and off-dry Johannisberg Riesling from the Napa Valley. A dry Rosé made from the Gamay grape is produced and a Napa Valley Red, a less expensive, medium-bodied Red made from Napa Valley Zinfandel and Cabernet grapes. Also a 20 year old Madeira (sweet).

SAUSAL WINERY *Sonoma County*
7370 Hwy. 128, Healdsburg, CA 95448
(707) 433-2285 Founded: 1973
Storage: Oak, stainless steel.
Owners: David, Edward and Roselee Demostene, Lucinda Nelson. Winemaker: David Demostene.

120 acre vineyards are in the Alexander Valley and at

winery. The Demostene family has a long history of winemaking in Alexander Valley.

Varietal, vintage-dated, estate bottled wines produced are Zinfandel, Cabernet Sauvignon and Chardonnay. Also produced is Sausal Blanc.

Sauterne

Sauterne wines are golden-hued, fragrant, full-bodied, white dinner or table wines ranging from dry to sweet. In California, there are three types of Sauterne—Dry Sauterne, Sauterne, and Sweet, Haut or Chateau-type Sauterne. They vary greatly because the sweetness of the three Sauterne types is not defined by regulations. Generally, California Sauternes are drier than those of France. Sauvignon Blanc and Semillon are predominant varietals and are discussed under their individual names. Generic Sauterne is traditionally a blend of Semillon, Sauvignon Blanc and Muscadelle du Bordelais.

Award wines to look for: Barengo, Brookside, Cadenasso, Christian Brothers, Concannon, Giumarra, Perelli-Minetti, San Antonio, Verdugo.

Sauvignon Blanc

(White Table Wine) A varietal grape producing a white table wine that ranges from dry to sweet. When produced "dry", the wine is excellent with seafood and poultry. When sweet it is delightful to sip after being well chilled. Also a good accompaniment for cake and fresh fruit.

One of the principal grapes of the Sauterne district of France. The Sauvignon Blanc also has several aliases using the Fumé name before or after the Blanc. Fumé Blanc, Blanc Fumé Sauvignon and Blanc de Sauvignon. The wines carrying the Fumé tend to be drier with a grassy or smoky taste. Sauvignon Blanc is richer, sweeter and fruitier unless indicated as "dry".

Award wines to look for: Almaden (Dry & Fumé), Ballard Canyon, Beaulieu (Sweet), Bel Arbres, Beringer (Fumé), Boeger, Brander, Buena Vista (Dry), Davis Bynum, Cakebread Cellars, California Hillside, Callaway, Cambiaso (Fumé), J. Carey (Dry), Richard Carey (Dry), Chateau St. Jean (Fumé & Sweet), Christian Brothers (Fumé & Sweet), Concannon, R. & J. Cook (Fumé), Cordtz Brothers, DeLoach (Fumé & Sweet), Devlin (Dry), Diamond Oaks (Fumé), Dry Creek, Estrella River, Fenestra (Dry), Fetzer (Fumé), Filsinger (Fumé), Firestone (Dry), Flora Springs, Foppiano (Fumé), Franciscan, Gallo, Geyser Peak (Dry, Fumé, Sweet), Girard (Dry), Glen Ellen (Dry), Grand Cru, Grgich Hills (Fumé), HNW Cellars, Husch, Iron Horse, Kenwood (Dry), Konocti, (Fumé), J. Lohr (Late Harvest), Los Vineros (Dry), Lou-Dell, Maddalena, Mastantuono, Mayacamas, Mirassou (Fumé), Robert Mondavi, Monterey (Sweet), Montevina (Dry), Monticello Cellars, Mount Palomar (Dry), Napa Creek (Fumé), Napa Wine Cellars, Obester Winery, Papagni (Fumé & Sweet), Parducci, J. Pedroncelli (Dry), Pellegrini Brothers, Joseph Phelps (Dry), Pope Valley, Preston, River Road (Dry), San Martin (Fumé), San Pasqual, Santa Ynez Valley (Dry), Shenandoah, Souverain (Dry & Fumé), St. Clement

(Dry), Stephens, Stevenot (Dry), Stonegate (Dry), Taylor California, Turner (Fumé), Veedercrest, Ventana (Dry & Sweet), Vose (Fumé), Wente Brothers, Whitehall Lane, Wilson Daniels, Zaca Mesa.

SAUVIGNON VERT

A varietal grape that is mainly used for blending because of its high acidity. Not a true Sauvignon.

SCHARFFENBERGER CELLARS *Mendocino County*

303 Talmage Road, Ukiah, CA 95482
(707) 462-8996 Founded: 1981
Storage: Stainless steel.
Owner: John Scharffenberger. Winemaker: Robert W. Porter.

The production of sparkling wine in the tradition of method champenoise is the main object of the winery. Also produced under the "Eaglepoint" label are the varietal, vintage-dated Chardonnay and Blanc de Noir.

Scheurbe

In 1916, German botanist George Scheu developed a new wine grape by crossing Sylvaner and Riesling. Riesling-like but strongly floral. In 1956 the grape was officially named Scheu Rebe. See Joseph Phelps Vineyards.

SCHRAMSBERG VINEYARDS ★ *Napa County*

Calistoga, CA 94515
(707) 942-4558 Founded: 1862
Storge: Bottles.
Managing Director: Jack Davies. Winemaker: Gregory Fowler.

Established by Jacob Schram, this was the first winery on the hillsides of the Napa Valley. The 40 acre vineyards are located at the winery. Designated as a Historical Landmark in 1957, Robert Louis Stevenson wrote of Schramsberg in his "Silverado Squatters" when he visited in 1880.

Champagnes produced are bottle fermented Reserve, Blanc de Blancs, Blanc de Noirs, Cuveé de Pinot and Cremant.

['81 OC] (G) '75 SW, (S) '78 SW; ['82 OC] (G) '77 CHA, (S) '79 CHA, (B) '79 CHA.

SEA RIDGE WINERY *Sonoma County*

P.O. Box 433, Cazadero, CA 95421
(707) 847-3434 Founded: 1980
Storage: French oak.
Owners: Timothy Schmidt & Daniel Wickham. Winemaker: Daniel Wickham. Vineyards: 14 acres.

Vineyard recently planted at 1,200 ft. elevation. Grapes are purchased on a select vineyard basis. Label indicates vineyard and/or appellation.

Varietal, vintage-dated wines produced are Chardonnay and Pinot Noir.

SEBASTIANI VINEYARDS ★ *Sonoma County*

389 Fourth Street East, Sonoma, CA 95476
(707) 938-5532 Founded: 1904
Storage: Oak, redwood, stainless steel.
Owner: the Sebastiani family. Winemakers: Doug Davis, J. Carter.

The original vineyard was founded in 1825 by the Padres of the Mission de Sonoma. It was the first vineyard north of San Francisco. In 1904 Samuel Sebastiani bought the vineyard and started the winery.

Vintage-dated, varietal wines produced as "Proprietor's Reserve" are Zinfandel, Cabernet Sauvignon, Chardonnay, Barbera and Brut Three-Star.

['81 OC] (S) '80 CH, (B) '73 PN, (S) NV TP, (B) NV CA; ['82 OC] (B) '76 B, (S) '80 G, (B) '79 PN; ['82 SJP] (B) '81 GAR.

Sec

French word for "dry". Usually applied to Champagne, it actually means medium sweet.

Sediment

The solids which are contained in a wine. They do not signify that a wine is not drinkable, rather sometimes prove that it has perfected itself in the bottle.

SEGHESIO WINERY *Sonoma County*

P.O. Box 24035—Redwood Highway, Cloverdale, CA 95695

(707) 857-3581 Founded: 1902

Owners: Eugene and Edward Seghesio. Vineyards: 300 acres.

Select Late Harvest

Equivalent to the Auslese and Beerenauslese wines of Germany. Picked only from grapes that have been infected by Botrytis.

THOMAS SELLARDS WINERY *Sonoma County*

6400 Sequoia Circle, Sebastopol, CA 95472

(707) 823-8293 Founded: 1981

Storage: French & American oak.

Grapes are purchased on a select vineyard basis from Sonoma County. The first vintages will be released in late 1983.

Semillon

(White Table Wine) A varietal grape that is a companion to the Sauvignon Blanc in the Sauternes region of France. The wine is made in both a dry and sweet version. Dry it has a perfumey, aromatic flavor. Goes well with poultry and cream sauces. Sweet it is rich and full. Good to sip or with desserts.

Award wines to look for: Ahlgren, Chateau Bethune, Concannon, Congress Springs, Lawrence, San Martin, Stony Ridge, Ventana, Wente Bros.

SENRYO MIRIN (*See* Numano Sake Co.)

Serving Temperatures

Champagne: 50 degrees; Red Table Wine: 65-70 degrees; Sherry: 65-70 degrees; Port: 65-70 degrees; Rosé: 50 degrees; White Table Wine: 55 degrees.

SEQUOIA CELLARS *Yolo County*

1110 Lincoln Ave., Woodland, CA 95695

(916) 756-3081 Founded: 1977

Owners, Winemakers: Carol Gehrmann and Patricia Riley.

Varietal wines produced are Carnelian, Gewurztraminer, Zinfandel, and Cabernet Sauvignon.

SEQUOIA GROVE VINEYARDS ★ *Napa County*
8338 St. Helena Hwy., Napa, CA 94558
(707) 944-2945 Founded: 1980
Storage: French oak, stainless steel.
Owners: the Allen family. Winemaker: James W. Allen.
Vineyards: 21 acres at winery.

The winery is located in a 110 year old building surrounded by Sequoias. Grapes are also purchased on a select vineyard basis. Label indicates vineyard and/or appellation.

Varietal, vintage-dated, estate bottled wines produced are Chardonnay and Cabernet Sauvignon.

['82 SJP&C] (S&B) '80 C.

SETRAKIAN VINEYARDS *Tulare County*
P.O.Box 21, Yettem, CA 93670
(415) 398-1122 Founded: 1936
by Arpaxat "Sox" Setrakian
Owner: the Setrakian family.

Vineyards are located at winery. Varietal, vintage-dated wines produced are Cabernet Sauvignon, Petite Sirah, Grenache Rosé, Chenin Blanc, French Colombard, Emerald Riesling, and Johannisberg Riesling. Also produced are Blanc de Blanc Brut Champagne, Sherry and Port.

SHAFER VINEYARDS ★ *Napa County*
6154 Silverado Trail, Napa, CA 94558
(707) 944-2877 Founded: 1979
Owners: John and Elizabeth Shafer. Winemaker: Doug Shafer. Vineyards: 37 acres in Stag's Leap region.

Varietal, vintage-dated wines produced are Chardonnay, Gewurztraminer, Cabernet Sauvignon and Zinfandel.

['81 OC] (B) '78 CA; ['82 OC] (S) '80 C.

CHARLES F. SHAW VINEYARD ★ *Napa County*
1010 Big Tree Road, St. Helena, CA 94574
(707) 963-5459 Founded: 1978
Storage: French oak, stainless steel.
Owner, Winemaker: Charles "Chuck" Shaw. Vineyard: 47 acres at the winery.

Varietal, vintage-dated wine produced is Napa Gamay Method Beaujolais. Also produced is varietal, vintage-dated, estate bottled Chardonnay.

['82 SJP] (B) '81 GA.

SHELL CREEK VINEYARD—Cabernet Sauvignon, Petite Sirah, and Barbera Vineyard in San Luis Obispo County.

SHENANDOAH SPRINGS VINEYARD *Amador County*
P.O. Box 876, Fiddletown, CA 95629
(415) 595-1181 Founded: 1980
Owners: Joe Peri, Richard Martella, Michael Hoey, John Lewis and Richard Krayenhagen. Winemaker: Scott Harvey. Vineyards: 40 acres.

The vineyards and winery are located at elevation of 1,800 to 2,000 feet in Amador County. Currently 20 acres are planted in Zinfandel and Sauvignon Blanc. Chardonnay and Semillon will be planted on remaining 20 acres.

Varietal, vintage-dated, estate bottled wines produced

are Zinfandel and Sauvignon Blanc.

SHENANDOAH VINEYARDS ★ *Amador County*
12300 Steiner Rd., Plymouth, CA 95669
(209) 245-3698 Founded: 1977
Owners: Leon and Shirley Sobon. Winemaker: Leon Sobon.

The 10 acre vineyards are located in the Shenandoah Valley. Grapes are also purchased on a select vineyard basis. Varietal, vintage-dated wines produced are White Zinfandel, Chenin Blanc, Zinfandel, Zinfandel Special Reserve, Black Muscat, Zinfandel Port, Mission Cream Sherry and Mission Del Sol.

Varietal, vintage-dated, estate bottled wines are Cabernet Sauvignon and Sauvignon Blanc.

The winemaker's favorite wine is Zinfandel.

['81 OC] (S) '79 Z, (G) '78 Z, (G) NV P; ['82 OC] (B) '79 Z; ['82 SJC] (B) '81 SB, (P) (B) '79 Z, (P) (B) '80 ZP.

Shermat
Short for "Sherry material." Young wine, adjusted by the addition of wine spritis to the desired alcohol content, destined to be made into Sherry by one of several different methods.

SHERRILL CELLARS *Santa Clara County*
P.O. Box 4155, Woodside, CA 94062
(415) 851-1932 Founded: 1973
Owners: Nathaniel and Jan Sherrill. Winemaker: Nat Sherrill.

Vineyard being planted at winery location. Grapes purchased on a select vineyard basis. Label indicates vineyard and/or appellation. Varietal, vintage-dated wines produced are Cabernet Sauvignon, Zinfandel, Petite Sirah, Sauvignon Blanc, and Gamay. Under Skyline label blended wines are produced.

The winemaker's favorite wines are Zinfandel and Petite Sirah.

Sherry California
The most popular appetizer wine of all, is often made from Palomino, Mission or Pedro Ximenes. Sherry has a characteristic "nutty" flavor. Its color ranges from pale gold to dark amber, and it is either dry, medium dry or sweet. The sweet is often called "cream" Sherry.

The sweeter Sherries are usually served with dessert, or between meals refreshment.

Sherry, California Dry
Light straw to light amber in color with a nutty sherry character. Light in body, but mellow. Sugar content should be lower than 2.5%.

Sherry, California, Dry Flor and Medium Flor
Same characteristics and sugar content of corresponding sherries with the exception of a pronounced flor or mild yeasty flavor.

Sherry—California, making
Although many different grapes are used to make Sherry, in California, many winemakers use Mission, Palomino, Thompson Seedless and Pedro Ximenes. After fermentation of the juice has reached the desired stage—when the

wine is as dry as the producers style requires—brandy is added to stop fermentation. The new wine is called shermat in the California wine industry. Then many wineries age the wine at a warm temperature in lined or stainless steel or concrete tanks or in redwood containers. This process, at temperatures anywhere between 100 to 140 degrees F (38 to 60 degress C) continues from three months to a year. Sometimes it is done in a heated room, sometimes in tanks heated by coils, and sometimes by the heat of the sun. Later, the Sherry is allowed to cool gradually to cellar temperature and it is then aged like other wines. The heating, the oxidation due to the prolonged contact of the warm wine with air and the aging in wood barrels all combine to develop the pleasant "nutty" flavor characteristic of California Sherry. In addition, other California wineries produce a "flor" Sherry, using either the Spanish method which allows a film—yeast growth called "flor" to form on the surface of the wine in partially-filled containers or the "submerged flor" process. These also impart a distinctive flavor to the wine. Some other wineries offer blends of baked and "flor" Sherries.

Some California wineries operate Sherry Soleras. A solera consists of barrels lying one on top of another four or five tiers high, the oldest at the bottom and the youngest at the top. At periodic intervals, the matured Sherry is drawn from the bottom barrel to be bottled. This barrel is then replenished from the one above, and so on. The top barrel is filled with new wine. By this method the young wine mixes with the older to provide a uniform product of high quality year after year.

Sherry, California, Medium

Light golden amber to medium golden amber in color. Medium bodied, nutty character. Sugar content should be between 2.5 and 4.0%.

Sherry, California, Sweet (Cream)

Medium to dark amber in color. Full bodied, rich and nutty with well developed Sherry character. Sugar content should not be less than 4.0%.

Sherry

Award wines to look for: Almaden, Bargetto, Brookside, Buena Vista, Christian Bros., Concannon, Cresta Blanca, East-Side, Franciscan, Gallo, Gibson, Hecker Pass, Inglenook, Charles Krug, Llords & Elwood, Louis Martini, Paul Masson, Monterey Peninsula, Papagni, Perelli-Minetti, Rancho de Philo, Richert, Sebastiani, Setrakian, Sonoma, Weibel.

SHIN MIRIN (*See* Numano Sake Co.)

SHOWN & SONS VINEYARDS ★ *Napa County*

8643 Silverado Trail, Rutherford, CA 94573

(707) 963-9004 Founded: 1979

Owners: Richard L. Shown and Gary Gouvea. Winemaker: Jim Vahl.

The vineyards are in Rutherford. Varietal, vintage-dated wines produced are Cabernet Sauvignon, Zinfandel, Johannisberg Riesling, Chardonnay and Chenin Blanc.

['81 OC] (S) '80 CH; ['82 OC] (B) '79 CA; ['82 SJC] (B) '81 JR, (P) (B) '78 CA.

SIERRA VISTA WINERY ★ *El Dorado County*
4560 Cabernet Way, Placerville, CA 95667
(916) 622-7221 Founded: 1977
Storage: Small oak, stainless steel.
Owners: John and Barbara MacCready. Winemaker: John MacCready.

The winery and vineyard is located in the Pleasant Valley region at an elevation of 2800 feet; to the east is the Crystal range of the Sierra Nevada. Varietal, vintage-dated wines produced are Zinfandel, Fumé Blanc, Cabernet Sauvignon, Chardonnay, Chenin Blanc, and Sauvignon Blanc.

['81 OC] (S) '79 Z, (S) NV Z; ['82 OC] (S) '79 CA, (S) '81 CH; ['82 SJP] (B) '80 C, (P&C) (S&S) '79 CA, (P) (S) '79 Z.

SILKWOOD CELLARS *Napa County*
P.O. Box 2757, Yountville, CA 94599 Founded: 1979
Owner: John D. Knapp. Winemaker: B. B. Levy.

Grapes are purchased on a select vineyard basis. Label indicates vineyard and/or appellation.

Varietal, vintage-dated wines produced are Chardonnay and Sauvignon Blanc.

SILVER MOUNTAIN *Santa Clara County*
P.O. Box 1695, Los Gatos, CA 95031
(408) 353-2278 Founded: 1979
Storage: French oak.
Owner, Winemaker: Jerold O'Brien.

Grapes are purchased on a select region basis. Varietal, vintage-dated wines produced are Zinfandel and Chardonnay.

SILVER OAK CELLARS ★ *Napa County*
915 Oakville Cross Road, P.O. Box 414, Oakville, CA 94562
(707) 944-8808 Founded: 1972
Storage: Oak.
Owners: Justin R. Meyer and Raymond T. Duncan. Winemaker: Justin R. Meyer.

Grapes are purchased on a select vineyard basis. Label indicates vineyard and/or appellation. 100% varietal, vintage-dated wine produced is Cabernet Sauvignon (aged 5 years).

['82 SJP] (B) '77 CA.

THE SILVERADO VINEYARD *Napa County*
6121 Silverado Trail, Napa, CA 94558
(707) 257-1770 Founded: 1981
Storage: Stainless steel, oak and small cooperage.
Owners: Mrs. Walter E. Disney, Ron & Diane Miller. Winemaker: John Stuart. Vineyards: 185 acres.

The vineyards, part of the original Rancho Yajome Landgrant, are on both sides of the Napa River. The winery is on the property of one of the vineyards. Label indicates vineyard and/or appellation.

Varietal, vintage-dated, estate bottled wines produced are Cabernet Sauvignon, Sauvignon Blanc and Chardonnay.

SIMI WINERY ★ *Sonoma County*
Box 698, Healdsburg, CA 95448
(707) 433-6981 Founded: 1876
Storage: Oak, stainless steel.
Owner: Moet-Hennessy. Winemaker: Zelma Long.

Moet-Hennessy is the French company that also owns Champagne Moet & Chandon, Mercier and Ruinart, Hennessy Cognac and Dior Perfumes.

Label indicates appellation. Varietal, vintage-dated wines produced are Zinfandel, Chenin Blanc, Chardonnay, Gewurztraminer, Pinot Noir, Cabernet Sauvignon, Rosé of Cabernet Sauvignon.

['81 OC] (B) '74 CA, (S) '79 CH; ['82 OC] (B) '81 C; ['82 SJP] (B) '80 C, (P) (S) '81 CH, (P) (B) '81 CAR.

SKY VINEYARDS *Napa County*
1500 Lokoya Road, Napa, CA 94558
Owner: Lore Olds. Vineyards: 20 acres.

Wine produced is vintage-dated, estate bottled Zinfandel.

SKYLINE (*See* Sherrill Cellars.)

SMITH & HOOK VINEYARD *Monterey County*
P.O. Box 1010, Gonzales, CA 93926
(408) 678-2132 or (408) 675-2311 Founded: 1974
Storage: Small oak, stainless steel.
Owner: Ltd. Partnership. President: Gerald McFarland. Winemaker: Duane DeBoer. Vineyards: 255 acres planted on 652 acre mountain ranch west of Soledad on east slope of Santa Lucia Mts.

Only one product: Vintage-dated, estate bottled Cabernet Sauvignon.

SMITH-MADRONE VINEYARDS *Napa County*
4022 Spring Mountain Road, St. Helena, CA 94574
(707) 963-2283 Founded: 1977
Owner/Winemaker: Stuart Smith.

The 38 acre vineyard and winery are located at 1700 ft. level on Spring Mountain in Napa Valley. Varietal, vintage-dated, estate bottled wines produced are Chardonnay, Cabernet Sauvignon and Pinot Noir. Also vintage-dated, varietal Johannisberg Riesling.

SMOTHERS-VINE HILL WINES ★ *Santa Cruz County*
2317 Vine Hill Road, Santa Cruz, CA 95065
Owner: R. R. Smothers. Winemaker: William Arnold.

A relatively new winery that won the Grand Prize for its Gewurztraminer '77 in 1978 at the L. A. County Fair. The 12 acre vineyard is located at the winery in the Santa Cruz mountains. Grapes are also purchased on a selected vineyard district basis.

Label idicates vineyard and/or appellation. The 100% varietal, vintage-dated wines produced are Cabernet Sauvignon, Gewurztraminer, Zinfandel. The varietal, vintage-dated wines produced are White Riesling, Chardonnay, and Gewurztraminer.

['81 OC] (S) '80 C, (S) '80 G; ['82 OC] (S) '80 C, (G) '81 G, (B) '81 JR, (S) '80 JR.

SODA ROCK WINERY *Sonoma County*
8015 Hwy. 128, Healdsburg, CA 95448

(707) 433-1830 Founded: 1880
Storage: Oak, stainless steel.
Owner: Charles Tomka, Jr. Winemaker: Charles Tomka, Sr.

Varietal, vintage-dated wines produced are Zinfandel, Cabernet Sauvignon, Chenin Blanc and Johannisberg Riesling.

Soft Wines

New low alcohol, (7-10%), wines.

SOLANO COUNTY

North Coast Inland from Napa.

Solera

The Spanish system of progessively blending Sherries in tiers of small casks—to blend Sherries of the same type but varying ages.

SOMMELIER WINERY ★ *Santa Clara County*
2560 Wyandotte Street, Mountain View, CA 94043
(415) 969-2442 Founded: 1976
Owner: the Keezer family. Winemaker: Richard C. Keezer.

Grapes are purchased on a selected vineyard district basis. Varietal wines produced are Zinfandel, Cabernet Sauvignon, Petite Sirah and Pinot Chardonnay.

['82 SJP] (B) '79 C.

SONOMA COUNTY

North Coast, Appellations: Sonoma Valley, Russian River Valley, Alexander Valley, Dry Creek, and Geyserville.

SONOMA-CUTRER VINEYARDS *Sonoma County*
4401 Slusser Road, Windsor, CA 95492
(707) 528-1181 Founded: 1973
Storage: Oak, stainless steel.
President: Brice C. Jones. Winemaker: William Bonetti.

Vintage-dated, estate bottled Chardonnay is only wine produced.

SONOMA COUNTY CELLARS *Sonoma County*
P.O. Box 925, Healdsburg, CA 95448
(707) 433-4366
Owner: F. M. Passalacqua.

SONOMA COUNTY COOPERATIVE *Sonoma County*
P.O. Box 36, Windsor, CA 95492
(707) 838-6649 Founded: 1935

Under contract to E. & J. Gallo.

SONOMA VINEYARDS (WINDSOR) ★ *Sonoma County*
11455 Old Redwood Hwy., Windsor, CA 95492
(707) 433-6511 Founded: 1961
Storage: Limousin, Troncais, Nevers and American oak.
Ownership: publicly held corporation. Winemaker: Rodney D. Strong.

Rodney Strong was the original founder who also selected the seven locations and planted the vineyards in Sonoma County. 800 acres on the east and west side of the Russian River. 450 acres throughout the surrounding countryside.

Label indicates vineyard and/or appellation. Varietal, vintage-dated wines produced are Cabernet Sauvignon, Chardonnay, Fumé Blanc, Merlot, Pinot Noir, Johannisberg Riesling, Petite Sirah, Zinfandel, Chenin Blanc, Grey Riesling, French Colombard, Ruby Cabernet, Grenache Rosé, Brut and Blanc de Noir Champagne.

Varietal, vintage-dated, estate bottled wines are produced only in exceptional years and are bottled in a special, gold-script label. They are Chardonnay, Johannisberg Riesling, Pinot Noir, Zinfandel, and Cabernet Sauvignon. Other brands: Windsor Vineyards and Tiburon Vintners.

The winemaker's preferred wines are Alexander's Crown Cabernet Sauvignon, River West and Chalk Hill Chardonnay.

['81 OC] (B) '77 PN, (S) '79 WR; ['82 OC] (G) '80 C, (G) '81 CH, (S) '81 GB, (G) '81 G.

SOTOYOME WINERY ★ *Sonoma County*

641 Limerick Lane, Healdsburg, CA 95448
(707) 433-2001 Founded: 1974
Storage: American oak, redwood, stainless steel.
Owner: C. S. Wines, Inc. Winemaker: William Chaikin.

The 8 acre vineyards are located at the winery. Grapes are also purchased on a select vineyard basis. The name comes from Rancho Sotoyome, a Mexican land grant of 1840.

Varietal, vintage-dated wines produced are Zinfandel, Petite Sirah, Cabernet Sauvgnon and Chardonnay.

The winemaker's favorite wine is Petite Sirah.

['81 OC] (S) '78 CA, (B) '78 PS; ['82 SJP&C] (S&B) '77 CA, (P) (B) '79 PS. ['82 SJMN] (S) '79 CA.

Sour

A sour wine is a spoiled wine. It is inaccurate to call a dry, astringent, or tart wine "sour".

SOUTH COAST CELLAR *Los Angeles County*

12901-B South Budlong Ave., Gardena, CA 90297
(213) 324-8006 Founded: 1977
Storage: Small oak cooperage.
Owners: Doug Anderson and Geoff Anderson. Manager: Bruce Sterten. Winemaker: Doug Anderson.

Grapes are purchased on a selected vineyard district basis.

Label indicates vineyard and/or appellation. Varietal wines produced are Cabernet Sauvignon, Merlot, Petite Sirah and Zinfandel.

SOUVERAIN CELLARS ★ *Sonoma County*

P.O. Box 528, Geyserville, CA 95441
(707) 433-8281 Founded: 1943
Owners: General partner, the North Coast Grape Growers Association. Winemaker: Bob Mueller. Director of Winemaking: Thomas G. Eddy Jr.

The vineyards of the North Coast Grape Growers are located in the counties of Sonoma, Napa and Mendocino. Souverain varietal wines are produced 100% from the grapes for which each wine is named and they are all vintage dated. All the grapes for the premium wines are grown in the North Coast. The white wines produced are: Chardonnay, Fumé Blanc, Grey Riesling, Johannisberg Riesling, Chenin Blanc, Gewurztraminer and Muscat

Canelli. The two blended whites are Chablis and Colombard-Blanc. The red varietals include: Gamay Beaujolais, Merlot, Zinfandel, Pinot Noir, Petite Sirah, Charbono and Cabernet Sauvignon. Burgundy is also produced. Exceptional wines are designated "Vintage Selection" and include a Cabernet Sauvignon, Merlot and Zinfandel. In the Fall of 1982, Souverain will release the first Estate Bottled Vintage Selection wines starting with a 1978 Cabernet Sauvignon and 1981 Fumé Blanc with Chardonnay to be added to the line in 1983. These hand-selected grapes come from the most outstanding vineyard growing the varietal that year. Bottled in 1.5 liters and 3 liters are White, Rhine, Rosé and Red table wines.

Produced under the North Coast Cellars label are Chardonnay, Chenin Blanc, White Riesling, French Colombard, Napa Gamay, Pinot Noir, Zinfandel, Cabernet Sauvignon and Cabernet Sauvignon (Limited Release).

['81 OC] (S) '77 PN, (B) '79 WR; ['82 OC] (B) '78 CB, (B) '81 C, (G) '81 CH, (S) '80 G, (S) '81 MC; ['82 SJP&C] (S&B) '81 FB, (P) (S) '81 PNR.

Spanada (*See* E. & J. Gallo.)

Sparkling Burgundy

A red wine made sparkling by secondary fermentation in closed containers. It is usually semi-sweet or sweet. Barbera, Carignane, Petite Sirah and Pinot Noir are the grapes most used for its production.

Sparkling Wines

Sparkling wines are wines which have been made naturally effervescent by a second fermentation in closed containers. Sparkling wines can be red, pink or white, with an alcohol content of 10-14 percent.

Sparkling wines: Champagne, Cold Duck, Sparkling Burgundy, Sparkling Muscat, Sparkling Rosé.

Award wines to look for: Andre, Christian Bros., Cresta Blanca, Cribari, Crystal Valley, Domaine Chandon, Franzia Bros., Gallo, JFJ Bronco, LaMont, Paul Masson, Mirassou, Papagni, Perelli-Minetti, Sonoma, Stanford, Stony Ridge, Weibel.

Spatlese

The German word for "late picking". This word is prohibited from use by American vineyards and in its place the wines are called "Late Harvest". Grapes that are picked in an over-ripe condition with some incidence of Botrytis.

SPAULDING VINEYARD—Chardonnay vineyard in Napa Valley.

Special Select Late Harvest

Equivalent to the Beerenauslese or Trockenbeerenauslese wines of Germany. Wines produced only from grapes totally affected with Botrytis and in some cases the berries are fully raisined.

SPRING MOUNTAIN VINEYARDS ★ *Napa County*

2805 Spring Mountain Road, St. Helena, CA 94574

(707) 963-5233 Founded: 1968

Storage: French oak, stainless steel.

Owner: Michael Robbins. Winemaker: John Williams.

Vineyards are located in the Napa Valley, 35 acres on Spring Mountain, 88 acres in Rutherford and 18 acres near Napa.

Varietal, vintage-dated, estate bottled wines produced are Cabernet Sauvignon, Chardonnay, Sauvignon Blanc and Pinot Noir. Also, Falcon Crest Chardonnay and Gamay Beaujolais.

['82 SJP] (B) '80 C, (P) (B) '79 CA.

STAG'S LEAP WINE CELLARS ★ *Napa County*

5766 Silverado Trail, Napa, CA 94558

(707) 944-2020 or 944-2782 Founded: 1972

Storage: American, French oak, stainless steel.

Owner: Ltd. partnership. General Partner/Winemaker/Manager: Warren Winiarski.

The 44 acre Cabernet Sauvignon and Merlot vineyards are 1/4 mile from winery in the Napa Valley. It was the 1973 Stag's Leap Cabernet Sauvignon that set the French on their ear in 1976 when it came in first in the Paris tasting. Mouton-Rothschild '70 was second.

Label indicates vineyard and/or appellation. Varietal, vintage-dated, estate bottled wines produced are Cabernet Sauvignon and Merlot. Varietal, vintage-dated wines produced are Cabernet Sauvignon, Chardonnay, Johannisberg Riesling, Gamay Beaujolais, Petite Sirah and Sauvignon Blanc. Also produced under the Hawk Crest label is Cabernet Sauvignon and Johannisberg Riesling.

Winemaker's favorite wines are Stag's Leap Vineyards Cabernet Sauvignon and Napa Valley Vineyard Chardonnay.

['81 OC] (B) '78 CA, (G) '78 M, (G) '78 PS; ['82 OC] (G) '79 M, (G) '79 C.

STAGS' LEAP WINERY ★ *Napa County*

6150 Silverado Trail, Napa, CA 94558

(707) 253-1545 Founded: 1972

Storage: French oak, stainless steel.

Owners: Carl & Joanne Doumani. Winemaker: John Henderson.

The 100 acre vineyards are located at the winery.

Varietal wines produced are Chenin Blanc, Petite Sirah, Cabernet Sauvignon and Merlot.

The winemaker's favorite wine is Petite Sirah.

['82 OC] (G) '79 C, (S) '81 CH, (B) '78 PS.

P AND M STAIGER *Santa Cruz County*

1300 Hopkins Gulch Road, Boulder Creek, CA 95006

(408) 338-4346 Founded: 1973

Storage: French oak, stainless steel.

Owners: Paul and Marjorie Staiger. Winemaker: Paul Staiger.

Original vineyard was planted in 1900. Replanted by the Staigers in 1973. The 5 acre vineyard is at winery north of Boulder Creek at elevation of 1100 feet.

Varietal, vintage-dated wines produced are Chardonnay (estate bottled), Cabernet Sauvignon (estate bottled).

ST. ANDREWS WINERY *Napa County*

2921 Silverado Trail, Napa, CA 94558

(707) 252-6748 Founded: 1980

Owner: I. Vizkelety. Consulting Winemaker: Charles Ortman. Vineyards: 82 acres Chardonnay at winery.

Grapes are also purchased on a select vineyard basis. Label indicates vineyard and/or appellation.

Varietal, vintage-dated, estate bottled wine produced is Chardonnay under the St. Andrews Vineyard Label. Under the Charles Ortman name varietal, vintage-dated Chardonnay and Sauvignon Blanc are produced.

Stanford (*See* Weibel Champagne Vineyards.)

ST. CLEMENT VINEYARDS ★ *Napa County*

2867 St. Helena Hwy. North, St. Helena, CA 94574

(707) 963-7221 Founded: 1975

Storage: French oak, stainless steel.

Owners: Doctor William and Mrs. Alexandra Casey. Winemaker: Dennis Johns.

The house that appears on the label is a Napa Valley landmark that was built in 1876 and it is in the cellars of this Victorian home that the first wines of Spring Mountain Vineyards were made. The Casey's purchased the property in 1975. The vineyards are located at the winery and in St. Helena, Rutherford and Yountville.

The varietal, vintage-dated wines produced are Chardonnay, Sauvignon Blanc and Cabernet Sauvignon.

['81 OC] (G) '80 SB; ['82 OC] (S) '81 SB.

ST. AMANT VINEYARD—Zinfandel vineyard in Amador County.

ST. FRANCIS VINEYARDS ★ *Sonoma County*

8450 Sonoma Hwy., Kenwood, CA 95452

(707) 833-4666 Founded: 1979

Storage: French oak, stainless steel.

Owner: Joseph Martin. Winemaker: Bob Robertson.

The 100 acre vineyards are in the Sonoma Valley. Varietal, vintage-dated, estate bottled wines produced are Chardonnay, Gewurztraminer, Merlot, Pinot Noir and Johannisberg Riesling.

['81 OC] (B) '79 C, (B) '79 M, (B) '79 JR; ['82 OC] '81 G.

ST. MARTIN (*See* The Martin Winery.)

STANISLAUS COUNTY

Central San Joaquin Valley.

STEARN'S WHARF VINTNERS *Santa Barbara County*

217 G. Stearn's Wharf, Santa Barbara, CA 93101

(805) 966-6624 Founded: 1982

Owners: Douglas & Candace Scott. Manger: David Delapa.

Stearn's Wharf Vintners is situated on historic Stearn's Wharf in the Santa Barbara Harbor. Grapes are purchased on a selected vineyard basis from nearby Santa Ynez vineyards. Varietal, vintage-dated wines produced are Johannisberg Riesling, Chenin Blanc and Cabernet Sauvignon Blanc.

ROBERT STEMMLER WINERY *Sonoma County*

3805 Lambert Bridge Road, Healdsburg, CA 95448

(707) 433-6334 Founded: 1977

Storage: French oak, stainless steel.

Owners: Robert Stemmler, Trumbull W. Kelley. Winemaker: Robert Stemmler.

Robert Stemmler was formerly winemaker at Charles Krug, Inglenook and Simi. 4 acre vineyard (Chardonnay) located at the winery. Grapes are also purchased on a select vineyard basis. Label indicates vineyard and/or appellation.

Varietal, vintage-dated wines produced are Fumé Blanc, Cabernet Sauvignon and estate bottled Chardonnay.

STEPHENS ★ (*See* Girard Winery.)

['82 OC] (G) '81 SB; ['82 SJP&C] (S&B) '81 SB.

STERLING VINEYARDS *Napa County*

1111 Dunaweal Lane, Calistoga, CA 94515

(707) 942-5151 Founded: 1964

Storge: French oak, stainless steel.

Owner: The Coca-Cola Co. (The Wine Spectrum). President: Gregory DeLucca. V.P. of cellar operations: Theo Rosenbrand. Assistant Winemaker: Bill Dyer.

The vineyards are located in the Napa Valley.

The varietal, vintage-dated, estate bottled wines produced are Chardonnay, Cabernet Blanc, Sauvignon Blanc, Cabernet Sauvignon and Merlot. Under the label "Sterling Reservé' a vintage-dated, estate bottled Cabernet Sauvignon is produced.

The winemaker's favorite wine is the "Reservé' Cabernet Sauvignon.

STEVENOT ★ *Calaveras County*

2690 San Domingo Road, Murphys, CA 95247

(209) 728-3436 Founded: 1978

Storage: French, American oak, stainless steel.

Owner: Barden E. Stevenot. Winemakers: Barden E. Stevenot and Steve Millier. Vineyard: 20 acres at the winery.

Grapes are also purchased on a select vineyard basis. Label indicates vineyard and/or appellation. The varietal, vintage-dated wines produced are Chenin Blanc, Chardonnay, Zinfandel Blanc, Cabernet Sauvignon, Zinfandel, and Sauvignon Blanc.

Winemaker's favorite wine is Mendocino Chardonnay.

['81 OC] (B) '79 C, (B) '80 SB; ['82 OC] (S) '80 C; ['82 SJP] (S) '81 SB, (B) '81 CH.

STONEGATE WINERY ★ *Napa County*

1183 Dunaweal Lane, Calistoga, CA 94515

(707) 942-6500 Founded: 1973

Storage: Oak, stainless steel.

Owners: James C. and Barbara G. Spaulding. Winemaker: David B. Spaulding.

Winery has two vineyards. A hillside 20 acre vineyard above the city of Calistoga at 800 feet and a 15 acre vineyard located at the winery.

Label indicates vineyard appellation. Wines produced are all varietal, vintage-dated, Cabernet (with Merlot for blending), Cabernet Sauvignon, Chardonnay, Sauvignon Blanc and Merlot.

['81 OC] (S) '79 C, (S) '80 SB; ['82 OC] (S) '78 CA, (B) '80 C.

STONERIDGE *Amador County*

13682 Ridge Road East, Sutter Creek, CA 95685

(209) 223-1761 Founded: 1975
Owners/Winemakers: Gary and Loretta Porteous.

The 7 acre vineyard is located at the winery.

Vintage-dated, estate bottled varietal wines produced are Zinfandel, White Zinfandel and Ruby Cabernet.

STONEY CREEK VINEYARDS *El Dorado County*
8221 Stoney Creek Road, Somerset, CA 95684
(209) 245-3467 Founded: 1980
Storage: Oak, stainless steel.
Owners: Vernon and Marcia Gerwer. Winemaker: Vernon Gerwer.

10 acre vineyard located at winery. Grapes are also purchased on a selected vineyard basis. Label indicates vineyard and/or appellation.

Varietal, vintage-dated wines produced are Ruby Cabernet, Sauvignon Blanc, Semillon and Zinfandel. Also produced is Fairplay Red.

STONY HILL VINEYARD *Napa County*
P.O. Box 308, St. Helena, CA 94574
(707) 963-2636 Founded: 1953
Storage: Oak.
Owner: Mrs. Eleanor W. McCrea. Winemaker: Michael A. Chelini.

Owned by the McCreas since 1943. Mr. McCrea passed away in 1977. The 35 acre vineyard is in the foothills north of St. Helena.

100% varietal, vintage-dated, estate bottled wines produced are Chardonnay, White Riesling, Gewurztraminer and Semillon de Soleil (A sweet dessert wine).

The winemaker's favorite wine is Chardonnay.

STONY RIDGE WINERY ★ *Alameda County*
1188 Vineyard Ave., Pleasanton, CA 94566
(415) 846-2133 Founded: 1975
Owners: Henry & Joanne Schneider. Winemakers: Sam Balderas and Bob Atkinson.

The 590 acre vineyards are located at the winery in the Livermore Valley. Label indicates vineyard and/or appellation. The original Ruby Hill Winery was established in 1887. The winery changed the name when it was restored in 1975.

The varietal, vintage-dated, estate bottled wines produced are Chardonnay, Zinfandel, Malvasia Bianca Champagne, Chevrier Fumé (Dry Semillon), Blanc de Noir Champagne, Pinot Noir, Barbera and Sauvignon Blanc. Also produced is vintage-dated Cabernet Sauvignon.

The winemaker's favorite wines are the Chardonnay and Chevrier.

['81 OC] (G) '75 CA, (B) '79 C, (B) '79 PN, (S) '79 WR, (G) '79 WR; ['82 OC] (G) '79 CA, (G) '79 PN, (B) '79 PN, (S) CHA; ['82 SJP] (B) '80 C, (C) (S) '79 CA, (P) (S) '81 LHJ.

Stop Fermentation
The term that describes how in winemaking, a little pure grape brandy is added to a sweet dessert wine to check the fermentation. This prevents complete conversion of the natural grape sugar into wine alcohol and carbon dioxide so that the wine is sweeter than if fermentation

had run its course. Never use the word "fortify" in conjunction with wine. It is unlawful, under Federal regulations plus many States.

STORM CELLARS (*See* Winters Winery.)

STORY VINEYARDS ★ *Amador County*

10851 Bell Rd., Plymouth, CA 95669
(209) 245-6208 Founded: 1973
Storage: Oak, stainless steel.
Owner: Ann Story. Vineyards: 33 acres located at winery.

Varietal, vintage-dated, estate bottled wines produced are Zinfandel and Premier White Table Wine.

['82 OC] (B) Z.

STORYBOOK MOUNTAIN VINEYARDS *Napa County*

3835 Hwy. 128, Calistoga, CA 94515
(707) 942-5310 Founded: 1979
Owner, Winemaker: Dr. J. Bernard Seps.

The 36 acre vineyard is in the Napa Valley. This vineyard was originally established by Adam and Jacob Grimm in the early 1880's. To this day, the wine caves are still in use under Storybook Mountain.

As conditions warrant, there will be two Zinfandel bottlings. The regular will carry the white on blue label, the reserve will be white on ivory. The only varietal, vintage-dated, estate bottled wine produced will be Zinfandel.

Sugar Content

The following are average sugar percentage contents: Aperitif: 0.5-3.5%; Red: 0-1.5%; White: 0-4.0%; Rosé: 0-2.0%; Dessert: 5.0-14%; Champagne: 0.5-5.0%.

Note: Late harvest white wines might go from 4% to 6% or more.

Sugars

Ripe grapes have around 20% of their weight as sugar, but this is changed into about 12% alcohol by the yeast during fermentation. About 0.2% in fully fermented (dry) wine analyzes out as reducing sugar. Supposition is that 0.2%, more or less, is made up of odd sugars that the yeast cannot handle. Normal threshold for sugar is around 0.5%. Sugar content is the main index of grape ripeness; normally the higher the sugar content (expressed as degress Balling or Brix), the riper the grapes are.

In warm climate zones the sugar content of grapes tends to increase to high levels while the natural acidity, at the same time, drops to very low levels and eventually the wine quality is poor. In cool climate zones (California Coastal regions, Monterey for example) the acidity remains high during ripening, even as the sugar content in the grapes builds to optimum ripeness levels, and the eventual quality of the wine can be outstanding.

SULLIVAN VINEYARD WINERY *Napa County*

1090 Galleron Lane, Rutherford, CA 94573
(707) 963-9646 Founded: 1979
Storage: Oak, stainless steel.
Owners: James and Jo Ann Sullivan. Winemaker: James Sullivan. Vineyard: 30 acres at the winery.

Varietal, vintage-dated, estate bottled wines produced are Chenin Blanc, Chardonnay, Zinfandel and Cabernet Sauvignon.

SUMMERHILL VINEYARDS ★ *Santa Clara County*
3920 Hecker Pass Hwy., Gilroy, CA 95020
(408) 842-3032 Founded: 1917
Storage: Oak, redwood, stainless steel.
President: H. T. "Red" Johnson. Sec., Treas.: Debra A. Dodd. Winemaker: Gary L. Hada.
Purchased by present owners in 1980. Grapes are purchased on a select vineyard basis.
Varietal wines produced are Cabernet Sauvignon, Riesling, Chenin Blanc, Zinfandel, and French Colombard. Also Aleatico and fruit wines.
['82 SJMN] (S) Fruit.

Summit (*See* Geyser Peak Winery.)

SUNRISE WINERY ★ *Santa Cruz County*
16001 Empire Grade Rd., Santa Cruz, CA 95060
(408) 423-8226 Founded: 1976
Storage: Small oak barrels, stainless steel.
Owners: Keith Hohlfeldt, Rolayne and Ronald Stortz. Winemaker: Keith Hohlfeldt.
Grapes are purchased on a select vineyard basis.
Varietal, vintage-dated wines produced are Pinot Noir, Cabernet Sauvignon and Chardonnay.
The winemaker's favorite wines are the Cabernet Sauvignon and Pinot Noir.
['81 OC] (G) '78 CA, (B) '79 C; ['82 SJP&C] (S&B) '79 CA, (P) (B) '79 PN (P&C) (S&B) '65 VP.

SUSINÉ CELLARS *Solano County*
301 Spring St., Suisun City, CA 94585
(707) 425-0833 Founded: 1981
Storage: American, French oak, stainless steel.
Owner and Winemaker: Edward O'Brien.
Grapes purchased on a select vineyard basis. Varietal, vintage-dated wines produced are Johannisberg Riesling, Chenin Blanc, Cabernet Sauvignon, Zinfandel, Sauvignon Blanc and Gewurztraminer. Also produced are Red, White and Rosé Bouquet.

SUTTER BASIN VINEYARD—Zinfandel vineyard in Yolo County.

SUTTER HOME WINERY, INC. ★ *Napa County*
277 St. Helena Hwy. South, P.O. Box 248, St. Helena, CA 94574
(707) 963-3104 Founded: 1874
Storage: Wood and stainless steel.
Owner: the Trinchero family. Manager: Roger J. Trinchero. V.P. Winemaker: Louis "Bob" Trinchero Pres.
A 15 acre vineyard is in Calistoga. The winery was originally built in 1874. The Trinchero's purchased it in 1946.
Grapes are also purchased on a select vineyard basis. Label indicates vineyard and/or appellation. The varietal, vintage-dated wines produced are Zinfandel, White Zinfandel, Dessert Zinfandel, and Muscat Amabile.
The winemaker's favorite wine is Amador County Zin-

fandel.
['81 OC] (S) '77 Z; ['82 OC] (B) '79 Z.

JOSEPH SWAN VINEYARDS *Sonoma County*
2916 Laguna Rd., Forestville, CA 95436
(707) 546-7711 Founded: 1969
Owners: Joseph A. and June Swan. Vineyards: 10 acres are in Sonoma at the winery. Grapes are also purchased on a select vineyard basis.

Varietal, vintage-dated wines produced are Chardonnay, Pinot Noir and Zinfandel.

T. J. SWANN (*See* Heublein.)

Sweet Dessert Wines
Full bodied wines served with desserts and as refreshments. Under California standards, the total fixed acidity calculated as tartaric acid shall not be less than 0.25 grams per 100cc; the alcoholic content not less than 17% for Sherry, 18% for all other dessert wines, and not more than 21% by volume and the volatile acidity calculated as an ascetic acid, not in excess of 0.12 grams for white wines and 0.14 grams for red wines per 100cc after SO2 correction. They range from medium sweet to sweet and in color from pale gold to red.

SWEETWATER SPRINGS (*See* Hop Kiln Winery.)

SYCAMORE CREEK VINEYARD ★ *Santa Clara County*
12775 Uvas Road, Morgan Hill, CA 95037
(408) 779-4738 Founded: 1976
Storage: French, American oak, stainless steel.
Owners: Terry and Mary Kaye Parks. Winemaker, Manager: Terry Parks.

Originally started in 1906 by the Marchetti family who came as settlers. The 16 acre vineyard is located at the winery.

Label indicates vineyard and/or appellation. Varietal, vintage-dated wines produced are Cabernet Sauvignon, (dry and semi-sweet) Johannisberg Riesling, Gewurztraminer (off-dry), Zinfandel (estate bottled), Carignane (estate bottled), (estate bottled) Chardonnay and Pinot Noir.

['81 OC] (S) '79 CA, (G) '80 WR; ['82 OC] (G) '80 Z; ['82 SJP&C] (S&B) '81 SJR (P) (B) '79 Z, (C) (S) '80 CAG, (B) '80 Z.

Sylvaner
(White Table Wine) A varietal grape that produces a semi-dry to just a touch of sweetness, soft, clean and fruity wine. Not a Riesling, although sometimes labeled as Riesling or Franken Riesling. Goes well with shellfish, poultry and light meats.

Award wines to look for: Davis Bynum, Gundlach-Bundschu, Hoffman Mt. Ranch (HMR), St. Francis.

T

Table Or Dinner Wine
The "right" name for all still wines with not over 14%

alcohol content by volume. Most table or dinner wines are dry, but it is wrong to call all of them "dry" wines. That was formerly the practice but it has been discontinued because many dinner wines, like Sweet Sauterne, are actually semi-sweet or sweet, while some wines of the dessert or appetizer class, like Sherry, are nearly dry. "Tablé' or "dinner winé' is the "right" term because most wines of that class are used with meals and also because the term guides the consumer in selecting wines of this class for mealtime use. The class includes the wines sometimes referred to as "light wines," "dry wines," or "natural wines".

TAFT STREET WINERY *Sonoma County*

Box 878, 6450 First Street, Forestville, CA 95436
(707) 887-2801
Storage: Stainless steel, French oak.
Owners: John Tierney, Mike Martini and Arleigh Sanderson. Winemaker: John Tierney.

Grapes are purchased on a select vineyard basis. Varietal, vintage-dated wines produced are Chardonnay and Pinot Noir.

Tannins or Phenols

Give the wine its red color, astringent or bitter taste (but not "tart") and much of what the tongue senses as "body" in the wine.

Tannin in wine comes from grape skins, stems (even seeds if they happen to get crushed) but also, important to the eventual wine flavor, from barrels the wine was aged in at the winery. Most white wines are lower in tannin than most red wines, but no grape wine is completely free of it. However, white wines aged in wood (Chardonnay, Sauvignon Blanc and a few others) can contain lots of tannin, one of the reasons that these wines live longer in the bottle than others. Tannins are natural antioxidants and, since oxygen is the greatest enemy of aging wine, tannins are responsible for extending the life of bottled wine. "Fresh and Fruity" white wines, not aged in wood and not fermented in contact with skins or stems, don't contain much tannin and don't taste bitter or astringent and don't have long lives in the bottle.

Tart

Possessing agreeable acidity; in wine, tartness reflects the content of agreeable fruit acids.

Tasting Wine

In tasting wines the color, clarity, aroma, bouquet, tartness, flavor, astringency, degree of sweetness and balance are all to be considered.

Look for judging color and clarity.
Smell for aroma and bouquet.
Taste for flavor.

Tavola (*See* Heublein.)

Tawny

Wines having turned from red and brownish in color during maturation. Also a style of cask-matured Port.

TAYLOR CALIFORNIA CELLARS ★ (*See* The Monterey Vineyard)

Wines labeled Taylor California Cellars are developed and controlled by Dr. Richard Peterson.

['81 OC] (B) NV CH; ['82 OC] (S) CA, (S) SB, (S) JR; ['82 SJP] (B) CA.

TELDESCHI VINEYARD—Cabernet Sauvignon and Zinfandel vineyard in Dry Creek Valley.

THOMAS VINEYARDS *San Bernardino County*
8916 Foothill Blvd., Cucamonga, CA 91730
(714) 987-1612 Founded: 1839
Owner: the Filippi family. Winemaker: Joe Filippi, Jr.

Designated as a historical landmark, on March 3, 1839, Tiburcio Tapia was given the Cucamonga land grant by Juan Alvarado, Governor of Mexico. Tapia built an adobe home, planted a vineyard and started California's first winery.

Now owned by the Filippi family who started when Joseph and his father Giovanni came to America in 1922 to plant their first vineyard. The 10 acre vineyard is located in Mira Loma.

Wines produced are Zinfandel, Grenache Rosé, Chablis Blanc, Rhine and Burgundy.

Thunderbird (*See* E. & J. Gallo.)

TIBURON VINTNERS (*See* Sonoma Vineyards.)

TIJSSELING VINEYARDS *Mendocino County*
2150 McNab Ranch Road, Ukiah, CA 95482
(707) 462-1034 Founded: 1981
Storage: Oak, stainless steel.
Owners: Herman and Alida Tijsseling. General Manager: Dick Tijsseling. Winemaker: Miles Karakaseuic.

This 35 acre vineyard is part of a 3500 acre ranch. Varietal, vintage-dated, estate bottled wines produced are Chardonnay, Sauvignon Blanc, Cabernet Sauvignon and Petite Sirah. Also produced are White and Red Table Wines and Champagne.

Tinta Madeira Grape
Famous in Portugal and grown in the warm districts of California. Used in the best of California Ports.

Tinta Ruby Port Wine
A fortified wine produced from Tinta Madeira grapes. Ruby red in color and rich, with a fruity bouquet. Full bodied and sweet.

Tirage (or Liquer de Tirage)
The sugar or sweetner added to still wine to induce yeast cells to begin secondary fermentation.

TOBIAS VINEYARDS *San Luis Obispo County*
P.O. Box 733, Paso Robles, CA 93446
(805) 238-6380 Founded: 1980
Owners: Pat and Marty Wheeler. Winemaker: Pat Wheeler. Vineyards: 25 acres.

Vineyards are on a hilltop west of Paso Robles. Label indicates vineyard and/or appellation.

Varietal, vintage-dated wines produced are Zinfandel and Petite Sirah.

Tokay
Tokay is midway in sweetness between Sherry and Port. It is amber-colored with a slightly "nutty" or Sherry-like

flavor. It is a blend of dessert wines, usually Angelica, Port and Sherry. California Tokay is not to be confused with Tokay wines from Hungary or with the Flame Tokay grape, which may or may not be used in its production.

Award wines to look for: Christian Bros., Gibson, Perelli-Minetti.

TOPOLOS AT RUSSIAN RIVER ★ *Sonoma County*
5700 Gravenstein Hwy., North Forestville, CA 95436
(707) 887-2956 Founded: 1964
Storage: French, American oak, stainless steel.
Owners: Michael, Jerry and Christine Topolos. Winemaker: Michael Topolos.

25 acre vineyard at winery and 50 acres on Sonoma Mt. Label indicates vineyard and/or appellation. Varietal, vintage-dated wines produced are Chardonnay, Zinfandel, Petite Sirah, Pinot Noir and Cabernet Sauvignon.

Winemaker's favorite wines are Chardonnay, Petite Sirah and Cabernet Sauvignon.

['81 OC] (B) '79 Z; ['82 OC] (G) '79 PS, (B) '80 PN.

TOROSA VINEYARDS (*See* Richard Carey Winery.)

TOYON VINEYARDS ★ *Sonoma County*
427 Allan Court, Healdsburg, CA 95448
(707) 433-6847 Founded: 1973
Owner, Winemaker: Donald Holm.

Vineyard is located in Alexander Valley. Grapes are also purchased on a select vineyard basis. Label indicates vineyard and/or appellation.

Varietal, vintage-dated wines produced are Gewurztraminer, Chardonnay, Cabernet Sauvignon (estate bottled), Sauvignon Blanc and Zinfandel.

['81 OC] (B) '78 CA, (B) '80 G; ['82 SJP] (B) '79 CA.

TRADERS JOE'S WINERY ★ *Los Angeles County*
538 Mission St., South Pasadena, CA 91030
(213) 441-1177
President: Joe Columbe. Winebuyer: Bob Berning.

(Private labels Trader Joés. Raymond Hill, Chateau Arroyo and Schloss Josef for own stores).

['81 OC] (S) '79 Z; ['82 OC] (B) '79 Z, (S) CHA.

Traminer
(White Table Wine) A varietal grape that produces a light, fruity, semi-dry, soft wine. Originally from the Alsace province of France. Serve with shellfish and poultry.

Transfer Method
A method used to produce Champagne. After secondary fermentation is completed in the bottle, wine is passed through a filter to remove sediment and transferred to another bottle saving having to manually remove sediment.

TRAULSEN VINEYARDS *Napa County*
2250 Lake County Hwy., Calistoga, CA 94515
(707) 942-0283 Founded: 1980
Owners: John & Patricia Traulsen. Winemaker: John Traulsen. Vineyards: 2 acres at winery.

Grapes are also purchased on a select vineyard basis.

Label indicates vineyard and/or appellation.

Varietal, vintage-dated, estate bottled wine produced is Zinfandel. Also non-estate Zinfandel.

TREFETHEN VINEYARDS ★ *Napa County*

1160 Oak Knoll Ave., Napa, CA 94558

(707) 255-7700 Founded: 1973

Storage: Oak, stainless steel.

Owner: the Trefethen family. Winemaker: David Whitehouse, Jr.

Founded in 1886 and known as "Eschol" ranch, the owners won a first award for Cabernet Sauvignon at the San Francisco Viticultural Fair in 1880. The Trefethen family acquired the property in 1968. The 600 acre vineyards are located in Napa Valley.

The 100% varietal, vintage-dated, estate bottled wines produced are Chardonnay, White Riesling, Pinot Noir and Cabernet Sauvignon (sometimes blended with Merlot).

Also produced are Eshcol White wine and Eshcol Red wine.

['81 OC] (S) '79 CA, (G) '78 C, (G) '80 WR; ['82 OC] (B) '78 CA, (G) '81 JR, (S) '79 C.

TRENTADUE WINERY ★ *Sonoma County*

19170 Redwood Hwy., Geyserville, CA 95441

(707) 433-3104 Founded: 1969

Storage: Oak, redwood and stainless steel.

Owners: Leo and Evelyn Trentadue. Winemakers: Leo and Victor Trentadue.

The 200 acre vineyard is located at the winery in the Alexander Valley of Sonoma County.

100% Varietal, vintage-dated, estate bottled wines produced are Semillon, Chardonnay, Johannisberg Riesling, French Colombard, Chenin blanc, Zinfandel, Carignane, White Zinfandel, Petite Sirah, Merlot, Gamay, Cabernet Sauvignon and Aleatico. Also produced are Early Burgundy and Burgundy.

Winemaker's favorite wines are Petite Sirah and Zinfandel.

['82 OC] (B) '77 PS; ['82 SJC] (B) '80 LHZ.

TRIBUNO VERMOUTH (*See* Franzia Winery.)

Trockenbeerenauslese

The German word for "dried berry selection". Refers to the overripe grapes as a result of Botrytis that are allowed to stay on the vine until they shrink and the water evaporates thus giving the appearance of raisins. They must be picked raisin by raisin.

TRUCHARD VINEYARD—Cabernet Sauvignon vineyard in Napa Valley.

TUDAL WINERY *Napa County*

1015 Big Tree Road, St. Helena, CA 94574

(707) 963-3947 Founded: 1979

Storage: French oak, stainless steel.

Owners: Arnold and Alma Tudal. Winemaker: Arnold Tudal. Consulting enologist: Charles Ortman.

The vineyard is 10 acres in the Napa Valley. Varietal, vintage-dated, estate bottled wine produced is Cabernet Sauvignon. Also produced is Chardonnay.

TULOCAY WINERY ★ *Napa County*
Box 53, Oakville, CA 94562
(707) 255-4064 Founded: 1975
Storage: Oak, stainless steel.
Owners: William C. and Barbara Cadman. Winemaker: William Cadman.

Grapes are purchased from selected growers on a district basis.

100% varietal, wines produced are Cabernet Sauvignon, Pinot Noir, Zinfandel and Chardonnay. 100% Napa Valley grapes.

Winemaker's favorite wine is Pinot Noir.

['81 OC] (S) '77 PN; ['82 OC] (S) '78 PN.

TULARE COUNTY
San Joaquin Valley.

TUOLUMNE COUNTY
Sierra Foothills.

TURGEON & LOHR WINERY/J. LOHR WINES & JADE WINE CO. ★ *Santa Clara, Monterey Counties*
1000 Lenzen Avenue, San Jose, CA 95126
(408) 288-5057 Founded: 1974
Storage: American, French oak, stainless steel.
Owners: Bernard J. Turgeon and Jerome J. Lohr. Winemaker: Barry Gnekow.

The winery was converted from the historic Falstaff Brewery in San Jose. The 280 acre vineyards are located at Greenfield in Monterey County.

Label indicates vineyard and/or appellation. The varietal, vintage-dated wines produced are Chenin Blanc, Chardonnay, Johannsiberg Riesling, Pinot Blanc, Fumé Blanc, Gamay Rosé, Gamay, Zinfandel, Petite Sirah, Cabernet Sauvignon, Cabernet Sauvignon Trois Cuveés, Sauvignon Blanc and Selected Clusters Chardonnay (limited bottling) and Late Harvest Johannisberg Riesling (Special Selection and Select).

Also produced is Jade, a white wine.

The winemaker's favorite wine is Monterey Gamay.

['81 OC] (B) '80 CH, (B) '79 Z; ['82 OC] (S) '81 GA, (G) '78 PS, (B) '81 SB, (G) '81 JR, (B) '81 M, (B) '80 SB; ['82 SJP] (B) '80 C, (B) (C) '80 PB (P) (B) '81 CH, (P&C) (B&B) '81 SJR.

JOHNSON TURNBULL VINEYARDS *Napa County*
P.O. Box 41, 8210 St. Helena Hwy., Oakville, CA 94562
(707) 963-5839 (Winery) Founded: 1979
(415) 563-0807 (Office)
Storage: Oak.
Owners: Reverdy and Marta S. Johnson, William Turnbull, Jr. Winemaker: Lawrence Wara.

20 acre vineyards are located in Napa Valley.

Varietal, vintage-dated, estate bottled wine produced is Cabernet Sauvignon.

TURNER WINERY ★ *Lake County*
3750 E. Woodbridge Rd., P.O. Box R, Woodbridge, CA 95258
(209) 368-5338 Founded: 1970
Owners: the Turner family. John Turner—Exec. Wine-

maker, Ben White—Winemaker. Vineyards: 600 acres.

The winery was built at the turn of century and called Urgon Winery which stems from Urgon Station, a railroad switching terminal which today is the town of Woodbridge. The winery was the first built in Lodi. It was purchased by the Turner family in 1979. The vineyard is nestled in north coast Lake County.

Varietal, vintage-dated wines produced are Lake County Cabernet Sauvignon, Lake County Zinfandel, Lake County Merlot, Mendocino County Chardonnay, Lake County Fumé Blanc, Lake and Mendocino County Johannisberg Riesling, Lake County Chenin Blanc and Lake County Rosé of Cabernet Sauvignon. Also produced are California Burgundy, Chablis, Rosé and Rhine.

['82 OC] (B) '81 M, (B) '80 SB, (B) '80 M; ['82 SJC] (B) '80 Z.

TYLAND VINEYARDS ★ *Mendocino County*

2200 Mc Nab Ranch Road, Ukiah, CA 95482

(707) 462-1810 Founded: 1979

Storage: American, French oak, stainless steel.

Owners: Dick and Judy Tijsseling. Winemaker: Miles Krakasevic.

The 250-acre vineyard is in Mendocino County.

Varietal, vintage-dated, estate bottled wines produced are Cabernet Sauvignon, Zinfandel, Chardonnay, Pinot Noir Blanc, Chenin Blanc and Gamay Beaujolais. Varietal, vintage-dated wine produced is Gewurztraminer.

['81 OC] (G) '79 C; ['82 SJP] (B) '79 CA.

Tyrolia (*See* E. &. J. Gallo.)

U

ULLAGE

The amount of air-space above a wine in a bottle or cask which is no longer full. Excessive ullage leads to spoilage.

UNITED VINTNERS, INC (*See* Heublein.)

UPTON RANCH—Zinfandel vineyard in Amador County.

URAS (*See* Kirigin Cellars.)

V

VACHE ★ (*See* Brookside.)

['81 OC] (B) '80 CH, (G) '79 PS; ['82 OC] (B) '80 PS, (S) '81 JR.

VAIL VISTA—Chardonnay and Cabernet Sauvignon vineyards in Alexander Valley.

VALLEY OF THE MOON WINERY *Sonoma County*

777 Madrone Road, Glen Ellen, CA 95442

(707) 996-6941 Founded: 1944

Owners: E. & H. Parducci. Winemaker: Otto Toschi.

The name Valley of the Moon comes from the Wappo, Miwok and Pomo Indians. Originally "Valley of the Seven Moons," Jack London, the writer, shortened the name. Originally a portion of the Agua Caliente Rancho granted by the Mexican Government to Lazaro Pena, the land was purchased by General M. G. Vallejo. In 1851, Joseph Hooker took over 640 acres and planted a vineyard. He went on to become the famous "Fighting Joe Hooker" of the Union Army. These are the vineyards that surrounded the winery. Enrico Parducci bought the winery and vineyard in 1941.

The varietal, vintage-dated, estate bottled wines produced are Zinfandel, White Zinfandel, Zinfandel Rosé Dry, Zinfandel Rosé, French Colombard Dry, French Colombard, Semillon, Pinot Noir Blanc & Pinot Noir. Also produced are Claret, Burgundy, Vin Rosé and Chablis.

Varietal

When a wine is named for the principal grape variety from which it is made it is said to have a varietal name. Cabernet Sauvignon, Chardonnay, Muscatel, Pinot Noir are some of the varietal names for wine types in the United States.

VEGA VINEYARD WINERY ★ *Santa Barbara County*

9496 Santa Rosa Road, Buellton, CA 93427
(805) 688-2415 Founded: 1979
Storage: Oak, stainless steel.
Owner, Winemaker: William M. Mosby. Vineyard Mgr.: Michael Mosby.

30 acres of vineyards are located in the Santa Ynez Valley. Varietal, vintage-dated Rieslings produced are Late Harvest and Dry, Dry Gewurztraminer and Pinot Noir (Burgundian style).

['81 OC] (S) '79 WR, (G) '80 WR; ['82 OC] (B) '81 JR, (B) '81 JR, (B) '81 JR; ['82 SJP] (B) '81 WR, (P) (S) '81 SWR.

VELVET CORK WINE COCKTAILS (*See* Frasinetti Winery.)

VENTANA VINEYARDS WINERY ★ *Monterey County*

P.O. Box G, Soledad, CA 93960
(408) 678-2606 Founded: 1978
Storage: French, American oak, stainless steel.
Owners: J. Douglas and Shirley Meador. Winemaker: Doug Meador. Winery Supervisor: John Kerr.

Vineyard is on Arroyo Seco River in Monterey County.

Varietal, vintage-dated estate bottled wines produced are Chardonnay, Chenin Blanc, White Riesling, Petite Sirah, Pinot Noir, Cabernet Sauvignon, Sauvignon Blanc and Gewurztraminer. Also produced are Sauvignon Blanc and Sauvignon Musque.

['81 OC] (G) '79 C, (G) '79 PS, (G) '80 SB, (S) '80 WR; ['82 OC] (G) '80 C, (B) '81 CH, (G) '81 JR, (B) '81 JR; ['82 SJP&C] (B&B) '81 SWR (P) (B) '81 PSR.

Vermouth

A wine flavored with herbs and other aromatic substances. The two principal types are dry (pale) and sweet (dark) and usually fortified with Brandy.

For Vermouth, neutral white wines are first selected and aged. Then they are flavored by an infusion of herbs, and more ageing follows. Vermouth ranges from 15-20 percent alcohol content.

NICHOLAS G. VERRY *Fresno County*
400 First St., Parlier, CA 93684
(209) 646-2785 Founded: 1933
Owner, Winemaker: John N. Verry.

Specialized in Greek style resin flavored wines. Resin imported from Greece. Only current producer of Retsina in America.

CONRAD VIANO WINERY *Contra Costa County*
150 Morello Ave., Martinez, CA 94553
(415) 228-6465

VICHON WINERY *Napa County*
1595 Oakville Grade, P.O. Box 363, Oakville, CA 94562
(707) 944-2811 Founded: 1980
Storage: Oak, stainless steel.
Owners: Douglas Watson, Peter Brucher and George Vierra. Winemaker: John McKay.

Grapes are purchased on a select vineyard basis. Label indicates vineyard and/or appellation.

Varietal, vintage-dated wines produced are Cabernet Sauvignon and Chardonnay. Also produced is Chevrier Blanc (Semillon and Sauvignon Blanc).

VIEW'S LAND VINEYARD & WINERY *Sonoma County*
18701 Gehricke Rd., Sonoma, CA 95476
(707) 938-3768 Founded: 1979

The vineyard is located at the winery and Cabernet is purchased.

Varietal, vintage-dated wines produced are Gewurztraminer, Chardonnay and Cabernet Sauvignon.

VIKINGS FOUR (*See* Copenhagen Cellars.)

VILLA ARMANDO WINERY *Alameda County*
553 St. John St., Pleasanton, CA 94566
(415) 846-5488 Founded: 1903
Owner: the Scotto family. Winemaker: Anthony Scotto, Jr.

Vineyards are located in nearby Sunol Valley. The Scotto's have been a winemaking family for over 100 years. Their wines are primarily distributed on the East Coast.

Varietal, vintage-dated, estate bottled wines produced are Chardonnay, Cabernet Sauvignon, Malvasia Bianca and Petite Sirah. Varietal, vintage-dated wines produced are Cabernet Sauvignon, Chardonnay, Napa Gamay Rosé, Chenin Blanc, Valdepenas and Muscat Canelli. Also produced are Rustico Red, Rustico Mellow White, Rustico Mellow Red, Rustico Mellow Rosé, Orobianco and Rubinello.

VILLA MT. EDEN ★ *Napa County*
620 Oakville Crossroads, Oakville, CA 94562
(707) 944-2414 Founded: 1974
Owners: James K. and Anne McWilliams. Winemaker: Mike McGrath.

The 87 acre vineyards are located at the winery in the heart of the Napa Valley. Both vineyard and winery have existed since the early 1880s.

100% varietal, vintage-dated, estate bottled wines pro

uced (all dry style) are Cabernet Sauvignon, Chenin Blanc, Chardonnay, Pinot Noir, Gewurztraminer.

['81 OC] (B) '78 CA, (B) '79 C, (B) '78 PN; ['82 OC] (B) '79 PN.

VILLA PARADISO VINEYARDS *Santa Clara County*
1840 W. Edmundson Ave., Morgan Hill, CA 95037
(408) 778-1555 Founded: 1981
Storage: Oak, stainless steel.
Owner: Henry L. Bogardus II.

Vineyard is located at winery. Label indicates vineyard and/or appellation. Varietal, vintage-dated wines produced are Zinfandel and Petite Sirah.

VINA VISTA VINEYARDS *Sonoma County*
Chianti Road, Geyserville, CA 95441
(415) 939-3160 Founded: 1971
President: Keith Nelson.

VIN de BLANE FRES (*See* Brookside.)

VINE FLOW (*See* Bella Napoli Winery.)

VIN MONT (*See* Napa Valley Cooperative Winery.)

Vinosity
The grape character, and the effect of the winés actual alcohol strength.

Vintage
The gathering of grapes and their fermentation into wine; also the crop of grapes or wine of one season. A vintage wine produced in the U.S. is one labeled with the year in which at least 95% of its grapes were gathered and crushed and the juice therefrom fermented. A vintage year is one in which grapes reach full maturity. Particularly applicable in Europe where growing conditions vary greatly from year to year. Less applicable in California where grapes reach maturity every year.

Viticultural Area
A new class of appellation in the United States; a significant grape growing region whose geography and boundaries are recognized and strictly defined by the Federal Government. Previous regulations requiring that at least 75 percent of the wine comes from the vineyards in the labeled appellation remained unchanged, except when a "Viticultural Area" is used; then the minimum is 85 percent. The federally established "Viticultural Area" is also a factor in defining "estate bottled".

VOLCANIC HILL (*See* Diamond Creek Vineyard.)

VOSE VINEYARDS ★ *Napa County*
4035 Mt. Veeder Road, Napa, CA 94558
(707) 944-2254 Founded: 1970
Storage: Small oak, stainless steel.
Owner, Winemaker: Hamilton Vose III. Business Manager: Lourdes Vose.

Vineyards, 40 acres on Mt. Veeder. Varietal, vintage-dated wines produced are Chardonnay (estate bottled), Cabernet Sauvignon (estate bottled), Fumé Blanc, Zinfandel (estate bottled) and White Zinfandel (Zinblanca).

['81 OC] (S) '80 SB; ['82 OC] (S) '79 Z.

W

WALKER WINES ★ *Santa Clara County*
P.O. Box 11198A, Palo Alto, CA 94306
(415) 858-2310 Founded: 1979 Storage: Small oak.
Owner, Winemaker: Russ Walker.

Grapes are purchased on a select region basis. Label indicates vineyard and/or appellation. Varietal, vintage-dated wines produced are Chardonnay, Gamay, Cabernet Sauvignon, Barbera, White Zinfandel and Petite Sirah.

['81 OC] (B) '79 B; ['82 SJP] (B) '79 PS.

WATSON VINEYARDS *San Luis Obispo County*
Adelaide Road, Paso Robles, CA 93446
(805) 238-6091 Founded: 1981
Partners: Charles Bryan & Jennifer Ann Watson.

WEIBEL VINEYARDS ★ *Alameda, Mendocino Counties*
1250 Stanford Ave., Mission San Jose, CA 94538
(415) 656-2340 Founded: 1869
Storage: Oak, redwood, stainless steel.
Owner: Fred E. Weibel, Sr. Winemaker: Rick Casqueiro.

The vineyards are 450 acres at Mission San Jose and 400 acres in Mendocino County. They date back to 1806. The winery was established in 1869 by Leland Stanford. California's first Governor and founder of Stanford University.

Varietal, vintage-dated, estate bottled wines produced are Pinot Noir, Petite Sirah and Cabernet Sauvignon. Label indicates appellation. Vintage-dated, varietal wines are Chardonnay, Johannisberg Riesling, Pinot Noir, Cabernet Sauvignon, Gamay Beaujolais, Pinot Noir Blanc, Grey Riesling, Chenin Blanc, Petite Sirah, Cabernet Sauvignon Rosé, White Zinfandel, Zinfandel, Fumé Blanc, Riesling and White Cabernet Sauvignon. Also non-vintage Green Hungarian and Zinfandel.

Generics are Chablis, Burgundy and Vin Rosé.

Mountain wines are Mountain Chablis, Mountain Burgundy and Mountain Vin Rosé.

Proprietor's Special Reserve are Pinot Noir, Cabernet Sauvignon and Petite Sirah.

Bottle fermented wines, Chardonnay Brut, Brut Champagne, Extra Dry Champagne, Sparkling Burgundy and Blanc de Pinot Noir.

Crackling Wines, Champagne Blanc de Blanc, Crackling Rosé, Sparkling White Zinfandel, Muscato Spumante and Sparkling Green Hungarian.

Dessert Wines: Dry Bin Sherry, Classic Medium Sherry, Amber Cream Sherry, Rare Port, Cream of Black Muscat and Tangor.

Vermouths: Dry Vermouth and Sweet Vermouth.

Stanford: Extra Dry Champagne.

The winemaker's favorite is Fumé Blanc and estate bottled Pinot Noir.

['81 OC], (S) '80 CH, (B) '75 PN, (S) '80 WR; ['82 OC] (S) CHA, (B) CHA, (G) CHA; ['82 SJP] (B) '81 WZ, (C) (B) '81

WCA, (B) SW.

WEIDMAN VINEYARD—Zinfandel vineyard in Santa Clara County.

WEINGARTEN CASTLE
19920 Geyserville Ave., Geyserville, CA 95448
(707) 433-4400
Owner: Leroy Rasmussen. Winemaker: Dan Teldeschi.

WENTE BROS ★ *Alameda County*
5565 Telsa Road, Livermore, CA 94550
(415) 447-3603 Founded: 1883
Storage: Oak, redwood, stainless steel.
Owner: the Wente family. Winemaker: Eric Wente.

Wente Bros. was founded in 1883 when Carl Wente planted the vineyard and built the winery in the Livermore Valley. Vineyards are 900 acres at the winery and 600 acres in the Arroyo Seco area of Monterey County. Philip, Carolyn and Eric, fourth generation run the vineyards and winery.

100% varietal, vintage-dated wines produced are Gamay Beaujolais, Petite Sirah (estate bottled), Pinot Noir (vintner grown), Blanc de Noir, Dry Semillon (estate bottled), Johannisberg Riesling, Pinot Blanc (vintner grown), Zinfandel, Sauvignon Blanc (estate bottled), Pinot Chardonnay, and Grey Riesling.

Also produced are Chablis, Rosé, and Le Blanc de Blanc.

There are Wente Bros. Special Selections which are Arroyo Seco Riesling (100% Late Harvest White Riesling), Gewurztraminer (100%), and Chateau Wente (58% Sauvignon Blanc, 42% Semillon).

The winemaker's favorite wines are Pinot Chardonnay, Sauvignon Blanc, Petite Sirah, Johannsiberg Riesling and Arroyo Seco Riesling.

['81 OC] (B) NV CH, (G) '79 PS, (G) '79 WR; ['82 OC] (G) '79 PS, (B) '80 PB, (S) '79 JR; ['82 SJP] (B) '80 SB, (P&C) (S&S) '79 SR.

WHALER VINEYARD *Mendocino County*
6200 Eastside Rd., Ukiah, Ca 95482
(707) 462-6355 Founded: 1973
Storage: American oak, stainless steel.
Owners: Russell & Ann Nyborg. Winemaker: Russ Nyborg. Vineyards: 23 acres at winery.

A new winery specializing in vintage-dated, estate bottled Zinfandel.

WM. WHEELER WINERY ★ *Sonoma County*
130 Plaza Street, Healdsburg, CA 95448
(707) 433-8786
Owners: William & Ingrid Wheeler. Winemaker: Julia Baird Iantosca.

Located in Dry Creek Valley in Sonoma County. Ranch and vineyard is 175 acres. Tasting room and ageing cellars are located in Healdsburg, 5 miles from vineyards.

Varietal, vintage-dated wines produced are Cabernet Sauvignon, Chardonnay and Sauvignon Blanc.

['82 SJP] (S) '80 C, (P) (B) '79 CA.

WHITEHALL LANE WINERY ★ *Napa County*
1563 St. Helena Hwy., St. Helena, CA 94574
(707) 963-9454 Founded: 1980
Owners: Alan & Charlene Steen, and Art & Bunnie Finkelstein. Winemaker: Arthur Finkelstein. Vineyard: 23 acres at winery and 4 acres in Rutherford.

Grapes are also purchased on a selected vineyard basis. Label indicates vineyard and/or appellation. Varietal, vintage-dated wines produced are Chardonnay, Cabernet Suavignon, Sauvignon Blanc and Blanc de Noir.

['81 OC] (S) '80 SB; ['82 OC] (B) '81 PN; ['82 SJP] (B) '80 C, (P) (B) '81 RT.

WHITE OAK VINEYARDS *Sonoma County*
208 Haydon St., Healdsburg, CA 95448
(707) 433-8429 Founded: 1981
Owners: R. Terry & Carolyn Gibson and William & Barbara Myers. Winemaker: R. Terry Gibson.

Winery was designed by Bill Myers and built by Bill and Terry. Label indicates vineyard and/or appellation.

Varietal, vintage-dated wines produced are Chardonnay, Cabernet Sauvignon, Johannisberg Riesling, Sauvignon Blanc and Zinfandel. Also produce under the Fitch Mountain Cellars label.

White Pinot
(White Table Wine) (*See* Chenin Blanc.)

White Riesling
(White Table Wine) (*See* Johannisberg Riesling.)

White Table Wines
White dinner or table wines vary from extremely dry and tart to sweet and full-bodied. Their color ranges from pale straw to deep gold and their alcohol content from 10 to 14 percent. Most popular white dinner wines fall into three generic types: Chablis, Rhine or Sauterne. The varietal white wines are all discussed under their varietal name.

White Dinner Wines—Generic: Chablis, Moselle, Rhine, Sauterne, Vino Bianco.

White Table Wines—Varietal: Chardonnay (Pinot Chardonnay), Chenin Blanc, Emerald Riesling, French Colombard, Gewurztraminer, Pinot Blanc, Pinot Noir Blanc, Sauvignon Blanc, Semillon, Sylvaner Riesling, Traminer, White Riesling (Johannisberg), Zinfandel Blanc.

Award wines to look for: Barengo, Brookside, Buena Vista, Richard Carey, Chateau St. Jean, Colony, Congress Springs, R. & J. Cook, Conn Creek, Cordtz Brothers, ENZ, Filippi, Foppiano, Jacare, Kenwood, Mirassou, J. W. Morris, Papagni, Parducci, Pedroncelli, Preston, Rancho Yerba Buena, Raymond, River Oaks, San Antonio, San Martin, Sebastiani, Sonoma, Stony Ridge, Turgeon & Lohr, Ventana.

WILDWOOD VINEYARD—Cabernet Sauvignon and Chardonnay vineyard in hills of Sonoma Valley.

WILLOW CREEK VINEYARD *Humboldt County*
1904 Pickett Road, McKinleyville, CA 95521
(707) 839-3373 Founded: 1976
Storage: French, American oak, stainless steel.
Owners: Dean and Judy Williams. Winemaker/Manager:

Dean Williams.

2-1/2 acre vineyard is located at Willow Creek in the mountains. Some are grown, produced and bottled in Humboldt Co.

Varietal, vintage-dated, estate bottled wines produced are Zinfandel, Chardonnay, White Zinfandel, Gewurztraminer, Petite Sirah and Cabernet Sauvignon.

WILLOWSIDE VINEYARDS *Sonoma County*
1672 Willowside Rd., Santa Rosa, CA 95401
(707) 528-1599 and (707) 544-7504 Founded: 1975
Owner: the Beliz family. Winemaker: Berle Beliz.

Varietal, vintage-dated wines produced are Zinfandel, Pinot Noir, Pinot Chardonnay and Gewurztraminer. Vineyards, 24 acres in Sonoma County.

WINDSOR VINEYARDS (*See* Sonoma Vineyards.)

WINEMASTERS (*See* Guild Wineries.)

WINE BY WHEELER (*See* Nicasio Vineyards.)

WINERY LAKE VINEYARD—Chardonnay, Johannisberg Riesling, Pinot Noir and Merlot vineyard in Carneros district of Napa.

Wine Tasting and Scoring

These are the quality factors and score weighting as recommended by U. C. Davis:

APPEARANCE—This refers to clarity, not color. Wine should be free of cloud or sediment (unless it is very old red). "Unfiltered" wines don't often rate high in appearance. Give the wine 2 points if brilliant, only 1 if not crystal clear, and 0 if dull or cloudy.

COLOR—You need an idea of what color is right for each wine. Golden or amber is unacceptable for white or pink table wines, but exactly right for many dessert wines. Rosé should be distinctly pink, with only a suggestion of orange or red. Whites can be yellow, gold or straw color; flaws are amber or too "water white'. Red can have violet tints if young, amber tints if aged. But brown is a flaw, as is too little red color. Perfect color for type: 2 points; reduce points if unacceptable tints or tones begin to predominate.

AROMA AND BOUQUET—Aroma may be a "varietal" or simply wine-like, "vinous". Intensity of aroma and bouquet may be light, medium or high. Give the wine 4 points for having a clean and unmistakeable aroma, 3 points for good varietal overtones, 2 for being pleasantly vinous, etc. Subtract points for off odors such as moldy, mousey, corked, sulfur dioxide, sewer-like, excess wood, bacterial, carmel, raisiny, rubbery, etc.

ACESCENCE—Volatile acidity (vinegar) is an index of aerobic bacterial spoilage in wine. If you smell no vinegar, give the wine 2 points; a faint vinegar aroma rates 1 point. If the smell is strong and interferes with the normal wine aroma and bouquet, give the wine 0.

TOTAL ACID—Finally, for the first time, you taste the wine. Too high acidity tastes excessively sharp or sour, low acid makes the wine seem flat, flabby or even soapy. Rate the acidity level 0, 1 or 2 points.

SUGAR—The taste of sugar (sweetness) and acid are

evaluated together. Good balance: 1 point; too high or too low in sugar, 0.

BODY—Evaluate the mouth-feel of the wine as it is swished about in the mouth. Too thin or too heavy are defects: 0 points. Good balance: 1 point.

FLAVOR—Is the flavor pleasant, and appropriate for the wine type? Does it correspond well with the smell? 2 points is perfect, 1 if the flavor is slightly marred by the off-tastes, and 0 if off-tastes are distinct.

ASTRINGENCY—This is the taste of tannin (sometimes bitter or mouth puckering) and it should be in balance with the other taste components. Score 0, 1 or 2, depending upon your judgement of the balance.

GENERAL QUALITY—If your overall impression is high, give it 2 points; average 1 point; poor 0 points.

20 is maximum, 17-20 is an outstanding wine, 13-16 sound commercial wine, below 9 is commercially unacceptable wine.

WINTERS WINERY *Yolo County*

15 Main St., Winters, CA 95694
(916) 795-3201 Founded: 1980
Owners: David & Leona Storm. Winemaker: D. R. Storm.

Winery is in an 1897 brick building on banks of Putah Creek. Grapes are purchased on a select vineyard basis. Label indicates vineyard and/or appellation.

Varietal, vintage-dated wines produced are Amador Late Harvest Zinfandel, Chardonnay, Sauvignon Blanc, White Riesling, Chenin Blanc, Petite Sirah, and Cabernet Sauvignon.

WITTWER WINERY *Humboldt County*

2440 Frank Avenue, Eureka, CA 95501
(707) 433-8852 Founded: 1969
Storage: Oak, stainless steel.
Owner, Winemaker: J. R. Wittwer.

Varietal wines produced are Cabernet Sauvignon and French Colombard.

WOODBRIDGE VINEYARD ASSN. *San Joaquin County*

4614 W. Turner Rd., Lodi, CA 95240
(209) 369-2614 Founded: 1905
Storage: Oak, stainless steel.
Owner: Growers Cooperative. Winemaker: James W. Riley.

WOODBURY WINERY *Marin County*

32 Woodland Ave., San Rafael, CA 94901
(415) 454-2355 Founded: 1977
Storage: Oak, redwood, stainless steel.
Owner, Winemaker: Russell T. Woodbury.

Grapes are purchased from Alexander Valley vineyards. Port wine is only wine produced.

Favorite wine of winemaker is Vintage Port.

WOODEN VALLEY WINERY *Solano County*

4756 Suisun Valley Rd., Suisun, CA 94585
(707) 864-0730 Founded: 1932
Owners: Mario and Richard Lanza. Vineyards: 125 acres.

Varietal wines produced are Riesling, Sauvignon Blanc,

Zinfandel, Pinot Noir, Cabernet Sauvignon, Gamay Beaujolais, French Colombard, Pinot Chardonnay, Johannisberg Riesling, Green Hungarian, Gewurztraminer, Chenin Blanc, Pinot Noir Blanc, Zinfandel, Blanc and Cabernet Rosé.

WOODSIDE VINEYARDS *San Mateo County*
340 Kings Mountain Road, Woodside, CA 94062
(415) 851-7475 Founded: 1960
Owners: Robert and Polly Mullen. Winemaker: Bruce Hart. Vineyards: 8 acres.

The vineyard is located at the winery.

Varietal, vintage-dated wines produced are Cabernet Sauvignon, Pinot Noir and Chardonnay.

Woody
The characteristic odor of "wet oak" is apparent in wine aged too long or in faulty wood. The term comes into use when this characteristic is excessive.

Y

YANKEE HILL WINERY *Tuolumne County*
11755 Coarsegold Lane, Columbia, CA 95310
(209) 532-3015 Founded: 1974
Owner, Winemaker: Ron Erickson.

Varietal, vintage-dated wines produced are Golden Bonanza Zinfandel and Columbia Cellars Zinfandel.

YERBA BUENA *San Francisco County*
Pier 33, San Francisco, CA 94111
(415) 397-5944 Founded: 1977
Owner: Yerba Buena Industries, Inc. Winemaker: Brian R. R. Whipple. Vineyards: 22 acres in Sonoma County.

Varietal wines produced are Pinot Noir (red, white, rosé) and Gewurztraminer.

YOLO COUNTY
Northern San Joaquin Valley.

YORK CREEK VINEYARD—Petite Sirah, Zinfandel, and Cabernet Sauvignon vineyard in Napa on Spring Mountain.

YORK MOUNTAIN WINERY ★ *San Luis Obispo County*
Rt. 2, Box 191, Templeton, CA 93465
(805) 238-3925 Founded: 1882
Storage: Oak, redwood, stainless steel.
Owner: Max Goldman. Winemaker/Manager: Steve Goldman.

Founded by the York family, the winery was sold to Max Goldman in 1970. Max Goldman is former president of the American Society of Enologists. The 50 acre vineyard being replanted is located at the winery, York Mountain, Templeton.

Varietal, estate bottled, vintage-dated wines produced are Zinfandel, Pinot Noir, Cabernet Sauvignon, Chardonnay, Merlot and Merlot Rosé (not estate bottled).

Also produced is a Red wine (Barbera, Merlot-Ruby Cabernet Blend) and White wine (Chenin Blanc and

Chardonnay blend). A Dry Sherry and two Champagnes are also available.

The winemaker's favorite wine is Zinfandel.

['82 SJP] (B) '77 M.

YOSEMITE ROAD (*See* Franzia Winery.)

ROBERT YOUNG VINEYARDS

Johannisberg Riesling, Chardonnay and Gewurztraminer vineyards in Alexander Valley.

YVERDON VINEYARDS ★ *Napa County*

3787 Spring Mountain Road, Saint Helena, CA 94574

(707) 963-4270 Founded: 1970

Owner/Winemaker: Fred Aves.

One vineyard is located at the winery site on Spring Mountain Road, a second in St. Helena and a third in the Napa Valley at the foot of Mt. St. Helena totalling 100 acres.

Label indicates vineyard and/or appellation. Varietal, vintage-dated wines produced are Cabernet Sauvignon, Gamay, Chenin Blanc, Johannisberg Riesling and Gewurz raminer.

['82 SJP] (B) '79 G, (P&C) (B&S) '78 Z.

Z

ZACA CREEK (*See* Ross-Kellerei.)

ZACA MESA WINERY ★ *Santa Barbara County*

P.O. Box 547, Foxen Canyon Road, Los Olivos, CA 93441

(805) 688-9339 Founded: 1978

Administration: 2920 Grand Avenue, P.O. 547, Los Olivos, CA 93441

President: Louis M. Ream. Winemaker: Ken Brown.

240 acre vineyard and winery is located on Zaca Mesa Ranch. Varietal, vintage-dated, estate bottled wines pro duced are Cabernet Sauvignon, Chardonnay, Johannsiberg Riesling, Sauvignon Blanc, Pinot Noir and Zinfandel. Also produced are Toyon Blanc, and Toyon Noir.

['81 OC] (B) '78 CA, (B) '79 C, (B) '78 PN, (B) '80 WR, (B) '79 Z; ['82 OC] (S) '78 CA, (B) '79 M, (G) '79 PN, (S) '81 JR.

ZD WINES ★ *Napa County*

8383 Silverado Trail, Napa, CA 94558

(707) 963-5188 Founded: 1969

Storage: Oak.

Owners/Winemakers: Norman DeLeuze and Gino Zepponi.

A 3 acre vineyard was planted in 1981. Grapes are purchased on a select vineyard basis.

Label indicates vineyard and/or appellation. Varietal, vintage-dated wines produced are Chardonnay, Pinot Noir, Cabernet Sauvignon and Zinfandel.

The winemaker's favorite wines are Chardonnay and Pinot Noir.

['81 OC] (B) '79 C; ['82 OC] (S) '79 CA, (B) '79 PN, (B) '80 C; ['82 SJP] (B) '80 C, (P) (B) '79 CA.

STEPHEN ZELLERBACH VINEYARD *Sonoma County*

14350 Chalk Hill Road, Geyserville, CA 95448

(707) 433-WINE Founded: 1981
Storage: American, French oak, stainless steel.
Owner: Stephen Zellerbach Vineyards, Inc. Winemaker: John Jaffray.

The property of 160 acres is planted in 69 acres of vines. The vineyard is in the Chalk Hill area at the southern tip of the Alexander Valley. Stephen Zellerbach is joined in his efforts by his wife "Cici" whose family founded the Nervo Winery in 1850.

Varietal, vintage-dated, estate bottled wines produced are Cabernet Sauvignon and Merlot. Varietal, vintage-dated Chardonnay is also produced.

ZIN BLANCA (*See* Vose Vineyards.)

ZINFANDEL

(Red Table Wine) A varietal grape that produces three styles of wine: Light—spicy flavor with a berry-like aroma and a tang. It should be consumed in one to three years, serve with pastas and barbecues; Oak aged—intense, berry-like and spicy aroma, full bodied with some tannin and dark in color. Should be aged 3-8 years. Serve with sausages, pastas and stews; Late Harvest—rich, dark, full-bodied, lots of alcohol and tannin. May be aged 8 to 16 years. Serve with Roquefort and rich game dishes.

Award wines to look for: Ahern, Almaden, Baldinelli/Shenandoah, Bargetto, Beau Val, Bel Arbres Berkeley, Boeger, Brenner, David Bruce, Buena Vista, Burgess, Davis Bynum, Cakebread, Calera, Callaway, Richard Carey, Carneros Creek, Cassayre-Forni, Channing Rudd, Chateau Montelena, Christian Bros., Clos du Val, Colony, Congress Springs, Conn Creek, Conrad Viano, Cordtz Bros., H. Coturri, Cresta Blanca, Cribari, Cuvaison, Dehlinger, DeLoach, Devlin, Dry Creek, Edmeades, Estrella River, Farview Farm, Fetzer, Foppiano, Fortino, Gemello, Geyser Peak, Giumarra, Granite Springs, Grgich Hills, Gundlach-Bundschu, Hacienda, Haraszthy, Harbor, Hoffman Mt. (HMR), Hop Kiln, Inglenook, Karly, Kenwood, Kenworthy, Las Montanas, Lawrence, Leeward, Lytton Springs, Madrona, Louis Martini, Mastantuono, McDowell Valley, McLester, Milano, Mirassou, Montclair, Monterey Peninsula, Montevina, J. W. Morris, Napa Wine Cellars, Obester, Page Mill, Parducci, Pedroncelli, Pesenti, Joseph Phelps, Pope Valley, Preston, Ranchita Oaks, Raymond, Richardson, Ridge, Ridgewood, River Oaks, River Road, Rosenblum, Roudon-Smith, Round Hill, Rutherford Hill, San Martin, Santa Barbara, Santino, Sarah's Vineyard, Shenandoah, Sherrill, Sierra Vista, Simi, Smothers, Sommelier, Sonoma, Stony Ridge, Story, Sunrise, Sutter Home, Sycamore Creek, Topolos, Trader Joe's (Raymond Hill), Trentadue, Turner Winery, Valley of the Moon, Veedercrest, Verdugo, Vose, Wente Bros., Woodbury, Yverdon, Zaca Mesa.

Zinfandel—Late Harvest

Award wines to look for: Bynum, Calera, Charles Le Franc, Devlin, Dry Creek, Fetzer, Gemello, Grand Cru, Hop Kiln, Johnson's Alexander Valley, Milano, Monterey Peninsula, Montevina, Mount Veeder, Ridge, Roudon-

Smith, Rutherford Hill, Santino, Sutter Home, Woodbury.

Zinfandel Blanc

Award wines to look for: Bel Arbres, DeLoach, Greenstone, Konocti, Mastantuono, San Antonio, Weibel.

California Vintage Chart

Unlike the wine growing regions of Europe, California has a relatively stable climate with consistent sunshine to ripen the grapes and produce reliable wine. However, there are some years that are truly outstanding in certain areas, particularly in the premium varietals. There are, of course, exceptions.

	North Coast (Napa, Sonoma, Mendocino)		Central Coast (Monterey, Santa Clara, etc.)	
	REDS	WHITES	REDS	WHITES
1968	★★★★	★★★★	★★★★	★★★★
1969	★★★	★★★	★★★	★★★
1970	★★★★	★★	★★★	★★★
1971	★★	★★	★	★
1972	★★	★	★	★
1973	★★★	★★	★★★	★★
1974	★★★★	★★★	★★★★	★★★
1975	★★★	★★★★	★★★	★★★
1976	★★★	★★★	★★★	★★★★
1977	★★★	★★★★	★★	★★★
1978	★★★★	★★★★	★★★★	★★★★
1979	★★★	★★★	★★★	★★★
1980	★★★★	★★★	★★★	★★★
1981	★★★	★★	*too early*	★★
1982	*too early*	*mixed**	*too early*	*mixed**

★★★★ EXCEPTIONAL ★★★ VERY GOOD
★★ GOOD ★ FAIR

**1982 was a difficult and mixed vintage due to spring frosts, a cool summer and early September rains. Although it was the largest harvest on record, the overall quality was poor; but the early varieties look exceptional.*

California Vintage Chart

WINE RATINGS

Wine, like music and art is very subjective when it comes to personal taste. When it comes to judging the best, the sum total of a large panel of experts is the closest one can get when seeking an objective professional opinion. In my effort to be as objective as possible, with the cooperation of the Orange County Wine Society, I bring to you the results of the 1982 Orange County Fair Commercial Wine competition.
William I. Kaufman.

ORANGE COUNTY FAIR
1982 Wine Judging Awards

The 1982 competition included seventeen (17) different wine varieties . . . Barbera, Cabernet Sauvignon, Charbono, Chardonnay, Chenin Blanc, Gamay Beaujolais, Gewurztraminer, Merlot, Muscat, Petite Sirah, Pinot Blanc, Pinot Noir, Sauvignon (Fumé) Blanc, White (Johannisberg) Riesling, Zinfandel, and Sparkling Wine (all methods).

This competition judges every wine in each category that is commercially available in Orange County. The wine samples for judging are obtained either from the wineries, or when unobtainable from a winery, are purchased off the shelf from local retail outlets.

The judging is performed by professionals. Each judge is either a winemaker or winery principal with each traveling to Orange County for the competition. All judging is performed "blind;" the judging panels have no knowledge of the identity of the wines being evaluated. Scoring is done using a 20-point rating system. Each wine is evaluated on such attributes as appearance, color, aroma, bouquet, total acidity, sweetness, body, flavor, bitterness, astringency, and general quality. Each wine is judged by a panel of judges and is placed in a price grouping identified as inexpensive, moderate and premium. The white wines are further grouped by subcategories of residual sugar percentage. Each grouping is judged individually on the basis of entries in that grouping alone. This system of judging, and the reporting of results by category, is to assist the consumer in purchasing wines considered by the judges to be the best of their class.

MEDAL WINNERS

BARBERA
($5.51 and UP—3 entries)

GOLD
None
SILVER
Monterey Peninsula Winery, 1979, Northern California Vineyard View
BRONZE
Sebastiani Vineyards, 1976, Northern California, Proprietors Reserve

BARBERA
($4.51 to $5.50—6 entries)

GOLD
None
SILVER
None
BRONZE
Parducdi Wine Cellars, 1977, North Coast
Walker Wines, 1979, Solano County, Nyland Vineyard
Borra's Cellar, 1978, California, Estate Bottled

BARBERA
(Up to $4.50—4 entries)

No Awards

CABERNET SAUVIGNON
($11.01 and UP—59 entries)

GOLD
Monterey Peninsula Winery, 1979, Monterey, Arroyo Seco
SILVER
Chateau Montelena Winery, 1978, Sonoma
Conn Creek, 1978, Napa Valley, Lot 1
Clos du Bois, 1978, Alexander Valley, Marlstone Vineyard
Stonegate, 1978, Napa Valley
Joseph Phelps Vineyards, 1978, Napa Valley, Backus
Kenwood Vineyards, 1979, Sonoma Valley, Jack London Vineyard
Heitz Wine Cellars, 1977, Napa Valley, Martha's Vineyard
ZD Wines, 1979, California
BRONZE
Beaulieu Vineyard, 1977, Napa Valley, Private Reserve
Charles Krug, 1977, Napa Valley, Vintage Select

Jekel Vineyard, 1978, Monterey, Private Reserve, Estate Bottled
Shown & Sons Vineyards, 1979, Rutherford, Napa Valley, Estate Bottled
Robert Mondavi Winery, 1977, Napa Valley, Reserve
Buena Vista Winery & Vineyards, 1978, Sonoma Valley, Special Selection, Carneros, Estate Bottled
Mount Eden Vineyards, 1978, Santa Cruz Mountains, Estate Bottled

CABERNET SAUVIGNON
($7.01 to $11.00—101 entries)

GOLD

Stony Ridge Winery, 1979, Monterey County, Smith & Hook Vineyard
Field Stone Winery, 1979, Alexander Valley, Estate Bottled
Carmel Bay Winery, 1978, Monterey County, D & M Junction Vineyards

SILVER

HMR Hoffman Vineyards, 1979, Central Coast
McDowell Valley Vineyards, 1979, Mendocino County, Estate Bottled
Fenestra, 1979, Monterey
Pine Ridge Winery, 1979, Napa Valley, Rutherford District
Zaca Mesa Winery, 1978, Santa Ynez Valley, Special Selection

BRONZE

Cordtz Brothers Cellars, 1980, Upper Alexander Valley
Grand Cru Vineyards, 1980, California
Davis Bynum Winery, 1979, Sonoma
Beaulieu Vineyard, 1978, Napa Valley, Rutherford, Estate Bottled
Obester Winery, 1979, Sonoma County, Batto Ranch
Dry Creek Vineyard, 1979, Sonoma County
Trefethen Vineyards, 1978, Napa Valley, Trefethen Vineyards
Girard Winery, 1980, Napa Valley, Estate Bottled
Clos du Bois, 1978, Alexander Valley
Estrella River Winery, 1978, San Luis Obispo, Estate Bottled
Raymond Vineyard & Cellar, 1979, Napa Valley, Estate Bottled
Marietta Cellars, 1978, Dry Creek
Ahlgren Vineyard, 1979, Napa Valley, Rutherford
J. Pedroncelli Winery, 1978, Sonoma, Vintage Selection
Jekel Vineyard, 1978, Monterey, Estate Bottled
Mirassou Vineyards, 1979, Monterey County, Harvest Reserve
Veedercrest Vineyards, 1979, Napa Valley, North Ranch Vineyard
Pommeraie Vineyards, 1979, Sonoma County
Boeger Winery, 1979, El Dorado County, Estate

Bottled
Rutherford Hill Winery, 1978, Napa Valley

CABERNET SAUVIGNON
(Up to $7.00—60 entries)
GOLD
Bel Arbres Vineyards, 1979, Lake County
Geyser Peak Winery, 1977, California
SILVER
Alexander Valley Vineyards, 1979, Alexander Valley, Estate Bottled
Sierra Vista Winery, 1979, El Dorado County
Taylor California Cellars, N.V., California
J. Pedroncelli Winery, 1979, Sonoma
BRONZE
Cambiaso Winery and Vineyards, 1978, Sonoma
Fortino Winery, 1978, Santa Clara County
Fetzer Vineyards, 1980, Lake County
River Oaks Vineyards, 1979, Alexander Valley
Montevina Wines, 1979, Amador County, Estate Bottled
Fetzer Vineyards, 1979, Mendocino County
Beaulieu Vineyard, 1979, Napa Valley, Beau Tour, Estate Bottled

CHARBONO
($6.01 and UP—3 entries)
GOLD
None
SILVER
None
BRONZE
Souverain Winery, 1978, North Coast

CHARBONO
($4.51 to $6.00—3 entries)
GOLD
None
SILVER
None
BRONZE
Fortino Winery, 1978, Santa Clara County

CHARBONO
(Up to $4.50—No entries)

CHARDONNAY
($12.01 and Up—58 entries)
GOLD
Stag's Leap Wine Cellars, 1979, Napa Valley, Haynes
Chateau St. Jean, 1980, Alexander Valley, Robert Young Vineyards
Veedercrest Vineyards, 1980, Napa Valley, Winery Lake Vineyards
Dry Creek Vineyard, 1980, Sonoma, Vintners Reserve
Milano, 1980, Mendocino, Redwood Valley, Lolonis

Vineyards

SILVER

Chateau Chevalier Winery, 1980, Edna Valley

Kenwood Vineyards, 1980, Sonoma Valley, Beltane Ranch

Clos du Bois, 1980, Alexander Valley, Barrel Fermented, Reserve

Smothers, 1980, Sonoma, Green Pastures Vineyard

Burgess Cellars, 1980, Napa

Robert Mondavi Winery, 1980, Napa Valley

BRONZE

Chateau St. Jean, 1980, Alexander Valley, Jimtown Ranch

ZD Wines, 1980, California

Robert Keenan Winery, 1980, Napa Valley

Edmeades, 1980, Mendocino County, Anderson Valley Reserve

CHARDONNAY
($8.01 to $12.00—103 entries)

GOLD

Ventana Vineyards Winery, 1980, Monterey, Estate Bottled

Raymond Vineyard & Cellar, 1980, Napa Valley, Estate Bottled

Alexander Valley Vineyards, 1980, Alexander Valley, Estate Bottled

Ballard Canyon Winery, 1981, Santa Barbara

Sonoma Vineyards, 1980, Sonoma County, Chalk Hill Vineyard, Estate Bottled, Second Release

SILVER

J. Carey Cellars, 1980, Santa Ynez Valley

Jekel Vineyard, 1980, Monterey

Conn Creek, 1979, Napa Valley

Chateau St. Jean, 1980, Sonoma County

Napa Cellars, 1980, Alexander Valley, Black Mountain Vineyard

Shafer Winery, 1980, Napa Valley, Spicer Ranch, Monticello Vineyards

DeLoach Vineyards, 1980, Russian River Valley

Stevenot Winery, 1980, Mendocino County

Trefethen Vineyards, 1979, Napa Valley, Tefethen Vineyards

Flora Springs Wine Co., 1980, Napa Valley

Parsons Creek Winery, 1980, Sonoma, Dry Creek, Vogenson Ranch

Parsons Creek Winery, 1981, Mendocino

Bargetto Winery, 1980, Santa Barbara County, Tepusquet Vineyard

Santa Ynez Valley Winery, 1980, California

Ahern Winery, 1981, Edna Valley, San Luis Obispo, MacGregor Vineyard

BRONZE

Rutherford Hill Winery, 1980, Napa Valley

Dry Creek Vineyard, 1980, Sonoma

Mill Creek Vineyards, 1980, Sonoma County, Dry

Creek Valley, Estate Bottled
David Bruce Winery, 1980, California
McDowell Valley Vineyards, 1980, Mendocino County, Estate Bottled
Lakespring Winery, 1980, Napa Valley
Hacienda Wine Cellars (Inc.), 1980, Sonoma County, Clair de Lune
Cordtz Brothers Cellars, 1980, Upper Alexander Valley
Souverain Winery, 1981, North Coast
Parducci Wine Cellars, 1980, North Coast, Cellar Masters
Conn Creek, 1979, Napa Valley, Yountville
Stonegate, 1980, Napa Valley
Christian Brothers Winery, 1979, Napa Valley
Simi Winery, 1981, Mendocino County
Charles Ortman, 1980, Napa Valley

CHARDONNAY
(Up to $8.00—47 entries)
GOLD
Filsinger Vineyards & Winery, 1980, Temecula, Estate Bottled
Geyser Peak Winery, 1980, Sonoma County
Clos du Bois, 1980, Alexander Valley
SILVER
Conn Creek, 1980, North Coast, Chateau Maja
San Martin Winery, 1980, California
Husch Vineyards, 1980, Anderson Valley, Mendocino, Estate Bottled
BRONZE
Fetzer Vineyards, 1980, Mendocino County, Barrel Aged
Fetzer Vineyards, 1981, Mendocino County, Early Bottling
J. Pedroncelli Winery, 1980, Sonoma
The Monterey Vineyard, 1979, Monterey County
River Oaks Vineyards, 1981, Alexander Valley

CHENIN BLANC Residual Sugar: 0.0% to 0.70%
($7.01 and Up—3 entries)
GOLD
R & J Cook, 1980, Northern California, Estate Bottled, Extra Dry
SILVER
Stag's Leap Winery, 1981, Napa, Stag's Leap
BRONZE
Lawrence Winery, 1980, California

CHENIN BLANC Residual Sugar: 0.0% to 0.70%
($4.01 to $7.00—32 entries)
GOLD
Ronald Lamb Winery, 1981, Monterey, Ventana Vineyards
Bel Arbres Vineyards, 1981, North Coast
Congress Springs Vineyards, 1980, Santa Cruz Mountains, St. Charles Vineyard

Raymond Vineyard & Cellar, 1980, Napa Valley

SILVER

Sierra Vista Winery, 1981, Clarksburg, Northern California

BRONZE

Martin Brothers, 1981, Central Coast, Sisquoc River Vineyards

Fenestra, 1981, Monterey

L. Foppiano Wine Co., 1980, Northern California

CHENIN BLANC Residual Sugar: 0.0% to 0.70%
(Up to $4.00—6 entries)

9GOLD

None

SILVER

Cambiaso Winery and Vineyards, 1981, Northern California

California Hillside Cellars, 1980, California

BRONZE

None

CHENIN BLANC Residual Sugar: 0.71% and above
($7.01 and Up—3 entries)

GOLD

None

SILVER

None

BRONZE

Fenestra, 1981, Monterey, Select Harvest, Ventana Vineyards

CHENIN BLANC Residual Sugar: 0.71% and above
($4.01 to $7.00—29 entries)

GOLD

Sonoma Vineyards, 1981, Sonoma County

Beringer Vineyards, 1981, Napa Valley

Souverain Winery, 1981, North Coast

SILVER

Parducci Wine Cellars, 1981, North Coast

Congress Springs Vineyards, 1981, Santa Cruz Mountains

BRONZE

Ventana Vineyards Winery, 1981, Monterey, Estate Bottled

Bargetto Winery, 1981, Santa Barbara County, Tepusquet Vineyard

CHENIN BLANC Residual Sugar: 0.71% and above
(Up to $4.00—29 entries)

GOLD

San Antonio Winery, 1981, California

SILVER

Colony Wines, N.V., California Colony Classic

The Wine Cellars of Ernest & Julio Gallo, California

BRONZE

Bogle Vineyards, 1981, Clarksburg

Cresta Blanca Vineyards, 1980, Santa Barbara
Lost Hills Vineyards, 1981, California
Giumarra Vineyards, 1981, California

GAMAY
($7.01 and Up—2 entries)
GOLD
None
SILVER
Lawrence Winery, 1981, San Luis Obispo, French Camp Vineyard Selection
BRONZE
None

GAMAY
($5.01 to $7.00—7 entries)
GOLD
None
SILVER
Alta Vineyard Cellar, 1978, Napa Valley, Commemorative Bottling
San Pasqual Vineyards, 1979, San Pasqual Valley, Indian Summer Harvest
BRONZE
Hop Kiln, 1980, Russian River Valley

GAMAY
(Up to $5.00—8 entries)
GOLD
None
SILVER
Preston Vineyards, 1981, Sonoma, Dry Creek Valley, Estate Bottled
J. Lohr, 1981, Monterey, Greenfield Vineyards
BRONZE
None

GAMAY BEAUJOLAIS
($6.01 and Up—2 entries)
No Awards

GAMAY BEAULOLAIS
($4.51 to $6.00—17 entries)
GOLD
Buena Vista Winery & Vineyards, 1981, Sonoma Valley, Carneros, Estate Bottled
SILVER
Sonoma Vineyards, 1981, Sonoma County, Prime
Robert Pecota, 1981, Napa Valley
BRONZE
Paul Masson Vineyards, 1980, California
Chateau Nouveau, 1981, Napa Valley

GAMAY BEAUJOLAIS
(Up to $4.50—17 entries)
GOLD

Fetzer Vineyards, 1981, Mendocino County
SILVER
Davis Bynum Winery, 1981, Sonoma, Vineyard of Joe Rochioli, Jr., Nouveau
BRONZE
Round Hill Cellars, 1981, Napa, Round Hill
Parducci, Wine Cellars, 1981, North Coast
Giumarra Vineyards, 1981, California

GEWURZTRAMINER Residual Sugar: 0.0% to 0.70%
($7.51 and Up—one entry)
GOLD
None
SILVER
None
BRONZE
Chateau St. Jean, 1981, Alexander Valley, Robert Young Vineyards

GEWURZTRAMINER Residual Sugar: 0.0% to 0.70%
($5.51 to $7.50—12 entries)
GOLD
None
SILVER
Navarro Vineyards, 1980, Mendocino, Estate Bottled
Sebastiani Vineyards, 1980, Sonoma Valley
BRONZE
Gundlach-Bundschu Winery, 1980, Sonoma Valley, Estate Bottled, Rhinefarm
Hacienda Wine Cellars, 1981, Sonoma Valley
Evensen Vineyards & Winery, 1980, Napa Valley, Estate Bottled
Monticello Cellars, 1981, Napa Valley

GEWURZTRAMINER Residual Sugar: 0.0% to 0.70%
(Up to $5.50—one entry)
GOLD
None
SILVER
None
BRONZE
Louis M. Martini Winery, 1980, California

GEWURZTRAMINER Residual Sugar: 0.71% to 3.0%
($7.51 and Up—5 entries)
GOLD
None
SILVER
Chateau St. Jean, 1981, Sonoma Valley, Frank Johnson Vineyards
BRONZE
Grand Cru Vineyards, 1981, Alexander Valley, Garden Creek Ranch
Milano, 1981, Mendocino County, Anderson Valley Vineyard, Late Harvest

GEWURZTRAMINER Residual Sugar: 0.71% to 3.0%
($5.51 to $7.50—38 entries)

GOLD

Sonoma Vineyards, 1981, Sonoma County
St. Francis Vineyards, 1981, Sonoma Valley, Estate Bottled

SILVER

Veedercrest Vineyards, 1980, Napa Valley, Winery Lake Vineyards
Souverain Winery, 1980, North Coast
Parsons Creek Winery, 1981, Mendocino, Anderson Valley, Philo Foothills Ranch
Donna Maria Vineyards, 1981, Chalk Hill, Sonoma County
Beringer Vineyards, 1980, Napa Valley

BRONZE

Clos du Bois, 1981, Alexander Valley, Early Harvest
Joseph Phelps Vineyards, 1980, Napa Valley

GEWURZTRAMINER Residual Sugar: 0.71% to 3.0%
(Up to $5.50—9 entries)

GOLD

Husch Vineyards, 1981, Anderson Valley, Mendocino, Estate Bottled

SILVER

J. Pedroncelli Winery, 1981, Sonoma

BRONZE

Almaden Vineyards, 1980, San Benito
The Monterey Vineyard, 1981, Monterey County

GEWURZTRAMINER Residual Sugar: 3.1% to 6.0%
($7.51 and Up—No entries)
($5.51 to $7.50—one entry)

GOLD

None

SILVER

None

BRONZE

Fetzer Vineyards, 1981, California

GEWURZTRAMINER Residual Sugar: 3.1% to 6.0%
(Up to $5.50—2 entries)

GOLD

None

SILVER

River Oaks Vineyards, 1980, Alexander Valley, Early Harvest

BRONZE

Lost Hills Vineyards, 1980, Alexander Valley

GEWURZTRAMINER Residual Sugar: 6.1% to 12.0%
($7.51 and Up—3 entries)

GOLD

Navarro Vineyards, 1981, Mendocino, Late Harvest
Smothers, 1981, Alexander Valley, Late Harvest

SILVER

None
BRONZE
None

GEWURZTRAMINER Residual Sugar: 6.1% to 12.0%
($5.51 to $7.50—No entries)
(Up to $5.50—No entries)

GEWURZTRAMINER Residual Sugar: 12.1% and Up
($7.51 and Up—2 entries)
GOLD
Chateau St. Jean, 1980, Alexander Valley, Late Harvest, Jimtown Ranch
SILVER
None
BRONZE
Felton-Empire Vineyards, 1981, Santa Barbara, Tepusquet Vineyards, Select Late Harvest

GEWURZTRAMINER Residual Sugar: 12.1% and Up
($5.51 to $7.50—No entries)
(Up to $5.50—No entries)

MERLOT
($11.01 and Up—5 entries)
GOLD
Lawrence Winery, 1981, California, Bien Nacido Vineyard Selection
Stag's Leap Wine Cellars, 1979, Napa Valley, Stag's Leap Vineyard
SILVER
Duckhorn Vineyards, 1979, Napa Valley
BRONZE
Clos du Val, 1979, Napa Valley

MERLOT
($7.01 to $11.00—12 entries)
GOLD
Gundlach-Bundschu Winery, 1979, Sonoma Valley, Rhinefarm Vineyards
Rutherford Hill Winery, 1979, Napa Valley
SILVER
Chappellet Vineyard, 1978, Napa Valley
Robert Keenan Winery, 1979, Napa Valley
BRONZE
Caperone Winery, 1980, Templeton, Unfined
Clos du Bois, 1979, Napa Valley
Calafia Cellars, 1979, Napa Valley

MERLOT
(Up to $7.00—14 entries)
GOLD
None
SILVER
Lawrence Winery, 1981, Southern Central Coast of California

BRONZE
Turner Winery, 1980, Lake County
Zaca Mesa Winery, 1979, Santa Ynez Valley
Farview Farm Vineyard, 1979, Templeton

MUSCAT Residual Sugar: 0.0% to 0.70%
($7.01 and Up—No entries)
($5.01 to $7.00—one entry)
No awards
(Up to $5.00—No entries)

MUSCAT Residual Sugar: 0.71% to 3.0%
($7.01 and Up—No entries)
($5.01 to $7.00—4 entries)
GOLD
None
SILVER
Pat Paulsen Vineyards, 1981, Sonoma County (Muscat Canelli)
BRONZE
Concannon Vineyard, 1981, Livermore Valley, Estate Bottled (Muscat Blanc)
Chateau St. Jean, 1981, Alexander Valley, Jimtown Ranch (Muscat Canelli)

MUSCAT Residual Sugar: 0.71% to 3.0%
(Up to $5.00—one entry)
No awards

MUSCAT Residual Sugar: 3.0% to 6.0%
($7.01 and Up—2 entries)
No awards

MUSCAT Residual Sugar: 3.0% to 6.0%
($5.01 to $7.00—7 entries)
GOLD
None
SILVER
Souverain Winery, 1981, North Coast (Muscat Canelli)
BRONZE
Ballard Canyon Winery, 1981, Santa Ynez, Estate Bottled (Muscat Di Canelli)
Estrella River Winery, 1980, San Luis Obispo, Estate Bottled (Muscat Canelli)
Parducci Wine Cellars, 1981, North Coast (Muscat Canelli)

MUSCAT Residual Sugar: 3.0% to 6.0%
(Up to $5.00—2 entries)
GOLD
None
SILVER
None
BRONZE
Beringer Vineyards, 1980, Madera (Malvasia Amabile)

MUSCAT Residual Sugar: 6.0% to 12.0%
($7.01 and Up—one entry)
GOLD
None
SILVER
Chateau St. Jean, 1980, Alexander Valley, Selected Late Harvest, Jimtown Ranch (Muscat Canelli)
BRONZE
None

MUSCAT Residual Sugar: 6.0% to 12.0%
($5.01 to $7.00—3 entries)
GOLD
None
SILVER
Papagni Vineyards, N.V., California, Estate Bottled (Moscato d'Angelo)
BRONZE
None

MUSCAT Residual Sugar: 6.0% to 12.0%
(Up to $5.00—2 entries)
No awards

MUSCAT Residual Sugar: 12.0% and Up
($7.01 and Up—one entry)
GOLD
None
SILVER
None
BRONZE
Estrella River Winery, 1979, San Luis Obispo, Estate Bottled, Late Harvest (Muscat Canelli)

MUSCAT Residual Sugar: 12.0% and Up
($5.01 to $7.00—No entries)
(Up to $5.00—No entries)

PETITE SIRAH
($7.01 and Up—13 entries)
GOLD
McDowell Valley Vineyards, 1979, Mendocino County Estate Bottled
Hop Kiln, 1979, Russian River Valley
Parducci Wine Cellars, 1978, North Coast, Cellar Masters
SILVER
Cilurzo Vineyard & Winery, 1979, Temecula
Rosenblum Cellars, 1980, Napa, St. George & Rich Vineyard
BRONZE
Stag's Leap Winery, 1978, Napa

PETITE SIRAH
($5.01 to $7.00—23 entries)
GOLD

Wente Bros., 1979, Livermore Valley, Estate Bottled
Fenestra, 1979, San Luis Obispo, Shell Creek Vineyard
Beringer Vineyards, 1977, Napa Valley, Spring Lane Vineyard
J. Lohr Winery, 1978, Northern California, Wilson, Spenker, Greenfield Vineyards
Topolos at Russian River Vineyards, 1979, Sonoma County Hillside, Unfined

SILVER
Estrella River Winery, 1979, San Luis Obispo, Estate Bottled
Hultgren and Samperton, 1979, Sonoma County
Fetzer Vineyards, 1980, Mendocino
Paul Masson Vineyards, 1979, California

BRONZE
Pedrizzetti Winery, 1977, Shell Creek
Trentadue Winery, 1977, Sonoma, Alexander Valley, Estate Bottled
Round Hill Cellars, 1978, Napa, Round Hill
Concannon Vineyard, 1978, California

PETITE SIRAH
(Up to $5.00—13 entries)

GOLD
R. & J. Cook, 1979, Northern California

SILVER
Parducci Wine Cellars, 1978, Mendocino
Mirassou, 1978, Monterey County

BRONZE
Fortino Winery, 1978, Santa Clara County
Giumarra Vineyards, 1979, California
Emilio Guglielmo, 1977, Santa Clara Valley, Estate Bottled
Vache, 1980, Temecula

PINOT BLANC
($6.51 and Up—5 entries)

GOLD
Jekel Vineyards, 1980, Monterey, Estate Bottled

SILVER
Monterey Peninsula Winery, 1981, Monterey, Cobblestone Vineyards

BRONZE
Congress Springs Vineyards, 1980, Santa Cruz Mountains, St. Charles Vineyard

PINOT BLANC
($4.51 to $6.50—3 entries)

GOLD
None

SILVER
Mirassou Vineyards, 1981, Monterey County (Labeled White Burgundy)

BRONZE
Wente Bros., 1980, Monterey

PINOT BLANC
(Up to $4.50)

GOLD
The Monterey Vineyard, 1979, Monterey County

SILVER
None

BRONZE
None

PINOT NOIR
($10.01 and Up—18 entries)

GOLD
Zaca Mesa Winery, 1979, Santa Ynez Valley, Special Selection
Bacigalupi, 1979, Sonoma County

SILVER
Hacienda Wine Cellars, 1979, Sonoma Valley, Buena Vista Vineyard

BRONZE
Mount Eden Vineyards, 1979, Santa Cruz Mountains
Villa Mt. Eden, 1979, Napa Valley
ZD Wines, 1979, California
Robert Mondavi Winery, 1977, Napa Valley, Reserve
David Bruce Winery, 1979, Santa Cruz Mountain, Estate Bottled

Pinot Noir
($6.01 to $10.00—46 entries)

GOLD
Lazy Creek Vineyards, 1979 Mendocino
Stony Ridge Winery, 1979, Monterey County, Vinco Vineyards

SILVER
Husch Vineyards, 1979, Anderson Valley, Mendocino, Estate Bottled
Tulocay, 1978, Napa Valley
Buena Vista Winery and Vineyards, 1979, Sonoma Valley, Carneros, Estate Bottled
Edmeades, 1980, Mendocino County, Anderson Valley
Louis M. Martini Winery, 1976, California, Special Selection
Frick Winery, 1979, Monterey County

BRONZE
Topolos at Russian River Vineyards, 1980, Sonoma County, Hillside, Unfined
Alatera Vineyards, 1979, Napa Valley
Mill Creek Vineyards, 1980, Sonoma County, Dry Creek Valley, Estate Bottled
Firestone Vineyard, 1978, Santa Ynez Valley

PINOT NOIR
(Up to $6.00—29 entries)

GOLD
Pendleton Winery, N.V., Monterey
J. Pedroncelli Winery, 1979, Sonoma

SILVER

Geyser Peak Winery, 1977, California
Fetzer Vineyards, 1978, Mendocino
Parducci Wine Cellars, 1979, Mendocino
Carmel Bay Winery, 1979, Monterey County, Sleepy Hollow Vineyards

BRONZE

Beringer Vineyards, 1978, Sonoma
Stony Ridge Winery, 1979, Monterey County, Tom Jones/Sleepy Hollow Vineyards
Sebastiani Vineyards, 1979, California, August Sebastiani Country (1.5 liter size)
Whitehall Lane Winery, 1981, Fleur D'Helene
Christian Brothers Winery, N.V., Napa Valley

SAUVIGNON BLANC Residual Sugar: 0.0% to 0.70%
($8.51 and Up—13 entries)

GOLD

H.N.W. Cellars, 1981, Napa Valley, H.N.W. Vineyards
Chateau St. Jean, 1981, Alexander Valley, Murphy Ranch (Fumé)

SILVER

St. Clements, 1981, Napa Valley

BRONZE

Robert Mondavi Winery, 1980, Napa Valley (Fumé)
Concannon Vineyard, 1981, Livermore Valley, Estate Bottled
Grand Cru Vineyards, 1981, Northern California
Wilson Daniels Cellars, 1980, Napa Valley

SAUVIGNON BLANC Residual Sugar: 0.0% to 0.70%
($5.01 to $8.00—72 entries)

GOLD

Napa Cellars, 1981, Napa Valley
Stephens, 1981, North Coast (Fumé)
Husch Vineyards, 1980, Mendocino, Estate Bottled
Montevina Wines, 1981, Amador County, Estate Bottled

SILVER

Dry Creek Vineyard, 1981, Sonoma County (Fumé)
Richard Carey, 1980, San Luis Obispo Library Reserve (Fumé)
Beringer Vineyards, 1981, Napa Valley (Fumé)
Konocti Winery, 1981, Lake County, Isabel Downs Vineyard (Fumé)
L. Foppiano Wine Co., 1980, Sonoma County (Fumé)

BRONZE

San Martin Winery, 1980, San Luis Obispo (Fumé)
Beringer Vineyards, 1980, Sonoma (Fumé)
Kenwood Vineyards, 1981, Sonoma Valley
J. Pedroncelli Winery, 1981, Sonoma
Cambiaso Winery and Vineyards, 1980, Sonoma (Fumé)
The Brander Vineyard, 1981, California
Monticello Cellars, 1981, Napa Valley
DeLoach Vineyards, 1981; Russian River Valley (Fumé)

SAUVIGNON BLANC Residual Sugar: 0.0% to 0.70%
(Up to $5.00—17 entries)

GOLD

Christian Brothers Winery, N.V., Napa Valley, Cuveé
809 Wine Warehouse, 1979, Sonoma County

SILVER

Filsinger Vineyards and Winery, 1980, Temecula, Estate Bottled, Lot #1 (Fumé)
Taylor California Cellars, N.V., California
The Wine Cellars of Ernest & Julio Gallo, N.V., California

BRONZE

Turner Winery, 1980, Lake County (Fumé)
California Hillside Cellars, 1980, San Luis Obispo
Maddalena Vineyard, 1981, Temecula

SAUVIGNON BLANC Residual Sugar: 0.71% and Up
($8.51 and Up—2 entries)

GOLD

None

SILVER

None

BRONZE

J. Lohr Winery, 1981, Monterey, Greenfield Vineyards, Late Harvest

SAUVIGNON BLANC Residual Sugar: 0.71% and Up
($5.01 to $8.50—5 entries)

GOLD

Parducci Wine Cellars, 1981, North Coast

SILVER

Konocti Winery, 1980, Lake County, Estate Bottled (Fumé)

BRONZE

Callaway Vineyard & Winery, 1980, Temecula

SAUVIGNON BLANC Residual Sugar: 0.71% and Up
(Up to $5.00—4 entries)

GOLD

None

SILVER

None

BRONZE

Christian Brothers Winery, N.V., Napa Valley

WHITE (JOHANNISBERG) RIESLING Residual Sugar: 0.0% to 0.70%
($8.01 and Up—one entry)

No Awards

WHITE (JOHANNISBERG) RIESLING Residual Sugar: 0.0% to 0.70%
($5.51 to $8.00—5 entries)

GOLD

Trefethen Vineyards, 1981, Napa Valley, Trefethen Vineyards

SILVER
Bargetto Winery, 1981, Sonoma
BRONZE
None

WHITE (JOHANNISBERG) RIESLING Residual Sugar: 0.0% to 0.70%
(Up to $5.50—8 entries)
GOLD
None
SILVER
San Antonio Winery, 1981, California
BRONZE
Vega Vineyards, 1981, Santa Ynez Valley (Labeled White Riesling)

WHITE (JOHANNISBERG) RIESLING Residual Sugar: 0.71% to 3.0%
($8.01 and Up—one entry)
No Awards

WHITE (JOHANNISBERG) RIESLING Residual Sugar: 0.71% to 3.0%
($5.51 to $8.00—63 entries)
GOLD
J. Lohr Winery, 1981, Monterey, Greenfield Vineyards
Obester Winery, 1981, Monterey County, Ventana Vineyards
Sarah's Vineyard, 1981, Mendocino County, Victor Matheu Vineyards
Haywood Winery, 1981, Sonoma Valley, Estate Bottled, Early Harvest
Ventana Vineyards Winery, 1981, Monterey, Estate Bottled
SILVER
Ballard Canyon Winery, 1981, Santa Ynez, Estate Bottled
Conn Creek, 1979, Napa Valley
Chateau St. Jean, 1981, Sonoma County
Santa Ynez Valley Winery, 1981, California
Field Stone Winery, 1981, Alexander Valley, Estate Bottled
Jekel Vineyards, 1981, Monterey, Home Vineyard, Estate
Bottled
Chateau St. Jean, 1981, Alexander Valley, Robert Young Vineyards
Estrella River Winery, 1981, San Luis Obispo, Estate Bottled
Parsons Creek Winery, 1981, Mendocino, Anderson Valley, Philo Foothills Ranch
Zaca Mesa Winery, 1981, Santa Ynez Valley, American Estate
BRONZE
Jekel Vineyards, 1981, Monterey
Concannon Vineyard, 1981, Livermore Valley, Estate

Bottled
Bargetto Winery, 1981, Santa Barbara County, Tepusquet Vineyard
Felton-Empire Vineyards, 1981, Santa Cruz Mountains
Fetzer Vineyards, 1981, Lake County
Smothers, 1981, California
Robert Mondavi Winery, 1980, Napa Valley
Raymond Vineyard & Cellar, 1981, Napa Valley, Estate Bottled

WHITE (JOHANNISBERG) RIESLING Residual Sugar: 0.71% to 3.0%
(Up to %5.50—20 entries)
GOLD
Veedercrest Vineyards, 1980, Napa, Steltzner and Winery Lake Vineyards
SILVER
Taylor California Cellars, N.V., California
BRONZE
Vega Vineyards, 1981, Santa Ynez Valley (Labeled Johannisberg Riesling)

WHITE (JOHANNISBERG) RIESLING Residual Sugar: 3.1% to 6.0%
($8.01 and Up—3 entries)
GOLD
None
SILVER
Smothers, 1980, Santa Cruz, Vine Hill Vineyard, Residual Sugar 4.2%
BRONZE
Charles Le Franc, 1977, San Benito, Late Harvest, Residual Sugar 5.6%

WHITE (JOHANNISBERG) RIESLING Residual Sugar: 3.1% to 6.0%
($5.51 to $8.00—5 entries)
GOLD
Ballard Canyon Winery, 1981, Santa Ynez, Estate Bottled, "Reserve", Residual Sugar 3.9%
SILVER
Veedercrest Vineyards, 1980, Napa, Winery Lake Vineyards, Late Harvest, Sugar at Bottling, 4.7%
Beringer Vineyards, 1980, Sonoma, Residual Sugar 4.5%
BRONZE
Vega Vineyards, 1981, Santa Ynez Valley, Special Selection

WHITE (JOHANNISBERG) RIESLING Residual Sugar: 3.1% to 6.0%
(Up to $5.50—4 entries)
GOLD
None
SILVER

Vache, 1981, Temecula "Soft"
BRONZE
Lost Hills Vineyards, 1980, California

WHITE (JOHANNISBERG) RIESLING Residual Sugar: 6.1% to 12.0%
($8.01 and Up—7 entries)
GOLD
None
SILVER
Wente Bros., 1979, Monterey, Arroyo Seco Vineyards, Late Harvest
BRONZE
HMR Hoffman Vineyards, 1979, San Luis Obispo, Late Harvest, Residual Sugar 11.25%
Ventana Vineyards Winery, 1981, Monterey, Estate Bottled, Botrytised, Residual Sugar 9%
Charles LeFranc, 1979, San Benito, Selected Late Harvest, Advanced Botrytis, Residual Sugar 11.7%

WHITE (JOHANNISBERG) RIESLING Residual Sugar: 6.1% to 12.0%
(5.51 to $8.00—4 entries)
GOLD
Bargetto Winery, 1981, Santa Barbara County, Late Harvest, Tepusquet
SILVER
None
BRONZE
Christian Brothers Winery, 1980, Napa Valley, Late Harvest, Residual Sugar 7.3%
San Martin Winery, 1980, Santa Barbara, "Soft"

WHITE (JOHANNISBERG) RIESLING Residual Sugar: 6.1% to 12.0%
(Up to $5.50—no entries)

WHITE (JOHANNISBERG) RIESLING Residual Sugar: 12.1% and Up
($8.01 and Up—7 entries)
GOLD
Milano, 1981, Mendocino, Philo, Anderson Valley Vineyards, Late Harvest, Individually Bunch Selected, Residual Sugar 17.7%
Chateau St. Jean, 1980, Alexander Valley, Belle Terre Vineyards, Late Harvest, Individual Bunch Selected, Residual Sugar 17.9%
SILVER
Jekel Vineyards, 1980, Monterey, Late Harvest, Estate Bottled, Residual Sugar 16%
Felton Empire Vineyards, 1981, Santa Barbara, Tepusquet Vineyards, Select Late Harvest, Residual Sugar 20%
BRONZE
Chateau St. Jean, 1981, Alexander Valley, Belle Terre Vineyards, Select Late Harvest, Residual Sugar 14.5%

WHITE (JOHANNISBERG) RIESLING Residual Sugar: 12.1% and Up
($5.51 to $8.00—No entries)
(Up to $5.50—No entries)

ZINFANDEL
($7.51 and Up—39 entries)

GOLD

- Sycamore Creek Vineyards, 1980, California, Estate Bottled
- David Bruce Winery, 1979, El Dorado
- Mastantuono, 1980, Paso Robles

SILVER

- Montevina Wines, 1979, Amador County, Estate Bottled
- Edmeades, 1980, Mendocino County, Pacini Vineyards
- Sarah's Vineyard, 1980, San Benito County
- Vose Vineyards, 1979, Napa Valley

BRONZE

- Sarah's Vineyard, 1980, Sonoma County, Les Vignerous Vineyard
- Burgess Cellars, 1979, Napa Valley, Estate Bottled
- J.W. Morris Winery, 1980, Sonoma
- Edmeades, 1980, Mendocino County, Ciapusci Vineyards

ZINFANDEL
($4.51 to $7.50—103 entries)

GOLD

- Raymond Vineyard & Cellar, 1979, Napa Valley, Estate Bottled
- Cordtz Brothers Cellars, 1980, Upper Alexander Valley
- Montevina Wines, 1980, Amador County, Estate Bottled, Montino
- Madrona Vineyards, 1980, El Dorado County, Estate Bottled
- Ahern Winery, 1980, Amador County
- Kenworthy Vineyards, 1979, Amador, Potter-Cowan Vineyards

SILVER

- Richard Carey, 1979, Amador, Library Reserve
- Parducci Wine Cellars, 1980, North Coast
- Conn Creek, 1978, Napa Valley
- Santino, 1979, Amador County, Shenandoah Valley
- Dry Creek Vineyard, 1979, Sonoma County
- San Martin Winery, 1979, Amador County

BRONZE

- Shenandoah Vineyards, 1979, Amador County
- McLester, 1980, San Luis Obispo County, Radike Vineyard
- Obester Winery, 1979, Sonoma County, Forchini Vineyard
- Round Hill Cellars, 1979, Napa, Round Hill
- Hacienda Wine Cellars, 1979, Sonoma County
- Bargetto Winery, 1980, San Luis Obispo County,

Farview Farm Vineyard
Sutter Home Winery, 1979, Amador County
Santino, 1979, Amador County, Fiddletown
L. Foppiano Wine Co., 1978, Sonoma County

ZINFANDEL
(Up to $4.50—33 entries)

GOLD

Christian Brothers Winery, N.V., Napa Valley
Ridgewood Winery, 1979, Lytton Springs, Polk Vineyard (This wine was inadvertently judged in this category. It should have been judged in the $4.51 to $7.50 category.)

SILVER

Cresta Blanca Vineyards, 1978, Mendocino
Cribari & Sons Winery, N.V., California

BRONZE

Mirassou Vineyards, 1978, Monterey County, Unfiltered
Santino, 1980, Amador County, Shenandoah Valley
Fetzer Vineyards, 1980, Lake County
Trader Joe's Winery, 1979, Mendocino
Paul Masson Vineyards, 1980, California
Raymond Hill (Trader Joe's), 1979, Mendocino, Unfiltered, Unfined
J. Pedroncelli Winery, 1979, Sonoma
Story Vineyards, N.V., Amador County, Estate Bottled

ZINFANDEL: Late Harvest—Dry
($8.51 and Up—3 entries)

GOLD

None

SILVER

None

BRONZE

Monterey Peninsula Winery, 1977, Amador, Late Harvest
Monterey Peninsula Winery, 1978, Amador, Ferrerro Old Ranch, Late Harvest

ZINFANDEL: Late Harvest—Dry
($6.01 to $8.50—2 entries)

No awards

ZINFANDEL: Late Harvest—Dry
(Up to $6.00—No entries)

ZINFANDEL: Late Harvest—Sweet
($8.51 and Up—3 entries)

GOLD

None

SILVER

None

BRONZE

Monterey Peninsula Winery, 1980, Amador, Sweet

Late Harvest

ZINFANDEL: Late Harvest—Sweet
($6.01 to $8.50—one entry)

GOLD
None
SILVER
Charles Le Franc, 1980, San Benito, Royale, (Sweet—3.1% Residual Sugar)
BRONZE
None

ZINFANEL: Late Harvest—Sweet
(Up to $6.00—No entries)

SPARKLING WINE Residual Sugar: 0.0% to 0.50%
($9.51 and Up—13 entries)

GOLD
Schramsberg Vineyards, 1977, Napa Valley, Blanc de Noir
Mirassou Vineyards, 1978, Monterey County, Blanc de Noir
SILVER
Schramsberg Vineyards, 1979, Napa Balley, Cuveé de Pinot
Korbel, N.V., California, Natural, Extremely Dry
BRONZE
Mirassou Vineyards, 1979, Monterey County, Au Natural
Cresta Blanca Vineyards, N.V., California, Chardonnay

SPARKLING WINE Residual Sugar: 0.0% to 0.50%
($5.01 to $9.50—11 entries)

GOLD
None
SILVER
Weibel Vineyards, N.V., Bottle Fermented, Brut
Korbel, N.V., California, Brut
Stony Ridge Winery, N.V., California, Blanc de Noir
Trader Joe's Winery, N.V., Sonoma, Bottle Fermented, Brut
BRONZE
Weibel Vineyards, N.V., Bottle Fermented, Blanc de Pinot Noir

SPARKLING WINE Residual Sugar: 0.0% to 0.50%
(Up to $5.00—3 entries)

GOLD
None
SILVER
None
BRONZE
Stanford, N.V., California, Governor's Cuveé, Dry

SPARKLING WINE Residual Sugar: 0.51% to 1.40%
($9.51 and Up—3 entries)

GOLD
None
SILVER
None
BRONZE
Domaine Chandon, N.V., Napa Valley, Brut

SPARKLING WINE Residual Sugar: 0.51% to 1.40%
($5.01 to $9.50—5 entries)
GOLD
None
SILVER
None
BRONZE
Papagni Vineyards, 1979, California, Estate Bottled, Brut

SPARKLING WINE Residual Sugar: 0.51% to 1.40%
(Up to $5.00—one entry)
GOLD
None
SILVER
Crystal Valley Cellars, N.V., California, Robins Glow, Blanc de Noir, Brut
BRONZE
None

SPARKLING WINE Residual Sugar: 1.41% to 2.40%
($9.51 and Up—No entries)
($5.01 to $9.50—4 entries)
GOLD
Weibel Vineyards, N.V., Bottle Fermented, Extra Dry
SILVER
None
BRONZE
Christian Brothers Winery, N.V., California, Brut

SPARKLING WINE Residual Sugar: 1.41% to 2.40%
(Up to $5.00—3 entries)
No Awards

SPARKLING WINE Residual Sugar: 2.41% and Up
($9.51 and Up—one entry)
GOLD
None
SILVER
None
BRONZE
Schramsberg, 1979, Napa Valley, Cremant Demi Sec

SPARKLING WINE Residual Sugar: 2.41% and Up
($5.01 to $9.50—10 entries)
GOLD
None
SILVER
Papagni Vineyards, N.V., California, Estate Bottled,

Spumante d'Angelo
BRONZE

SPARKLING WINE Residual Sugar: 2.41% and Up
(Up to $5.00—15 entries)
GOLD
None
SILVER
Crystal Valley Cellars, N.V., California, Spumante
BRONZE
Franzia Brothers Winery, N.V., California, Extra Dry

TOTAL ENTRIES—1387
GOLD MEDALS—91
SILVER MEDALS—149
BRONZE MEDALS—204

PANEL OF JUDGES

Jerry D. Mead, *Chairman*
Jim Ahern, *Ahern Winery*
Bill Arnold, *Smothers Vine Hill Wines*
Richard Arrowood, *Chateau St. Jean*
Fred Brander, *Santa Ynez Winery & Brander Vineyards*
Ken Brown, *Zaca Mesa Vineyards*
Jim Bundschu, *Gundlach-Bundschu Winery*
Jim Carter, *Sebastiani Vineyards*
Jim Concannon, *Concannon Vineyards*
David Cordtz, *Cordtz Brothers Cellars*
Charles M. Crawford, *E. & J. Gallo*
Kerry Damsky, *San Pasqual Vineyards*
Joseph Franzia, *JFJ Bronco Winery*
Don Harrison, *Buena Vista Winery and Vineyards*
Bill Jekel, *Jekel Vineyards*
Josh Jensen, *Calera Wine Company*
Tor Kenward, *Prager Winery & Port Works*
John Kenworthy, *Kenworthy Vineyards*
Bob Kozlowski, *Kenwood Vineyards*
Ray Krause, *Farview Farm Vineyard*
James Lawrence, *Lawrence Winery*
Jerry Lohr, *J. Lohr Wines*
Zelma Long, *Long Vineyards & Simi Winery*
Richard Longoria, *J. Carey Cellars*
John Merritt, *Bandiera Winery*
Bonny Meyer, *Silver Oak Cellars*
Daniel Mirassou, *Mirassou Vineyards*
Myron Nightingale, *Beringer Vineyards*
Paul Obester, *Obester Winery & Gemello Winery*
Steve O'Donnell, *Callaway Vineyards and Winery*
Angelo Papagni, *Angelo Papagni Vineyards*
John A. Parducci, *Parducci Wine Cellars*
Phyllis Pedrizzetti, *Pedrizzetti Winery*
Brian Pendleton, *Pendleton Winery*
Richard G. Peterson, *The Monterey Vineyard*
Jim Prager, *Prager Winery & Port Works*
Dawnine Sample-Dyer, *Domaine Chandon*
David Stare, *Dry Creek Vineyards*
George Starke, *Napa Cellars*
Rodney D. Strong, *Sonoma Vineyards*
John Turner, *Turner Winery*
Nils Venge, *Villa Mt. Eden*
Carolyn Wente, *Wente Bros.*
Warren Winiarski, *Stag's Leap Wine Cellars*

Key map

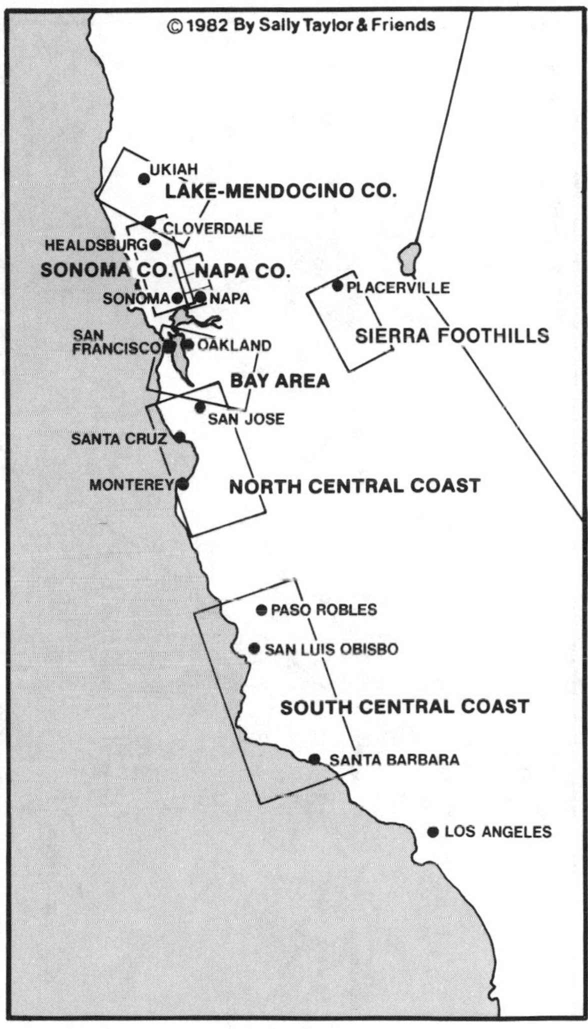

©1982 By Sally Taylor & Friends
UKIAH
LAKE-MENDOCINO CO.
CLOVERDALE
HEALDSBURG
SONOMA CO.
NAPA CO.
SONOMA
NAPA
PLACERVILLE
SIERRA FOOTHILLS
SAN FRANCISCO
OAKLAND
BAY AREA
SAN JOSE
SANTA CRUZ
MONTEREY
NORTH CENTRAL COAST
PASO ROBLES
SAN LUIS OBISBO
SOUTH CENTRAL COAST
SANTA BARBARA
LOS ANGELES

Lake-Mendocino County

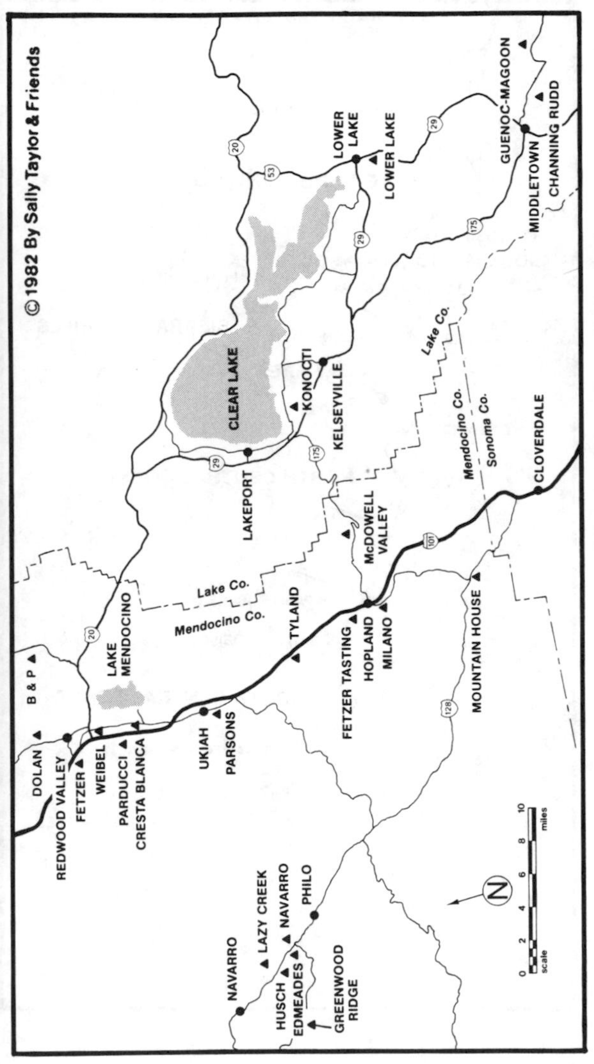
© 1982 By Sally Taylor & Friends
CLEAR LAKE
LOWER LAKE
LOWER LAKE
GUENOC-MAGOON
MIDDLETOWN
CHANNING RUDD
KONOCTI
KELSEYVILLE
LAKEPORT
Lake Co.
Mendocino Co.
Lake Co.
Mendocino Co.
Sonoma Co.
CLOVERDALE
McDOWELL VALLEY
TYLAND
FETZER TASTING
HOPLAND
MILANO
MOUNTAIN HOUSE
LAKE MENDOCINO
B & P
DOLAN
REDWOOD VALLEY
FETZER
WEIBEL
PARDUCCI
CRESTA BLANCA
UKIAH
PARSONS
NAVARRO
LAZY CREEK
NAVARRO
PHILO
HUSCH
EDMEADES
GREENWOOD RIDGE
20
53
29
175
101
128
N
0 2 4 6 8 10
scale
miles

Sonoma County

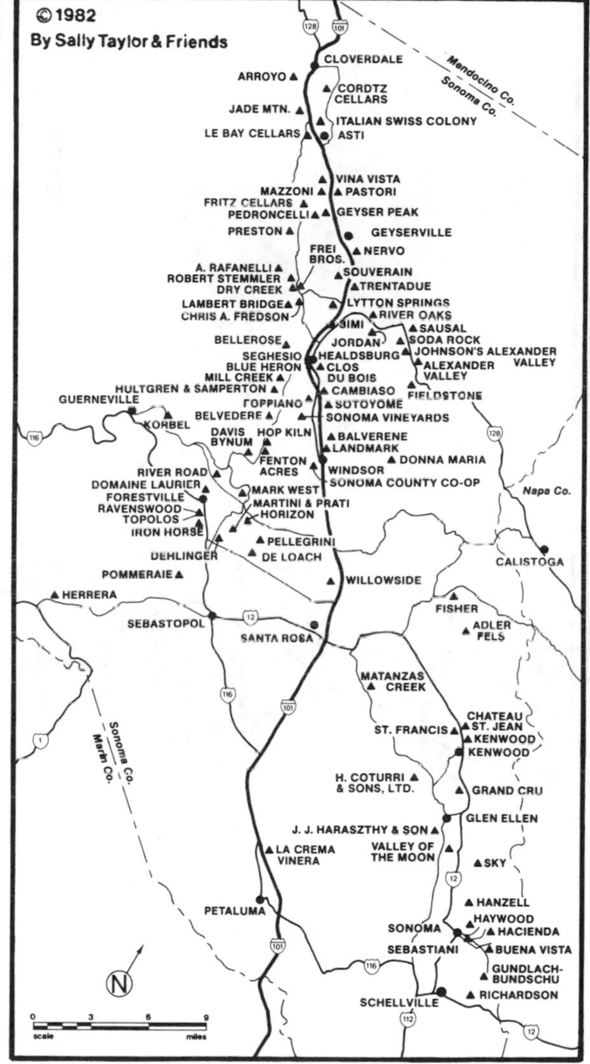

Napa County-North

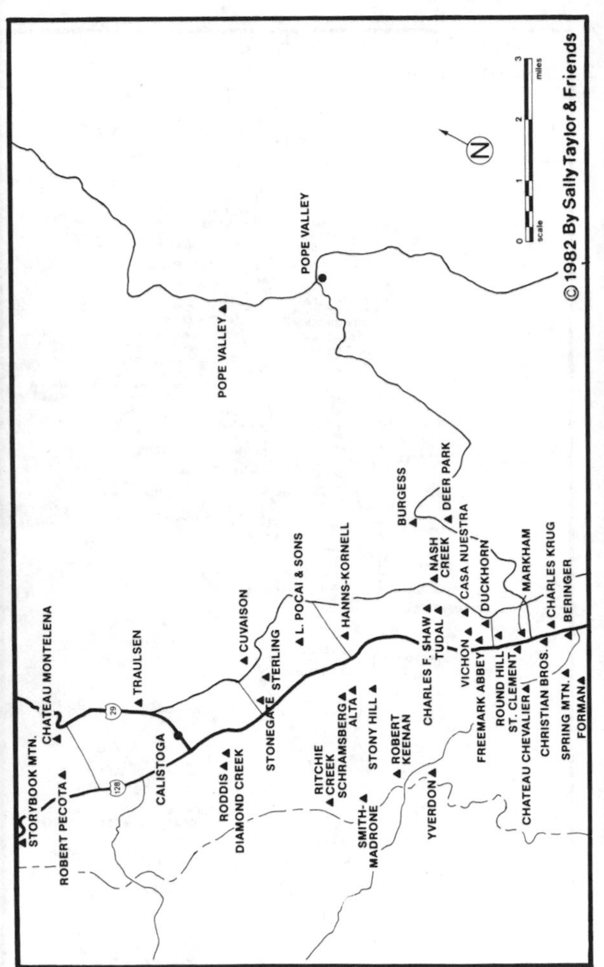

Napa County-Central

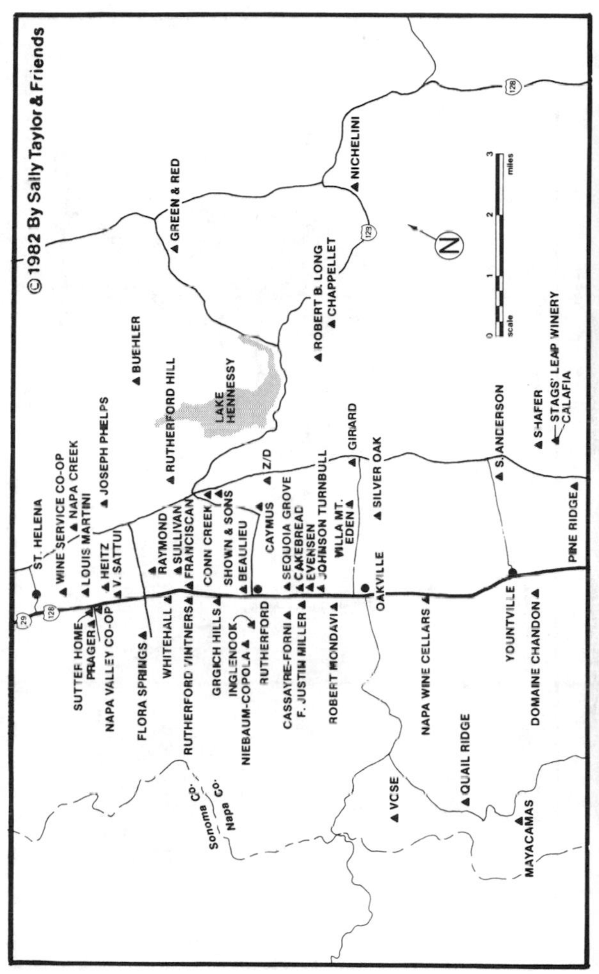

Napa County-South

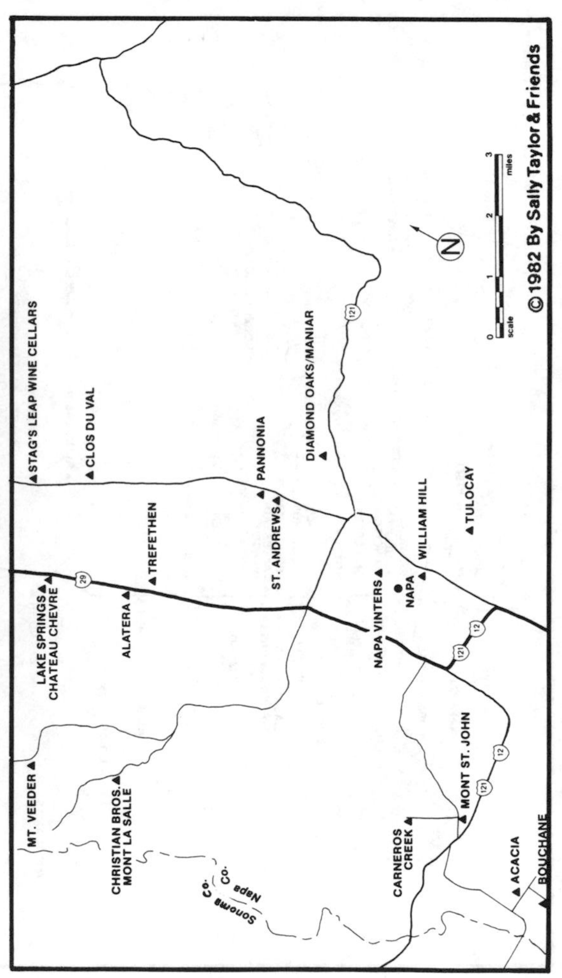
STAG'S LEAP WINE CELLARS
CLOS DU VAL
PANNONIA
DIAMOND OAKS/MANIAR
121
TREFETHEN
ST. ANDREWS
WILLIAM HILL
TULOCAY
LAKE SPRINGS
CHATEAU CHEVRE
29
ALATERA
NAPA VINTERS
NAPA
12
121
MT. VEEDER
CHRISTIAN BROS.
MONT LA SALLE
MONT ST. JOHN
CARNEROS
CREEK
ACACIA
BOUCHANE
Sonoma Co.
Napa Co.
N
0
1
2
3
scale
miles
© 1982 By Sally Taylor & Friends

Sierra Foothills

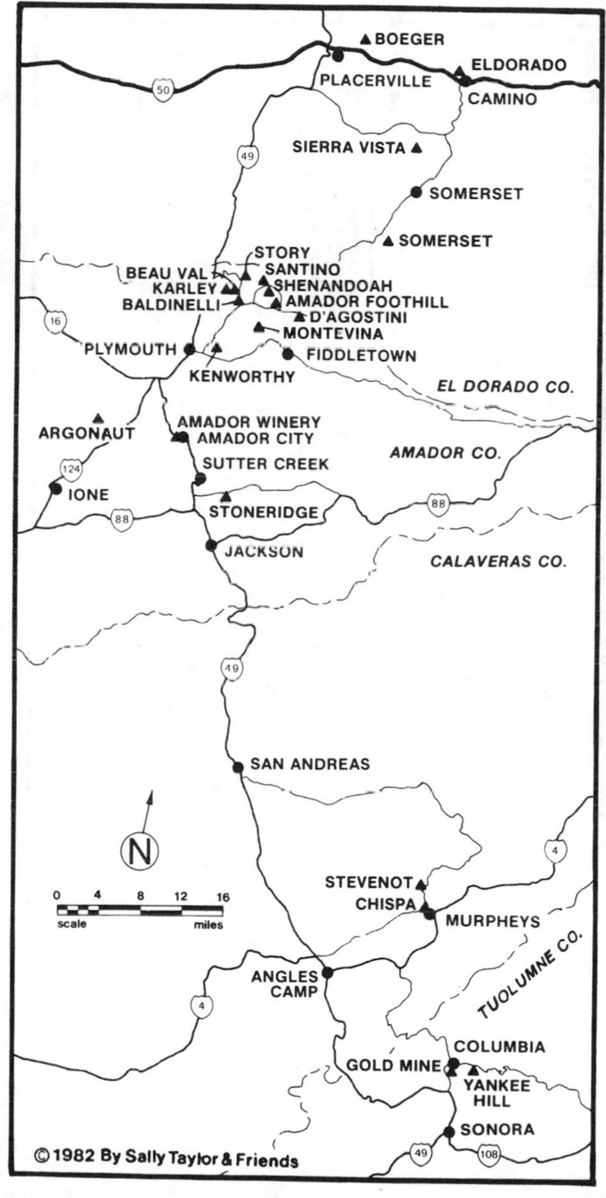

BOEGER
PLACERVILLE
ELDORADO
CAMINO
50
49
SIERRA VISTA
SOMERSET
SOMERSET
STORY
SANTINO
BEAU VAL
KARLEY
SHENANDOAH
BALDINELLI
AMADOR FOOTHILL
D'AGOSTINI
MONTEVINA
16
PLYMOUTH
FIDDLETOWN
KENWORTHY
EL DORADO CO.
ARGONAUT
AMADOR WINERY
AMADOR CITY
124
SUTTER CREEK
AMADOR CO.
IONE
STONERIDGE
88
88
JACKSON
CALAVERAS CO.
49
SAN ANDREAS
N
0 4 8 12 16
scale
miles
STEVENOT
CHISPA
MURPHEYS
4
TUOLUMNE CO.
ANGLES CAMP
4
COLUMBIA
GOLD MINE
YANKEE HILL
SONORA
49
108
© 1982 By Sally Taylor & Friends

Bay Area

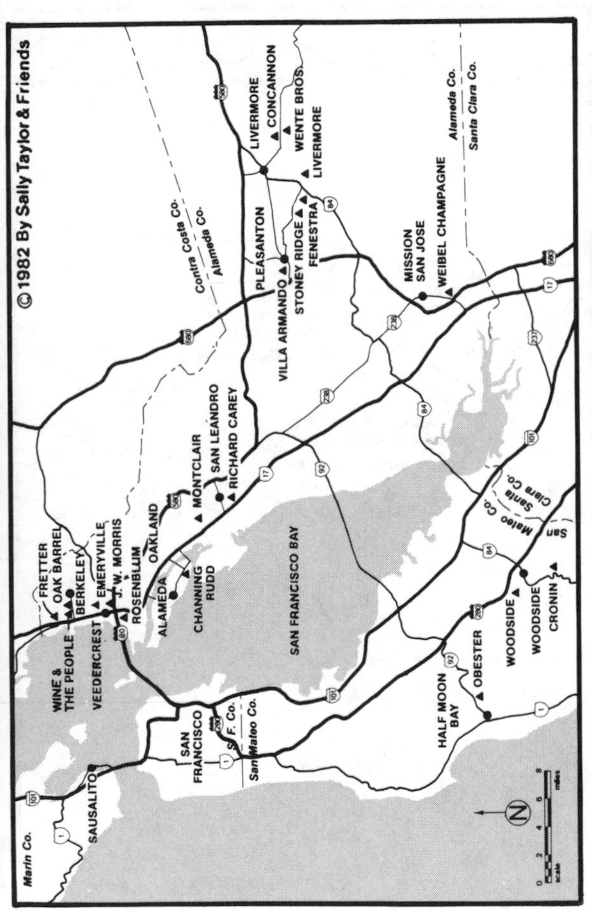
© 1982 By Sally Taylor & Friends
Marin Co.
SAUSALITO
WINE & THE PEOPLE
VEEDERCREST
FRETTER
OAK BARREL
BERKELEY
EMERYVILLE
J. W. MORRIS
ROSENBLUM
OAKLAND
ALAMEDA
CHANNING RUDD
MONTCLAIR
SAN LEANDRO
RICHARD CAREY
SAN FRANCISCO BAY
SAN FRANCISCO
S. F. Co.
San Mateo Co.
Contra Costa Co.
Alameda Co.
PLEASANTON
VILLA ARMANDO
STONEY RIDGE
FENESTRA
LIVERMORE
CONCANNON
WENTE BROS.
LIVERMORE
MISSION SAN JOSE
WEIBEL CHAMPAGNE
Alameda Co.
Santa Clara Co.
San Mateo Co.
Santa Clara Co.
WOODSIDE
WOODSIDE
CRONIN
HALF MOON BAY
OBESTER
scale
miles

North Central Coast

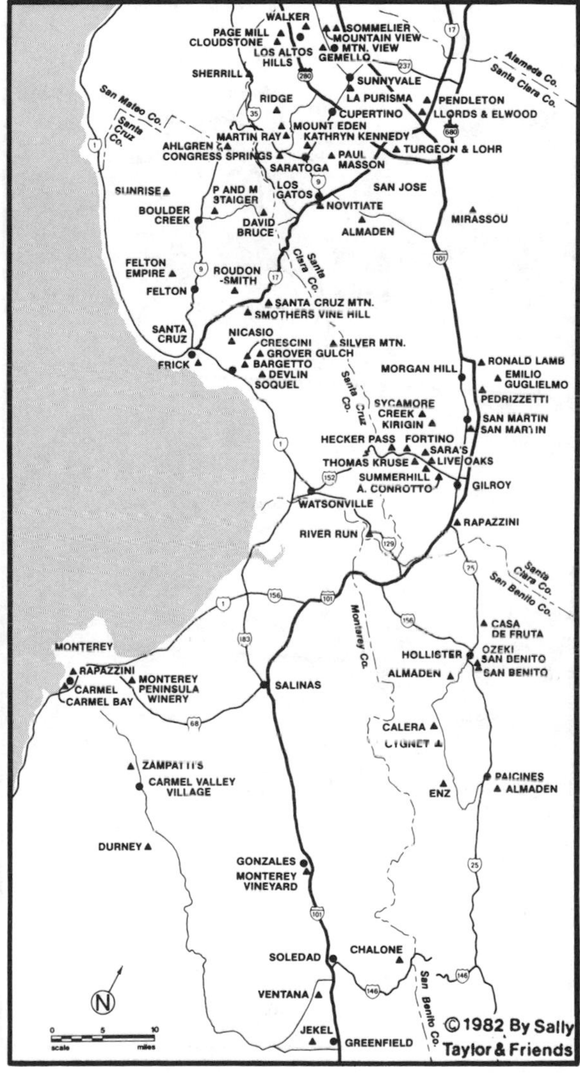

WALKER
PAGE MILL
CLOUDSTONE
SOMMELIER
MOUNTAIN VIEW
MTN. VIEW
LOS ALTOS HILLS
GEMELLO
Alameda Co.
Santa Clara Co.
SHERRILL
SUNNYVALE
San Mateo Co.
Santa Cruz Co.
RIDGE
LA PURISMA
PENDLETON
CUPERTINO
LLORDS & ELWOOD
MOUNT EDEN
MARTIN RAY
KATHRYN KENNEDY
AHLGREN
CONGRESS SPRINGS
TURGEON & LOHR
PAUL MASSON
SARATOGA
SUNRISE
P AND M STAIGER
LOS GATOS
SAN JOSE
NOVITIATE
BOULDER CREEK
DAVID BRUCE
MIRASSOU
ALMADEN
Santa Clara Co.
FELTON EMPIRE
ROUDON -SMITH
FELTON
SANTA CRUZ MTN.
SMOTHERS VINE HILL
SANTA CRUZ
NICASIO
CRESCINI
SILVER MTN.
GROVER GULCH
FRICK
BARGETTO
DEVLIN
SOQUEL
RONALD LAMB
MORGAN HILL
EMILIO GUGLIELMO
PEDRIZZETTI
Santa Cruz Co.
SYCAMORE CREEK
KIRIGIN
SAN MARTIN
HECKER PASS
FORTINO
SARA'S
THOMAS KRUSE
LIVE OAKS
SUMMERHILL
A. CONROTTO
GILROY
WATSONVILLE
RAPAZZINI
RIVER RUN
Santa Clara Co.
San Benito Co.
Monterey Co.
CASA DE FRUTA
MONTEREY
HOLLISTER
OZEKI
SAN BENITO
SAN BENITO
RAPAZZINI
MONTEREY PENINSULA WINERY
ALMADEN
CARMEL
CARMEL BAY
SALINAS
CALERA
ZAMPATTI'S
CARMEL VALLEY VILLAGE
PAICINES
ALMADEN
ENZ
DURNEY
GONZALES
MONTEREY VINEYARD
SOLEDAD
CHALONE
San Benito Co.
VENTANA
JEKEL
GREENFIELD
scale
miles
©1982 By Sally Taylor & Friends

South Central Coast

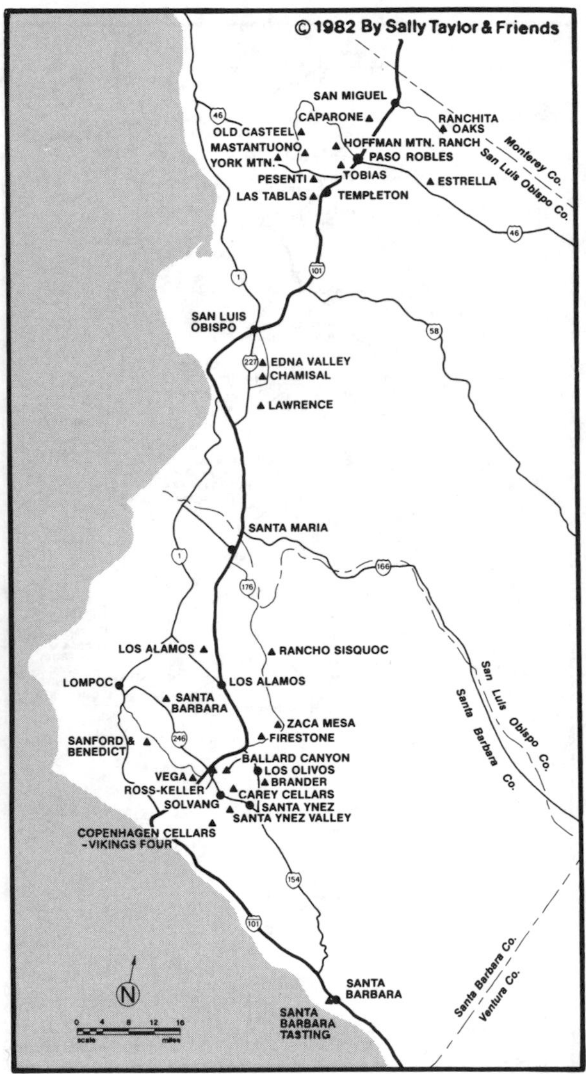
© 1982 By Sally Taylor & Friends
SAN MIGUEL
CAPARONE
RANCHITA OAKS
OLD CASTEEL
MASTANTUONO
HOFFMAN MTN. RANCH
PASO ROBLES
YORK MTN.
TOBIAS
PESENTI
ESTRELLA
LAS TABLAS
TEMPLETON
Monterey Co.
San Luis Obispo Co.
46
101
1
58
SAN LUIS OBISPO
227
EDNA VALLEY
CHAMISAL
LAWRENCE
SANTA MARIA
166
176
LOS ALAMOS
RANCHO SISQUOC
LOMPOC
LOS ALAMOS
SANTA BARBARA
ZACA MESA
FIRESTONE
SANFORD & BENEDICT
246
BALLARD CANYON
LOS OLIVOS
VEGA
BRANDER
ROSS-KELLER
CAREY CELLARS
SOLVANG
SANTA YNEZ
SANTA YNEZ VALLEY
COPENHAGEN CELLARS -VIKINGS FOUR
San Luis Obispo Co.
Santa Barbara Co.
154
SANTA BARBARA
SANTA BARBARA TASTING
Santa Barbara Co.
Ventura Co.
N
0 4 8 12 16
scale
miles

Touring California Wine Country

CALIFORNIA WINERIES OPEN TO VISITORS*

The wineries listed by county on the following pages have stated that they are open to the public as shown. Their facilities for visitors are indicated by the following symbols noted in parentheses after the winery's name and nearest town:

H—Access for handicapped
P—Picnic facilities available
R—Retail sales at winery
T—Tasting
TR—Retail Sales outlet only

Data relative to individual wineries was correct when this book went to press but is subject to change. Visitors planning tours in advance are advised to call wineries to avoid delay or disappointment. Large groups should always be booked in advance. Some wineries close on certain major legal and religious holidays and not others. Visitors should check with wineries as to holiday hours. It is strongly suggested that visitors obtain a current California state road map to supplement individual winery directions. Check exact address and telephone # under winery listing.

ALAMEDA COUNTY

Berkeley Wine Cellars, Berkeley (R,T)—Call for hours.

Channing Rudd Cellars, Alameda—By appt. only.

Concannon Vineyard, Livermore (H,P,R,T)—From Hwy. 580, S on Vasco 3 mi. Turn R on Tesla Rd. M-Sa 10-5, Su 12-5. Tours avail. on req.

Fenestra Winery, Livermore (R,T)—Tasting by appt. only.

Fretter Wine Cellars, Berkeley (H,R)—Visitors by appt. only. (415) 525-3232.

Livermore Valley Cellars, Livermore (P,R,T)—S on Arroyo Rd., R on Wetmore Rd. By appt. only.

Montali Winery, Berkeley—Fourth & Allston Street.

J. W. Morris Wineries, Emeryville (R)—Powell St. exit Hwy. 17 to Emeryville, 2-1/2 blks. W of San Pablo Ave. Visitors by appt. only.

Numano Sake Co., Berkeley (H,R,T)—4th & Addison Sts., off University. Daily 12-6. Tours: weekends only 12-4. Special grp. tastings by appt.

Oak Barrel Winery, Berkeley (TR)—1 blk. E of San Pablo Ave., M-Sa 10-6:30.

Rosenblum Cellars, Oakland—tours & tastings by appt. only.

Stony Ridge Winery, Pleasanton (H,P,R,T,)—From Hwy. 680 to Sunol Blvd. toward Pleasanton to Vineyard Ave. R to 1188 Vineyard Ave. Tasting daily 12-5. Tours by appt.

Veedercrest, Emeryville (R)—100 yds. SW corner of Hollis and Stanford. Visitors by appt. only. Days (415) 652-3103; eves. & weekends (415) 849-3303.

Villa Armando Winery, Pleasanton (R,T)—Open daily 12-5:30 except major Holidays.

Weibel Champagne Vineyards—Mission San Jose (P,R, T)—From Hwy. 680, 1.1 mi. S on Mission Blvd., 0.5 mi. L on Stanford Ave. From Hwy. 17, exit & 1.5 mi. E on Mission Blvd., 0.5 mi. R on Stanford Ave. Daily 10-5.

Wente Bros., Livermore (R)—From Hwy. 580, S on Vasco, 3 mi. to Tesla Rd., turn rt, M-Sa 9-4:30, Su 11-4:30. Touring weekdays only 9:30-3:30. Picnic facils. limited.

Wine and the People, Berkeley (H,R,T)—Hours M-Sa 10-6, Su 11-5. 907 University Ave.

AMADOR COUNTY

Amador Foothill Winery, Plymouth (R,T)—At Steiner Rd. Weekends 10-4. Call ahead.

Amador Winery, Amador City (T,R)—Hwy. 49 to winery. Open daily 10-6.

Argonaut Winery, Ione (R,T)—5 mi. NE of Ione on Willow Creek Rd. Tours & tasting by appt. only.

Baldinelli Vineyards, Plymouth (H,R,T)—4-1/2 mi. N of Plymouth on Shenandoah Rd. Tours & tasting by appt. only.

Beau Val Wines, Plymouth (R,T)—4.5 mi. NE of Plymouth on Shenandoah Valley Rd., L on Bell, L to 10671 Valley Dr. Tours & tasting by appt.

D'Agostini Winery, Plymouth (R)—8 mi. NE of Plymouth on Shenandoah Rd. Daily 9-4:30.

Greenstone Winery, Ione (R,R,T)—Hwy. 88 & Jackson Valley Rd. at the gateway to California's gold country & the Sierra Nevadas. Sa-Su 10-4; July-Aug Tu-Su 10-4.

Karly Wines, Plymouth (R,T)—Bell Rd. 4 mi. E off Shenandoah Rd., by appt.

Kenworthy Vineyards, Plymouth (R,T)—Located on Shenandoah Rd., 1/2 mi. N of Fiddletown Rd. junct. Tasting 12-5 Su, or by appt.

Montevina, Plymouth (R,T)—3 mi. NE of Plymouth on Shenandoah School Rd. Daily 1-3.

Santino Winery, Plymouth (H,P,R,T)—From Plymouth drive 5.4 mi. E on Shenandoah Rd., L on Steiner Rd. to corner of Steiner & Upton Rds. Normally tasting from 9-4

M-F. Sa-Su by appt. only. Tours by appt. only.

Shenandoah Vineyards, Plymouth (R,T)—From Plymouth drive 5 mi. E on Shenandoah Rd., L on 12300 to Box 23. Tasting on Sa & Su & Holidays, 12-5, or by appt.

Stoneridge, Sutter Creek (P,R,T)—Open Sa 1-4 or by appt.

CALAVERAS COUNTY

Chispa Cellars, Murphys—Located corner of Murphys Grade Rd. & French Gulch Rd. at 425 Main St. By appt. only.

Stevenot Winery, Murphys (P,R,T)—3 mi. N of Murphys on San Domingo Rd. Open daily 10-4 year round.

CONTRA COSTA COUNTY

J. E. Digardi Winery, Martinez (R)—2.3 mi. SE on Pacheco Blvd. M-F 9-3. Tours by appt.

J. W. Morris Wineries, Concord (T,R)—Visitors by appt. only.

Conrad Viano Winery, Martinez (R)—1 mi. E of VA Hospital on Hwy. 4, 1 mi. N of Morello Ave., daily 9-12, 1-5.

EL DORADO COUNTY

Boeger Winery, Placerville (P,R,T)—Open W-Su 10-5. Closed M-Tu.

Carson Ridge Vineyard, Camino (R)—Visitors by appt. only.

Eldorado Vineyards, Camino (H,P,R,T)—Hwy. 50 at Camino turnoff 4 mi. E of Placerville. Most Sa 12-4 or by appt. Open daily 10-4 Sept thru Dec.

FBF WINERY, Somerset (P,R,T)—Fairplay Rd., Somerset. By appt. only.

Granite Springs Winery, Somerset (P,R,T)—Off Hwy. E16. Sa-Su 11-5 or by appt.

Madrona Vineyards, Camino Rd., Open Sa 10-5, Su 1-5 or by appt.

Madrona Vineyards, Camino (H,R,T)—Gatlin Rd., N off Carson Rd., 5 mi. E of Placerville. Sa 10-5 & Su 1-5, or by appt.

Sierra Vista Winery, Placerville (R,T)—Located at end of Leisure Ln. off Pleasant Valley Rd. in Pleasant Valley. Open Sa & Su 12-5 or by appt.

Somerset Vineyards, Somerset (R)—2-1/2 mi. SW of Post Office on Fairplay Rd. Visitors by appt.

Stoney Creek Vineyards, Somerset (R,T)—Off Fairplay Rd. Call ahead.

Wineyards Historic Winetasting Cellar, Rescue (TR, T)—Off Hwy. W of Shingle Springs on Green Valley Rd. at Cameron Park Dr. Open daily except Tues. Call for hrs. Tasting of the largest selection of Sierra Foothill wines.

FRESNO COUNTY

B. Cribari & Sons Winery, Fresno (H,R,T)—From Hwy. 99, at Jensen exit E to 2nd signal, left to Church Ave., R to 3223 E Church Ave, M-Sa 10-5, Su 12-5. Large grps. welcome.

Farnesi Winery, Sanger (R)—2426 Almond Ave., Jensen Ave. exit from Hwy. 99. Retail sales only, M-F 8-5, Sa 8-noon.

Gibson Wine Co., Sanger (R,T)—Call for hrs.
A. Nonini Winery, Fresno (R,T)—7.5 mi. W of Hwy. 99 on McKinley, 0.5 mi. N on Dickenson Ave. Tours 9-4, tasting 9-5. Closed Su.
Nicholas G. Verry, Parlier (T)—Open daily 8-6 for tasting & tours. No retail sales.
Villa Bianchi Winery, Fresno (R)—13 mi. W on Shaw Ave., from Hwy. 99, M-F 9-4.
HUMBOLDT COUNTY
Willow Creek Vineyards, Mckinleyville (R,T)—Visitors by appt. only.
Wittwer Winery, Eureka (R)—No tastings. Call for hours.
KERN COUNTY
Giumarra Vineyards, Edison (R,T)—Edison Rd. at Edison Hwy., 9 mi. E of Hwy. 99, off Hwy. 58. Tasting rm. open Tu-Sa 9-5.
LaMont Winery, Di Giorgio (R,T)—Located 10 mi. E of Hwy. 99 on Hwy. 58, 5 mi. S on Comanche Rd. to Bear Mtn. Winery Rd. Tasting room open M-F, 1-5.
Sierra Winery (formerly Perelli-Minetti), Delano (P,R, T)—Adj. to Fwy. at Pond Rd. & Hwy. 99. 3 mi. S of Delano & 28 mi. N of Bakersfield. Open daily from 10-5.
Villa Bianchi Vineyards, Kerman (T,R)—M-F 9-4.
LAKE COUNTY
Chateau du Lac, Lakeport (R)—Off Highland Springs Rd. 2 mi. S of Lakeport on Hwy. 29. Call for appt.
Guenoc Winery, Middletown (R)—Visitors by appt. only.
The Konocti Winery, Kelseyville (H,P,R,T)—Hwy. 29 at Thomas Dr., midway bet. Kelseyville & Lakeport. Tasting daily 11-5. Grp. tours by appt. Harvest Festival second week in Oct.
Lower Lake Winery, Lower Lake (H,P,R,T)—Hwy. 29 1 mi. S of Lower Lake. Open Sa & Su 10-5. Weekday visitors call.
Turner Winery, Woodbridge (P,R,T)—From Hwy. 99, go W on Woodbridge Rd. for 1/4 mi., just before RR crossing. M-F 9-6, Sa-Su 10-5.
LOS ANGELES COUNTY
Ahern Winery, San Fernando—Visitors by appt. only.
Barengo Vineyards, Los Angeles (TR)—Farmers Market, 6333 W. Third at Fairfax, daily 9-7.
Brookside Winery, Agoura (TR,P,T)—28650 W Canwood Rd., Kanan Rd. offramp from Ventura Fwy., 10-6 M-Sa, 12-6 Su.
Brookside Winery, Glendale (TR,T)—1101 Air Way, San Fernando Rd. at Grandview. 10-6 M-Sa, 11-5 Su.
Brookside Winery, Long Beach (TR,T)—4515 E Pacific Coast Hwy., 10-6 M-T-W-Sa, 10-7:30 Th-F, 10-5 Su.
Brookside Winery, Northridge (H,TR)—9677 Reseda Blvd. 11-7 Tu-Sa, 12-5 Su, Closed Monday.
Brookside Winery, Pasadena (TR,T)—3589 E Colorado Blvd., 2 blks. off Rosemead, 10-7 M-Sa, 11-5 Su.
Brookside Winery, San Pedro (TR,T)—Berth #77, Ports of Call Village, daily 11-9.
Brookside Winery, Torrance (TR,T)—25352 Crenshaw Blvd. in Rolling Hills Plaza Shopping Center, 10-6 M-Sa,

11-5 Su.

Brookside Winery, Van Nuys (TR,T)—6100 Sepulveda Blvd. btwn. Burbank & Victory, 10-6 M-Sa, 12-5 Su.

Donatoni Winery, Inglewood (R,T)—Call for hours.

J. Filippi Vintage Co., El Monte (TR)—9613 Valley Blvd., 1 blk. W of Temple City Blvd., daily 10-6.

J. Filippi Vintage Co., Hawthorne (TR)—5107 El Segundo Blvd., 1 blk. E of San Diego Fwy., daily 10-6.

J. Filippi Vintage Co., Pico Rivera (TR)—8447 Rosemead Blvd., 1 blk. N of Telegraph Rd., daily 10-6.

J. Filippi Vintage Co., Sun Valley (TR)—8522 Sunland Blvd., btwn. San Fernando Rd. & Golden State Fwy., daily 10-6.

The Martin Winery, Culver City (R)—11800 W Jefferson from San Diego Fwy. Tasting daily 11-8. Chateau cafe 11-6. No tours.

McLester, Inglewood (R,T). Weekends.

Ranchita Oaks Winery, San Miguel (P,R,T)—From Hwy. 101 take Cross Canyon turn off at San Miguel. Tasting by appt. only.

San Antonio Winery, Los Angeles (P,T,R)—Downtown LA. 737 Lamar St. M-Th 8-7, F 8-8, Sa 8-7, Su 10-6.

South Coast Cellars, Gardena (R)—12 mi. S of LA Civic Center. Harbor Fwy. to El Segundo Blvd., W 1 mi. to Budlong Ave. Visitors by appt. only.

MADERA COUNTY

Coarsegold Wine Cellar, Coarsegold (R)—On Hwy. 41, 3 mi. S of Coarsegold, tasting daily 10-5.

Ficklin Vineyards, Madera (R)—30246 Ave. 7-1/2. By appt. only.

Papagni Vineyards, Madera (R)—6 mi. S on Hwy. 99 & Ave. 9, SE corner. Tours by appt. only.

Quady Winery, Madera (R,T)—13181 Rd. 24. By appt. only. Call eves.

MARIN COUNTY

Grand Pacific Vineyard Co., San Rafael (R,T)—Hwy. 101 N from San Francisco to Freitas Parkway exit, approx. 1/2 mi. on frontage rd. to 134 Paul Dr., #9, Northgate Industrial Park, daily 11-5:30.

Kalin Cellars, Novato—Visitors by appt. only.

Pacheco Ranch Winery, Ignacio (R)—5495 Redwood Hwy. 101 N from San Francisco to Alameda Del Prado exit—over overpass to West Farnlage Rd., R at stop 3/10 mi. N. By appt. only.

Sonoma Vineyards (Tiburon Vintners), Tiburon (TR)—Hwy. 101 N from San Francisco at Tiburon-Belvedere exit, 4 mi. to 72 Main St., Su-Th 10-6, F-Sa 10-8.

Woodbury Winery, San Rafael (R)—Hwy. 101 N from San Francisco to Francisco Blvd. exit, 1 mi. to 32 Woodland Ave. By appt. only.

MENDOCINO COUNTY

Bel Arbres, Hopland (R,T)—Located on US Hwy. 101 less than 2 hrs. N of San Francisco Bay Area. Tours & tasting 10-5.

Cresta Blanca, Ukiah (H,P,R,T)—From Hwy. 101 S take Lake Mendocino exit, R 1 mi. to winery. From Hwy. 101 N take North State St. exit, R 1/2 mi. to winery. Guided weekday tours, tasting rm., daily 9-5. Grps. welcome.

Dach Vineyards, Philo (R)—5 mi. N on Hwy. 128 from Philo (due W of Ukiah on road map). By appt. only.

Edmeades Vineyards, Philo (H,P,R,T)—5500 Hwy. 128, 3 mi. N of Philo. Tours by appt. only. Daily 10-6 summer, 11-5 winter.

Fetzer Vineyards, Hopland (H,P,T,R)—on Hwy. 101 in Hopland. Wine tasting, art gallery, gift shop, delicatessen, picnic facil. Open daily 9-5.

Fetzer Vineyards, Redwood Valley—23 mi. N of Hopland. Tours by appt. only.

Frey Vineyards Ltd., Redwood Valley (R)—1400 Tommi Rd. (northern end of Redwood Valley). 8 mi. N of Ukiah on Hwy. 101 to Hwy. 20. Turn E 1 mi. to Redwood Valley turnoff. N 5 mi. to Tomki Rd. Retail sales & tours by appt.

Greenwood Ridge Vineyards, Philo (R)—7 mi. NW of Philo (11 mi. E of Elk) on Greenwood Rd. Visitors by appt. only please.

Hidden Cellars, Talmage—5 mi. E of the Ukiah Valley. Visitors by appt. only.

Husch Vineyards, Philo (P,R,T)—5 mi. NW Philo on Hwy. 128. Open daily 10-5. Tours by appt.

McDowell Valley Vineyards, Hopland (R)—4 mi. E of Hopland (Hwy. 101) on Hwy. 175. By appt. only.

Milano Winery, Hopland (R.T)—1 mi. S of Hopland. Open for tasting Tu-Su 10-5. Tours by appt. only.

Mountain House Winery, Cloverdale—by appt. only.

Navarro Vineyards, Philo (R,T)—3 mi. N of Philo. Tasting daily 10-6. Tours by appt. only.

Parducci Wine Cellars, Ukiah (P,R,T)—2 mi. N on Hwy. 101, rt. on Lake Mendocino Dr., left to 501 Parducci Rd., daily 9-6. Tours 10-4 on the hour.

Parsons Creek, Ukiah (R)—by appt. only.

Tyland Vineyards, Ukiah (R,P,T)—6 mi. S of Ukiah & 2.5 mi. W of Hwy. 101, at 2200 McNab Ranch Rd. Open for tours, tasting & retail sales most weekends & weekdays during summer, 10-4:30, or by appt.

Villa Baccala Winery, Ukiah—6 mi. S of Ukiah.

Weibel Champagne Vineyards, Redwood Valley (H,P,R, T)—7051 N State St., Redwood Valley, from Hwy. 101, N of Hwy. 20, daily 9-6.

Whaler Vineyard, Ukiah—5 mi. S of Talmage. By appt. only.

MONTEREY COUNTY

Bargetto Winery, Monterey (TR)—Corner of Cannery Row & Prescott. Daily 10-7 (winter), 10-10 (summer). Tasting room & gift shop.

Carmel Bay Winery, Carmel (R,T)—Visitors by appt. only.

Chalone Vineyard, Soledad—Retail sales & tours by appt. only. Closed weekends. Write.

Durney Vineyard, Carmel Valley—Retail sales & tours by appt. only.

Fortino Winery, Gilroy (R,T)—Open daily 9-6.

Jekel Vineyard, Greenfield (H,P,R,T)—Walnut Ave. bet. 12th & 13th Sts., 1 mi. W of Hwy. 101 (use Walnut Ave. off-ramp). Guided tours, grp. tours by appt. Daily except Tu & W 10-5.

Paul Masson Pinnacles Vineyard, Soledad—Metz Rd. on rd. to Pinnacles Nat. Monument E of Hwy. 101. Tours by appt. only. Contact Paul Masson Vineyards, Saratoga.

Mirassou Vineyards, Soledad—Arroyo Seco Rd., 3 mi. W of Hwy. 101, daily (vineyards only). Appt. only.

The Monterey Vineyard, Gonzales (R,T)—Hwy. 101 at S edge of Gonzales, daily 10-5, tours 11-4. Grps. by appt.

Monterey Peninsula Winery, Monterey (H,P,R,T)—Corner of Monterey-Salinas Hwy. 68 and Canyon Del Rey Hwy. 218, 2 mi. E of Hwy. 1. Open daily 10-dusk. Informal tours. Restaurant adjacent.

Rapazzini's Stage Coach Cellars, Aromas (TR)—Hwy. 101, 15 mi. N of Salinas, daily 9-8 (summer), 10-6 (winter).

Smith & Hook, Soledad (P,T)—Arroyo Seco Rd. exit, R at Ft. Romie Rd., L on Colony, R on Foothill. Tours & tasting by appt.

Ventana Vineyards Winery, Soledad (R,T)—5.8 mi. SW of Soledad. Take Arroyo Seco exit off Hwy. 101, 3 mi. L at Los Coches Rd. for 1 mi. Tours and tastings by appt.

Zampatti's Cellar, Carmel (R)—Call ahead.

NAPA COUNTY

Acacia Winery, Napa—Visitors by appt. only.

Alatera Vineyards, Yountville—By appt. only. Write or call.

Alta Vineyard Cellar, Calistoga—5 mi. N of St. Helena off Hwy. 29. Retail sales & winery tours by appt.

S. Anderson Vineyard, Yountville—by appt. only. No tasting. Write or call.

Beaulieu Vineyard, Rutherford (R,T)—60 mi. N of San Francisco, take Hwy. 101 N. On Hwy. 29. Tours & tasting 10-4. Grps. welcome but adv. reservations.

Beringer Vineyards, St. Helena (R,T)—Left off Hwy. 29 just N of St. Helena. Daily 9-4:45. Guided tours 9:30—last tour 3:45. Grp. tours by appt.

Burgess Cellars, St. Helena (R)—3.4 mi. from Hwy. 29. Retail sales. Daily 10-4. Tours by appt.

Cakebread Cellars, Rutherford (R)—1 mi. S of Rutherford on Hwy. 29, by appt. only.

Calafia Wines, St. Helena—No tours or tasting, not even by appt. Retail sales by mailing list only.

California Meadery/Winery of the Roses, Napa—Visitors by appt. only.

Carneros Creek Winery, Napa (R)—Retail sale M-F 10-4, tours on Sa by appt.

Casa Nuestra, St. Helena (R)—Retail sales but no tours or tasting.

Cassayre-Forni Cellars, Rutherford (R)—1/2 mi. S of Rutherford at 1271 Manley Ln. off Hwy. 29. By appt. only.

Caymus Vineyards, Rutherford. Retail sales & visitors by appt. only.

Chappellet Vineyard, St. Helena—Tours on Fr. afternoon

by appt.

Chateau Boswell Winery, St. Helena (H,R)—Visitors by appt. only. Retail sales.

Chateau Bouchaine, Napa—Visitors by appt. only. No tasting.

Chateau Chevalier Winery, St. Helena (R)—2 mi. NW Madrona & Spring Mtn. Rd. By appt. only; no visitors Su & holidays.

Chateau Chevre Winery, Yountville (H,R,T)—By appt. only.

Chateau Montelena Winery, Calistoga (R)—Tours & tasting by appt. only.

The Christian Brothers Mont la Salle Vineyards and Winery, (R,T)—8 mi. NW of Napa on Redwood Rd., off Hwy. 29, daily 10:30-4. Grps. of 20 or more by appt. only.

The Christian Brothers Wine and Champagne Cellars, St. Helena (H,R,T)—1/3 mi. N of St. Helena on Hwy. 29, daily 10:30-4:30. Grps. of 20 or more by appt. only.

Clos du Val, Napa (P,R)—5 mi. N of Napa. Retail sales M-Sa 10-4. Tours by appt.

Conn Creek Winery, St. Helena—intersection of Rt. 128 and Silverado trail. Tasting, retail sales & winery tour by appt. only.

Cuvaison, Calistoga (H,P,R,T)—just S of Dunaweal Ln., 6 mi. N of St. Helena, W-Su 10-4.

Deer Park Winery, St. Helena (R)—3 mi. E from Hwy. 29. Retail sales & tours by appt.

Diamond Creek Vineyards, Calistoge (P)—Invited guests & wine society grps. only.

Domaine Chandon, Yountville (H,R)—Exit Hwy. 29 at Yountville, go W on California Dr. toward Veterans Home, turn rt. into winery after crossing railroad tracks. Tours, (paid) tasting of sparkling wines 11-5:30. Restaurant serves lunch & dinner (res. adv. 707-944-2892). The winery is open & lunch is served daily from May-Oct. During the winter (Nov-Apr) the winery & restaurant are closed Mo & Tu.

Duckhorn Vineyards, St. Helena (R)—1 mi. N of St. Helena, corner Lodi Ln. & Silverado Trail N. No tours or tastings, visitors by appt. only.

Evensen Vineyards & Winery, Oakville (R)—1 mi. N of Oakville on Hwy. 29. By appt. only.

Far Niente Winery, Oakville—by appt. only.

Flora Springs Wine Co., St. Helena—1 mi. W of Hwy. 29. Visitors by appt. only.

Franciscan Vineyards, Rutherford (H,R,T)—1 mi. N on Hwy. 29 at Galleron Rd. Tasting & retail sales 10-5 daily; self-guided tour & gift shop; sensory evaluation at 2 daily.

Freemark Abbey Winery, St. Helena (R)—1 mi. N of St. Helena on Hwy. 29. Sales daily 10-4:30, tour daily at 2. No tasting, grps. by appt. Restaurant for lunch-dinner. Winery No. 707-963-9694. Restaurant No. 707-963-2706.

Frog's Leap Winery, St. Helena—Visitors by appt. Retail sales by mailing list only.

Girard, Oakville (H,R)—On Silverado Trail just N of Oakville Crossroad. Retail sales 1-4 weekdays, 2-4 weekends & holidays (May-Sept). Tours & tasting by appt.

Grgich Hills Cellar, Rutherford (H,R,T)—2 mi. N of Rutherford on Hwy. 29. Retail sales 10-4, tours by appt. only.

Heitz Wine Cellars, St. Helena (H,R)—Sales rm. at 436 St. Helena Hwy., 0.5 mi. SE on Jy 29, open daily 11-4:30. Tours by appt. only.

William Hill Winery, Napa—Visitors by appt.

HNW Cellars, Rutherford (R)—Call for hours.

Inglenook Vineyards, Rutherford (T,R)—From Napa, Hwy. 29 N to intersection 128, turn L. Daily Sa, Su 10-5. Tours on the hour 10-4.

Johnson Turnbull Vineyards, Oakville—1 mi. N of Oakville on Hwy. 29, by appt. only.

Robert Keenan Winery, St. Helena—From Hwy. 29, 5 mi. W on Spring Mtn. Rd. Visitors by appt. only.

Hanns Kornell Champagne Cellars, St. Helena (R,T)—3 mi. N of St. Helena on Hwy. 29, 1/4 mi. E on Larkmead Ln., daily 10-4.

Charles Krug/CK Mondavi, St. Helena (R,T)—E side of Hwy. 29 N limit of St. Helena (2800 Main St.) Daily 10-4:45—last tour 4. Gps. by appt.

Lakespring Winery, Napa (R,T)—By appt. only.

Long Vineyards, St. Helena—By appt. only. Write or call for appt. and directions.

Markham Winery, St. Helena (H,R,T,)—Hwy. 29, 1-1/4 mi. N of St. Helena at Deer Park Rd. Open daily 11-4. Tours by appt.

Louis M. Martini, St. Helena (R,T)—Hwy. 20, 1-1/2 mi. S of St. Helena, daily 10-4:30.

Mayacamas, Napa (R)—Visitors by appt. only. Closed weekends.

Louis K. Milhaly Vineyard, Napa—Visitors by appt. only.

F.J. Miller, Napa (R)—Located 1 mi. N of Oakville on W side of Rte. 29. Visitors by appt. only.

Robert Mondavi Winery, Oakville (R.T)—Hwy. 29, 12 mi. N of Napa, daily 10-4:30. May 1-Oct 31, 9-5. Prearranged group lunches & dinners catered by appt.

Mont St. John Cellars, Napa (H,P,R,T)—Tasting 10-4:40 daily.

Mount Veeder Winery, Napa (R)—No tasting. Call for appt., weekdays only.

Napa Cellars, Oakville (H,P.R,T)—7481 Hwy. 29, 10 mi. N of Napa, daily 10-5:30. Jan 1-Mar 31 10-4:30. Prearranged picnic lunches by appt.

Napa Creek Winery, St. Helena (H,R)—Daily 10-4.

Napa Vintners, Napa—Sales & tasting by appt. only.

Newton Winery, St. Helena (R)—Call for hrs.

Newlan Vineyards & Winery, Napa (R)—4 mi. N of Napa on frontage rd. of Hwy. 29. Tours by appt.

Nichelini Vineyard, St. Helena (R)—From Hwy. 29 at Rutherford E 11 mi. on Hwy. 128, Winery on R. Sa, Su 10-6. Weekdays by appt.

Niebaum-Coppola Estate, Rutherford—Visitors by appt. only.

Pannonia Winery, Napa (R,T)—Tasting by appt. only. Retail sales at winery.

Robert Pecota Winery, Calistoga—0.4 mi. N on Bennett Ln. Visitors by appt. only.

Robert Pepi Winery, Oakville (R)—No tasting. Visitors by appt.

Joseph Phelps Vineyards, St. Helena (R)—off Silverado Tr. 1 mi. S of St. Helena. Retail sales M-F 8-5, Sa 9-4. Tours by appt.

Pine Ridge Winery, Napa (H,P,R,T)—Open W-Su 11-3:30. Picnic & hiking trails open to public.

Pope Valley Winery, Pope Valley (P,T.R)—12 mi. E of St. Helena. Hwy. 29 N to Deer Park Rd. Weekends 11-5 or by appt.

Prager Winery & Port Works, St. Helena (R)—Just S of St. Helena. Lewelling Ln. off Hwy. 29. Visitors by appt. only.

Quail Ridge, Napa—1 mi. S of entrance to Silverado Country Club. Visitors & sales by appt. only.

Raymond Vineyard & Cellar, S. Helena—S of St. Helena 3 mi. Visitors by adv. appt. only.

Ritchie Creek Vineyards, St. Helena (R.T)—call ahead.

Roddis Cellar, Calistoga—1 mi. S of Calistoga on Hwy. 29, 1/2 mi. W on Diamond Mtn. Rd. By appt. only.

Don Charles Ross Winery, Napa (R,T)—by appt. only.

Round Hill Vineyards, St. Helena (R)—1 mi. N of St. Helena. Tours by appt. only.

Rutherford Hill Winery, Rutherford (P,R,T)—2 mi. E of Rutherford on Silverado Tr. Daily 10-4:30. Grps. larger than 6 call for appt.

Rutherford Vintners, Rutherford (R,T)—1 mi. N of Rutherford on W side of Hwy. 29, daily 10-4:30. Grp. tours by appt.

Sage Canyon Winery, Rutherford—Visitors by appt. only.

V. Sattui Winery, St. Helena (R,P,T)—2 mi. S. on Hwy. 29 at White Ln. Cheese shop & gourmet deli, picnic area, gift shop. Tasting & informal tours. Daily 9-6. All wines sold only at the winery.

Schramsberg Vineyards, Calistoga—5 mi. N of St. Helena on Hwy. 29, no tasting. Retail sales & winery tours by appt.

Sequoia Grove Vineyards, Rutherford (R,T)—bet. Oakville & Rutherford on Hwy. 29. Daily 11-5.

Shafer Vineyards, Napa (R)—3/4 mi. S of Yount Cross Rd. on Silverado Tr., no tasting. By appt. only.

Charles F. Shaw Vineyard & Winery, St. Helena (R)—4.4 mi. N on Hwy. 29, go E on Big Tree Rd. 5 mi. Sales daily 11-5, tours by appt. only.

Shown & Son's Vineyards, Rutherford (H,P,R)—M-F 10-3 & by appt.

Silver Oak Cellars, Oakville—1 mi. E of Hwy. 29. By appt. only.

Silverado Vineyards, Napa (R)—Visitors by appt.

Smith-Madrone, St. Helena (R)—M-Sa, 9-5 by appt. only.

Spring Mountain Vineyards, St. Helena—1 mi. NW

Madrona & Spring Mtn. Rd. Retail sales M-F 9-5; Tours M-F, 2:30 by appt.

St. Andrews Winery, Napa—Visitors by appt. only.

St. Helena Wine Co., St. Helena—1 mi. N of St. Helena, Corner Lodi Ln. and Silverado Trail. By appt. only.

Stag's Leap Wine Cellars, Napa (R)—6 mi. N of Napa. Tours 1-3 M-F, 10-4 Sa-Su by appt. only.

Stag's Leap Winery, Napa—Visitors by appt. only.

Sterling Vineyards, Calistoga (H,P,R,T)—From Hwy. 29, 7 mi. N of St. Helena, E 0.5 mi. on Dunaweal Ln. Apr 1-Oct 31 open daily 10:30-4:30; closed M, Tu Nov 1-Mar 31. $3.50 tramway fee for visitors 16 & over.

Stonegate, Inc., Calistoga (P,R)—1.25 mi. S of Calistoga on Hwy. 29. Retail sales. Tours by appt. only. 10-noon, 1-4.

Stony Hill Vineyard, St. Helena—2 mi. W of Hwy. 29, no tasting. By appt. only.

Storybook Mountain Vineyards, Calistoga—4 mi. NW of Calistoga on Hwy. 128. Visitors by appt. only.

Sullivan Vineyards Winery, Rutherford (R)—1 mi. N of Rutherford. E of Hwy. 29. Tasting by appt. only.

Sutter Home Winery, St. Helena (H,R,T)—1.5 mi. S of St. Helena on Hwy. 29, sales daily 9-5, tasting 10-4:30.

Trefethen Vineyards, Napa—3 mi. N of Napa on Hwy. 29. Tours only by appt. Retail sales weekdays 10-12, 1-4.

Tudal Winery, St. Helena—4 mi. N of St. Helena on Big Tree Rd. Visitors by appt. only.

Tulocay Winery, Napa (R)—By appt. only.

Vichon Winery, Oakville (H,R)—1 mi. up Oakville Grade. Tours & tasting by appt. only.

Villa Mt. Eden Winery, Oakville (R.T)—N from Napa on Hwy. 29, 2 mi. E of Oakville on Oakville Crossroads. By appt. only.

Vose Vineyards, Napa (R)—Hwy. 29 N to Oakville Grade, 3 mi. to Mt. Veeder Rd. Visitors by appt. only.

Whitehall Lane Winery, St. Helena (H,P,TR)—3 mi. S of St. Helena on Hwy. 29. Summer daily 12-6. Winter F, Sa, Su 12-5. Private tours & tasting by appt.

Yverdon, St. Helena (R)—Write for adv. appt.

ZD Wines, Napa (R,T)—By appt. only.

NEVADA COUNTY

Nevada City Winery, Nevada City (R,T)—Located in heart of Historic Nevada City. Winery open tours-tasting daily 12-Sunset.

ORANGE COUNTY

Brookside Winery, Anaheim (TR,T,P)—711 S. Brookhurst St. btwn. Lincoln & Ball, 10-6 M-Sa, 11-5 Su.

Brookside Winery, Costa Mesa (TR,T)—2925 Bristol St. 10-6 M-Sa, 12-6 Su.

Brookside Winery, Dana Point (TR,T)—24292 Del Prado, 10-6 daily.

Brookside Winery, La Habra (TR,T)—2050 W. Lambert Rd. at Beach Blvd., 10-6 M-Sa, 11-5 Su.

J. Filippi Vintage Co., Garden Grove (TR)—12872 S Harbor Blvd., btwn. Chapman & Garden Grove Blvd., daily 10-6.

RIVERSIDE COUNTY

Callaway Vineyard & Winery, Temecula (H,P,R,T)—31 mi. S of Riverside on Hwy. 15E, take off-ramp Rancho California Rd., travel E approx. 4 mi. to winery. Open daily 10-5. Free guided tours on the hour until 4. Call to arrange private grp. tour, tastings & luncheons.

Cilurzo Vineyard & Winery, Temecula/Rancho California (P,R,T,)—Bet. San Diego & Riverside on Hwy. 15E. Exit Rancho California Rd., travel E approx. 6 mi., R on Calle Contento 1/4 mi. Open weekends 9-5, weekday by appt. Informal tasting & tours. Some picnic tables avail.

Filsinger Vineyards & Winery, Temecula (R,T)—32 mi. S of Riverside on Hwy. 15 exit at Hwy. 79 (Warner Springs Rd.). E 4 mi. to Anza, 1 blk. to De Portola then E 4 mi. Open weekdays June thru Aug 10:30-5:30. Weekends 11-5. Tours by appt.

Galleano Winery, Inc., Mira Loma (H,P,R,T)—M-Sa 8-6. Tours M-F 8-4.

Glen Oak Hills Winery, Temecula—By appt. only.

Hart Winery, Temecula (R)—Rancho California Rd. about 4 mi. E of Hwy. 15. Visitors by appt. only.

Mount Palomar Winery, Temecula (H,P,R,T)—Btwn. San Diego & Riverside on Hwy. 15 Exit at Rancho California Rd. and 5 mi. E to winery. Gourmet deli, picnic facils. for 80 or more, gift items. Open daily 9-5.

Opici Winery, Alta Loma (T,R)—5 mi. from Hwy. 10. Haven Ave. exit N to Highland. Daily 10-6.

Prestige Vineyards, Cabazon (T,R)—16 mi. W of Palm Springs on I-10. Located in Hadley Fruit Orchards store. Open 8-8 year around.

Rubedoux Winery, Riverside (R)—Visitors by appt. only.

SACRAMENTO COUNTY

Brookside Winery, Sacramento (H,P,TR,T)—4.5 mi. NE on Hwy. 50, 9910 Folsom Blvd., daily 10-7.

Cache Cellars, Davis (R)—3 mi. S of Putah Creek on Pedrich Rd. Visitors by appt. only.

Jas. Frasinetti & Sons, Florin/Sacramento (P,R,T)—Hwy. 99 to Florin Rd., E to Frasinetti Rd. to winery. M-F 8:40-7, Sa 11-6, closed Su.

Gibson Wine Company, Elk Grove (TR,P,T)—Hwy. 99 at Grant Line Rd., 3 mi. S of Elk Grove, tasting daily, no tours.

SAN BENITO COUNTY

Alamaden Vineyards, Pacheco Pass Hwy. (TR)—6 mi. N of Hollister, 12 mi. E of Gilroy at Rts. 152-156, daily 10-5.

Calera Wine Company, Hollister (R)—11 mi. S of Hollister. Tour & sales Sa at 11. By appt. only.

Casa de Fruta, Hollister (P,TR,T)—13 mi. E of Gilroy on Hwy. 152, Pacheco Pass 1 hr. S of San Jose. Open daily 9-6 (winter) 8-8 (summer), 24 hr. coffee shop, deli, recreational facils. & trailer park.

Cygnet Cellars, Hollister (R,P,T)—12 mi. S of Hollister. By appt. only. 408-733-4276.

Enz Vineyards, Hollister—16 mi. S of Hollister on Limekiln Rd. By appt. only.

Ozeki San Benito, Hollister (R)—M-F 8-5. Tours by appt.

Rapazzini Winery, San Juan Bautista (TR)—Mission Plaza, 10-5 daily.

San Benito Vineyards, Hollister (R)—M-F 9-5. Tours by appt.

SAN BERNARDINO COUNTY

Brookside Winery, Colton (TR,T,P)—22900 Washington Ave. off Riverside Fwy., 9-6 Su-Th, 9-7 F-Sa.

Brookside Winery, Guasti (R,P,T)—Guasti Rd. at Archibald Ave. off San Bernardino Fwy., 8-6 daily.

Brookside Winery, Victorville (TR,P)—14820 7th St. (Desert Knolls & 7th, entrance to fairgrounds). Daily 10-6.

Louis Cherpin Winery, Fontana (R)—Hwy. 10 btwn. Cherry & Citrus. Daily 8-5.

Cucamonga Vineyard Company, Cucamonga (R,P)—2 mi. N of San Bernardino Fwy., 10013 E. 8th St., btwn. Archibald and Turner Ave., daily 8-7.

J. Filippi Vintage Co., S. Fontana (R,P)—1-1/4 mi. S of San Bernardino Fwy. on Etiwanda Ave., daily 9-6.

Opici Winery, Alta Loma (R)—5 mi. from Hwy. 10 on Haven Ave. off-ramp N to Highland, daily 10-6.

Rancho de Philo, Alto Loma (H,R,T)—approx. 3.5 mi. N of Foothill Blvd. on Archibald Ave. (in Cucamonga), E on Wilson for 0.5 mi. M-Sa 9-5. Call ahead.

Thomas Vineyards, Cucamonga (R,P)—(Hwy. 66), 0.5 mi. W of Cucamonga on Foothill Blvd. & Vineyard Ave., daily 8-6.

SAN DIEGO COUNTY

Bernardo Winery, Escondido (H,P,R,T)—Pomerado Rd. off Rt. 15 (Hwy. 395) 7 mi. S of Escondido. Daily 9-5.

Bianchi Vineyards/Hadley Fruit Orchards, Carlsbad (TR)—6115 Paseo de Norte.

Brookside Winery, Bonita (TR,P,T)—3901 Bonita Rd. Chula Vista area, 10-7 M-Sa, 10-6 Su.

Brookside Winery, El Cajon (TR,T)—707 Arnele St., nr. Arnele & Johnson, M-Sa 10-7, Su 10-6.

Brookside Winery, Escondido (TR,P,T)—2402 S. Escondido Blvd., Hwy. 395 exit at Felicita Rd., turn E to S Escondido Blvd. 10-6 M-Sa 12-6 Su.

Brookside Winery, San Diego (Pacific Beach) (TR,T)—4730 Mission Bay Dr., 10-7 M-Sa, 10-6 Su.

Ferrara Winery, Escondido (R)—W on Felicita Ave. from Centre City, Pkwy., rt. on Redwood Ave. to 15th Ave., daily 9-6:30. Self-conducted tours.

J. Filippi Vintage Co., Vista (TR)—On rd. to Fallbrook, daily 10-6.

Point Loma Winery, San Diego—By appt. only.

San Pasqual Vineyards, San Diego (H,P,R,T)—3 mi. S of Escondido on Hwy. 15, take Via Rancho Pkwy. turnoff, then E approx. 1 mi. to San Pasqual Rd. Sales daily, tasting facility, in winery. Open Th-Su 11-5. Grp. tours by appt.

SAN FRANCISCO COUNTY

Buena Vista Winery, San Francisco—at Pier 39. Daily 10:30-8:30.

Cannery Wine Cellars, San Francisco (TR)—Daily 9:30-

6:30.

Havelock Gordon Negociants (Stanford Wine Co.), (R,T)—No tours. Call for appt.

San Benito Vineyards, San Francisco (TR,H)—Located on street level at the end of Pier 39 (Nth Point nr. Fisherman's Wharf). Daily 10-8:30.

Sonoma Vineyards, San Francisco (TR)—Corner of Union St. & Fillmore at 2191 Union. Su-Th 10-6, F-Sa 10-7.

The Wine Museum, San Francisco—Presenting The Christian Brothers Collection of wine in the Arts. 633 Beach St. (opp. the Cannery, near Fisherman's Wharf). Tu-Sa 11-5, Su 12-5. Closed M. Free.

Yerba Buena Winery, San Francisco—Pier 33, tours & tasting by appt.

SAN JOAQUIN COUNTY

Barengo—Lost Hills Vineyards, Acampo (R,P)—1 mi. W of Hwy. 99 at Acampo off-ramp. Tasting rm. open daily 9-5, tasting, retail sales.

Bella Napoli Winery, Manteca (R)—1/2 mi. S Hwy. 99 at 21128 S. Austin Rd. 9:30-5.

Borra's Cellar, Lodi—3 mi. W of Hwy. 99, open by appt. only.

Ciriaco Borelli Winery, Stockton (R)—10 mi. E of Stockton, 1-1/2 mi. N Hwy. 26, 5 mi. W of the community of Linden. Open by appt.

Cadlolo Winery, Escalon (R)—approx. 12 mi. E of Manteca on Hwy. 120 in Escalon, M-Sa 10-5:30 (closed 12-1).

Coloma Cellars, Escalon—McHenry Ave. at Escalon. Tu thru Su 10-5. Tasting & sales.

Coloma Cellars, Lodi (R,T)—N Ny. 99 Frontage Rd. Open daily.

Delicato Vineyards, Manteca (H,R,T)—From Hwy. 99, 4.2 mi. N of Manteca, 1/4 mi. S of French Camp Rd., daily 9-5. Tours F at 2 exc. dur. Aug, Sept, Oct.

East-Side Winery, Lodi (P,R,T)—Call for hrs.

Franzia Brothers Winery, Ripon (H,P,R,T)—6 mi. E of Manteca on Yosemi.te Ave. (Hwy. 120), daily 10-5.

Granite Springs Winery, Somerset (P,R,T)—1.7 mi. of E16 on Fairplay Rd. Tasting 11-5 weekends & by appt.

Guild's Central Cellars, Lodi (H,P,R,T)—0.5 mi. E of Hwy. 99 on Hwy. 12, L on Myrtle Ave. to One Winemaster's Way, Daily 10-5. Large grps. welcome.

The Lucas Winery, Lodi—Hwy. 99 W on Turner, or I-5 E on Turner, to N Davis Rd. Appt. only. Retail Sales Oct 1-Dec 20 9-6.

Oak Valley Winery, Oakdale (R)—Visitors by appt. only.

SAN LUIS OBISPO COUNTY

Caparone, Paso Robles—By appt. only.

Chami.sal Vineyard, San Luis Obispo (R,T)—M-F 10-4.

Coloma Cellars, Cayucas (TR)—Tu-Su 10-5.

Edna Valley Vineyard, San Luis Obispo (R)—No tasting, call for appt.

Estrella River Winery, Paso Robles (P,R,T)—6 mi. E of Paso Robles on Hwy. 46. Tasting rm. open daily 10-5.

HMR (Hoffman Vineyards), Paso Robles (R)—Winery, by appt. only. (TR) Black Oak Corner in Paso Robles, just W of Hwy. 101 on 24th St. M-Th 11-5, F-Su 10:30-6:30. Summer hrs. (June-Sept) daily 10:30-6:30.

Las Tablas Winery, Templeton (H,P.R,T)—3 mi. W of Hwy. 101 on Winery Rd. btwn. Vineyard Dr. & Las Tablas Rd. Daily 9-5.

Lawrence Winery, San Luis Obispo (P,R,T)—6 mi. SE of San Luis Obispo, take Hwy. 227 to Corbett Cyn Rd., then E on Corbett Cyn Rd. 1/3 mi. (6 mi. E of Pismo Beach & 6 mi. No. of Arroyo Grande.) Daily 10-4.

Martin Brothers Winery, Paso Robles (R)—1 mi. N of Hwy. 46 on Buena Vista Dr. just E of Paso Robles. By appt. only.

Mastantuono, Paso Robles (R)—Go 4 mi. W of 101 on Vineyard Dr., then R on Willow Creek Rd., 3 mi. Call for appt.

Old Casteel Vineyards, Paso Robles. By appt. only.

Pesenti Winery, Templeton (R,T)—3 mi. W of Hwy. 101. Self-conducted tours 9-5. M-Sa 8-6, Su 10-6.

Ranchita Oaks Winery, San Miquel (R)—Visitors by appt.

Tobias Vineyards, Paso Robles—By appt. only.

Watson Vineyards, Paso Robles—2 mi. W of Naciemento Rd. on Adelaide Rd. By appt. only.

York Mountain Winery, Templeton (H,R,T)—off Hwy. 46, 9 mi. W of Hwy. 101 or 12 mi. E of Hwy. 1, daily 10-5.

SAN MATEO COUNTY

Brookside Winery, Belmont (TR)—1645 El Camino Real, 10-6 daily.

Cronin Vineyards, Woodside (R)—By appt. only.

Thomas Fogarty, Portola Valley (R,T)—Call ahead.

Obester Winery, Half Moon Bay (R,T)—12341 San Mateo Rd. (Hwy. 92), 6 mi. W of Hwy. 280 on Hwy. 92, or 1 mi. E of the city of Half Moon Bay on Hwy. 92. Open Sa & Su bet. 10-5.

Woodside Vineyards, Woodside (R,T)—1.4 mi. W of Woodside Town Center on Kings Mtn. Rd. Sa-Su by appt.

SANTA BARBARA COUNTY

Ballard Canyon Winery, Solvang (P,R,T)—Daily 10-4, Grp. tours by appt.

The Brander Vineyard, Los Olivos (R,T)—Call ahead.

J. Carey Cellars, Solvang (R,P,T)—3 mi. outside of Solvang. Open Tu-Su 10-4.

Copenhagen Cellars-Vikings Four, Solvang (TR,T)—Located in the Old Danish community offering CA-Import wines for tasting & sales. Open daily 10-5. Danish Days fest., Sept.

The Firestone Vineyard, Los Olivos (H,R,T)—1/4 mi. N of junct. Hwy. 154 and Hwy. 101, go 2-1/2 mi. E on Zaca Station Rd. Tours M-Sa, 10-4. Closed Su.

Hale Cellars, Los Alamos (R)—Open Tu-Su 10-5.

Los Vineros Winery, Santa Maria (R,T)—Take Stowell Rd. off-ramp, W 2.5 mi. to 618 Hanson Way. Open M-F 10-4.

Rancho Sisquoc Winery, Santa Maria (R,P)—18 mi. E of Santa Maria on Foxen Canyon Rd. From Hwy. 101 take Sisquoc off-ramp E to Foxen Canyon Rd. By appt. only.

Ross-Kellerei, Buellton (R,T)—1 mi. N of intersection of Hwy. 246 and McMurray Rd., Hwy. 101 N—on E frontage rd. Tasting and tours daily 11-5.

Sanford & Benedict Vineyards, Lompoc (P,R,T)—9 mi. W of Buellton. Pl. call for appt.

San Martin Winery, Solvang (TR)—475 Alisal Rd., from Hwy. 101 (or Hwy. 154 N) via Hwy. 246 to Solvang. M-Th 9:30-6, F-Su 9:30-7. 805-688-7217.

Santa Barbara Winery, Santa Barbara (R,T)—1 blk. E of State St., 2 blks. N of ocean on Anapaca St. Tasting daily 9:30-5. Self-conducted tours.

Santa Ynez Valley Winery, (R.T)—approx. 1 mi. S of Hwy. 246 btwn. Santa Ynez and Solvang on Refugio Rd. Weekdays by appt., Sa open for tours & tasting 10-4.

Stearn's Wharf Vintners, Santa Barbara (TR,P)—Situated on historic Stearn's Wharf in Santa Barbara Harbor. Offers CA & Imported wines for tasting & retail sales daily 10-6.

Vega Vineyards Winery, Buellton (H,P,R,T)—At Hwy. 101 & Santa Rosa Rd. Take Santa Rosa Rd. off-ramp located 1/4 mi. S of Buellton. Daily 11-5.

Zaca Mesa Winery, Los Olivos (P,R,T)—1/4 mi. N of junct. Hwy. 154 and Hwy. 101, go 9 mi. E on Zaca Station/Foxen Canyon. Tastings & tours daily 10-4.

SANTA CLARA COUNTY

Almaden Vineyards, San Jose—From N, Hwy. 101 or Hwy. 280 to Hwy. 17 (take Santa Cruz exit), cont. on Hwy. 17 to Campen Ave. exit left, cont. on Camden Ave. 4 mi. to Blossom Hill Rd. L, approx. 0.4 mi. to winery of S st. side (look for US Flag at main entrance).
From S, Hwy. 101 to Hwy. 82 (Old Monterey Hwy.), 0.5 mi. to Blossom Hill Exit, approx. 5 mi. to winery on S st. side. Tours-tastings-retail sales M-F by appt. only.

Casa de Fruta, Gilroy (H,P,R,T)—Hwy. 152, 17 mi. E of Gilroy, daily 8-8 (summer), 9-6 (winter), 24-hr. rst., gourmet deli, recreational facils., trailer park, motel.

Congress Springs Vineyards, Saratoga (R)—approx. 3.5 mi. from village of Saratoga on Hwy. 9 (Congress Springs Rd.). Address on mailbox on L side of rd. Tasting and retail sales by appt. only.

Conrotto Winery, Gilroy (R,T)—Call ahead.

Fortino Winery, Gilroy (H,P,R,T)—From Hwy. 101, Watsonville Rd. at Morgan Hill to Hecker Pass Hwy., approx. 5 mi. W on Hwy. 152, tours, tasting daily 9-6. Picnic facils. for small grps.

Gemello Winery, Mountain View (R)—0.8 mi. S of San Antonio Rd. Tasting and tours. By appt.

E. Guglielmo Winery (Emile's Wines), Morgan Hill (P,R,T)—1.5 mi. E on Main Ave. from Monterey St. (El Camino), Picnic facils. Daily 9-5.

Hecker Pass Winery, Gilroy (R,T)—Hwy. 152, 5 mi. W of Gilroy, daily 9-6.

Kathryn Kennedy Winery, Saratoga (R)—Visitors by appt.

Kirigin Cellars, Gilroy (P,R,T)—From Hwy. 101, 5 mi SW on Watsonville Rd., or 2 mi. N of Hwy. 152 on Country

Rd. G8. Tasting daily 9-6, Gps. & tours by appt. Picnic Facils.

Thomas Kruse Winery, Gilroy (R,P)—From Hwy. 101 at Morgan Hill, Watsonville Rd. to Hecker Pass Hwy. Tasting daily 12-6.

La Purisima Winery, Sunnyvale (R)—From Hwy. 85, 1 mi. E on El Camino Real, corner of El Camino & Sunnyvale-Saratoga Rd. Tu-F 11-2 & 4:30-6:30. Weekends 11-6.

Ronald Lamb Winery, Morgan Hill (R.T)—Weekends by appt.

Live Oaks Winery, Gilroy (R,P)—From Hwy. 101 W on First St., 4.5 mi. W (look for sign on rt.), daily 8-5. Close to Mt. Madonna Park. Tasting for grps. 40 to 50 people, by appt.

Llords & Elwood Winery, Fremont & San Jose (R.T)—By appt. only. Contact Woodland Hills office. 213-716-7794.

Martin Ray, Saratoga (R)—Dir. given by winery. By appt. only.

Paul Masson Champagne & Wine Cellars, Saratoga (H,R,T)—Tours & tasting daily 10-4. From Hwy. 280, 3 mi. SW on Saratoga Ave. From Hwy. 101, Lawrence Expressway to Saratoga Ave. On unique 30 min. tour visitor walks to own pace with hand-held private radio receiver listening to narration about wine-making. 408-725-4270.

Mirassou Vineyards, San Jose (P,R,T)—Capitol Expwy., E from Hwy. 101, turn R on Aborn Rd. for 2 mi. Tasting Rm. open daily M-Sa 10-5, Su 12-4; Tours daily M-Sa 10:30; noon; 2 & 3:30; Su 12:30 & 2:30. Priv. tours & tasting by appt. only. 408-274-4000.

Mount Eden Vineyards, Saratoga (R)—Dir. given by winery. By appt. only.

Mountin View Winery, Mountain View (H,R,T).

Novitiate Wines, Los Gatos (R,P,T)—Hwy. 17 to E Los Gatos turnoff, turn R on LG Blvd., becomes Main St., turn L at College Ave. to Prospect Ave., turn R into Jesuit Center Property. Tours M-F 1:30, 2:30; Sa 11-1. Retail and tasting rm. daily 10-5. Facils. for pvt. picnics, lunches, dinners with tastings & grp. tours. By appt.

Page Mill Winery, Los Altos Hills (R,T)—0.7 mi. W of Hwy. 280 on Page Mill Rd. By appt. only.

Pedrizzetti Winery, Morgan Hill (R,P)—1.5 mi. from Hwy. 101 on San Pedro Ave., grp. tours by appt. only. Tasting rm. in Madrone, Hwy. 101 N of Morgan Hill, daily 9-7.

Pendleton Winery, San Jose (H,R,T)—2156G O'Toole Ave., 1/4 mi. S of Montague Expressway (bet. Hwy. 17 & 101).

Rapazzini Winery, Gilroy (H,R,T)—3 mi. S of Gilroy on Hwy. 101, Box 247, Private tasting & tours by appt. Daily 9-6.

Rapazzini Winery, San Juan Bautista (H,P,T)—Across from historical San Juan Mission, Daily 10-4; closed Tu in winter.

Richert Cellars, Winery in Morgan Hill. By appt. only.

Ridge Vineyards, Inc., Cupertino (R,T)—4.4 mi. from Stevens Creek Reservoir. Tastings, Sa 11-3; Sales, W & Sa 11-3.

San Martin Winery, Gilroy (TR,P)—4210 Monterey Hwy. at Bloomfield, daily 9-8 (June-Sept), 9-6 (Oct-May).

San Martin Winery, Morgan Hill (TR,P)—(Vintage 1892) at 1110 San Pedro Ave.

San Martin Winery, San Martin (R,P)—Hwy. 101 to San Martin (btwn. Gilroy & Morgan Hill).

Sarah's Vineyard, Gilroy (P,R,T)—Sa-Su 12-4. Weekdays by appt. only.

Sherrill Cellars, Palo Alto (H,R,T)—Approx. 1 mi. S of Alpine intersection on Skyline Blvd. (Hwy. 35) at 1185 Skyline. By invitation & appt. only.

Sommelier Winery, Mtn. View (R)—Take San Antonio Rd. to Middlefield, S on Middlefield, veer left onto Old Middlefield, L on Independence, L on Wyandotte Ave., R into complex at 2560 Wyandotte. Sales & tasting by appt. only.

Summerhill Vineyards, Gilroy (R,P)—From Hwy. 101, 4 mi. W on Hwy. 152, Noon-dusk.

Sycamore Creek Vineyards, Morgan Hill (P,R,T)—From Hwy. 101 at Morgan Hill, 3.9 mi. on Watsonville Rd. to 12775 Uvas Rd. (winery located on corner of Uvas Rd. and Watsonville Rd. btwn. Thousand Trails Park and Oak Dell Park). Tasting Sa-Su only 12-5. Weekdays by appt. only.

Turgeon & Lohr Winery, San Jose (H,R,T)—Off the Alameda 1/4 mi. S of Hwy. 17 at 1000 Lenzen Ave. Tasting, daily 10-5.

Villa Paradiso Vineyards, Morgan Hill (R,T)—from Hwy. 101. Tasting Sa-Su 11-5.

Walker Wines, Los Altos Hills—1.0 mi. W of Foothills Expressway on Estacada Dr. By appt. only.

SANTA CRUZ COUNTY

Ahlgren Vineyard, Boulder Creek (R)—Very limited appts. avail. Call or write in adv.

Bargetto's Santa Cruz Winery, Soquel (H,R,T)—3535 N Main St., Hwy. 1, 4 mi. S of Santa Cruz, L from Capitola-Soquel off-ramp, daily 9-5:30.

David Bruce, Los Gatos—exactly 5 mi. W of Hwy. 17, retail sales Tu-Sa, tasting Sa 11.

Cook-Ellis Winery, Corralitos (R,T)—Located 1 hr. from San Jose or Santa Cruz. Tasting on weekends by appt. only.

Crescini Wines, Soquel (R,T)—Call for hours.

Devlin Wine Cellars, Soquel (R,T)—Visitors by appt. only.

Felton-Empire Vineyards, Felton (P,R,T)—.2 mi. from Hwy. 9 on Felton-Empire Rd. Tours & tasting Sa & Su 11-3. Retail sales at winery weekends only.

Frick Winery, Santa Cruz (H,R,T)—Downtown Santa Cruz off River St. M-F by appt. F & Sa summer hrs., but call ahead.

Grover Gulch Winery, Soquel (R,T)—Call ahead for appt. & directions.

McHenry Vineyards, Santa Cruz—Visitors by appt. only.
Michael T. Parsons Winery, Soquel—By appt. only.
Nicasio Vineyards, Soquel (R,T)—Sa by appt.
River Run Vintners, Watsonville—By appt. only.
Roudon-Smi.th Vineyards, Santa Cruz—5 mi. N of Santa Cruz at 2364 Bean Cr. Rd. Retail sales & tasting on Sa 12-4, Apr thru Dec; call ahead please.
Santa Cruz Mountain Vineyard, 8 mi. N of Santa Cruz. By appt. only.
Silver Mountain, Los Gatos (R)—Call for hrs.
Smothers-Vine Hill Wines, Santa Cruz—Visitors by appt. only.
P & M Staiger, Boulder Creek (R)—By appt. only.
Sunrise Winery, Santa Cruz (R,P)—Write or call for appt.

SOLANO COUNTY

Cache Cellars, Davis (R,T)—.3 mi. S of Putah Creek. By appt. only.
Cadenasso Winery, Fairfield (R)—Off Hwy. 80 at Fairfield-Rio Vista exit, daily 8-5.
Chateau De Leu, Suisun (P,R,T,TR)—3 mi. N on Green Valley Rd. exit at Hwy. 80. Daily 11-4:30.
Diablo Vista, Benicia (R)—674 E H St. Retail sales & tours by appt.
Susine Cellars, Suisun City (R,T)—Tu-Sa 10-6.
Wooden Valley Winery, Suisun Valley (H,R,T)—4.5 mi. NW on Suisun Valley Rd., exit at Hwy. 80, daily 9-5, closed M, no tours.

SONOMA COUNTY

Adler Fels, Santa Rosa (T)—2.2 mi. off Hwy. 12, by appt. only.
Alexander Valley Vineyards, Healdsburg (P,R,T)—8 mi. E of Healdsburg. Tours by appt., tasting & sales, 10-5 weekdays, 12-5 weekends.
Arroyo Sonoma Winery (California Wine Company), Cloverdale (R,T)—Sales-tasting daily 10-5. Tours by appt.
Balverne Winery & Vineyards, Windsor (R)—Visitors by appt. only.
Belvedere Wine Co., Healdsburg—Visitors by appt. only.
Braren Pauli Winery, Potter Valley (R)—10 mi. NW Ukiah off Hwy. 20. Take Potter Valley exit, 6 mi. to winery. By appt. only.
Buena Vista Winery-Haraszthy Cellars, Sonoma (H,P,R, T)—End of Old Winery Rd., 1 mi. E of Sonoma. A historical center, tasting and retail salesroom open to the public daily, 10-5.
Bynum Winery, Healdsburg (R)—Take Westside Rd. from Healdsburg W 8 mi. to winery. Daily 9-5. Tours by appt.
Cambiaso Vineyards, Healdsburg (TR)—1.5 mi. SE of Healdsburg, Fwy. N to Healdsburg Ave. off-ramp turn E on Grant Ave. to end, M-Sa 10-4. Closed Su. Retail sales, no tasting.
Chateau St. Jean, Kenwood (H,P,R,T)—Hwy. 12, 8 mi. E of Santa Rosa. Tasting, retail sales & picnic area 10-4. Self guided tours 10:30-4. Adv. res. req. for grps. of 8 or more.
Clos du Bois, Healdsburg (H,R,T)—Tasting/retail 10-4 M-

S; winery tour 2 M-F; vineyard tours (limited-call for info. & resvns.).

Cordtz Brothers Cellars, Cloverdale (R,T)—Daily 10-4.

H. Coturri & Sons Ltd., Glen Ellen—By appt. only.

DeLoach Vineyards, Santa Rosa (H,P.R,T)—Daily 10-4:30. **Domaine Laurier**, Forestville (H,R,T)—Off Hwy. 116. Tours & tasting by appt. only.

Donna Maria Vineyards, Healdsburg (H,R,T)—Tasting by appt. only.

Dry Creek Vineyard, Healdsburg (H,P.R,T)—3.2 mi. NW on Dry Creek Rd. Exit from Hwy. 101, daily 10:30-4:30.

Georges Duboeuf & Son, Healdsburg (T)—2 blocks from Healdsburg Town Square. Hrs. 9:30-4.00 M, Th & F. Call for appt.

Field Stone Winery, Healdsburg (H,P,R,T)—Corner of Chalk Hill & Hwy. 128, halfway bet. Healdsburg & Calistoga, daily 10-4, retail sales & tasting daily. Tours by appt. only.

Fisher Vineyards, Santa Rosa—By appt. only.

Foppiano Vineyards, Healdsburg (H,P,R,T)—12707 Old Redwood Hwy., 2 mi. S. of Healdsburg, W of Hwy. 101, daily 10-4.

Fritz Cellars, Cloverdale (P,R,T)—N on Hwy. 101, take Dutcher Creek Rd. exit, L on Dutcher Creek Rd., 2.3 mi. down rd. on right side. Open W-Su 12-5 for tasting, picnic facilities, tours by appt.

Geyser Peak Winery, Geyserville (H,P,R,T)—Hwy. 101 at Canyon Rd. overpass, daily 10-5, tours by appt., tasting. Picnic area.

Grand Cru Vineyards, Glen Ellen (P,R,T)—from Hwy. 12 S take Dunbar Rd. exit (2 mi. N of Glen Ellen) to Henno, then W 200 ft. Tasting rm. open daily 10-5.

Gundlach-Bundschu Winery, Sonoma (H,P,R,T)—Daily 11-4:30. From Sonoma Plaza go E on Napa St. to Old Winery Rd.—turn L; R on Lovall Vly. Rd. R on Thornsberry Rd.

Hacienda Wine Cellars, Sonoma (R,PT)—pvt. rd. ext. off Castle Rd., 1.5 mi. NE of Sonoma Plaza, in historic Buena Vista Vineyards, daily 10-5. Tours by appt.

Hanzell Vineyards, Sonoma—Visitors by appt. only.

J. J. Haraszthy & Son, Glen Ellen—In London Glen Village 1/2 mi. S of Glen Ellen. By appt. only.

Haywood Winery, Sonoma—Take 4th St. E to Lovall Valley Rd., turn R 1 blk. to Gehricke Rd., turn L and proceed about 0.5 mi. Visitors by appt. only.

Healdsburg Wine Company, Healdsburg (H,R,T)—Downtown Healdsburg, adj. to the Plaza. M-F 10-4, weekends by appt.

Hop Kiln Winery, Griffin Vineyards, Healdsburg (R, P)—6-1/2 mi. SW of Healdsburg. Open daily 10-5. Picnic Facils. for retail patrons.

Horizon Winery, Santa Rosa (R)—Tours by appt. only.

Hultgren & Samperton, Healdsburg—2.2 mi. SW on Westside Rd. by appt. only.

Iron Horse Vineyards, Sebastopol—Tours & Tasting by appt. only.

Italian Swiss Colony, Asti (P,R,T)—80 mi. N of San Francisco, Hwy. 101 N to Asti exit. Daily 10-5 except major holidays. Tours 10,12,2 & 4, hourly during summer.

Johnson's Alexander Valley Wines, Healdsburg (H,P,R, T)—Hwy. 128 1-3/4 mi. S of Jimtown Store in Alexander Valley, daily 10-5.

Jordan Vineyards & Winery, Healdsburg—Visitors by appt. only.

Kenwood Vineyards, Sonoma (R,T)—8 mi. N of Sonoma, on Hwy. 12, daily 10-4:30.

Korbel Champagne Cellars, Guerneville (R,T)—3 mi. N of Santa Rosa on Hwy. 101, 14 mi. W on River Rd. Daily 9-5. Grp. tours by appt.

La Creama Vinera, Petaluma—Tours by appt.

Lambert Bridge, Healdsburg—3-1/2 mi. W on Dry Creek Rd. to Lambert Bridge Rd., L to W Dry Creek Rd., L 1/2 mi. to Winery. By appt. only.

Landmark Vineyards, Windsor (P,R,T)—Hwy. 101 N of Santa Rosa, exit at Windsor, cont. straight, crossing Old Redwood Hwy. onto Los Amigos Rd. (fwy. frontage rd.) for 1/4 mi. Sa-Su 10-5.

Laurel Glen Vineyard, Glen Ellen—By appt. only.

Lytton Springs Winery, Healdsburg (H,R,T)—From Hwy. 101, 1 mi. W on Lytton Springs Rd. M thru F 8-5, tours by appt. only.

Mark West Vineyards, Forestville (H,P,R,T)—Hwy. 101 N of Santa Rosa to River Rd., 5-1/2 mi. W. to Trenton-Healdsburg Rd., R 1/2 mi. to winery. Daily 10-5. Grp. tastings & picnic luncheons by appt.

Martini & Prati Wines, Inc., Santa Rosa (R,T)—Hwy. 101 at Guerneville Rd., 8.1 mi. NW on Laguna Rd., M-F 9-4. No tours.

Matanzas Creek Winery, Santa Rosa—Hwy. 101 N to Hwy. 12 E to Bennett Valley Rd., 5 mi.les to winery. Tours by appt. only.

McDowell Valley Vineyards, Hopland (R.T)—4 mi. E of Hopland on Hwy. 175 (off Hwy. 101), Th-Su 10-6.

Mill Creek Vineyards, Healdsburg (H,P.R.T)—1 mi. W of Healdsburg on Westside Rd. Daily 10-4:30.

Mountain House Winery, Cloverdale (R,T)—Visitors by appt. only.

Nervo Winery, Geyserville (R,P)—Hwy. 101, Independence Ln. E, 4 mi. N of Healdsburg, daily 10-5. Picnic area.

Pastori Winery, Geyserville (R)—Canyon Rd. exit to Geyserville Ave. N 1 mi., daily 9-5.

Pat Paulsen Vineyards, Cloverdale (R)—Visitors by appt. only, no tasting.

J. Pedroncelli Winery, Geyserville (R,T)—Hwy. 101, 1 mi. N of Geyserville, 1 mi. W on Canyon Rd., daily 10-5. Tours by appt.

Piper-Sonoma, Windsor (R,T)—Open daily 10-5.

Pommeraie Vineyards, Sebastopol—By appt. only.

Preston Vineyards, Healdsburg (TR)—In Dry Creek Valley, 1.5 mi. N of Yoakim Br. on W. Dry Creek Rd. By appt. only.

A. Rafanelli, Healdsburg—Exit from Hwy. 101 Dry Creek

Rd. 3-1/2 mi. NW on Dry Creek Rd. to Lambert Bridge Rd. L to West Dry Creek Rd., then R 400 yds. By appt. only.

Ravenswood Winery, Sonoma (R)—Retail sales by mail (pls. write). Visitors by appt. only.

River Oaks Vineyards, Healdsburg—Soon to have retail sales & tasting. Call for info.

River Road Vineyards, Forestville—Visitors by appt. only.

Sausal Winery, Healdsburg—Visitors by appt. only.

St. Francis Winery & Vineyards, Kenwood (H,R,T)—(Hwy. 12, 8 mi. E of Santa Rosa). Tasting & retail sales 10-4:30 daily. Tours by appt.

Seaview Winery, Cazadero—Tours by appt.

Sebastiani Vineyards, Sonoma (H,R,T)—daily 10-5.

Simi Winery, Healdsburg (H,P,R,T)—Dry Creek exit off Hwy. 101, E to Healdsburg Ave., N 1 mi., daily 10-5. Grps. by appt.

Soda Rock Winery, Healdsburg (R,T)—Daily 10-5.

Sonoma-Cutrer Vineyards, Windsor—Visitors by appt. only.

Sonoma Vineyards, (Windsor Vineyards), Windsor (R,P, T)—Hwy. 101 N of Santa Rosa to Windsor exit, go L, 3 mi. on Old Redwood Hwy., daily 10-5.

Sotoyome Winery, Healdsburg—On Limerick Ln. 1-1/2 mi. S off Old Redwood Hwy. Visits by appt. only.

Souverain Winery, Geyserville (R,T)—Independence Ln. exit from Hwy. 101. Open daily 10-5. Tours (on the hour) & tastings. Restaurant (H) open daily for lunch 11-3; W-Su for dinner 5-9. Restaurant phone 707-433-3141.

Robert Stemmler Winery, Healdsburg—Off Hwy. 101, 3.2 mi. NW on Dry Creek Rd. to Lambert Bridge Rd., L on Lambert Br. Visit & sales by appt. only.

Topolos at Russian River Vineyards, Forestville (R, T)—5700 Gravenstein Hwy., N 1 mi. S of Forestville. Tours by appt. only, tasting & sales 11-5 W-Su. Restaurant only daily for lunch 11-3, W-Su dinner 6-9:30. Su Brunch 10:30-2:30. 707-887-1562.

Toyon Winery & Vineyards, Healdsburg (H,TR)—By appt. only.

Trentadue Winery, Geyserville (R)—4 mi. N of Healdsburg on Hwy. 101 to Independence turnoff to 19170 Redwood Hwy., tasting daily 10-5.

Valley of the Moon, Glen Ellen (R,T)—Off Hwy. 12 on Madrone Rd., daily 10-5, except Thurs. No tours.

Views Land Co., Sonoma (R)—Visitors by appt.

Vina Vista, Geyserville—N on Hwy. 101, exit at Canyon Rd. then 1.9 mi. N on Chianti Rd. Tours by appt. only.

White Oak Vineyards, Healdsburg—By appt. only.

William Wheeler Winery, Healdsburg (R,T)—Tasting by appt. only.

STANISLAUS COUNTY

Oak Valley Winery, Oakdale (R)—Visitors by appt. only.

Pirrone Wine Cellars, Salida (R)—From Hwy. 99, 6.5 mi. N of Modesto on Pirrone Rd., M-F 9-5.

TEHAMA COUNTY

Barengo Vineyards, Red Bluff (TR)—Hwy. 5 at Motel

Orleans, daily 9-5.

TULARE COUNTY

Anderson Wine Cellars, Exeter (TR)—9 mi. E of Visalia on Hwy. 198, then 1 mi. N. By appt. only.

California Growers Winery, Inc., Yettem (R)—Approx. 1/2 mi. W of Yettem, E on Ave. 384 from Hwy. 99, M-F 1-4. Tours by appt.

TUOLUMNE COUNTY

Gold Mine Winery, Columbia (TR)—4 mi. N of Sonora near entrance to Columbia State Park, daily 10-5.

Yankee Hill Winery, Columbia (P,R,T)—1 mi. E of Columbia-Yankee Hill Rd. Open 10-5 daily for tours & tastings. Museum & historic park. Stage shows Jul & Aug.

VENTURA COUNTY

Brookside Winery, Ventura (TR,P)—6580 Leland St., on Hwy. 101, 10-6 M-Sa, 12-5 Su.

Leeward Winery, Ventura (H,R,T)—2784 Johnson Dr. Pl. call for appt.

Old Creek Ranch Winery, Oakview (R,T)—From Ventura go N on Hwy. 33 approx. 10 mi. Turn rt. on Old Creek Rd., approx. 3/4 mi.; rd. ends at winery. Sa, Su 10-4 (call ahead). M-F by appt. Picnic for retail customers.

YOLO COUNTY

Bogle Vineyards Winery, Clarksburg (R,T)—By appt. only.

R & J Cook Winery, Clarksburg (P,R,T)—Netherlands Rd. Informal tours daily except Sa & Su, pl. call for appt.

Harbor Winery, West Sacramento—Visitors by appt. only.

Orleanes Vinicultural Association, Woodland (R,T)—Sa 10-2 or by appt.

Satiety, Davis—Visitors by appt.

Winters Winery, Winters (H,R,T)—15 Main St. just off Hwy. 128 in Winters. Tasting daily 10-5 except Christmas, Easter and New Year.

About the Author

THE POCKET ENCYCLOPEDIA OF CALIFORNIA WINE is Master Knight of the Vine, William I. Kaufman's 136th published book. Writer, lecturer, photographer, song writer, television spokesman and creator of television ideas, he has covered the fields of food, wine, entertaining and travel. His most recent wine books have been the *California Wine Drink Book, The Whole World Catalog of Wine* and *The Travelers Guide to the Vineyards of North America.* One of the most beautiful wine books ever created was *Champagne* which he wrote and illustrated. *Perfume* is another example of his magnificant photography. His books have been translated into many languages. Mr. Kaufman is recipient of the coveted wine book award the Gold Vine Award and many foreign honors including the Chevalier de l'Ordre du Merite Agricole from the French Republic and three Medallions for artistic achievement for writing and photography. He received the Christopher Award for his UNICEF childrens books, songs, poems, prayers and legends. He has had twenty major photographic exhibitions including two major color exhibitions by Kodak. His publishers include: Jove, Berkeley, Doubleday, Harper & Row, Penquin, Viking, Dell, Simon & Shuster. He is a member of the Southern California Wine Writers, Bontemp de Medoc, Authors Chevalier du Taste Vin, A.S.C.A.P., Screen Actors' Guild, Knight of Vine, Overseas Press Club, Friars Club, Commanderie de Bordeaux, Wine Media Guild, and is active on wine tasting and judging panels.

Gold Vine Award

William I. Kaufman was awarded the prestigious "Gold Vine Award" in May by the Brotherhood of the Knights of the Vine. The Brotherhood selected this book due to its usefulness, accuracy and timeliness of information.

The Brotherhood of the Knights of the Vine is the American branch of the Universal Order of the Knights of the Vine which traces its history to 13th Century France. The brotherhood supports the cause of American wine, its healthy virtues and its appreciation within the restraints of reason and good living.

Tasting Notes